*To: My dear friend, Shirley from Sun Gil Pra*

"The quintessential teacher!
He began with chalk and a blackboard. Now he uses a computer."
-GC

"We live! We die!
What we do with our time on Earth makes all the difference.
Prof. Krupp has traveled the world. Along with him, enjoy his
adventures as you read this entertaining and delightful book!"
-SS

"A pioneer in Distance Learning!
From the classroom to PBS-TV to the Internet."
-LG

"We are lucky to personally know Robert Krupp!
His kindness, generosity, and friendship mean a great deal to us."
-BK/SS

*I hope you enjoy reading this book and that it brings to mind many of your own pleasant memories!*

*Bob*

*P.S. Enjoy the mountains of Utah!*

*Dec. 2021*

Laura And Grandpa, Inc.

*My Marvelous Memories*

## First Edition © 2021 Dr. Robert H. Krupp

All rights reserved. No part of this publication may be reproduced, stored in a retrieval system, or transmitted in any form or by any means—electronic, mechanical photocopying, recording, or otherwise without written permission of the publisher.

ISBN-13: 978-0-9998993-6-6
ISBN-10: 0-9998993-6-6

In cooperation with Laura and Grandpa, Inc., Bradenton, FL.

www.LauraAndGrandpa.com

**Graphic Design/Art Direction**
**Kristina Edstrom**
www.KristinaEdstromDesigns.com

Printed in the United States of America

# Dedication

## Marie Rembowicz-Krupp and Harry Krupp
My Parents—who taught me to love, respect, and help others!

June 23, 1962
Betty and Ron's Wedding

St. John the Baptist Church, Winfield, IL

# Table of Contents

**Chapter One- The Early Years (1929 - 1943)**     7

**Chapter Two- The Preparation (1943 - 1949)**     33
- *Preparatory Novitiate: (March, 1944 - June, 1946)*
- *Novitiate: (June, 1946 - August, 1947)*
- *Scholasticate: (September, 1947- August, 1949)*

**Chapter Three- A Teacher's Beginning (1949 - 1960)**     53
- *CBC, St. Louis, MO (September, 1949 - June, 1951)*
- *St. Patrick, Chicago (September, 1951-June, 1953)*
- *De La Salle High School, Chicago (September, 1953 - July, 1955)*
- *De La Salle, KC, MO (September, 1955 - June, 1956)*
- *CBC, Memphis TN (June, 1956 - July, 1958)*
- *Graduate Student (September, 1958 - December, 1959)*

**Chapter Four- Genesis I (1960 - 1967)**     91
- *Wilber Wright (September, 1962 - March, 1967)*

**Chapter Five- The Transition (1967 - 1970)**     127

**Chapter Six- The West Coast (1970 - 1973)**     145

Chapter Seven- **The East Coast (1973 - 1978)**     167

Chapter Eight- **The Frozen Tundra (1978 - 1979)**     201
   -Minuteman Press  (September, 1979 - July, 1980)

Chapter Eight- **The Frozen Tundra (1978 - 1979)**     201
   -Minuteman Press-  (September, 1979 - July, 1980)

Chapter Nine- **Genesis II  (1980 - 1996)**     229
   -Wright Community College, Chicago-  (January 19, 1981 - June 30, 1996)

Chapter Ten- **Retirement  (1996 - 2001)**     251
   -College Preparatory Center (CPC)
    Saudi Arabia- (June 2, 1997 - Dec. 23, 2000)

Chapter Eleven- **Phenomenal Travels**     269

Chapter Twelve- **The Searing Sands of Arabia  (1998 - 2001)**     325

Chapter Thirteen— **Genesis III  (2001 - 2021)**     345

Chapter Fourteen- **A Literary Artist  (2009 - 2021)**     377

Epilogue     388
Appendix     390
Postscript     393

# Author's Note

In 1944, a young Army Air Corps veteran of WWII moved to Chicago. He began broadcasting on radio station WENR, an ABC affiliate. For the rest of his life, he was a radio broadcaster. He died in 2009 at the age of 90. Upon hearing of his passing, President George W. Bush said, "a friendly and familiar voice in the lives of millions of Americans is gone."

That man was Paul Harvey Aurandt.

He was known professionally as Paul Harvey. In 1976, he began a radio series called The Rest of the Story. It grew to six broadcasts a week and continued until his death. Harvey and his radio network stated that these stories, although entertaining, were completely true. This was challenged by some critics who claimed that many were urban legends.

I mention Paul Harvey because memoirs are nothing more than stories of a person's life. They are just images of one's trip on Earth.

As you read The Rest of My Story (***MS***) you may not find things laid out in a nice, logical, smooth flowing tale—like what is found in a novel, mystery, or documentary.

However, ***MS*** is true—not dreams, fantasies, or urban legends!

# Chapter One
## The Early Years
## (1929-1943)

### 1929 was a very eventful year!

- On February 14, the infamous St. Valentine's Day Massacre occurred in Chicago.
- On June 2, I was born, also in Chicago.
- On October 29, the Great Depression began and lasted a decade.

All of these had an impact on my life and are part of My Story (**MS**).

I'll start by mentioning my ancestors. My grandmother, Mary, was born in 1867. She emigrated from Poland in 1882, when she was 15 years old. Her family settled in Chicago after the Great Fire of 1871. In 1884, she met my grandfather, Frank Rembowicz. He too had come from Poland with his family in 1883, when he was 19. They met, fell in love, and were married in 1885. In 1898, their fifth child was born and named Mary (Marie), my mother. Mom was baptized and raised a Roman Catholic along with her four sisters and five brothers.

After eight years in a parochial school, mom went to work in the garment industry. She did what young children of immigrants did at that time to help ends meet. There were no laws preventing this. Her two younger sisters, Berniece and Emily, followed her. All three worked for Hart, Schaffner, and Marx (HS&M), one of the leading manufacturers of mass-produced clothing at the time.

Frank and Mary Rembowicz

My grandparents, Solomon and Chaja Krupitsky (Krupp), were Ashkenazi Jews from the Ukraine. They married in 1889. My father, Elia Hersch (Harry) was born in 1899. His three brothers and three sisters were also born in the Ukraine. He was 14, when they immigrated to the US in 1913 and settled in Chicago. Dad attended a public school for two years to learn English. He too went to work in the garment industry at B. Kuppenheimer and Company, a men's clothing manufacturing and retail sales operation. He specialized in the design and making of men's suits. I recall that throughout my early years he made knickers and pants for my younger brother and myself.

My parents met shortly after the end of WWI. They fell in love and married in 1922. Strangely, in an era when Catholics married Catholics, WASPS married WASPS, Italians married Italians, Poles married Poles, Jews married Jews, they managed to break the norm. They maintained a friendly relationship with both families. My father was accepted by all my mother's Catholic family. Mom, my brother, and I were warmly treated by dad's family. Best of all, Ron and I had Polish Catholic uncles, aunts, and cousins, as well as, Jewish uncles, aunts, and cousins. We lived in a harmonious, happy home!

In those times, it was not unusual for families to live together or near each other. Families bonded and helped each other through various means. There was much laughter and camaraderie.

I grew up on the near NW side of Chicago. My parents, Ron, my younger brother, and I lived on the third floor of a brick three story building. Grandpa Frank had purchased it before WWI. It was only occupied by family members. Mom's oldest brother Jack, and his son Lawrence, lived on the first-floor apartment. Lawrence's mother had died during the Great Influenza Pandemic of 1918.

*Me at age 4 with Skippy*

My grandmother, two aunts and two uncles lived on the second floor. They had a player piano in their apartment. I went there often and put a paper roll of music on the roller. I'd vigorously pump the pedals and as the roll moved around, the music would play automatically. I thought I was a wonderful musician! English was the only language spoken in our home because of my father. However, as I just mentioned, a floor below was my grandmother. She always had cookies and other treats for me. She only spoke to me in Polish. I was bilingual by the age of four! Sad to say, I lost my ability to speak Polish. I began kindergarten at Jonathan Burr public school in 1934, and my grandmother died shortly thereafter.

Dad managed to find work during the Great Depression. People still had money to buy clothes. He was a tailor and left early to go to work. When I awoke to go to school, he was gone. Every night at 5:30 pm, our family of four sat down together for supper!

Friday night was dad's night out with his boys. Supper on Friday evening was usually cold, smoked chubs or a tuna casserole, made from canned tuna. After dinner we'd walk to a movie. Most often to the Wicker Park theater on Milwaukee Ave. We had to go to see a weekly installment of a 15-week serial. It was essential for us to learn if the hero and heroine survived their weekly encounters with death.

Occasionally, we'd go to the Banner or Paulina theaters, on Damen or Paulina Avenues. I'm not sure if it was available in the 1930's, but we never bought popcorn or candy in a theater. We'd bring our own bag of candy or a box of Cracker Jack®.

By the age of 5, I was assigned chores. The first one I recall, was to wash and dry the supper dishes in a cold-water flat. Water was heated in a kettle on the stove. A large pan was placed in the sink. The dishes were placed in the pan, to which I added warm soapy water. After washing the dishes, I would rinse them in cold running water from the sink's faucet. The rinse water was drained from the dishes by placing them on a long arm of the sink. Finally, they were dried with a dish towel and put away.

As Ron got older, he'd help me with this task. I'd wash one week, and he'd dry. Next week, he'd wash, and I'd dry. Occasionally, we'd argue about whose turn it was to wash. In the summer, we'd hurry through this chore because we wanted to get back out to the field where we'd played all day.

No! Not to play more ball. We'd sit on the sidewalk and watch adults play softball. It was their turn to play and ours to watch. Monthly, we watched them play a hilarious game of donkey softball! The runners would circle the bases riding a mule! In the meantime, the outfielders chased the ball while mounted on a donkey!

*Donkey Softball Team!*

Depending on the season, I had additional chores. On winter mornings, I'd wake up and get dressed. Then I'd shovel ashes from the bottom of our coal-burning stove into a bucket. I'd carry them down to the alley and dump them into a garbage can. Afterwards, I'd go into a shed and fill the bucket with coal. Now came the real challenge. I would haul this heavy bucket of coal up three flights of stairs and place it next to the stove!

In summer, I had a different chore. On the back-stairway landing, midway between the 2nd and 3rd floor porches, was a wooden ice box. It kept food from spoiling. Water from melted ice dripped into a large pan underneath the ice box. My job was to empty the pan before it overflowed. This was an easy task! I'd pull the pan out and carry it down half a flight of steps. From the 2nd floor porch, I'd pour the water into the garden below.

Shopping for clothes, shoes, and other things was done at Wieboldt's Department store on Milwaukee Avenue. Ron and I loved to go to the shoe department! There we'd place our feet into the shoe-fitting machine called a Fluoroscope or Pedoscope. What a marvelous sight it was! Those X-rays showed the bones of our toes and feet inside our shoes.

We did not realize the danger of X-rays at that time. Now we know that overexposure from this invasive radiation can cause cancer!

We'd have several trips to downtown Chicago in the days before Christmas. We saw a marvelous sight on Randolph and State Streets! In a corner window of Marshall Field's, was a vast display of wonderful toys.

MARSHALL FIELD'S CHRISTMAS WINDOW 1900'S

Ron and I would gaze with awe and desire at all we saw. When we went inside Field's, our mother or aunts would shop in various departments. Meanwhile, Ron and I visited the Toy department. We'd wander about looking and touching those fantastic toys.

*Toy Dept at Fields*

Up and down, we would ride on that marvelous invention, the escalator. Imagine that, moving stairs! If we found a section empty, we'd try to run down the escalator moving up. We avoided running up an escalator moving downwards. That was too difficult. We didn't ride the elevators. They were run by employees of Field's who were not pleased with kids riding on their elevators.

We never had a bowl of soup or a hot chocolate in Field's Walnut Room. We didn't know it even existed!

Other holiday memories that I recall . . .

*The Walnut Room*

✓ Pączki or Bismarck Tuesday, the day before Ash Wednesday!

✓ Thanksgiving dinner, I usually got a drumstick!

✓ Holy Saturday, a basket filled with bread, colored eggs, Polish sausage, horseradish, ham, etc. was taken to the Polish Church for a blessing of food!

✓ Christmas dinner, I was given a shot glass, ½ full of Rock & Rye Whiskey to sip!

## Elementary School (1935-43)

I began classes at Annunciation parochial school in September 1935. The parish school was run by the Sisters of the Blessed Virgin Mary (BVM) nuns. I was ready for them. They weren't ready for me!

I never confronted or physically challenged a nun. I was placed at the end of every line because I was the tallest in my class. I was given a desk in the back of the room. I read every assignment and listened to the instructions given. I learned quite quickly and became bored. Consequently, I became the class mischief maker. I'd whisper, talk to, and distract students around me. Once a month, my mother was called in for a conference. At this meeting, all my sins were revealed. Usually, my penance was to wash and wax the floors in the convent on a Saturday morning. I cannot tell you the number of Saturdays I spent on my hands and knees repenting for my sins of boredom!

Though I caught on to academic subjects quickly, at times I was stupid in other matters. Near the end of 1st grade, in the spring of 1936, we received wonderful news from our pastor. He told us that he'd obtained tickets for the circus. It was being held indoors at the Chicago Stadium. We were given a holiday from school, a ticket, and told to be at the Stadium by 1:00 pm. The Wednesday matinee started at 2:00 pm.

I got up a little later than usual on circus day and dressed after breakfast. Just before leaving at noon, my mother wanted to give me a brown bag with a sandwich and some cookies. I said, "No thanks! Father Molloy said ALL would be taken care of!"

In my fantasy, I thought that once seated in the Stadium, I would be treated to a hot dog, soda, peanuts, popcorn, and maybe even a Cracker Jack®. My uncle Art gave me a quarter to take care of the 5¢ streetcar fare. That left me with 15¢ for anything else I wanted. What a treat! I was ready for a good time!

So, with a few friends, we boarded a southbound Ashland Avenue streetcar. We got off two blocks before the Stadium on Madison. Of course, once inside I found there were no free treats. Around 3:30 pm, there was a ½ hour intermission. I was starving and had to have something to eat! I bought a bag of popcorn and a Cracker Jack® for 20¢. Now I had no money for streetcar fare.

How did this six-year-old maverick get home? I walked home alone! It was almost 3 miles. I crossed 7 major thoroughfares. To their dying days, I never told this to my mother or father!

By the time I reached 6th grade, the nuns had figured out what to do with me. Since I was an altar boy, they made sure I served every funeral mass held on a weekday. In 7th and 8th grades, they sent me off to the parish rectory where I was assigned various chores. I stuffed, sealed, stamped, and mailed monthly notices to all members of the parish. In spring or fall, I'd caddy for one of the priests when they'd have time for 9 or 18 holes. But, the most interesting task of all occurred from the Monday after Thanksgiving until a week before Christmas. Three times a week, I would go for a ride with our pastor, Fr. Patrick J. Molloy. He was on a mission! He went to visit offices of relatives, friends, whomever, to receive his Christmas gifts! Usually, it was folding cash and a bottle of liquid refreshment. I leave it to the reader to guess what the liquid refreshment was.

I'd accompany him on all these trips. When he got downtown, he'd always park his car in a No Parking area. It might be a fire hydrant or a loading zone. He'd leave and I stayed in the car to guard his liquid treasures. I'd also been coached on what to do if a policeman started writing him a parking ticket. If this happened, and it frequently did, I got out of the car, approached the policeman, and said, "Officer, I'm supposed to tell you that this is the car of Father Patrick J. Molloy." He never got a ticket, in the two years I accompanied him! He always gave me a candy bar to eat as we drove home!

A benefit of my two years of doing these chores in the rectory was Fr. Molloy learned I was a hard worker. Consequently, he allowed me to operate the newsstand in front of the church on Sunday mornings. His blessing was necessary to run this newsstand. For two years my father, aunt Emily, and Ron helped me sell newspapers every Sunday morning from around 6:00 am to 1:00 pm. Our efforts netted me a profit of $4 to $6 for the day. My mother let me keep 50¢ for weekly expenses, i.e., candy, soda, gum, movies, etc. The rest she saved in a fund to pay for my high school tuition. When he was in 7th and 8th grades, Ron also operated this newsstand on Sunday mornings.

In the first few weeks of 8th grade, I'd come home every day in tears. It wasn't about my being bullied! I told my mother I was the last boy in class still wearing knickers. Everyone else was dressed in long pants. It took my mother almost two weeks to persuade my father to make me a pair of trousers. I recall the first time she brought up the subject at supper. My father groused and said, "He's a boy! Boys should wear knickers!"

*Me and Ron in Knickers*

In any case, I graduated from elementary school on June 1, 1943. During the ceremony I received a medal on a beautiful blue and white ribbon. It was for having the best academic record of the 1943 class. I know the 8th grade nun was not too happy with my earning this award. I beat out June and Teresa, her two favorite students. My mother treasured that medal until she died, but I don't know what happened to it.

Unrelated to events at the elementary school was my involvement in WWII activities. Six months before the bombing of Pearl Harbor, our Government established the Office of Civil Defense (OCD). It created a neighborhood watch program called the Air Raid Wardens. After December 7, 1941, I joined this program. Though I was only 12 years old, I was accepted. My height contributed to my looking like a high school student.

Twice a week, an elderly gentleman and I would go out together on patrol. From 9:00 pm to midnight, we'd wander through our assigned area. We were enforcing the blackout for homes, stores, bars, or factories in our neighborhood. Once a week, before our patrol duties, we met in a classroom setting. Earlier, we'd been given flash cards of German and Japanese aircraft. We were tested on identifying those airplanes. We were expected to recognize whether a plane was a German or Japanese bomber.

Twenty years later it dawned on me. What were we doing enforcing a blackout in Chicago? During WWII, neither Germany nor Japan, had an airplane that could fly across an ocean, continue inland over a thousand miles, and drop a bomb on Chicago!

If one can admit that war does produce some good, I would like to mention a benefit I received because of the war. In my opinion, WWII pulled our country out of the Great Depression. It opened factory jobs for women and enabled black men from the south to migrate north. Here they found work in the steel industry or in factories building trucks, jeeps, and tanks.

My benefit occurred in late 1940, when I acquired two bikes! One from my uncle Art and the other from my cousin Lawrence. Both men were drafted into the US Army that year. For eleven years of my life I never had a bicycle. We were too poor to afford one. Now I had two!

Art's bike was rather interesting as it was a racing bike. It had narrow wheels and tires. It also had no brakes! It did have straps on the pedals that went over the top of each foot. To slow down and stop, I had to *backpedal*.

One day, about 5:15 pm, I was scurrying home on this bike. I needed to be home in time for supper. The narrow wheels of the bike were in the streetcar track. I was flying! The track turned to the right. The wheels went with the track. I continued forward, sailed over the handlebars, landed on the pavement, and skinned both knees and an elbow. I was lucky I didn't break my nose! This was my first experience with Newton's First Law of Motion. I learned more about this Law, years later, when I went to college.

Another memory I recall was something quite irksome. You know that I was always very tall. About the age of eleven I'd obtained an ID card from the streetcar company (CTA) showing my correct age. It insured my riding the streetcar at the child's fare.

At times Ron, friends, and I would go to a movie by ourselves, no adult. Because I looked like I was a high school student, the ticket seller would demand I pay the adult price. I'd show my CTA card to try and persuade her to give me a child's ticket. Half the time it worked, and I got a ticket at the lower price. Other times, I was forced to pay full price. But this wasn't what bothered me. If I tried to buy a ticket for an *Adults Only* film, I was always told, "Get out of here kid!"

## Chapter One: The Early Years

Here is a memory that some may find interesting. The address of my home was 1731 N. Hermitage Avenue. This house faced west. The next street to the west was Wood Street, which ran parallel to Hermitage. On Wood street, at the rear of the building at 1729 N. Wood, stood a garage. A car would enter or leave the garage through an alley. As a kid, I sometimes played ball in that alley. At the end of the day, when I came home, my mother always asked where I'd been playing and with whom. If I told her I'd played in that alley, she'd get very upset and say, "I don't ever want you to play there!" She never explained why it was off limits. Fifty years later she told me!

*1731 N. Hermitage Ave.*

The garage at this house was once used by some Italian criminals who changed their Cadillac to look like a police car. On February 14, 1929, two mobsters dressed in the uniforms of Chicago policemen joined two criminals dressed in suits. The four left the garage in their modified Cadillac, drove 2 miles away to another garage on north Clark Street, where they killed 7 Irish gangsters. That event is known today as The St. Valentine's Day Massacre. After the murders, the assassins returned to the garage on Wood St. They changed clothes, set the garage, and car on fire. I guess my mother feared their evil spirits would possess me if I played in that alley!

*My Marvelous Memories*

At the age of nine I became the boy who sewed for our gang's softball team. During summers, Ron, our friends, and I played softball all day, every day but Sunday. We used the 16 inch softball, commonly found in Chicago. Over the summer, we probably destroyed a dozen balls. However, if a ball still had some life left, it might be temporarily salvaged.

When the threads on the seams broke, the ball would unravel. I would take a damaged, but still usable ball, and sew it together. Dad gave me a long, sturdy needle 4 to 5 inches long with a large eye. I used string from a roll of twine as the thread. First, I'd run the string over a wax candle. This made the new threads waterproof. The waxed string was drawn through the large eye of the needle. I'd push the needle through the holes in the leather seam, pull it through, and make sure it was tight. Usually, it took 3 to 4 hours to sew up a ball. To paraphrase a line from Professor Auguste Balls, which he spoke to Chief Inspector Clouseau, in *The Revenge of the Pink Panther* movie "When duty calls, go no further, I saved balls!"

A sad memory from my early years, I wish to mention. All families have good and bad times, sad and happy events, from which they need to move forward. This story is about my uncle Frank (Jerry), my mother's older brother. Jerry was a veteran of WWI, who fought with the US Army in France. He left with the rank of 1st Sergeant. During a three-month period, he was one of General Pershing's chauffeurs. He came home from the war, about 9 to 10 years before I was born. He had changed. Often, he didn't sleep at home, he drank frequently, and couldn't maintain a job.

Chapter One: The Early Years

From 1935 to 1936 he served in the Civilian Conservation Corps (CCC). During this time, he lived and worked in the Forest Preserve areas SW of Chicago. He cleared walking trails, picnic campsites, and even helped build a toboggan slide.

Once a month, on a Sunday, the family would drive out to visit him. We'd all have lunch with him in their mess hall. All the residents were fed first. Then a second seating was provided for the workers and their visitors to eat. After two years he was discharged from this program due to his drinking problem. He was an alcoholic!

He came home to live on Hermitage Avenue but was frequently absent. When at home, he would be drunk, hostile, often shouting and cursing. In 1937, the family arranged to have him placed in a state-operated facility. Back in the 1930's, the country was not yet Politically Correct (PC). This hospital was called the *Elgin State Insane Asylum*. While there, his sister, my Aunt Berniece, would go visit him and would take Ron and me along with her. We'd ride the Logan Square El (elevated train) to downtown Chicago. At Quincy and Wells, we'd board an Aurora and Elgin electric train. Upon reaching Elgin, we'd walk a mile to the hospital. While she and Jerry chatted, Ron and I played around on the grounds. Berniece would always bring a basket of sandwiches, cake, cookies, and fruit for our luncheon. Of course, there was always too much food! It was left with Uncle Jerry!

I hardly ever spoke to him. He was in his forties, and I was just a kid of nine or ten. But today I still weep and pray for uncle Jerry. He was a victim of Post-Traumatic Stress Disorder (PTSD). This affliction was not even recognized as a medical problem until after the Korean War in the 1950's.

One of my mother's younger brothers was Ed. At the age of seven I became Uncle Eddy's go-for. Many a time he'd hand me a small pail, a dime, and say, "Bobby, go get me a bucket of beer." Other times, he gave me a nickel and say, "Bobby, go get me three cigarettes at the candy store." Imagine, sending a child out today to buy beer or cigarettes! Who'd be arrested? Uncle Eddy? Me? The Bartender? My parents?

# My Marvelous Memories

I want to say more about some **special people** in my life. I'll start with my brother, Ron, who was born in 1933. My mother instilled in me that I was his protector. I was to care for him and see that he never got hurt.

One day, I brought him home with a broken right wrist. While playing basketball on a cement court, he fell and broke it. Mom took us to our family doctor. He set the bone and put a cast on Ron's wrist and lower arm. The doctor charged $15 or $20.

Ron couldn't play basketball while his arm was in the cast. When it came off, he begged to join us on the basketball court. For a few days, I didn't let him play. Eventually, I gave in. Of course, on that first day in playing again, he fell and broke the same wrist. I brought him home. My mother was furious. She shouted at me, "You take care of him!" She gave me $5. That's all the money she had. So, I took him to a local medicine man who lived nearby, in a basement apartment. He was not a doctor. He provided our community with minor medical services. He'd been an Army medical corpsman in WWI. Ron remembers him as an alcoholic. He too was probably a PTSD victim.

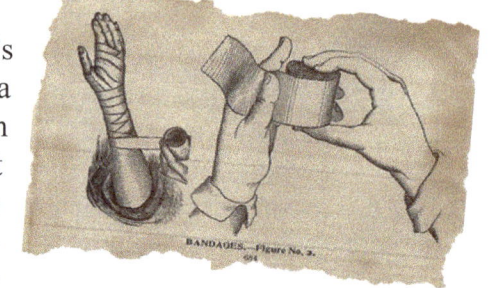

In any case, he set the bone in Ron's wrist. He used strips of cloth torn from a bed sheet instead of a cast. He tied them tightly to the wrist. He was happy to get the $5. Later, when the strips of cloth were removed, we saw a small bump on Ron's wrist. This bump didn't deter him from playing football in high school and college. It didn't prevent him from becoming a US Naval officer in 1955.

Half a block north of our home was an east-west running street called Bloomingdale Avenue. Along this street was an elevated concrete structure. It carried a single-track railroad line, a spur that delivered boxcars to factories alongside the track.

Mom never wanted us to play on this railroad track, so she told me a horror story. I'm not sure if it wasn't an urban legend! A boy who'd been playing in a boxcar on the track jumped off when it started to move. Unfortunately, he fell under the wheels, and was killed. Ron recalls another occasion when a boy fell off a moving boxcar and lost a leg.

Chapter One: The Early Years 21

In places along this elevated track, there were openings that allowed traffic to pass through. This elevated structure, called a viaduct was about fifteen feet high. It did not have any ladders or steps on which to climb up. However, half a block to the east of our home was Paulina Avenue, where there was a dirt hill up to the elevated track. This slope enabled us to climb up the elevation.

I was about 9 and Ron 5, when we were up there playing one day. Suddenly, we heard the noise of an approaching train. We weren't near Paulina, so we couldn't scramble down and get off the track. I grabbed Ron and pulled him under a wooden dock built alongside a factory. I held him tightly with both arms. While trembling, I kept assuring him we'd be OK. After a boxcar was uncoupled, the locomotive left. We quickly scurried off that railroad track and never told mom about this incident. The concrete structure exists today. It's been converted into a bicycle/walking path, known as The Bloomingdale Trail. It runs 2.7 miles west from Ashland to Central Park Avenue.

The next **special person** in my life was my father, Harry. He was 5' 9", but his older brother, Ike, was shorter. However, Ike's son, Gerry, had the same height as I did, 6' 5". Dad's younger brother and sister, Bill and Mary, were 6'. Since Ron was 6' 2", I guess we could say our height came from our father's genes!

Because he wasn't Catholic, dad never went to church on Sunday. He'd prepare our dinner while mom, Ron, and I were at Mass. It was always chicken! On Saturday, my mother would buy a fresh bird from the chicken store on Milwaukee Avenue. This store was stocked with cages holding live chickens, ducks, geese, and rabbits. She'd make her selection and pay for the bird. She'd then leave to do other shopping. An hour later, she'd return to get her chicken. It'd been killed, plucked, and cleaned out. She always brought home the feet, liver, and gizzards.

While we were at church, dad would start making chicken soup. Before the meat became too soft, he'd remove the chicken from the pot. He'd coat the pieces with flour, egg wash, and cracker crumbs. He'd then roast the pieces for about 20 minutes.

Sunday dinner began around 1:00 pm with chicken soup. A bowl of soup always contained a wedge of kugel, a savory Jewish pudding made with noodles. Dad always had the chicken feet in his bowl. On the occasions when mom was able to get extra livers from the chicken store, we would start dinner with an appetizer of chopped liver pâte on crackers. After the soup, we had a piece of chicken, another wedge of kugel covered with gravy, and some fresh vegetable. Because of my dad's preparing our Sunday dinner, I was never afraid to venture into a kitchen and try my hand at cooking. In coming chapters, you will hear about two periods in my life when I was a professional cook.

*Noodle Kugel Yummy*

When my children were young, they often had friends over for a Friday night sleepover. One Saturday morning, I made the kids a breakfast of green eggs and ham. Christine, who was 5 at the time, said, "Mom, why doesn't dad stay home and cook, while you go out and work?"

My father was a cigarette smoker, but not a drinker. I never remember him coming home drunk. He might have one or two beers on a Saturday night when he indulged his passion, to play pinochle. About 8:00 pm on Saturday, he'd walk half a block to a local bar to play cards. I recall occasions when our family joined our Jewish family for a social gathering. After dinner, he and his three brothers always played cards. Of course, it was pinochle! Frequently, his two younger brothers, Bill and Max, would get into a heated discussion. It was about how the cards had been played or should have been played. As they argued, dad and Ike just smiled and shuffled the deck.

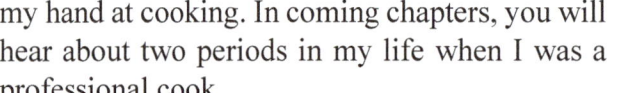

*Chapter One: The Early Years*

Earlier, I mentioned the basket of food taken for a blessing on Easter Saturday. The night before, dad would sit outside on the back porch. In his lap was a large wooden bowl and vegetable grader. With tears streaming down his face, he'd hand shred a horseradish root into tiny bits and pieces. He'd place the horseradish into two jars. One jar received a little beet juice to give it a red color. Both jars were placed into the basket that went to the church for a blessing on Easter Saturday!

Dad, as you know, was a tailor. For the last 25 years of his life, he specialized in making men's trousers. During the early part of this period, he was the production manager in a factory of 15 to 20 employees. He made sure that all the individual parts came together as a pair of trousers. In the last decade of his life, he and his business partner, Virginia, owned the factory. He supervised the production, while Virginia was the office manager, chief bookkeeper, and accountant.

On Saturday nights, Ron and I had a bath at home. We used a large metal tub, about 3 feet in diameter and 18" high. Once a month, dad took us to a bathhouse on North Avenue, just west of Damen. We placed our clothes in a locker of the dressing room, then descended the stairs to the washroom. Here dad lathered us with soap and scrubbed our bodies with loofahs. After rinsing off, we'd go into a steam room. Following this, we'd jump into a pool of cold water. It usually felt like ice water! After dressing, we'd stop in the cafe near the entrance. We'd share a plate of pickled herring and drink glasses of cold seltzer water.

This story reminds me that it was dad who introduced us to another wonderful delicacy. About once a month, a Sunday morning breakfast would consist of bagels, lox, cream cheese, onions, and tomatoes!

In 1955, my father began instructions in Catholicism and on Thanksgiving eve he was baptized. His partner, Virginia and her husband were his godparents. He also received the other Sacraments of the Roman Church.

Dad died in 1965 and was buried in St. Adalbert Catholic Cemetery in Niles, Illinois. My mom was buried alongside him in 1983. Before he passed, he had the privilege of seeing . . .

-His younger son finish college with a BA and the university with an MA, both in mathematics.

-His older son finish college with a BS in chemistry/math and the university with MS and PhD degrees in physics.

Two months after receiving my PhD, dad died. My father, an immigrant with only a 2nd grade education, was extremely proud of his sons!

I'm not sure when mom stopped working at HS&M. I suspect she worked during the early years of her marriage. When the Great Depression and I arrived in 1929, she became a stay-at-home mom. I would never say she wasn't a worker. Boy, did she work in the home!

Besides, all that was necessary to care for two infants born 4 years apart, she did the laundry every week for 11 to 12 people in our extended family. As I grew older, one of my chores was to help with the laundry. Monday was washday. In one corner of our kitchen was a Maytag washer. After moving the kitchen table and chairs aside, we'd roll the machine to the center of the room. Hot water was heated in kettles and pots on the stove. After washing a batch of clothes with hot soapy water, the water was drained into a bucket using a hose attached to the washer. I'd empty and flush this bucket of water in the toilet. We did not dump it into the kitchen sink. The lint would have clogged the sink and pipes. The washed clothes went back into the machine and run through a rinse cycle of cold water. They were squeezed dry using rollers on the top of the machine. The damp clothes were then put in a basket.

Spring, summer, and fall, the moist clothes were carried out to the back porches, hung on lines and fastened with pins. They remained there until dried. In the winter, or on rainy days, they dried on lines strung up in the 4th floor attic. After the clothes dried, mom ironed the shirts, blouses, and dresses. Other garments were folded and carried down and left in the proper apartment.

Laundry Day

In the attic just mentioned, mom had her workshop. There she had 2 or 3 sewing machines and a very large table, used to lay out and cut cloth. Nearby cabinets stored fabrics, scissors, patterns, and spools of thread. Mom sewed and made shirts for Ron and me. She made dresses for herself and her sisters.

Mom loved to garden! Her spring was spent in spading soil and planting flowers and vegetables. In summer, she was busy watering and weeding. In the fall, we'd enjoy the fruits and vegetables from her labor. She did all the food shopping for the entire family. Generally, she'd cook supper for only four: dad, Ron, herself, and me. Weekly she'd cook a big pot of spaghetti and much of it went downstairs to feed her sisters and brothers.

Once a month on a Thursday evening, she made a large pot of chop suey because her niece, Florence Irmen, stopped by for dinner. Florence worked in downtown Chicago as a secretary and she'd come by on her way home. After supper, mom taught her various skills in sewing and making dresses from patterns.

When shopping for food, mom would look and find great bargains. Because she was soft spoken and pleasant, her good friends in a Polish sausage shop on Milwaukee Avenue took care of her. Ham bones, from which slices were cut, were saved for her when the butchers got near the end of the bone. However, they always had a lot of meat left on them. She'd bring one home every week or two. Ron and I had wonderful sandwiches loaded with lots of ham for lunch. Best of all, she made the most delicious split pea and navy bean soups using the bone. These soups were always full of meat!

Her friends at the chicken store took care of her as well. Besides finding a nice chicken for her every Saturday, they'd save her chicken livers and gizzards when customers didn't want them. During the holidays, we always had a very nice, big, fresh turkey!

In August, fresh peaches became available. However, she didn't buy any at first. Her friends in the produce store saved peaches that were starting to spoil. They sold them to her at a discounted price. She'd bring them home, peel off the skins, and cut out the brown parts. From these pieces of fruit, she made the most delicious, sweetest pies I've ever eaten. She also made wonderful apple pies and strawberry-rhubarb pies using the products from her garden. But peach pie was my favorite!

Peach Pie

Finally, I wish to say that my mother, God bless her, was my protector! I don't believe I was a mischievous boy, just more inquisitive and adventurous. I'd come to her, confess my sins and tell her about something foolish I'd done. She'd listen, reprimand me, and advise me. She'd always finish by saying, "Let's not tell your father!"

Only once was dad told something about what I had done that was so bad, she just had to tell him. Maybe it was when I tried to smoke my first cigarette. Dad used a leather strap which hung on a hook inside the pantry door. He gave me a whipping. While wearing underpants, I only got 3 whacks across my butt. It was the only time he had to use it on me. I deserved it and have no animosity towards him! Ron never felt the sting of that whip!

In 1922, Chicago started building an island in Lake Michigan. It was one of the 5 islands proposed by Daniel Burnham in his **1909 Plan for Chicago**. His design called for 4 more islands to run southward from 12th Street to Jackson Park. This first island, called *Northerly Island*, was the only one ever built.

*Chapter One: The Early Years*  27

The Adler Planetarium opened on the north end of *Northerly Island* in 1930. Mayor William Thompson designated the rest of the island as an airport. However, during the Great Depression, funds were lacking. It wasn't until after WWII that Meigs Field was built and opened in December 1948.

*Northerly Island* was the location of The World's Fair of 1933, appropriately named **A Century of Progress**. It honored Chicago's 100 years of existence. It opened in May 1933 and was so popular, it was extended another year. It closed in October 1934. I went four or five times to this Fair with my parents or other family members. When I was five years old, I saw some *dream cars* in the American Automobile Manufacturers (AAM) Exhibit. However, I cannot recall the differences in a Cadillac VC-16 limousine, Lincoln-Zephyr, Nash Ambassador, Packard Deluxe, Pierce Arrow, or Studebaker Rockne.

As far as I was concerned, Chrysler stole the show. A dirt track was built adjacent to the AAM Exhibition. After waiting in line, one would board a Chrysler sedan for a ride around the track. Cars were lined up like cabs at a hotel. Best of all, the ride around the half mile track was **FREE**!

*1933 Studebaker Rockne*

Uncle Art, Cousin Lawrence, and I went to the Fair on July 15, 1933. We watched Italian seaplanes, called flying boats land in Lake Michigan. The planes were the Italian Air Armada led by General Italo Balbo. This Armada consisted of 24 seaplanes that landed on the shore of *Northerly Island* as part of the Fair. To commemorate the Armada's feat, Benito Mussolini sent a gift of a stone column, built in 300 BC, to Chicago. This monument, known as the Balbo Monument, and a street in Chicago, are named after the General.

A final ***Century of Progress*** story occurred after the Fair closed. I was only 5 years old. My two aunts, Berniece and Emily, took me to the State-Lake Theater in downtown Chicago in April 1935. At that time, the State-Lake theater showed a movie and staged a live vaudeville show. The movie ended. Out came the master of ceremonies (MC). A live band played a few tunes. A comedian told some jokes. A guitarist strummed and sang. The MC then introduced the featured performer ***fresh from her outstanding performance at the Century of Progress Fair!*** This was the reason my two aunts had come. They wanted to see her! They had no idea what kind of performance she was about to give!

The curtains parted and there was Sally Rand. Naked, except for a sheer body suit, much like nylon hose. She played peek-a-boo, while manipulating two large ostrich feathers in front and behind her. She swooped and twirled on the stage, while manipulating those fans to give the audience only a quick glimpse of her body. I was captivated!

As I gazed upwards, I noticed my two aunts who were seated on either side of me. They looked at each other in horror! The next thing I knew, I was dragged by both arms out of the theater. As we went up the aisle, I kept glancing back towards the stage. I wanted one last glimpse of Sally before we passed through the exit doors!

I have a few memories that relate to sports activities. Earlier, I mentioned the two bikes I'd acquired when Uncle Art, 18 years older, and cousin Lawrence, 12 years older, were drafted in 1940. These two men were my older brothers. They taught me to throw a ball, swing a bat, ride a bike, shoot a basketball, roller skate, and how to skate on ice.

## Chapter One: The Early Years

In winter, Lawrence would take me to Pulaski Park on Noble Street or Haas Park on Fullerton Avenue to ice skate. Art took me to the uptown area of Chicago. We rode three streetcars to get to Clarendon Park, east of Broadway and north of Montrose. Best of all, before boarding the first streetcar on our way home, we'd always stop for a hot chocolate! All three parks played waltzes over loudspeakers as we skated the evening away!

Art was a devoted White Sox fan and took me to my first major league baseball game. I was 6 when we went to see the Sox play the hated Yankees at Comiskey Park. Together, we'd shout out "Come on, Luke!" as Appling came to bat. We booed loudly when even a great player like Lou Gehrig came to the plate. Babe Ruth had retired before I ever attended a major league game. Despite all our loud shouting, the Yankees won!

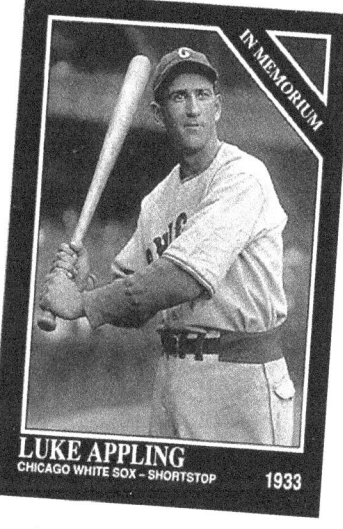

I can't recall the first Cub's game I saw, but I know it wasn't with an adult. It was in the fall, when a few of my friends and I went to Wrigley Field for the first time. All we needed was a nickel. This bought us a ride on a northbound Ashland Avenue streetcar. With a free transfer, we got on a bus heading east on Addison. When we got to Wrigley Field, we'd hang out behind right field on Sheffield Avenue. About the 7th inning the ushers in the right field corner would open some doors and let only kids in for FREE. We'd find empty seats in the stands and watch the rest of the game. If the park was full, which didn't happen too often, the gates wouldn't open. After the game we'd walk 3½ miles home!

My first Chicago Bears football game was also at Wrigley Field in the fall of 1943. I went to the game alone. All teams were scrambling for players during the middle of the war years. On Sunday, October 10, I went to see the Bears play the Chicago Cardinals. The radio and newspapers were touting that Bronko Nagurski was coming back to help the Bears. He'd retired from football 7 years earlier. He got into the game for 2 or 3 plays, but didn't do well. Later, in the championship game against the Washington Redskins, he scored a touchdown in the Bear's victory.

The Bears won the game I attended in October. In that game, a young Cardinal tackle from Auburn, named Chet Bulger, played in only his second year on the team. I met him a decade later and we became lifelong friends. He passed away in 2009. Chet taught me that there are no hated enemies among professional football players. He took me to several events in which former Cardinals, Bears, Packers, and Lions were present. I was amazed to hear these men chat and reminisce about different games they had played together. I sensed the respect they all had for each other because they had played the game!

The last **special person** in my life that I wish to mention was the pastor of Annunciation Church, Fr. Patrick J. Molloy.

During Prohibition, two major bootlegging operations supplied Chicago's speakeasies with beer and liquor. The *North Side Gang* (or *Irish Gang*) provided beer, whiskey, and gin for the downtown, north side, and Gold Coast areas of the city. This gang was led at first by Dean O'Banion, later by Bugs Moran, and then Hymie 'The Pole' Weiss. The *Chicago Outfit* (or *Italian Mob*) supplied the beer and liquor to the south side of Chicago and western suburbs. Johnny Torrio led these mobsters. Later, Al Capone was in charge.

In the 1920's, Fr. Molloy was a trusted go-between among these two warring gangs. In 1927, a $600,000 payment from one gang to the other went missing. What Fr. Molloy's involvement was in this *lost money* is not known. However, one night, a Capone henchman, phoned the head of the Roman Catholic Church in Chicago, Cardinal George Mundelein.

The Cardinal was informed that if Fr. Molloy was not out of town by midnight, he would be at the bottom of the Chicago River by morning. Fr. Molloy was immediately transferred far away, to Argentina.

In 1931, Capone went to prison and prohibition ended in 1933. Fr. Molloy returned from exile shortly thereafter. Upon his return, he was appointed pastor of Annunciation Church, less than a block from my home. He was just what our parish needed! Even during the Great Depression, he was a great fundraiser. He managed to collect money to pay for a new roof on the Church without incurring any debt. He refurbished the church basement into a modern hall for banquets and weekly bingos.

His annual carnival in late July, became a major fundraising event. Wabansia and Paulina streets were closed to traffic. A Ferris wheel, tilt-a-whirl, merry-go-round, etc. were erected. Canvas booths were placed on the sidewalks for games. Booths for food, beverages, and a beer garden, were located on the streets. Directly in front of the rectory was a large square booth. On four sides one could play a very special game of chance! Twenty-four slot machines were set up here! Nickel, dime, and quarter slots were present. No penny or dollar machines were to be found at our carnival!

Slot machines, of course, were illegal in IL during the 1930's. Throughout the 3-day festival, uniformed Chicago Police Officers, usually Irish, patrolled the carnival. They kept everything peaceful and orderly! During the 3 days of the carnival, I was one of Fr. Molloy's go-fors. The basement of the rectory was the bank for the event. Every hour, I canvassed all the booths to see if change was needed. I carried bills from the booths to the bank and returned with change. When the carnival closed each night at midnight, men carried the heavy slots into the rectory's basement. The back of a machine would be opened. Coins spilled out onto a table. Each slot was restocked and made ready for more action the next day. Other workers and I would place the remaining coins into trays of 40 nickels, 50 dimes, and 40 quarters. We'd then seal those coins into $2, $5, or $10 rolls. Throughout the year, these slot machines were found in the church basement.

They were available and used during the weekly bingos. In the late 1940's Fr. Molloy was transferred to St. Leo's parish on the south side. When he left Annunciation, the slots went with him!

A final story about Fr. Molloy. I was in 7th grade and served a weekday funeral mass as one of three altar boys. I'm convinced the deceased was a member of the *North Side Gang*. This notion is based on the observation that the departed person was not a member of our parish, and outside, lined up in front of the hearse, were four cars heaped with mounds of flowers. In addition, I received a $5 tip for my service. I'd never been tipped that amount!
Usually, I'd receive a $1 tip for a funeral mass or a wedding without a mass.

As this chapter ends, I wish to make a final point. It concerns a timeline. I graduated from elementary school in 1943. Six years later, in September 1949, I was teaching high school chemistry. Some of the students in my classes were only two years younger than me!

# Chapter Two
## The Preparation
## (1943-1949)

---

In September 1943, I started high school at St. Mel on the west side of Chicago. I was the first person, and probably the last, to attend St. Mel from Annunciation. For 2 years I'd planned, worked, and saved to attend a parochial high school. Why did I go to St. Mel? During my last year at Annunciation, I considered . . .

- Weber or Holy Trinity, 2 parochial schools less than a mile away.
- Wells public school, a mile from home.
- De Paul Academy, a distance of 2 miles.
- Lane Technical public school, only 3 miles.
- St. Patrick, just 4 miles away.
- St. Philip, less than 5 miles away.
- St. Mel High School... quite far!

St. Mel High School

Instead, I choose St. Mel nearly 7 miles from home. To get there I had to ride two street cars, Ashland and Madison. Considering my decision 75 years later, I think the choice was based on several factors. The country was in the middle of WWII. I wanted to enter the Army as an officer and St. Mel had a Junior Reserve Officers Training Corps (JROTC) program. Another factor was my two years of service as an air raid warden. Finally, my wish to be taught by brothers, not nuns. As a freshman, I was enrolled in six subjects: Religion, English, Latin, algebra, history, and military science.

Like my experiences in elementary school, my height contributed to my place in a line. The first day of military drill, I was put at the head of a 10-man squadron. Whenever we were called to Attention, the squad had to dress down, i.e., lineup alongside me.

I didn't go out for the freshmen football team. However, after a November tryout, I made the freshmen basketball team, and by January 1, I was the starting center! No! We didn't become city champions. We lost more than we won!

While in elementary school, no effort was ever made by anyone to encourage me to become a priest. I believe this was due to my being considered a mischief-maker. Starting in mid-October, the Brothers had a recruiter visiting all freshmen classes at St. Mel. His job was to encourage young men to join their religious community, known as the De La Salle Christian Brothers. He showed movies and slides of young men, just a few years older than me, who had joined this community. None of these young men planned to become priests, they were preparing to be brothers and teachers.

*La Salle Institute, Glencoe, MO*

Shortly before Christmas, I spoke to my homeroom teacher, Brother Leonard. I told him I was interested in becoming a Brother. He advised me to talk to my parents about this during the holidays. He needed to know in January whether I had their approval. A group of St. Mel freshmen were scheduled to leave in the 3rd week of January. They would continue their freshman year in Glencoe, MO. It was here the Brothers had a boarding school called La Salle Institute. Brother Leonard hoped I would join this group.

I returned in January and told him my parents had approved my going to Glencoe. However, I didn't want to leave St. Mel until March 1.

*Chapter Two : The Preparation*

I was the starting center on the freshman basketball team! Maybe that was a sign of where my major interests were. I finished the basketball season at the end of February. A week later I was in Glencoe, starting a new adventure.

Brother Leonard and I took a train from Chicago to St. Louis. We boarded a commuter train serving the southwest suburban area. I later learned this train was dubbed the Glencoe Hummer. We arrived in the dark of night. Someone met us at the Glencoe Depot. We drove up the hill to La Salle Institute. I was now at my new residence and high school. It was 7 miles from Eureka, MO, where Six Flags Amusement Park is located today. Of course, the park was not there when I arrived in March, 1944.

On that first night, Brother Gabriel, Director of the Preparatory Novitiate (PN), greeted me. He reintroduced me to Bob Finen, who was assigned to be my guardian angel. A guardian angel was a student at the PN, who showed a new boy around, and watched over him. I knew Bob, because he had been my classmate at St. Mel.

## Preparatory Novitiate
### (March 1944-June 1946)

•••••••••••

Except for military science, I had the same courses in the PN that I'd taken at St. Mel. My freshman class in March numbered 45 students. There were also 12 sophomores, 20 juniors, and 22 seniors at that time.

We ate our meals in the refectory, a large dining hall. Students sat at tables of 4 or 6. Each month we were assigned to different tables and companions. On a dais, a long table ran the width of the dining hall. The Brothers on our faculty, sat at this table, called the *high table*. Approximately 70% of the time, we didn't talk during a meal. A student would read aloud from a book about history or the life of a saint. The reader would stand on a platform at one end of the *high table*. Brother Paschal, our English teacher, sat at this end of the table. He was ready to help a reader pronounce a difficult word and signaled when a student was to be replaced. This usually occurred every 5 minutes.

I'm convinced that this activity helped us all become better teachers. We learned how to speak slowly, clearly, and loudly in a large room that contained 100 to 110 people listening in silence. However, there were ambient noises, as people passed dishes around and used their eating utensils.

*PN Dining Hall*

We all had many and varied chores. This was our home. We had to take care of it. Teams were assigned for washing dishes. One week, a team would wash and dry the breakfast dishes. Afterwards, they would reset the tables for lunch. The next week, this team would do the lunch dishes, and the week after the supper dishes. Finally, the team had a week off, before the cycle began again.

Other chores changed monthly. Examples would be (a) lavatories where toilets and sinks were scrubbed, and floors mopped, (b) similar scrubbing and mopping for shower rooms, and (c) sweeping and occasionally washing the floors in hallways, classrooms, study halls, dormitories, dining room, library, etc. Some chores involved a special assignment, for which one was trained. As a freshman, I was taught to cut hair. Over the next 16 years, I sheared many head, all men, of course!

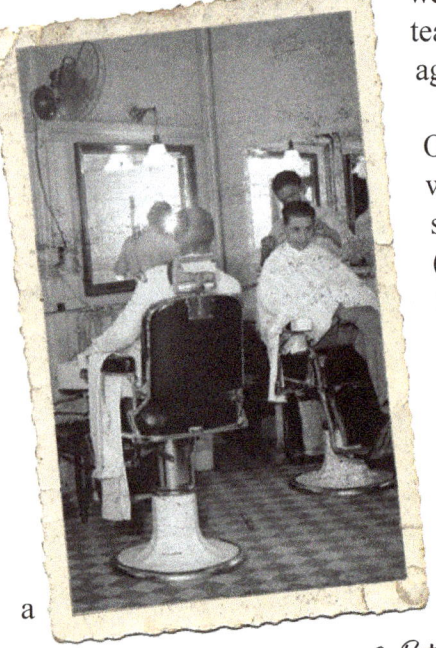
*Shave and A Haircut — 2 Bits!*

I enjoyed most sports activities, especially baseball, basketball, swimming, and handball. A new sport for me was soccer. I never did do well in using my feet to dribble or shoot the ball. I either played goalie or a defensive back.

## Chapter Two: The Preparation

Every morning started with prayers in the Chapel. We had Mass at 6:30 am, followed by breakfast. Then came an hour of chores including washing the dishes. Morning classes began at 8:45 am. We began lunch at 12:15 pm following a noon prayer session in the Chapel. Afterwards, we spent about 1½-hours playing games on the sports fields. After we washed-up, afternoon classes were held until 5:00 pm.

*Our Chapel for prayers and studies in the Common Room.*

Study periods were held before and after supper in the Common Room (CR). Our day ended around 9:00 pm with night prayers in the CR. My freshman year ended in early June 1944. During the summer I took two classes, one in typing and the other in ancient history. In August, we boarded the Glencoe Hummer and went home for a 30-day vacation.

*The Library*

My sophomore year (1944-45) was generally unspectacular. I took English II, Geometry, Latin II, French I, modern history, and music. I tried, with little success, to play the tuba, accordion, and oboe. My difficulty was that I couldn't read music! Consequently, I didn't join the band!

We did the general chores I mentioned earlier. I continued to shear scalps. In the fall I got a new job I loved immensely! I was assigned to clean the gym and stage. I would use a large dust mop, about 5 feet wide. First, I'd spray it with a chemical to pick up dust and shine the floor. Up and down, back and forth, over the gym floor and stage I'd run, pushing that mop. This left me 15 to 20 minutes before the work session ended. During this remaining time, I shot baskets with a ball I'd hidden in the gym!

*Shiny Gym Floors*

Another special job, for which I was trained, was to make ice cream. No! I didn't mix the cream, eggs, sugar, flavors, etc. This was done on Friday evening by the kitchen staff. On Saturday morning, during a 3-hour work period, Jim Krivich and I would start. In a walk-in cooler in the kitchen, we'd find a large metal cylinder, about 4 feet high and 20 inches in diameter. It contained the basic ingredients prepared by the cooks. We'd carry it outside to a nearby courtyard. After filling it with fresh cream from our farm, it was placed in a machine used to make the ice cream.

*Ice Cream — Yummy!*

The metal cylinder with the liquid was put in the center of a barrel-like structure on this machine. The space between the cylinder and barrel was filled with chipped ice and scoops of rock salt. An electric motor turned the cylinder. About two hours after starting the motor, we had ice cream. This dessert served 200 to 220 people on Sunday's noon dinner. Of course, Jim and I always had to test a sample of our ice cream, to be sure it was r e a d y for the next day!

A final memory from my ice cream story. One day the 220-volt fuse to the electric motor blew. The motor stopped before we'd finished. The courtyard was wet from melted ice. Jim refused to touch the fuse! I took it and started to carefully screw it into the socket. The next thing I knew, I was 8 feet from

Chapter Two: The Preparation    39

the fuse box, my back against a brick wall, and my butt on the concrete courtyard. I said, "Wow! That was something." Then I held the fuse with a dry cloth to screw it into the receptacle. An hour later, Jim and I enjoyed our dish of freshly made ice cream!

In June 1945, my sophomore year ended. The seniors graduated and moved over to the Novitiate. Juniors were now seniors and I was ready to become a junior. However, a new adventure was about to begin for this *maverick*.

The new senior class had only 7 students. At this time, our junior class numbered 26. Sometime that spring, the new Director of the PN, Brother I. Francis, and the faculty decided to increase the number of seniors. So, 7 new juniors were suddenly made seniors and I was one of the *Lucky 7*!

*Sophomore Class of 1945 —*
*Source of The Lucky 7!*

**The La Sallian**    15

## Our Sophomores

Bottom Row: L. Drbousek, E. Staub, J. Burke, J. Labelle, J. Downey, D. Vernon  Second Row: J. Krivich, L. Nolan, T. Bock, J. Schingle, C. Brosnan, E. Everett, G. Ranft, F. Twaragowski, Brother L. Rupert, H. Vaughn.  Third Row: D. Leitel, T. Sullivan, D. Harkin, P. McManaman, J. Foley, F. Donatelli.  Top Row: E. Bradtke, L. Boyle, R. Krupp, W. Monteith, J. O'Mara.

The Lucky 7 had to take extra courses to acquire enough high school credits to graduate in 1946. We took three courses in the summer of 1945 while all the other students took only two. I recall taking (1) phonetics, a speech credit, (2) ancient history II, and (3) trigonometry. All seven of us had trouble with trigonometry. I later realized this was due to not having taken algebra II before trigonometry. We took this algebra course in our senior year.

*Junior Class of 1945 —
The Lucky 7 Joined this Group!*

14     The La Sallian

## Our Juniors

Bottom Row: R. Botthof, G. Henlein, G. LaVaque, W. Carr, R. Rademacher, J. Finnegan
Top Row: G. Wegener, G. Castonguay, Brother J. Paschal, H. Sarnecki.

*Glencoe Depot,
Where's the Hummer?*

In August, we boarded the Glencoe Hummer and started our 30-day vacation at home. The summer of 1945 was somewhat special! WWII in Europe had ended in May, Little Boy, the 1st atomic bomb, destroyed Hiroshima on August 6, and Fat Man devastated Nagasaki on August 9.

## Chapter Two: The Preparation

*Here Comes the Hummer!*

Early Tuesday morning, August 14, six PN classmates and I boarded an electric train in Chicago. We left the Northwestern RR Depot and headed north towards Milwaukee. However, we got off in Waukegan, the hometown of Ray McManaman our fellow PN classmate. Ray and his father met us at the depot. We walked a mile to his home where Ray's mother served us a wonderful breakfast of pancakes, eggs, and milk. While eating and chatting, we listened to a radio and heard rumors that Japan was preparing to surrender.

After breakfast, Ray led us to a nearby park and gym. We played basketball for about five hours, with friends he knew from his elementary school. After showering, we returned to Ray's home around 5:30 pm for supper. We now heard the wonderful news! Japan had agreed to unconditional surrender. WWII was over!

Later, we walked to the depot and boarded the 7:30 pm train to Chicago. Shortly, we stopped at a station for 15 minutes.

We were inundated with young men, all dressed in white, climbing on board. They filled the seats, clogged the aisles, and crowded the platforms between cars. The train was full of ecstatic young men, only a year or two older than me. They were recruits from the Great Lakes Naval Training Station.

I cannot find the words to describe the joy and happiness I saw in these men. Just 24 hours earlier, they faced the completion of their basic training. After which, most would have been deployed to the Pacific. Here they would have fought in the invasion of Japan. They knew they faced death or injury. Many would never have returned!

When I spoke to them, they all told me various stories of how only a few hours earlier their officers, with huge smiles on their faces, had come into their barracks. The officers said, "Get out of here guys! Everybody's got three days leave. Be sure to wear your whites! Be back by midnight Friday! I don't care if you're drunk as a skunk! But, remember, to come back! You're still in the Navy. Don't go AWOL!"

Shortly after 9:00 pm, the train arrived in Chicago at the station on Randolph and Canal streets. I walked downtown to the Loop. State Street was congested with old and young people, sailors, soldiers, marines, and youngsters like me.

I wandered up and down State Street, joining the throng for hours. Every military person, male or female, was fair game! They were embraced, hugged, and kissed by everyone! It was a sight I never saw before or since! I got home around 3:00 am. My mother was waiting for me. She asked, "Where've you been?" I answered, "I was walking around downtown!" She smiled and hugged me tightly! As she kissed my forehead, I heard her say, "OK!"

*Aug 14th, 1945 — Chicago*

In the fall of 1945, I returned to Glencoe and continued as a member of the senior class. I took French, English literature, algebra II, chemistry, and American history. Each course was a 2-semester course. The Lucky 7 needed extra credits, so we took an additional course each semester, but I can't recall what they were.

*Chemistry Lab*

As far as my chores went, I continued to mop the gym—and shoot baskets. I sheared scalps and made ice cream. I'm not sure if this was a new chore, but another classmate and I, put out the equipment and chemicals for our weekly chemistry lab. Afterwards, we cleaned up and put everything away.

## Chapter Two: The Preparation

Being involved in seven courses, my senior year flew by quickly. It was not long before it was June 1946. I graduated from high school 3 years after finishing elementary school. I sent my diploma home to my mother and father. Parents did not attend high school graduations at La Salle Institute. As I end this segment of *MS*, I wish to mention the names of three classmates. In two years, we'd become the closest of friends. They were Ed Twaragowsky, Jim Krivich, and Ed Everett. We were all about the same age and came to Glencoe in 1944 as freshmen. I think we became close friends because we played pinochle together whenever we had a quiet, nonphysical recreation period. Throughout our lives, I kept in contact with them. Later, Mary, my wife, met and knew them all.

*Me and Ron at The Glencoe Pool*

Ed Twaragowsky started at St. Mel the same year I did. We first met at Glencoe. After leaving the religious community, he taught at a public high school in a suburb of St. Paul, MN. He retired and continued to help the young by teaching GED classes. Sad to say, like so many of my friends, Ed has passed on.

Jim Krivich, my fellow ice cream maker, was from the south side of Chicago. He began high school at De La Salle (DLS). When he left the religious community, he also continued in education. He was an administrator in the public schools of Atlanta, GA. His last position was as the principal of one of Atlanta's high schools. He retired at age 65. He wanted to enjoy the rest of his life traveling about the world. Regrettably, Jim died 6 months after he retired.

Ed Everett also started high school at DLS, Chicago. He was one of the Lucky 7 and was with me in Waukegan on August 14, 1945 playing basketball. Later known as Brother Dominic, he was the only one of the Lucky 7 who persevered in the religious community of Brothers. Sadly, he too has passed on. My wife, Mary, remembered him well, as that *crazy* Brother who visited us in IL and FL on his motorcycle. Yes, yes! Brother Dominic was a biker boy!

*Thinking about my years in high school has brought back both happy and sad memories.*

*I've shared many with you!*

## Novitiate
### (June 1946-August 1947)

•••••••••••••

The Novitiate is a period of 15 months in which one focuses entirely on the religious life. I learned what was expected of a person who planned to live a life of poverty, chastity, and obedience. I was also taught to follow the Rules of the Order, and to live in a community with fellow *Brothers*.

At the end of August 1946, our class donned the religious habit and were given new names. Henceforth, I was called Brother Hugh Conrad. I will not dwell on the time I spent reading, listening to seminars, or discussing the topics I mentioned above. My life was like a priest in a seminary, a minister in a divinity school, or a rabbi in a rabbinical school. We had little time to play organized games during the Novitiate.

## Chapter Two: The Preparation

Every Thursday afternoon, we took a long hike of 8 to 12 miles to give us some physical exercise. Throughout the year, we were enrolled in extension courses from Saint Mary's College (SMC). During the year, I earned 14 hours of college credit hours (CH) in Church History, French III, and Religion. There were, of course, many chores to be done. Some involved strenuous physical effort.

*Me, Age 17*

*Sacred Heart Grotto*

*Outdoor Stations of the Cross*

During the first 3 months, I worked on the farm under the direction of Brother Baldwin. Here I was, a boy raised on the streets of Chicago, now mucking out horse stables, harnessing mules to wagons, loading and riding those wagons, etc. I enjoyed it immensely! It was great fun to be a farmer! I continued shearing the scalps of my fellow Novices. In the summer of 1946, I was taught to be a cobbler. I replaced heels and saved soles. A machine was used to sew a leather sole onto a shoe. I was also a member of the coal crew.

The buildings at La Salle Institute were heated by a coal burning furnace. The buildings and furnace were at the top of a hill. In the valley, at the foot of the hill, was a railroad spur where a gondola of coal was left. I usually worked in the gondola. Three or four of us shoveled the coal into a dump truck. The truck was driven up the hill and dumped next to a manhole cover. Others shoveled the coal down into a bin, near the furnace below. Later, we'd all take a long shower to scrub the dust from under our fingernails and out of our hair and eyebrows. It was a great physical activity!

*Up the hill went the coal*

Because I was the tallest Novice in my class, I was assigned to be a grave digger. No! We didn't use a backhoe. Instead, my partner and I used a spade, shovel, and pickaxe. We needed the pickaxe to chip away at the limestone substrata we often encountered. I remember a grave I dug in the summer of 1946. We ran into a thick limestone slab only 3 feet from the earth's surface. It was the shallowest grave I ever dug!

August 31, 1947, we finished our Novitiate and took our first vows. We packed and then boarded the *Glencoe Hummer*, and off we went to St. Louis ⇨ Chicago ⇨ Winona, MN by train. There we began our college studies at SMC.

# Scholasticate
## (September 1947-August 1949)

•••••••••••

We Brothers were now college scholars, so our program was called the Scholasticate. We majored in subjects we planned to teach. Our freshman year at SMC began with 4 days of orientation. The first two days we took test after test. The third day, we heard presentations from Deans and Department Chairmen.

*Heffron Hall, 1st SMC Building*

On the 4th day I finally met with my academic advisor, Brother Emery. We were going to plan my schedule for the next 3 years. After greeting me, he looked over my test scores. He asked what I wanted to teach. Immediately, I said, "History!" I selected this because during my senior year, I had two semesters of American history. My teacher was excellent! He inspired a love of history in me. I wanted to be like him! Brother Emery said, "Fine! However, I want to say this to you. I just looked over your test results. You have outstanding scores in all subjects. You are well prepared to major in anything you want. I'd like to suggest you consider majoring in science or mathematics. We need science and math teachers. Not everyone I counsel has the skills you have. I want you to think about this for 24 hours. Talk to Brother Gregory, your Director. Come back tomorrow at 1:00 pm. If you still want to major in history, good! We'll plan out your program to pursue that degree. However, if you decide to follow my suggestion, we'll lay out a schedule in math and science."

I spent the next 24 hours thinking and seeking advice from others. Brother Gregory even let me phone my parents to discuss it with them. I came back to see Brother Emery the next day. I walked in and said, "Math and science it is." He smiled and started to plan my first semester. I've never looked back!

Seventy years ago, a full-time college student took a minimum of 12 credit hours a semester. Fifteen hours was considered average. A minimum of 120 was required for a BA degree. For a BS degree, 132 to 140 hours were needed. Including the summer school of 1948, I earned 48 credit hours in my first 12 months at SMC.

*The Physics Lab*

All grades were either A's or B's. During the next 12 months I earned another 47. Except for one C, all grades were A's or B's. By mid-August 1949, I had accumulated 109 hours—25 in chemistry, 18 in math, and 11 in physics. Things were soon to change for this maverick as *MS* continues.

Before I end this chapter, I wish to relate other aspects of my life at SMC during these 2 years. If I wished, I could attend and cheer for a SMC team in a sporting event. At this time, SMC had varsity teams in football, basketball and baseball. None of us, in the religious community, could be on any of these teams. While in the classroom, we were told not to engage in long conversations with the lay students. Exceptions to this *Rule of Silence* were made for group assignments or working together on a laboratory experiment.

Because all of us Scholastics were on different academic schedules, we couldn't have any organized physical activities together. Instead, we had a physically demanding chore assigned us on Saturday mornings, when no classes were scheduled. A morning work period was 3 to 4 hours long. Once a month I still cut hair. However, I acquired other new chores.

During the fall and spring, I was an *assassin*. No, not of humans, but of *nasty critters*. These varmints were moles and gophers. They left trails and mounds of dirt on the playing fields of the college. These deposits were dangerous! A player running to catch a ball would be looking upwards.

Chapter Two: The Preparation

Not seeing these mounds of dirt, he could trip over one, break an ankle, or suffer a bad sprain. I went out on Saturday mornings to set up traps for moles. However, these traps couldn't be used to kill a gopher. Instead, I would seed their tunnels with poisoned bait.

*A Mole Trap*

*A Gopher Mound*

In summer, while enrolled in 3 classes, I was on the paint crew. In 1948, we painted the buildings on the college farm. We didn't paint the buildings and barn red! We painted them battleship gray. The college had purchased 5-gallon buckets of paint for 50¢. This paint had been prepared during WWII for the US Navy to coat their ships. It was sold to SMC as part of the War Surplus Program. This paint was loaded with lead, to protect the ships from saltwater and rust.

An older, retired Brother supervised our crew. He would pour eight of these 5-gallon buckets into a large, empty drum. He'd stir it with a 2 x 4, because he wanted the consistency and color to be uniform. Our crew of five would fill small pails with the gray paint, and off we'd go to spread it onto the buildings. The wood in these structures had never seen a drop of paint before, so the first coat was soaked up like a sponge. A few days later, a building would get a second coat. To reach the higher parts of a building, we would stand on ladders or scaffolds.

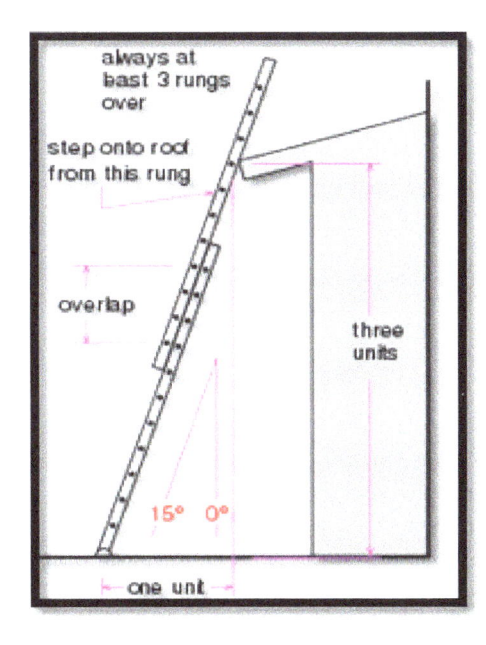

Since I was tall, I had the job of painting the silo. To do so, I used an extension ladder which was fully stretched to reach the top. It was about 35 to 40 feet above ground. The Occupational Safety and Health Administration (OSHA) did not exist, so no one stood at the ladder's base to prevent it from slipping. One day, I was at the top, painting away. I looked down and saw that the cows had been let into the stockade. The base of the ladder was resting in this enclosure. I quickly scurried down! I feared a cow would swish her tail against the ladder and I'd come tumbling down like Humpty Dumpty!

In the summer of 1949, I was again a member of the paint crew. This year we painted the wooden window frames of a building recently purchased by the college. It had been the Winona County poor farm, but was now the main dormitory for the Scholastics. First, we had to scrape away the old paint and dry caulk around the windowpanes. After re-caulking, we applied two coats of paint to the frame.

During the winter months, November-April, I had a Saturday morning chore I enjoyed immensely. I was a lumberjack! The college buildings were located on a bluff, 50 feet above a valley below. This bluff was about 600 to 700 feet long and was covered with various hardwood trees. In the fall of 1945, tiny evergreen saplings had been planted on its slope. In 1947, a program was started to remove all the old hardwood trees. In time, the bluff became covered entirely with evergreen trees as the hardwood trees were removed.

I was one of four on the lumberjack crew. We did not use any power saws! They didn't exist at this time. Instead, we had a 2-man handsaw, known as a misery whip. This saw was drawn, back and forth, by two people. We only had two misery whips, each about 6 feet long. Each Saturday we'd cut down two or three trees. Then we'd trim off light branches with axes. Large branches and the trunk were cut with our misery whips into 3-foot logs. Afterwards, we'd roll the logs down to the valley below. The branches, we pulled down. During the following week, farm workers carted the branches and logs away. They split the logs and sold them for firewood.

I loved working out in the crisp cold air, physically exerting myself, and coming in for a nice, hot shower. A luncheon of hot soup and sandwich never tasted better!

*A 12-foot Misery Whip in Oregon*

During the summer, we'd go on a picnic once a week on Wednesdays, when no classes were scheduled, and parks were virtually empty. We'd go to places within 50 miles of the campus, typically an hour's ride away. We'd play softball, walk the trails, and take a dip in the pool, if one was available.

On picnic days, I was assigned to the beverage crew. Shortly after breakfast, we'd leave for the park in a truck. An hour later, buses carrying the main group of Scholastics followed. Our job was to stop and buy cases of soda. No beer! We were all under 21! We'd also buy blocks of ice. When we got to the park, we'd fill 3 or 4 large vats with soda, ice, and water. By the time everyone arrived at the park, the drinks were nice and cold! Occasionally, our picnic was held at Merrick State Park, a few miles north of Fountain City, WI. The town was on the eastern shore of the Mississippi River. This park had wonderful trails along the shore and through the wetlands of the Mississippi. Fishing was pretty good too!

In Fountain City, we'd stop to buy ice at the Ice House where large blocks of ice were stored in a barn-like structure. The blocks came sliding down a ramp completely covered in sawdust. We had to rinse them off before loading them onto our truck. I learned that this ice had been cut out of the frozen Mississippi, the previous winter. The blocks were covered in sawdust, to insulate them from warming and melting.

*Harvesting Ice from a Frozen River*

Earlier, I mentioned that things were about to change for me in August 1949. A week before Labor Day, I received word to report to the Brother's high school near St. Louis. This school was just west of Forest Park, in the suburb of Clayton, MO.

The college phase of my preparation to become a teacher was over. It was time for me to go to work!

# Chapter Three
## A Teacher's Beginning
### (1949-1960)

••••••••••••

## CBC, St. Louis, MO
### (September 1949-August 1951)

••••••••••••

My teaching career began at the high school level. I joined the faculty of 30-35 Brothers teaching and living in the religious community at Christian Brothers College High School (CBC).

Brother Conrad, the Principal and Director, gave me a break. I only had two preparations, chemistry and plane geometry. Instead of 5 or 6 classes, I only taught 2 classes of each. In addition, I had only one extracurricular activity. I was the Band Coordinator, not the Band Director. A lay person, Major Sutter, was the Band Director and teacher of music. My job was to supervise the budget and arrange for two annual concerts, Christmas and the Spring Concert.

CBC had a Junior Reserve Officers Training Corps (JROTC) program. All the students were cadets. Each week ended with a military parade on Friday afternoon. Led by the Marching Band, the entire battalion passed in review. The band also played and entertained at home football games.

My lighter load enabled me to continue my college studies. I took two extension courses from SMC in the fall of 1949 and earned 6 credits. One, a course in education, was Observation & Practice Teaching. The other was in philosophy. During the second semester, I attended classes at St. Louis University (SLU) on Saturdays. There I earned a total of 5 credits in education and philosophy. I also went to SLU in the 1950-51 academic year and earned another 5 hours in education.

*Other memories from this time I recall are ...*

- I learned to drive, both an automatic and stick-shift car.

- I learned to be a motion picture projectionist. Once a week, on weekends, we showed a movie. Television was not available in 1949! Next to our recreation room was a small room which had two motion picture projectors, much like those found in any movie theater. Two small windows were in the wall separating the rooms. Light from the projectors streamed through them onto a screen in the recreation room.

- On Friday afternoon, when it was my turn, I'd drive to a warehouse. It supplied films to theaters throughout St. Louis. There, I'd pick up the movie scheduled for that weekend. Later, on Monday afternoon, I'd return it. An hour after Saturday night supper, I'd threaded the two projectors, made fresh popcorn, and stocked the refrigerator with Budweiser. Remember, this was St. Louis—Anheuser-Busch country!

- As a projectionist, I had to learn to watch for the spot on the upper right which flashed three seconds before the end of a reel. This was the signal to start the second projector. Doing so insured the movie flowed continuously, from reel-to-reel, without interruption. It took some time before I became skilled in seeing that this process went smoothly!

## Chapter Three: A Teacher's Beginning

I continued cutting the hair of my fellow Brothers.

In 1950, Ash Wednesday fell on February 22 and Lent began. The next day I had some great fun. After morning Mass, we went to breakfast. This morning, pancakes were served. I loaded my plate with 4 or 5. I also made 2 slices of toast and covered them with peanut butter and jelly. One of the Brothers at the table said, "Conrad, what are you doing? It's Lent!"
I responded gleefully, "Next year! Next year! I'm only 20!"

In the spring of 1950, I went on a trip with Major Sutter. He wanted to *reward* me for all the work and help I had given him during the year. Earlier in his life, he had taught music and been the band director at the public high school in West Frankfort, IL. He was invited to be the *Honorary Band Director* at their spring concert. He'd arranged and cleared this trip with Brother Conrad, the Director. One Saturday morning, we drove to West Frankfort, checked into a motel, and went to dinner before the concert. He treated me to my first ever *restaurant steak*! *Delicious!* Later that night, I slept in a *motel room* for the first time!

Here's a scary recollection. Early one Monday morning, I went into the chemistry stock room to get equipment and chemicals for an afternoon lab. I noticed some small bottles and beakers had been tipped over and left on the shelves and counters.

At supper that evening, I asked Brother Charles Roe, who also taught chemistry, if he had let some students into the stockroom. If so, I wanted him to know that they had left the room in disarray. He said, "Uh-oh!" He excused himself and left the table. Ten minutes later he returned and said, "Everything is OK now. I found him and put him in my biology room."
I asked, "What did you find?" He replied, "A copperhead. I found it Saturday afternoon while hiking in the woods." I was a little upset that I'd been working in the stockroom where a poisonous reptile was slithering around!

In January of 1950, I fell down a darkened stairway and broke a bone in my right wrist. I didn't know it was broken. I thought it was only a *bad sprain*. About two months later, I went to a doctor regarding another medical issue. At the end of my visit, I asked him about the pain that lingered in my *sprained wrist*. He took X-rays and showed me a small bone that was fractured in my wrist. It was held in place by surrounding bones. He put a cast on my wrist which I wore for two months. At the end of May, more X-rays were taken, and the doctor informed me that the bone was healing. He put on another cast to insure it continued to mend properly. He told me to leave the cast on until the end of July. I did as he said, and the wrist turned out just fine!

My first year of teaching ended. I returned to SMC in the summer of 1950 to take more classes. During this time, I earned 6 credits in physics and 3 in math.

My second year at CBC was not much different than the first. However, this year I taught 5 classes—2 beginning algebra, 1 plane geometry, and 2 chemistry. I mentioned earlier that I'd earned 5 credits in education at SLU during this academic year.

After attending summer school at SMC in 1951, I'd accumulated a total of 143 CH by mid-August. I finally received my BS in chemistry/mathematics, *cum laude* (outstanding scholastic honors), with a minor in physics.

There was no graduation ceremony in August. I picked up my degree at the Registrar's office, brought it home, and left it with my parents. I started my 3rd year of teaching following a two-week vacation at home.

*Chapter Three: A Teacher's Beginning*

# St. Patrick, Chicago
## (September 1951-June 1953)

The year I began teaching at St. Patrick, it was located on Des Plaines and Adams streets. It had opened in 1861, ten years before the Great Chicago Fire of 1871. It was, and still is, considered the oldest Catholic school in Chicago. It was the last year that St. Patrick Boys' HS would be at Des Plaines and Adams.

*Old St. Patrick's Church*

*Busy Union Station*

The school year began with about 25 to 30 in the community of Brothers on the faculty. I taught chemistry, physics, and algebra II. Since I'd earned my BS degree, I was also assigned to coach freshman basketball. I gave haircuts to most of the Brothers, since I was the only barber in the community. Once a month, I'd walk two blocks to the nearby Union RR Station. There I'd have my hair cut in a shop located in the station's arcade.

I was also assigned to be a bus driver. The school bus was an old, prewar yellow school bus, now painted green. I shuttled various sports teams to away games.

In 1950, the Catholic Church held its first Jubilee since 1933. Pilgrims were urged to travel to Rome to receive a special indulgence for their sins. Many were unable to travel to Rome during the Holy Year of 1950. Conscquently, the Church extended this opportunity in 1951 by letting pilgrims travel locally.

In Chicago, the conditions to obtain this special indulgence were for a pilgrim to visit and pray at 4 churches on a Sunday. The churches designated were . . .

1. Holy Name Cathedral on north Wabash Avenue.

2. Holy Family Church on Roosevelt Road.

3. St. Mary's Church on south Wabash.

4. St. Patrick Church, the oldest church in Chicago.

This extension of the Holy Year ended on December 31, 1951. Every Sunday, from September to December, the area around St. Patrick High School became congested with pilgrims. People arrived in busloads, from all over the metropolitan area.

*St. Patrick Church*

Des Plaines, a one-way street, ran south. The buses would stop in front of the school to deposit the passengers. Parish volunteers assembled the pilgrims into lines 4 abreast. The lines moved south, and people entered the Church through the main entrance in front. After praying, they were directed to exit by a side door onto Adams street, where their buses were waiting for them. Once loaded, a bus went off to the next church in their schedule. Four to eight policemen saw that traffic moved as smoothly as possible. On January 1, 1952 all of us Brothers celebrated the New Year and especially the end to the Sunday congestion in front of our home!

By this time, I was used to taking university courses as a part-time student. My first year at St. Patrick, I earned 10 hours in zoology and 3 in math at DePaul U. I never had a course in biology, so I wanted to see what I'd missed. I took a zoology course at DePaul's main campus on Fullerton Avenue during their fall and winter trimesters. On Saturdays, I was literally gone all day. A 3-hour lecture started at 9:00 am. We had an hour break for lunch, after which a lab was held from 1:00 to 4:00 pm. When I got home, it was time for supper. I took a math class in the spring trimester, which met one night a week at DePaul's downtown campus.

## Chapter Three: A Teacher's Beginning

Thanks to one of my chemistry students, I had a ride on a Chicago fireboat. His father worked for a company that had installed the pumps on the fireboat. Once a year, he would test the pumps on the boat to see that they functioned properly.

*Chicago Fireboats!*

*The Victor L. Schlaeger Fireboat*

On Saturday, December 29, my student, his father, and I boarded the Victor L. Schlaeger. It was moored on the south shore of the Chicago River, directly opposite the Merchandise Mart. We sailed out into Lake Michigan where all pumps were turned on, tested, and adjusted. As we sailed back home, the firemen treated us to lunch in their dining room, onboard the boat. The men seemed to be very happy and contended. They shared with us some of their escapades while fighting fires from a boat.

*My Marvelous Memories*

I mentioned earlier, that this was the last year for St. Patrick Boys High School at Adams and Des Plaines. Let me explain why. However, I must first describe the physical arrangement of St. Patrick parish in 1951.

On the northwest corner of Adams and Des Plaines was St. Patrick Church, the oldest church in Chicago. It is still there today. The priests' rectory or home was directly behind the church. A convent for the nuns was west of it. Further west of the convent was a 4-story building where the nuns taught an elementary school on the lower two floors. They also conducted a girls' high school on the top 2 floors.

Now let's come back to the corner of Adams and Des Plaines. A gymnasium was located north of the Church on Des Plaines. It was used primarily by the boys' high school basketball teams. On occasions, usually a Sunday, the parish held bingos and church suppers in this gym. The boys' high school was north of the gym and behind it, to the west, was the Brothers' residence.

These physical arrangements started to change, all due to the Kennedy Expressway which was built during the 1950's. The convent and school building used by the nuns was in the path of the expressway and both buildings were scheduled for destruction. In June 1952, the boy's high school closed. The Brothers moved out of their residence. The nuns moved into the vacant residence. The boys' high school building was now used as an elementary school and girls' high school.

*Kennedy Expressway Construction Begins*

It was during the spring of 1952 that I met several times with Dr. Paul Copeland, physics department chair at Illinois Institute of Technology (IIT). We discussed my desire to obtain a graduate degree in physics at IIT. He pointed out that though my credits in math (27 CH) were acceptable, I was *weak* in physics (17 CH). Consequently, I took a double summer session in 1952 at SLU. I earned 6 hours in physics and 6 hours in math during this summer. In the fall of 1952, I started at IIT as a *provisional graduate student* in physics.

## Chapter Three: A Teacher's Beginning

My second year at St. Patrick was a unique year. It was due to the closing just mentioned . . .

No freshmen were enrolled in the 1952-1953 academic year.

Classes were held for sophomores, juniors, and seniors only. Where did we hold these classes for 500 to 600 students?

We held classes at St. Mel HS because the religious community of Brothers was the same at both schools. St. Mel had a building on Madison and Kildare that accommodated 1000 students. Sophomores, juniors, and seniors were taught there. Half a block to the west was their freshmen building for 400 to 500 students. This is where I had begun my high school career in 1943.

In 1952, classes for St. Mel students started at 7:30 am and ended at noon for upper classmen. No lunch periods were scheduled. A short 20-minute restroom break was held in the middle of the morning. All St. Mel students had to be out of this building by 12:30 pm. St. Patrick students used this same building from 1:00 pm to 5:30 pm. The arrangements for no lunch periods, with a midafternoon restroom break, were similar. Meanwhile, construction on a new St. Patrick high school building at Belmont and Austin Avenues began in 1953.

The community of St. Patrick Brothers was now reduced to 12. We used a vacant convent on Hamlin, just north of Chicago Avenue, as our residence. This home was ½ block south of Our Lady of Angels (OLA) Church. Unfortunately, the parish school was the scene of a catastrophic fire in 1958. Ninety-two pupils and three nuns died in that tragic fire. While at this residence on Hamlin, I continued my barbering services and developed more of my culinary skills. Our cook was given the weekends off. Another Brother and I prepared the weekend breakfasts. Usually, I fried bacon and eggs and occasionally made pancakes.

I'll describe our typical school day, Monday to Friday, and how it benefited me as a scholar. Usually, we'd rise late and go to the 7:30 am Mass at OLA. Following breakfast, we'd spend the morning reading, preparing classes, grading papers, etc. After lunch, our bus would leave around 12:15 pm. We were at St. Mel 15 minutes later to meet and teach our St. Patrick students.

*IIT Main Hall*

Throughout this year, I followed a slightly different schedule. I'd rise early and go to the 6:00 am Mass at OLA on Monday/Wednesday. I'd rush home for a quick breakfast of toast and coffee.

I used the Chicago Transit Authority (CTA)—Pulaski bus, Lake Street *EL*, Jackson Park *EL*—to get to IIT for an 8:00 am class. The class ended at 9:50 am. After a short break, I took another class from 10:00 am to 11:50 am. When this class ended, I'd hustle to St. Mel, using the CTA. Meanwhile, one of the Brothers brought a bag of mine on the bus. It contained my high school books, papers, tests, etc., and a sandwich for lunch. I was ready to teach my high school classes!

During the 1952-1953 academic year, I earned 16 graduate credits in physics. A MS degree required only 32 CH. I was ½ way there! In addition, I justified Dr. Copeland's faith in me, because I earned A's in all four courses. I was no longer a provisional student!

*IIT Physics Building*

Chapter Three: A Teacher's Beginning

In the summer of 1953, I lived at DLS high school, at Wabash and 35th Streets. It was less than a ½ mile walk to the physics classrooms or laboratories at IIT. By the end of August, 12 months after I began my studies as a part-time provisional student, I had earned 25 hours—19 were in course work and 6 in research. I needed only 4 hours in research and 3 in course work to complete my MS degree!

## Chicago
### (September 1953-July 1955)

I was now assigned to DLS, where I taught chemistry, physics, and algebra II for the next two years.

In the fall of 1953, I took a 3-credit math course and received the only B in my MS degree. Over the next two summers, and at other times, I continued my research. All calculations were done by hand using a Marchant Calculator. No computers were available at IIT in the 1950's. In August 1955, my thesis paper was accepted. My transcript showed I had earned 32 CH with a GPA of 3.91. IIT did not hold a graduation ceremony during the summer of 1955.

*Marchant Calculator from the 1950's*

On January 28, 1956, I attended the winter graduation ceremony and received my MS degree in physics. This was the first graduation ceremony my mother and father attended, since my elementary school graduation in 1943!

## Various remembrances during these two years at DLS follow...

I continued to be a motion picture projectionist, barber, and one of the school's bus drivers. However, I learned a new skill because the school bus at DLS was an old, pre-WWII Greyhound. During the war, no buses were built for private use. Greyhound Corporation began building newer ones for their fleet in 1947. The old ones were sold when the new buses came into service. Several of the Brothers' schools had purchased these older Greyhounds. I had to learn a new skill called double clutching. I'd first push down on the clutch and shift the stick to neutral, in order to move out of one gear. Then, I'd push the clutch down a second time to shift into the next gear.

I drove the bus locally, on trips to Glencoe with new high school recruits, and on a long trip to Cleveland, OH. There were also several drives around Lake Michigan, one of which I want to share.

In August 1954, Bro. George Carney and I left Chicago in an empty bus. When we left around 9:00 am, it was already 90° with a humidity over 90% in the city. We only wore T shirts and brought a small overnight bag. We passed through Milwaukee as we drove north. We stopped for the night at a Brother's school and residence in Escanaba, Michigan. When we arrived, around 5:30 pm, the temperature was 45°. During the night it dropped to 35°. We went to downtown Escanaba and found a store open. Each of us bought a $10 sweatshirt because we didn't have much money between us. We had no credit cards in 1954. This was all we could afford. The sweatshirts helped keep us a bit warmer.

Street in Escanaba, MI

The next morning, we left at 5:00 am. I drove east through the Hiawatha

*Chapter Three: A Teacher's Beginning*

National Forest, along the northern shore of Lake Michigan. We were heading for the Straits of Mackinac. It was 35° outside. I was freezing! Bro. George was lying on a bench seat in the rear of the bus, trying to sleep and stay warm from the heat of the motor. You ask, "Why didn't you turn on the heat?"

Neither of us knew how! When we returned home, our mechanic showed us a valve in back, by the motor. If we'd given it a ¼ turn, we would have been toasty warm!

We arrived at the Straits and I drove the bus onto a ferry which carried us across water to the lower peninsula of MI. During the crossing, we observed the construction of a new bridge. The Mackinac Bridge had started in 1953 and opened in 1957.

You probably wonder about the reason for a trip with an empty bus. We were heading to Charlevoix, MI, a city on the eastern shore of Lake Michigan. We went to pick up a load of Brothers who had just finished a 30-day retreat on Beaver Island. As they got off the ferry from BI, we met them and drove them back to Chicago.

During my two years at DLS, one of my *extracurricular duties* was Athletic Director of Football. I did not coach any football team, and I was not involved in the basketball or baseball programs. I supervised the entire football budget. This meant I arranged for and paid the referees for all home games. I made sure that the bus was reserved and driven to all away games, varsity, JV, and freshmen. In cooperation with the Father's Club, I arranged for the annual football banquet in January. This last task included purchasing jackets, letters, trophies, certificates, etc. which were awarded at the banquet.

These recollections lead to several stories I wish to mention . . .

## The Eddie Carroll Story

A few years before I arrived at DLS, the school started to enroll black students. In the fall of 1953, three black players were on the varsity team. One of them was a 3rd string halfback named Eddie Carroll. I never met Eddie's father, who worked for the Chicago White Sox. He prepared their lunch or dinner, and served it in the clubhouse after each home game.

One day in mid-October, I was informed that Eddie was absent from school and would miss football practice for a week or two. His father had died. That day, I spoke to Frank Mannott, varsity head coach. I asked him to tell the players to remain in the locker room after practice. I wanted to meet with them.

When I spoke to them that afternoon, I told them to bring a dress suit, shirt, tie, and shoes to school the next day. After practice and showers, they were to get dressed in these clothes. We'd be going on a short trip together. Someone asked, "Where?" I answered, "We're going to the wake of Eddie Carroll's father." Most of the boys accepted that, but I saw frowns on a few faces. One of the disgruntled lads asked, "Why?" My curt answer was, "He's your teammate!"

The following evening, I herded all these well-dressed young men onto the bus. I drove them to the wake held at a Baptist Church on South Park Boulevard, now called Dr. Martin Luther King Jr. Drive. It was dark by the time I parked the bus near the church. I told the young men to lineup in a column of twos on the sidewalk. I informed them to follow me into the church, walk slowly past the open casket in front, and say a word or two to Eddie. I would speak to Eddie's mother.

This memory is one I've never forgotten! I marched down the middle aisle in the church, like a general leading his troops on parade. The boys walked behind me in a single column of twos. The church was occupied by 50 to 75 black folks sitting in various pews, conversing quietly. When they saw all these white young lads, all conversation stopped. We marched up that aisle in total silence! I spoke to Eddie's mother and said, "Eddie's teammates wanted to come and offer him their sympathy. Please accept our condolences and prayers." I recall seeing the tears in her eyes as she said, "Thank them all for coming. I know it will mean a lot to Eddie!"

Chapter Three: A Teacher's Beginning

## The McKown Story

Mr. McKown, a graduate of DLS, owned McKown's Restaurant on south Ashland and 85th Street. For years, all the sports banquets were held at his restaurant. I phoned him around Thanksgiving of 1953 to schedule and make plans for our football banquet. I mentioned we had 3 black football players on the varsity team, and about 12 others on the JV and freshman teams. These players and family members would be attending our banquet. At first, he said, "No problem!" He called me about two weeks later and suggested we find another location. He had discussed our banquet with others. He now felt his restaurant would lose business if it was held there.

Thanks to Al Lewendowski, a lay teacher at DLS, I found Margo's Restaurant on Ashland and 64th Street. We had our football banquet there in January 1954. All were welcomed, including Eddie Carroll, his mother, and grandparents. Our meal was like attending a Polish Wedding Reception. It started with a cup of soup and a small salad. The waitresses then brought out platters of polish sausage, sliced roast beef, and fried chicken. This was followed with bowls of sauerkraut, mashed potatoes, gravy, and green beans. Everything was served family style. Requests for seconds and thirds were readily satisfied. Throughout the evening, many of the boys, as well as, their parents thanked me.

When I left Margo's later that night, the two senior co-captains were standing on the sidewalk outside waiting for me. They approached me and said, "Brother Conrad, thank you for the best football banquet we've had in four years!"

DLS continued to have their football and basketball banquets for years at Margo's. When Margo changed her location a few years later, the teams followed her out to Narragansett and 63rd Street. Unfortunately, the restaurant closed in the 1970's and I lost contact with Margo. She was a dear friend for over twenty years. My wife, Mary, and our children met her, for my family often dined at Margo's on 63rd Street.

## The Jackie Murphy Story

The first year at DLS, I taught two chemistry classes. In one of them, I had a senior named Jackie Murphy. Jackie had all the features of an Irish Leprechaun. Though he lacked the beard, he had a head of fiery red hair and was somewhat of a scallywag.

He often spoke out in class and told jokes. I had to bite my tongue to keep from laughing. He really was a jester. After two weeks of this, I spoke to him about his behavior in class. He did quiet down for a day or two, but soon resumed speaking out.

Towards the end of September, I asked Brother Francis, the Assistant Principal, to remove him from my chemistry class. I was fearful that if he remained, I would end up failing him. It took a few days before he was rescheduled into a typing and a business class.

Jackie and his class graduated on the Sunday before Memorial Day. The ceremony was held in the school gym and afterwards refreshments were served outside in the courtyard. Pictures of graduates and family members were being taken everywhere. As I walked around, congratulating the graduates, Jackie brought his widowed mother over to meet me. He greeted me with a big smile and said, "Mom, I want you to meet the teacher who kicked me out of his class!" His mother smiled, and while giving me a kiss on my cheek whispered, "Please come over to my home tonight for some cake and coffee, and maybe a wee draft."

Later that night, I did stop at Jackie's home and met Mary and Jim Flannery. Mary was Jackie's aunt. For over forty years she and Jim were very good friends, until they both passed on. They often provided me with updates on Jackie's life. I guess the typing class helped, for he went on to be a court reporter! Jackie never married, but I heard that during his mid-thirties, he adopted an orphan, who had special needs. As a single parent, he raised a blind child!

## Chapter Three: A Teacher's Beginning

# The Chet Bulger and Len Kosiek Stories

During the time I was Director of Football, I became friendly with some of the coaches. Two of them I would like to mention.

Chet Bulger, an Assistant Football Coach, was much like me. He was 6' 3", and I was 6' 5", and we both weighed about 260 pounds. He played professionally for the Chicago Cardinals after playing football at Auburn U. He was a starting tackle on the 1947 Cardinal NFL Championship team.

I learned from him that professional athletes could be bitter opponents on the field. However, off the field, and especially in the years of retirement, they were quite friendly. He took me to gatherings of retired Cardinals, Bears, Packers, and Lions.

I saw these men all laughing and enjoying each other's company. They were all members of a select community that had *played the game!*

CHET BULGER - 1947 CHAMPION

## Len Kosiek —

Len Kosiek was the baseball coach at DLS. He and his wife Carol have been my friends for over 60 years. Regrettably, Len passed away about 10 years ago in 2010. I haven't heard from Carol in about 5 years.

Len Kosiek — Baseball Coach

During these two years at DLS, I seemed to develop more fun and enjoyment in my classes. It may have been due to the fact I was becoming an experienced teacher.

Because I was a bus driver, I often took my science classes on some great field trips. A few I recall were visits to the . . .

## Republic Steel Factory

Republic Steel factory at 95th Street and Lake Michigan to see iron smelting, blast and steel furnaces, and the rolling of steel I-beams and ingots.

## AMOCO Oil Refinery in Hammond, IN

to see gasoline and petroleum processing.

## Sanitary Ship Canal

Sanitary District of Chicago main facility at 39th and Central Avenue. Since 1889, this plant has treated wastewater from Chicago and Cook County. Its processed water led to the building of the Sanitary Ship Canal and the reversal of flow in the Chicago and Calumet Rivers.

During the 1950's, the country was in the middle of the *Cold War*. Chicago sounded sirens and alarms throughout the city at 10:30 am every Tuesday morning. This was the city's *Air Raid Warning* rehearsal drill. Students and faculty were instructed to take cover under desks or laboratory tables as preparation for the dropping of *The Bomb*. I was quite aware of the destructive force of an atom bomb. Instead, I would say to my students, "If it's really *The Bomb* falling, let's sit here and look out the windows. It's the last thing we'll ever see!"

Earlier, I mentioned that by August 1955, I had finished the requirements for my MS degree. My 2-year stint ended at DLS Chicago this summer. I left for my new assignment at DLS in Kansas City, MO.

## De La Salle, KC, MO
### (September 1955-June 1956)

*De La Salle Kansas City, MO*

I arrived in Kansas City to begin a 1-year assignment at DLS high school. These schools were like St. Mel and CBC, for both had JROTC programs. All students were cadets. The school and Brothers' residence were on The Paseo and east 16th Street. The cadets marched, drilled, and paraded in a broad, long park on the east side of The Paseo.

I taught chemistry, algebra II, and trigonometry classes. I coached freshman basketball, besides driving the school bus, and cutting hair. Our residence was only 1½ miles to the center of downtown KC. We could walk to see a matinee at a first-rate movie theater. No need to show movies in our house on weekends.

*Movie Theater*

In downtown KC, I saw an interesting sight. At major intersections, people waited at the signal lights. Every 3 minutes a signal to WALK appeared. All vehicles stopped! Pedestrians walked north, south, east, west, and diagonally! It was called a scramble crossing.

*Everyone, Scramble!*

I noticed something unusual about some of the players on my freshmen basketball team. Some boys were as young as 13 and others, as old as 15. This happened because in the Archdiocese of KC, MO, the Catholic elementary schools ended at 7th grade. Students who lived in KC, KS were in a different Archdiocese where the parochial schools finished elementary school after the 8th grade.

I didn't take any classes at the university this year. Instead, Brother Benedict Lidinsky and I played a lot of golf, at a great course, in a city park. The Swope Park Golf Course was adjacent to the KC Zoo, and the fees were very low. The school year ended in early June. It marked a significant change in my professional career. For the next 65 years, I was involved in higher education.

I had a week's vacation at home in Chicago during the first week of June. On June 12th, I boarded The City of New Orleans and headed for Memphis. I went early to the Dearborn Street RR depot and got a seat at the very back of the parlor car. Earlier, I had read H. L. Mencken's comment, "a parlor car was the best investment open to an American."

*A Parlor Car*

*Inside the Parlor Car*

What a wonderful trip that was! Once past Homewood, IL I gazed at the lush green prairies of IL. Kankakee, Champaign, Effingham, and Carbondale quickly flew by. After passing through KY and into TN, I was in Memphis. The 11-hour trip seemed like minutes as I sat drinking beer and Cokes and snacking on hot dogs and potato chips!

## CBC, Memphis TN
### (June 1956 - July 1958)

••••••••••••

CBC was the oldest collegiate degree granting institution in Memphis. It opened in 1871. Its first collegiate degrees were awarded in 1875. From its beginning, the school also offered high school courses. This program was known as CBC High School.

The enrollment in the college courses dropped significantly during the Great Depression and WWII era. The high school continued, but the college was reduced to a 2-year community college. In 1953, CBC began again offering four-year programs in Business and Electrical Engineering. The first graduates received their degrees in 1955. Today, it is a university, offering several graduate degrees.

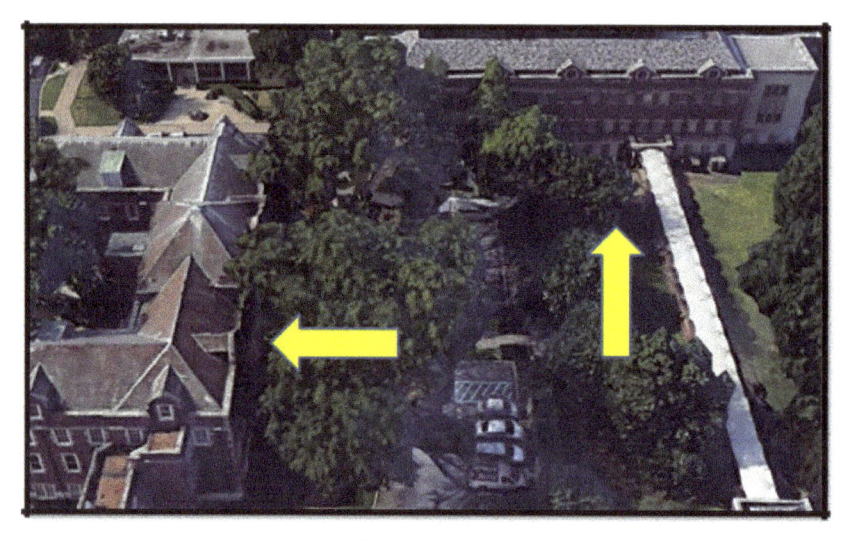

*CBC, Memphis*
*Main College Buildings 1956*

The college had started building its first dormitory a year or two earlier. The dorm was scheduled to open in the fall of 1956. I worked on a crew of Brothers who helped the maintenance staff in finishing the bedrooms. We put together bunk beds, designed and manufactured by the maintenance staff. Because these beds were to be used by young men, they were anchored to the wall by large bolts. Our crew also assembled two desks, with drawers, that were also home built. A bedroom was designed to hold two residents. Each student had a bed, desk, bookshelves, dresser, and closet with a sliding wooden door.

*Bell Tower (blue)*
*First Dorm (yellow)*

*Chapter Three: A Teacher's Beginning*

*Design of Two Apartments:*

| Bedroom #1 | Bedroom #2 | Showers, Toilets, Sinks, Mirrors | Bedroom #3 | Bedroom #4 |
|---|---|---|---|---|
| Parlor #1 | | | Parlor #2 | |

The bedroom I've been describing was part of an apartment. One entered from an open balcony and upon entering, you would be in a small parlor. It was intended for relaxing, smoking, chatting, and watching TV. Directly opposite the entry door were two other doors, each of which led to a bedroom. Thus, an apartment held two bedrooms, each containing two students, with the parlor shared by four. To the right of the entry door was another door to the bathroom which contained two toilets, two sinks/mirrors, and two showers. Beyond this bathroom, was an adjoining apartment. The bathroom served eight students. I have described an apartment because I want to tell you the tale of my Chair Story.

## My Chair Story

Brother Alfred, Director of Buildings and Grounds, oversaw the Dormitory project. He planned to furnish the parlors with a TV, small sofa and 2 or 3 comfortable chairs. These furnishings were to be purchased, not built. However, he wanted to be sure the furniture would be sturdy enough for use by our college students.

A salesman left him two new chairs, supposedly *indestructible*, to be tested for their durability. A chair had a steel frame of legs, seat, and back. Bolted to this frame was a large plastic bucket-shaped seat, like a tulip flower. Bro. Alfred placed these chairs in the Brother's recreation room. He also put an announcement on the bulletin board requesting our help in testing the toughness of the chairs. They were in the rec room for 3 or 4 days before I gave it a go! I did what many others had done. I sat in it, wiggled, and bounced my butt up and down. I pushed outwards using my back and arms. It did not break. It was indestructible! Then I had an inspiration. I put my arms on the outside and squeezed inwards. I heard a loud CRACK as the back of the plastic seat shattered down the middle.

A week later, the salesman returned ready to write up an order for 150 chairs. He could not believe the sight of the broken chair. None had ever shattered like that in the four years he'd been selling this product. Bro. Alfred phoned and asked me to come to his office. When I arrived, he told me to sit in the unbroken chair and see if I could break it. I sat in it, put my arms on the outside, and squeezed. Another CRACK and I broke my second chair! The salesman left without a purchase order, but with 2 broken chairs!

*Me at age 26*

Our dorm crew went out one evening after supper. We drove to a nearby Dairy Queen (DQ) to get each of us an ice cream cone. The car stopped in the DQ parking lot. The Brother driving, who had the money, got out and asked me what flavor I wanted. While he was getting our cones, I noticed a water fountain on the DQ wall. A sign above it read *For Colored Only*. I asked the Brothers sitting in back what it meant. I had never seen anything like that before. One of them said, "Conrad, you've only been in the mid-west. You are now in the south. Don't be surprised by what you may now experience!"

Another new experience I had that summer was because I was on the *dorm crew*. Shortly before we quit work one Friday afternoon, I was told to shower, and meet at the car in an hour. We were skipping supper with the community and going out to Vito's for pizza.

As we went into Vito's, one of the Brothers handed me a quarter and said, "Here, you'll need this!"

We entered the restaurant, which looked very small to me. On the left side were the ovens with a spacious area for preparing the pizzas. A small bar on the right side had no stools. The middle area held only three small unoccupied tables. We walked to the rear where a door led to a back room. It held 35 to 40 large circular tables. When I entered, a man sitting at a small table asked me for a quarter. I gave him a quarter and received ½ of a red raffle ticket. When we sat down I asked, "Is there going to be a raffle?" My four companions all laughed. One said, "No! Memphis and Shelby County are dry. You cannot buy a shot of whiskey, a glass of wine, or a bottle of beer anywhere in town. However, private clubs can sell you wine and beer." With a smile, he held up his raffle ticket and said, "We are now members of Vito's Private Pizza Club." I enjoyed being a member of this club, as I had several beers with my pizza!

## My Tim McCarver Story

Speaking of clubs, I am reminded of my Tim McCarver story. When I taught at CBC, high school and college buildings were on the same campus, but in different locations. In fact, some Brothers taught classes in both programs. At that time, the high school football team had an outstanding QB named Tim McCarver. I watched him play in several games. He led the football team to state championships in 1957 and 1958. He was named an All-State Player in both football and baseball. Tim went on to have a professional career in Major League baseball. He is among only a few who played in the Major Leagues for four decades (50's, 60's, 70's, and 80's). However, my story is not so much about Tim, as it is about his father and older brother.

Tim's brother was getting married, and some of the Brothers were invited to the wedding. Brothers William Rhody, "Moose" Edmund, Philip Morgan, Alfred Moroni, and I went to the wedding and reception.

The reception was held at the Catholic Club where liquor could have been served. But none was! Instead, we ate the wedding cake and drank a nice, cold punch made from lime sherbet. The bride, and her parents who were hosting the reception, were Baptists. They did not drink alcohol!

Tim's father, a lieutenant on the Memphis police force and of fine Irish stock, was initially upset by their plans for the reception. However, by the day of the wedding, he was in gay spirits for he had come up with a solution. The reception at the Catholic Club was held from 2:00 to 5:00 pm and during this time, Tim's father handed out a printed card to everyone, including the bride and groom, the bride's parents, and their family and friends. On the card was the address and directions to the McCarver home. At 5:30 pm a second reception would start there. The card didn't say it, but the kitchen was stocked with all manner of food, and the basement held all the beverages necessary for a grand Irish wedding. The other Brothers and I went to this second reception. We didn't get home until around 1:00 am. Yes, the bride's parents and other members of her family were there as well!

---

Classes at the college began in September. I was the chairman and only full-time member of the Mathematics & Physics Department. I taught all the calculus and most of the physics classes. As I mentioned, the CBC high school program was still operating on this campus. Some of the math teachers taught both high school and college courses as part of their full-time schedule. Having to teach calculus enabled me to finally understand it!

Besides my teaching and administrative duties, I had one other job. I was the Director of the dorm that had just opened. The building had 4 floors in the shape of an L. On the 2nd floor, where the short and long arms joined, was my suite. From the balcony corridor, you entered my office, furnished with a large desk, chair, bookshelves, typewriter, and chairs for students. My bedroom and bathroom were beyond the office. Outside my office was a large bulletin board, on which I posted announcements and notices for the students. The college had employees who weekly cleaned all bathrooms and floors in every student apartment. They left clean bed linen and towels but did not make beds. My office and apartment were also vacuumed and scrubbed by them.

In the 1950's, colleges were expected to exercise parental control, especially in housing facilities. Consequently, we still had Dormitory Rules which I had to enforce. Some of these were . . .

## Chapter Three: A Teacher's Beginning

- ✓ Sunday-Thursday every student was to be in bed with lights out at 11:00 pm. Using a large flashlight, I inspected every room and made a bed check from 11:10 pm to 11:30 pm.

- ✓ Friday and Saturday nights *lights out* was at 1:00 am.

- ✓ Clothing was not permitted to pile up on the floor of a bedroom or parlor. I checked on this once a week, usually on Saturday afternoon.

- ✓ Except for Friday and Saturday evenings, students were to be on campus from 6:00 to 11:00 pm. If necessary, a pass could be obtained from me, which allowed a student to be *off campus*.

- ✓ Penalties for infractions of rules would be a *campus* awarded by me. A *campus* meant a student could not leave campus on a Friday or Saturday night. More serious infractions were handled by the Dean of the College, Bro. Levian Thomas. He would phone the parents of a wayward chap and sometimes expel a student from the college for a very serious offense.

The enforcement of the above *Rules* led to several interesting and humorous stories I wish to share . . .

## My Beale Street Story

One Saturday night, I was sitting in my office reading, grading papers, preparing lessons, whatever. Ninety-five percent of the students were off campus. They were out and about in the city. About midnight my phone rang. It was a Memphis police lieutenant requesting my presence at the downtown police station ASAP.

When I arrived at the station a ½ hour later, I was ushered into his office. He said, "I'm sorry to tell you I have 8 men from CBC locked up in our jail." He bit his tongue to keep from laughing while he told me of their horrible crime. "Around 11:00 pm a squad car found them playing football in the middle of Beale Street, between 2nd and 3rd streets!" When he finished, we both had a good laugh. With a smile he said, "No fines! No tickets! No court dates! Just get them out of here!" Once they were released, I told them to come to my office when they got back on campus.

We all gathered in my office about 1:30 am. Several had to sit on the floor, because I didn't have enough chairs. In as solemn a voice as I could manage, I asked what possessed them to do such a thing. They told me that three weeks earlier, they'd been in downtown Memphis on Saturday night. While walking along Beale street around midnight, one of them had remarked, "This place is so dead! I bet we could play football in the middle of the street." Over the next few weeks, two teams of four were formed. Throughout the dorm, bets were placed. Last night was *game night*. They also mentioned that two dozen or more spectators were present along the sidewalks, cheering for their teams. When they saw the police car, they quickly fled, and returned to campus. The 8 players were all glad to hear that no tickets had been written, or any fines charged by the police. One of them asked, "What about you? Are we going to get a campus?" My answer was, "No! It's too funny! Get to bed. I'm tired!"

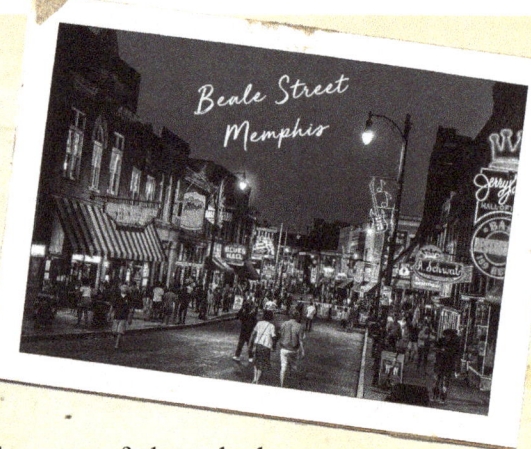

## My Moonshine Story

One Saturday afternoon, I was checking on the neatness of the bedrooms and apartments. In Bill's closet, I noticed a pile of clothes which I moved a bit. Underneath, I found a small, beautifully built, *brass still*.

I put a note on the bulletin board for Bill to come see me. When we met, I told him what I'd seen in his closet. However, I surprised him by complementing him on the excellent job he'd done in its construction. He told me that he'd been building it for several months. On the day I discovered it, he was in town buying cornmeal, sugar, yeast, and cheese cloth to start his first batch.

I told him he couldn't operate a *still* producing *moonshine* on campus. Later that week, he came to my office and showed me a cardboard box in which he'd packed his *still* and cushioned it tightly. He sealed the box and addressed it to his father in Kansas City. He took it to the post office and shipped it home. As he left, I said, "Bill, it's OK with me if you and your father want to make *moonshine* in your home. You just cannot do this at CBC!"

Sixty years after this occurrence, Bill and I reconnected, thanks to Facebook. We shared a laugh as this scallywag revealed how he had put one over on me! Everything about this story is true! Except on the Saturday I found his still, he was in town buying supplies to start his *3rd batch* of moonshine!

## My Bowling Alley Story

This story has several facets to it. You must remember that I was in Memphis in the latter years of the 1950's. American Machine and Foundry (AMF) and Brunswick Corporation (BC) had developed their *automatic pin setting machines*. These companies were installing them in bowling alleys around the country. Memphis got its first one in the summer of 1956. Shortly thereafter, this bowling alley was loaded with players and leagues every day of the week from noon to midnight. Then this alley started a wonderful program to encourage more individuals to come and play. A widely published ad read, "Monday-Friday, from midnight to 11:00 am, *ALL* the bowling you want for only $1!"

Many of our students were bowlers. They wanted to take advantage of this great opportunity! However, they faced a major problem—the rule of *lights-out* and *in-bed by 1:00 am* on Friday nights! So, a conspiracy was hatched.

One Friday evening, a student parked his station wagon off campus in a nearby neighborhood. He was back after a 2 block walk. The conspirators spent that evening in various activities, i.e., playing cards, going to the movies, shopping, etc. They were all back in their rooms getting ready for bed at 12:30 am. When I made my rounds after 1:00 am, they were all fast asleep. When I finished going around and retired, their plan was to quietly leave their rooms, descend the stairway furthest from my apartment, and walk to the waiting station wagon. They would then drive off and go bowling to their hearts' content!

*Unbeknown to them, I knew of their plans!*
*I had my own grapevine!*

As Paul Harvey would say, "Here's the rest of *MS!*"

I went through my inspection of all bedrooms and returned to my apartment. I turned out the lights after a few minutes. Instead of going to bed, I put on my jacket, brought my flashlight, and went down the stairway nearest my apartment. I walked to where the station wagon was stashed and hid in bushes, near a corner where they would pass. It wasn't long before the first student arrived. Within a few minutes ten were crammed into the wagon. The engine started, headlights came on, and the wagon slowly moved towards the corner. I stepped out of the bushes into the street. As they approached me, I turned on the flashlight to its brightest setting, shined it into the windshield, and shouted, "Stop!" The car halted immediately!

I walked towards the wagon and silently circled it while peering in. I made a mental note of all the occupants. When I passed in front, into the headlights, they finally realized who it was. I walked to the open driver's window, leaned in, and said, "Have a good evening, boys!" I quickly turned around and went home to sleep!

On Saturday afternoon, I met with all the renegades as a group. I began by asking if they'd enjoyed themselves. When did they come home? They told me they quit around 3:00 am and got back around 3:30 am. They left early, because they weren't having any fun. They were worried about their punishment. A campus? A call home to their parents? Could they be expelled from CBC? Sent home for a semester? Or for good?

I told them that their punishment was 2 nights of *campus*—the following Friday and Saturday nights. Several of them literally gave a sigh of relief! I sent them on their way with the following words, "You know, I have nothing against you guys bowling. In fact, I like to bowl myself. If you had asked me, I probably would have given you permission to go ahead and bowl all night long." The meeting was over, and we all parted.

Chapter Three: A Teacher's Beginning

The next aspect to this tale happened a month later. It was the week of the Thanksgiving holiday. Some students were going home for the holiday. Others, who had to travel great distances usually stayed on campus. They went home during the longer Christmas period. Two students came to my office on the Saturday before Thanksgiving. One said, "Do you remember, you told us to ask you about going bowling all night, if we wanted to? Some of us, who are not going home, would like to go bowling this coming Wednesday. How about it?" I quickly replied, "No problem! Just give me a list of those going by Wednesday afternoon." I forget how many went, but there were at least two carloads. To finish this segment, I want to mention what happened on Thursday morning.

On Thanksgiving, we had a late Mass in our chapel. I was walking to the Brother's dining room for breakfast around 8:30 am and saw one of the cars of bowlers returning. I waved them over and asked how it went. Did they have fun? How many games did they play? They said after a while they lost count of how many games they'd bowled. They all had a good time! However, when they began, they started using a heavier man's ball. After 3 to 4 hours of bowling, their arms started to hurt. They all switched to a woman's lighter bowling ball. They said their arms were sore. They planned to have a hot shower and a long nap, before dinner.

A final aspect to this *Bowling Alley* story occurred 10 years later. A lot changed in my life during this decade. Details about this will be found in the next chapter.

It happened in 1967, on the Friday night of the wedding rehearsal dinner for Colleen, my sister-in-law. Mary, my wife, was the maid of honor. Earlier, she had participated in the rehearsal. I was not a member of the wedding party, but I joined them at the rehearsal dinner. I was chatting with Bob, my future brother-in-law, and a few of the groomsmen. He and many of them were graduates of SMC, so we talked about teachers we knew. Bob knew I had been a Brother. He also had heard *My Bowling Alley* story. He managed to turn the conversation to chatting about CBC an asked me to tell *My Bowling Alley* story. While I was telling it, I noticed a young lady across the table listening very attentively. When I finished, she had a big smile on her face. She pointed at me and shouted, "You're the one!" Surprised, I replied, "What?" She answered, "Our family has laughed at that story for years. My older brother was in the back of that station wagon. He told us all about it when he came home at Christmas!"

I'd like to share some non-dorm related tales. In September 1956, the academic year began. It was the start of my college teaching career.

## The George Krupicka Story

In one of my calculus classes was a freshman named George Krupicka. He came to me for help about the 3rd week of class. George had grown up in Chicago and was two years younger than me. He'd graduated from Marshall HS on Kedzie and Adams, and then served in the Navy. His last years of naval service were at Millington Naval Air Station, Memphis. While there, he met, courted, and married Betty Moretta. When he finished his military service, the two moved to Chicago. They spent two years trying to settle in, but George couldn't find a well-paying, satisfying job. Betty pointed out to him that he lacked a college degree. She persuaded him to move back to Memphis. He could enroll at CBC and attend classes. She would get her old job back and be the family supporter. She'd been the secretary for a Battalion Chief of the Memphis Fire Department and managed to work for him again when she came back.

Betty phoned me on the weekend after my second meeting with George and begged me to talk to him. He was very discouraged, wanted to quit school, return to Chicago and find a job. Before our next help session, I did a little homework and checked his background. At the end of our next meeting I said, "George, I hear you are discouraged and want to quit." He was surprised! Betty hadn't mentioned her phone call. I went on and said, "I've done a little checking up on you. Your high school transcript shows that in mathematics you earned all A grades and only one B. I know Marshall, it's an excellent high school and has a fine reputation." He told me that when he was at Marshall, he liked math and his teachers. I went on to point out that he had been away from algebra and trigonometry for 5 or 6 years. If he didn't use his math skills during this time, it would be easy to forget what he had learned. I begged him not to quit. I promised that if he stayed in class and continued to see me at least once a week for help, he would be on track by Thanksgiving. He agreed to stay through the first semester. By Halloween, he was doing 'A' work in calculus.

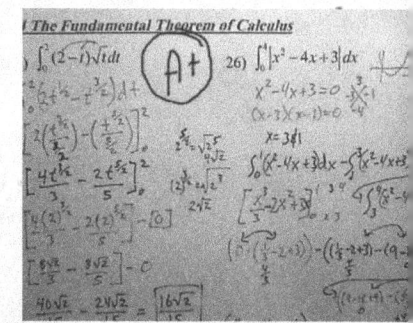

*Chapter Three: A Teacher's Beginning*

As you read further in **MS**, you will see I was not in Memphis when George graduated from CBC in 1960. I was not there when he began his professional career as an engineer. I was not present when he started graduate studies in Memphis, and earned his MS in Mechanical Engineering.

My family and I visited Memphis in the summer of 1967, during which time I reconnected with George and Betty. He was now teaching at his alma mater, CBC. He had introduced and helped establish a new degree for the College, a BS in Mechanical Engineering. Mary and I visited Memphis a few times over the next 40 years. When we last visited Memphis in 2003, we found that George had retired and was now enjoying his hobby, building and flying remote controlled model airplanes. Unfortunately, like so many of my friends, both Betty and George have passed.

## My Orval Faubus Story

All of us are the products of our experiences. I'm referring to the daily challenges, good and bad, which confront each of us. How we react, and move forward, is what makes us who we are! I've shared many stories in these memoirs that I was proud to tell you. I'm now going to relate an event that happened, for which I am ashamed. However, I first need to give some background for those unaware of the times.

Orval Faubus was the Governor of Arkansas in 1957. In early September, he stood in the main doorway of Little Rock Central HS. Around him, he stationed the Arkansas National Guard to prevent the integration of the school. Later that month President Eisenhower insured that racial desegregation occurred in Little Rock by using federal troops.

*Protestors in Little Rock*

The football teams, of Memphis and Arkansas Universities, played their game in Memphis in mid-October. The stadium was fully packed with 50,000 fans. I was one of them. When Governor Faubus entered his box seat on the 50-yard line, 50,000 fans stood and gave him a standing ovation. Sad to say, I was among them!

## My Cyril Conroy Story

A memory involving a new Memphis friend, Cyril Conroy. Early on the Saturday before Thanksgiving, he arrived on campus in his station wagon. Bro. William Rhody, three other Brothers and I were going with him for a 90-mile drive to Oxford, Mississippi. We first loaded up his wagon with coolers containing various cold cuts, cheeses, and cooked peeled shrimp. One cooler held beer and other liquid refreshments. Boxes with bread, crackers, chips, and other snacks were also piled into the wagon. We were going on a picnic, my first tail-gate picnic!

The University of Mississippi, in Oxford, was playing Mississippi State in their annual football game. This was a long standing, bitter rivalry, and we were going to the game. Bro. William was from Minnesota, and he decorated Cyril's wagon with festive banners and buntings. However, the colors he used were maroon and gold, the colors for the Golden Gophers of MN. The colors of Ole Miss were blue and red. He also pasted a poster with GO GOPHERS in the rear window! I noticed many quizzical stares and smiles at our outlandishly decorated wagon as we drove to Oxford. We arrived a few hours before the game, parked, and enjoyed our picnic! We went to the game, but none of us cared who won!

The game ended and we drove to Tunica, only 40-miles from Memphis. We stopped for supper at the home of Sam Watkins, a CBC student. He knew we were going to the game and even arranged for our tickets. His mother and father were waiting for us in Tunica. After a cocktail or two, we were served bowls of delicious *Brunswick Stew*. This traditional dish found only in the south is a tomato-based soup with lima beans, butter beans, corn, okra, and other vegetables. The meats vary, but are often chicken, pork, beef, and

Chapter Three: A Teacher's Beginning

small game meat. The stew we had that day had been simmering for almost two days. It was delicious, I loved it!

While sitting in the kitchen having my 3rd bowl, I questioned our hostess about its ingredients. She had not used any beef, only chicken, pork, rabbit, and squirrel.

Later, I made a mistake! Bro. William loved food, as I did. He too had eaten 3 bowls of the stew. When I told him about the meats in the stew, the thought of squirrel did not set well with his stomach. He immediately went outside and lost it all. His ride back home that night was not comfortable!

## My AAPT Story

In the fall of 1957 I joined the American Association of Physics Teachers (AAPT). I went to NYC to attend their annual meeting at the end of January 1958. I flew from Memphis to NYC. It was my first flight in an airplane.

While in New York, I made it a point to attend a few Broadway productions. I recall especially seeing Julie Andrews and Rex Harrison perform at the Mark Hellinger Theatre in My Fair Lady. I stood for the entire performance because the only tickets available were for Standing Room Only (SRO). I did manage to get a ticket and seat at the Cort Theatre. Here I enjoyed seeing Ralph Bellamy star as FDR in Sunrise at Campobello. I also saw a young actor, James Earl Jones, make his Broadway debut.

*My Fair Lady!*

## My John Giannini Story

John Giannini was the first *millionaire* I ever met. His parents had come from Italy to Memphis in 1920. They purchased *worthless bottomland* along the Mississippi River, about 12 miles southwest of the downtown area. They started growing vegetables, especially the best peppers in the world, outside of Italy. Every 4th or 5th year the river flooded. They might not have a crop for months, but they recognized these periodic floods as a blessing, rather than a tragedy. When the water receded, their fields were left with deposits of rich, black soil from IA, IL, IN, MN, MO, OH, and WI. No need to add any fertilizer! In addition, they bought more bottomland when some flooded fields were for sale.

When he was 16, John started driving a truckload of fresh vegetables into the Memphis market. A truck was loaded with fresh produce at night. The next morning, he drove to the market in Memphis at 4:00 am, where he sold the vegetables to stores and restaurants. He'd return home, shower, and get to his high school classes at CBC on time. This chore became easier once his brother, Jim, was old enough to drive.

In 1949, the Tennessee Valley Authority (TVA) started planning to build a coal fired power plant along the Mississippi River near Memphis. After examining several sites, they settled on the Giannini Farm and surrounding area. In 1951, their farm was sold for $10 million, which the two brothers and a sister split. Construction on the plant didn't start until 1956, so for 5 years, John and Jim continued farming and selling vegetables until construction began. During this time, they paid rent to use their farm at $1 a year!

TVA Power Plant

Chapter Three: A Teacher's Beginning

In the summer of 1957, I lived at DLS Chicago and attended IIT. I earned 4 hours in Electrical Engineering and 6 in Mechanical Engineering. Brother Lambert Thomas, President of CBC, had suggested I take some engineering courses.

I made a long retreat on Beaver Island in July of 1958, which prevented me from taking any summer classes. In August, dad and I drove to CA. It was our first trip to the West Coast. He had a chance to visit with his 2 brothers, 3 sisters, and their families. At that time, Ron was decommissioned from the Navy in Long Beach, CA. After which, we three drove back to Chicago on Route 66!

## Graduate Student
### (September 1958 - December 1959)

I lived at DLS, Chicago. I was not assigned to this religious community and had no teaching duties there. I was on leave, much like a sabbatical, to pursue graduate studies and earn a PhD in physics. Over the next 18 months, I earned 57 graduate CH at IIT. By the end of December 1959, I only needed one course of 4 hours and 10 hours of research to complete my PhD.

It was during these months that I began questioning my vocation. After much prayer and consultation, I left the religious community of the De La Salle Christian Brothers on December 31, 1959. January 1, 1960 I was back home on Hermitage Avenue in Chicago. It was a New Year and I was ready to embark on new adventures in my life!

As I end this chapter, I wish to mention two new friends I had just made. We first met in several classes and worked on our research topics in the same laboratory. You will hear more about both in the next chapter. They were my best friends in the 1960's! Without their help and assistance, I would never have earned my PhD!

Ed Piotrowski (1931-1980) grew up in Chicago near DePaul University. He attended DePaul Academy for high school and DePaul University to earn his BS and MS degrees in chemistry. He was working on his PhD in physics at IIT.

Bob Estin (1921-1987). I do not know much about Bob's early years. He was born in New Jersey but grew up in CA. Like Ed and I, he was working on his PhD in physics at IIT.

# Chapter Four

## Genesis I
## (1960-1967)

•••••••••••

## IIT, Chicago
## (January 1, 1960-August 15, 1962)

•••••••••••

The second semester started at IIT on January 18. I was now an Instructor in the Physics Department. Ed Piotrowski, Bob Estin, and I taught all the sections of the first course in physics for science/engineering majors.

We three were also given another major task. At this time, all science and engineering majors were required to take 3 courses in physics. Each one awarded 4 CH and required the use of calculus. Physics 111 and 112 were taken in the freshmen year and Physics 211 was taken in the sophomore year. Ed, Bob, and I were given a year to develop the curriculum, including laboratory experiments, for Physics 212, a 4 CH sophomore course. Our "full-time" teaching load was reduced one course so that we could do this and continue the research for our degrees.

At this point, I wish to summarize and finish the story regarding my PhD. In the last chapter, I tallied the credits I'd earned towards my PhD degree. I continued my graduate studies on a part-time basis, and by December 1962, I had accumulated 107 graduate CH with a GPA of 3.7. This was enough credit hours to receive a PhD, but I still needed to finish and publish my thesis.

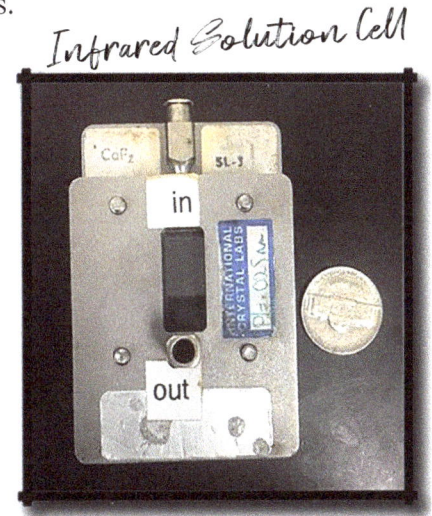

*Infrared Solution Cell*

It took me several years to double-check all my measurements and calculations. During this period, I presented two 15-minute papers, on my research at an International Conference, that was held annually at Ohio State University. Two additional years were spent in my writing and having a professional type my thesis. At the IIT graduation ceremony on June 11, 1965, I received my PhD degree. My father, mother, brother, wife, and other family members and friends were present!

In conclusion, I wish to acknowledge the help given to me by Ed and Bob. Ed showed me how to use the instruments in our laboratory, to collect and measure spectral data. Bob helped me to write in Fortran, the computer programs I used on an IBM-1620 to do all my calculations. Without their assistance, I would never have gotten my PhD!

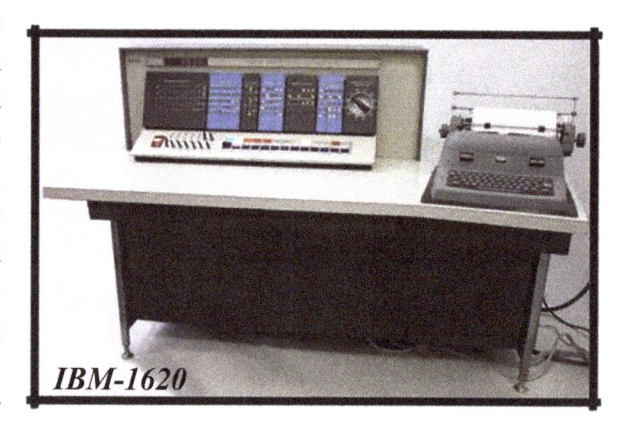

*IBM-1620*

For 1½ years, I was a member of the IIT faculty, with the rank of Instructor. In the fall of 1960, my good friend, Dr. Copeland, asked to meet with me. At our meeting, he told me about a new program, recently funded by the National Science Foundation (NSF) to help graduate students. The minimum requirement to apply for this funding, was to have taught 3 years of college science. My 2 years teaching at CBC and my 1½ years at IIT satisfied this stipulation. I filled out all the forms, and along with recommendations from Dr. Copeland and Dr. Cleveland, my Research Advisor, I forwarded everything to Washington, DC.

In April 1961, I received word that I'd been awarded an NSF Faculty Fellowship! For the 1961-62 academic year, I kept my office at IIT, worked in the research lab, and taught no classes. My $5200 salary was paid by NSF. Though the funds came through the IIT Business Office, it was nontaxable. Later, I received an additional $1000 payment for the summer of 1962. This fellowship allowed me to devote considerable time to my research activities.

## Chapter Four: Genesis I

Throughout these years, Ed, Bob, and I applied to NSF for other grants. All our proposals were accepted. These grants enabled IIT to conduct summer workshops in 1961, 1962, and 1963. These workshops were designed to improve the skills of high school physics teachers. All of them were four weeks long. Total expenses for the 24-28 participants were paid by NSF, which included round-trip rail travel to Chicago, housing, meals, tuition, fees, and books. These three workshops helped 75-80 high school educators improve their teaching skills in physics.

In the summer of 1962, I taught an evening physics class at Wright City College, one of the Chicago's community colleges.

From 1960 to 1963, other things were occurring in my life. When I started my *new life*, on returning home on January 1, 1960, many things had to change. For one thing, I had to get a new wardrobe. When a man left the religious community of Brothers, he was given $200. This was to be used to travel back to his hometown and to enable him to purchase new clothes.

I didn't spend anything in going from the southside to the northside of Chicago. On Saturday, January 2, 1960, I spent most of the day at the Hart, Schaffner, & Marx factory (HSM). My Aunt Emily gave me a pass to enter the private store on the ground floor of the factory. Only HSM employees and their family members could shop there. Uncle Art and Emily each had given me $50 as a Christmas gift. On that Saturday, I bought an overcoat, brown suit, two or three colored slacks, and a jacket. For $300, I purchased clothing worth about $650. No tax was charged in this store. In addition, my parent's Christmas gifts were brown shoes and colored socks.

*Magazine ad for Hart, Schaffner & Marx!*

Throughout these years, I'd read the notices on the graduate school bulletin board about recruiters visiting our campus. They interviewed graduate students for potential jobs. I probably had 8 to 10 such meetings. Two I would like to mention . . .

At the end of one interview, I was immediately offered a contract, which I could have signed right there and then. If I had, I would have moved to Moscow, ID and started the 1962-63 academic year as an Assistant Professor of Physics at the University of Idaho. Of course, if I played the if game, no Mary, no children, and *MS* would be quite different.

Another interview lasted only 20 minutes. I met with a recruiter from the National Aeronautics and Space Administration (NASA). He was very pleasant, gave me a cup of coffee, and filled out a form as we spoke. When we parted, he said, "Thanks for coming in and applying, Mr. Krupp, but I don't think we'll be calling you back." I wanted to go to the Moon! However, I was too large for the space vehicles that were built for those early trips.

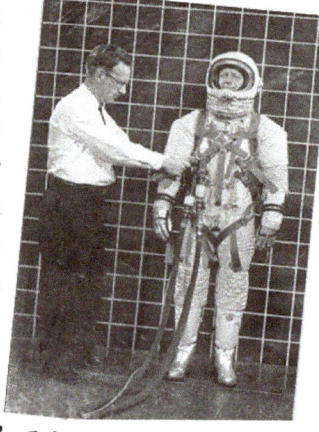

*1960's NASA Space Suit*

On Tuesday, July 5, 1960, just six months after leaving the religious community, I flew out of Chicago to Montreal, Canada. No summer teaching! No taking a class! No research! I was on a holiday adventure! A wonderful 6-week trip to Europe, at no cost!

How, you ask was this a free trip? Well, I was a tour escort, not a tour guide. I had the schedule, all the vouchers, American Express checks, and reservations to lead a group on their travel through Europe. I worked for a small agency in Chicago, named Regina Tours. I did not receive a salary. However, ALL expenses were taken care of!

## Chapter Four: Genesis I

After a night in Montreal, I was at the docks on the St. Lawrence River to meet and greet one of our tour groups. This group consisted of 40 tourists who were alums, family members, and five or six nuns from the College of St. Teresa, Winona, MN. We boarded the Isle de France, an ocean liner built in 1932. The ship set sail at 2:00 pm and headed NE on the St. Lawrence River.

We stopped briefly in Quebec to take on more passengers. We continued down the river. As we danced the evening away, our ship entered the Bay of Fundy. Shortly after midnight, we sailed into the north Atlantic. Two days later, we saw some icebergs floating a mile north of our vessel.

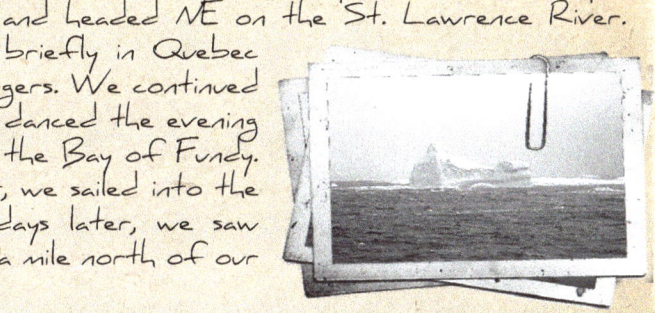

I shared a stateroom with three other gentlemen, one of whom was Lionel Bruneel. Like me, he was a tour escort. He worked out of an agency in Philadelphia, was very happy to meet me, and asked for my assistance. His tour consisted of 14 young, recent college graduates. Two were men; the other 12 were young women. He begged for my assistance, in keeping the ladies entertained, during our cruise across the Atlantic. Could I refuse? Of course not, I was very happy to oblige!

Lionel was born and raised in Belgium. He'd moved to the US in 1948. Later, you'll read about his move to Chicago, and how we were close friends in the 60's, 70's, and 80's before he retired to Belgium.

### Boat Train to London

After a wonderful 5-day cruise across the Atlantic, we docked in Liverpool on Monday, July 11. After passing through customs, we boarded the boat train to London. A bus was waiting for us, and in less than an hour, we were checked into our hotel. That night at dinner, I introduced them to Ed, their tour escort for the rest of their European trip. Ed had led another Regina tour through Europe in June. He was waiting for the St. Teresa Tour at our hotel.

On Tuesday afternoon, I boarded an empty chartered bus and left for Southampton. The driver and I stayed overnight near the docks. Early the next morning, we greeted my tour group, as they disembarked from the Queen Mary. This group, from St. Scholastica College, Duluth, MN consisted of about 30 alums, family members, and nuns. Using local guides, we spent three days visiting notable and historic sites in London and the surrounding countryside.

Early Friday evening, July 15, we left London's Liverpool station on another boat train, heading east to the channel. I recall that the locomotive on this train burned coal. I stood outside, on the back platform of the last car, enjoying the sights of London as we left the city. The train entered a tunnel. Before I could reenter the last car, I almost choked to death from the smoke and soot. I remember the nuns were very unhappy about this part of our trip. The main, and only course, for dinner on the train was chicken. I couldn't convince them that the Roman Church did permit an exemption for travelers in such a circumstance. In any case, we arrived at Harwich, on the east coast. Here we boarded a boat and I assigned people to their staterooms. While we slept, we crossed the channel to the continent.

Saturday morning, July 16, we landed in Hook-of-Holland. At a café, along the docks, we had a breakfast of zwieback (crisp, dry toast), fruit, and strong coffee. Afterwards, we boarded our tour bus and began our adventure on the continent.

## Chapter Four: Genesis I    97

We passed through Rotterdam and a flotilla of bikes. The scenery of Belgium was gorgeous! For the night, we stopped in Cologne. Sunday morning, July 17, we went to an early Mass at the Cathedral of Cologne. It was then, I realized the devastation caused by WWII. Fifteen years, after the end of the war, this Cathedral was only about 50% to 60% restored.

From Cologne, we drove south along the Rhine River. At Koblenz, we got off the bus, boarded a boat, and had a 4-hour cruise on the Rhine. While enjoying lunch and music on the open upper deck, we sailed past the Lorelei Rock. At Bingen, we left the boat, got on our bus, and drove to Frankfurt for two nights. When we left Frankfurt, we continued southward through Darmstadt and stopped in Heidelberg for a night.

*Rhine River & Lorelei Rock*

Before leaving Heidelberg, we rode through the campus of Heidelberg University. It is the oldest university in Germany, and one of the earliest built in Europe.

We continued southward passing through Karlsruhe. After a one-night stop in Stuttgart, we headed east and entered Bavaria and the Black Forest. We spent two wonderful nights in Baden-Baden! Here, we crossed paths with Lionel's tour.

I recall one fine evening out with his lovely ladies. We spent another evening at the elegant Versailles-inspired casino. Here, many of my group tried their luck at the gaming tables. In the meantime, I led the nuns through a stylish side entrance. We went to a gorgeous theatre attached to the casino. We enjoyed listening to a baritone and soprano entertain us with lovely arias. When we left Baden-Baden, we continued through the Black Forest and stopped one night in Freiburg.

We crossed into Switzerland, around Basel, and drove through the Alps. We stopped for a few days in Lucerne. It was here, one day, that we used the world's steepest cogwheel railway to ascend Mt. Pilatus. We came down by cable car.

When we left Lucerne, we drove eastward and stopped for lunch in Vaduz, Liechtenstein. We continued onwards for a two-night stay in Innsbruck, Austria. I now need to give you some background information to understand MS.

In 1633, Oberammergau, Bavaria, Germany was inflicted with the bubonic plague. The villagers made a promise to God! They pledged to produce a play for all time, every 10 years, depicting the life and death of Jesus, if He would only spare their village. The play started in 1634 and soon moved to a cycle of being presented in the years ending in zero.

Following WWI, the 1920 presentation was rescheduled to 1922. It was performed in 1930 and again in 1934 to commemorate its 300th anniversary. Due to WWII, it was cancelled. After obtaining permission from the American Occupation Authorities, it resumed in 1950. Though it was well attended by Europeans, not many crossed the Atlantic to see the 1950 production. Note that my trip to Europe was in 1960—the Oberammergau Passion Play was scheduled for this summer!

Starting in the fall of 1959, Regina Tours had been purchasing tickets for this play. Tourists who completed their total payment by March 1, 1960, were guaranteed a ticket and accommodations in Oberammergau. Of course, some people did not complete their final payment before this deadline.

All the proceeding was necessary to understand what now follows. On Thursday evening, July 21, my group, numbering 30, arrived in Innsbruck, Austria.

Chapter Four: Genesis I    99

That same evening Ed and the College of St. Teresa Tour (people from my cruise across the Atlantic), numbering 40, arrived at the same hotel. In addition, the St. Catherine College Tour (St. Paul, MN), numbering 34, joined us. Their tour escort was a woman named Helen.

After Friday's breakfast, we all toured the historic sites in Innsbruck. Before supper, in the hotel, Helen, Ed, and I met. We had to allocate the 75 tickets I had for the Oberammergau Play on Sunday, July 24 to the proper tourists. We had to accommodate 104 tourists, 3 escorts, and 3 bus drivers. At dinner, when all the tourists were gathered together, we explained the plan of the next three days . . .

On Saturday morning, following breakfast, 72 tourists and Ed left on two buses. After a drive of about 50 miles northwest, they spent the next two nights in Oberammergau. On Sunday, these people attended the Oberammergau Passion Play. Meanwhile, Helen and I took the remaining 32 tourists and drove 120 miles northeast to Erl, Austria.

Today, Erl is a town of around 1,400 inhabitants. It is on the Inn River, a tributary of the Danube. In this region, the river is the border between Austria and Bavaria, Germany. Sixty years ago, Erl had only 500 to 600 residents. Though Erl began its Passion Play in 1613, 21 years before Oberammergau, it is not as well-known.

About 4:30 pm that evening, we drove into Erl. There was a lot of traffic leaving town, for the play had ended at 4:00 pm. We stopped at the Tourist Center to obtain our play tickets, hotel accommodations, meal arrangements, etc. Was I in for a surprise! In 1960 there were no hotels in Erl! It had only one good restaurant!

*Erl Passion Play Theater*

I later learned that the woman Director of the Center, was one of only two or three people in town, who could speak English.

Quickly recovering from this shock, I want to tell you about the best two days of my entire European trip! While the tourists and driver remained in the bus, Helen and I sat inside the Center and chatted with the Director. We waited about 10 minutes for her husband to arrive. He walked over from the theater where he'd just finished his performance as St. Peter. When he arrived, we noticed his long beard, which he'd grown for his role in the Passion Play.

Peter joined us in the bus and directed us out into the countryside. We stopped at a crossroad in some beautiful farmland and several nearby farmhouses. Peter, our driver who was Dutch, Helen, and I stepped out of the bus. Three of us could speak English, but no German. Peter spoke only German. There we stood in the roadway, speaking, gesticulating, pointing, etc. We had to figure out if . . .

-this farmhouse had one room with two beds.

-that farmhouse had two rooms with four beds.

After understanding what accommodations were available, Helen and I had to figure out how to use them. Where would we put 6 nuns, a wife, her husband, and their two children? What about all the singles? Once that was determined, I informed each person to get their luggage and walk up to their farmhouse. That's right, no hotel porters! Before they left, I told them to be back down at the crossroads in an hour. The bus would be waiting to take them into town for supper. While they were getting settled into their accommodations, the four of us (our driver, Peter, Helen, and I) went back into town. I wanted to check on the restaurant. Peter showed us the restaurant and the four of us went in.

It was great, just what I hoped for! The interior was all wood, floors, walls, ceiling and beams, bar, tables, and chairs. The bar had no stools. The bartender/owner was expecting our group for dinner. I bought four steins of beer for our group. Peter started talking to some villagers who were seated at a table. All of them had beards and roles in the play. Helen and I bought them all, even the bartender, a stein of beer. We had great fun chatting with

Chapter Four: Genesis I

them and asking about their roles in the play. No one said he was Jesus. I learned that the role of Jesus was performed by a hired professional actor from Vienna. Sad to say, I never had a beer with Jesus! St. Peter and a few Disciples would have to do!

Later that evening, we had a delicious dinner in the restaurant. Towards the end of the meal, I told the group some bad news. There was nothing to see or do in Erl after 9:00 pm. During the time of the Passion Play, all places providing entertainment closed at 9:00 pm. But not to worry! I took them back to the crossroads and let them go back to their rooms. Twenty minutes later, 16 tourists, Helen, the driver, and I were starting on our Saturday Night Out in Germany. The couple with two children, 6 nuns, and 6 younger ladies from the St. Catherine tour stayed home. These young ladies planned to do their nails and hair.

The restaurant owner had given me some excellent advice. We drove south out of town along the Inn River. In six miles, we crossed a bridge into Bavaria. Nothing was closed there. Within a mile or two, we were in Oberaudorf where we found a large building with lights on and many cars parked around it. While all remained on the bus, I went in to see what it was. It was a dance hall with a 4-piece band, accordion, horn, drums, and bass fiddle. I spoke to the manager. In 10 minutes, we were all seated together at a line of tables he'd arranged. We ordered pitchers of beer and soon we were sipping and humming to the music. At the table were 17 ladies and two men, the driver and me. Shortly, a man who had been standing around the side of the dance floor came and spoke to me. Sitting at the head of the table, I was obviously the general or one in charge. He said to me, "I would like to dance with one of the ladies here. Do I have your permission to ask her?" I answered, "Yes, Yes!" As he started to leave, I called him back and said, "Any of your friends standing around there, also have my permission." Within 5 minutes every lady, including a 72 year-old grandmother, was out on the floor twirling around. I think we got back to Erl and the crossroads around 1:30 am. Sunday morning, we went to Mass at 8:30 am in the theater because the small church in town could not hold all the visitors. Afterwards, we wandered around the village, had some coffee, and returned to the theater at 11:00 am for the start of the play. There was an hour intermission at

1:00 pm. The play resumed at 2:00 pm and ended at 4:00 pm. We had Sunday dinner at the restaurant in town and spent another night in our farmhouses. After breakfast on Monday, we drove back to Innsbruck and reunited our separated groups.

Two final facets to my Passion Play story...

When we were together in Innsbruck, I asked one of the nuns who went to Germany, if she enjoyed the Oberammergau play. She answered, "No! It was too long! It started at 10:00 am and had a 20-minute intermission around noon. It resumed and ended at 2:00 pm for an hour break to have lunch. It began again at 3:00 and ended at 7:00 pm. I was so tired, that I went to my room at the lunch break, took a nap, and didn't attend the second half!"

*Sunday Mass*

At the end of our tour, when we were leaving to return home several people in my group spoke to me separately. Essentially, they said, "Thanks for a wonderful trip, Mr. Krupp! I liked our visit to Erl the best! I loved the two nights in the farmhouse, meeting the family, especially the children!"

We left Innsbruck on Tuesday, August 2nd, and went to Cortina d'Ampezzo for lunch. As the bird flies, it is only about 60 miles. But driving through the Alps, up and down and around the mountains, the distance is longer. In addition, it took time to pass through the Brenner Pass, where the border patrol checked and stamped all passports. Once beyond the border, we were in Italy! The winter Olympics had been scheduled in Cortina for 1944 but were cancelled due to WWII. They were held there in 1956.

We stopped at a lovely restaurant in Cortina for lunch. On a bright sunny day, we sat outside on a deck under umbrella-covered tables. I forget the food we ate, but the scenery was gorgeous! Everywhere I turned there was a mountain, still snowcapped in August!

However, we did have a situation develop here in Cortina. As we drove into town, we heard a loud clunk from the motor in back. Our driver stopped, checked the motor, returned, and took us to a restaurant for lunch. As I stepped off the bus, he told me he would be back in an hour. He had to find a garage and fix something. We sat down for lunch about 12:30 pm. An hour later, we were ready to board our bus, but it hadn't returned. By 2:30 pm, I was worried and talked to the restaurant owner. He phoned a few garages that might be servicing our bus, but didn't locate it. He then drove me to various repair shops hunting for our bus. About 3:30 pm we found it! Our driver informed me that the repairs were taking longer than he expected. It wouldn't be ready until 8:00 pm or 9:00 pm. I now faced a major crisis . . .

- I needed to find sleeping rooms for 32, an impossible task, during the summer tourist season.

- The reservations for rooms and supper at our hotel in Venice, could not be cancelled, since the 24-hour notice had passed.

- The 3:00 pm train to Venice had left and the next train wasn't scheduled until 8:00 pm.

What did I do? I found six taxis, brought them to the restaurant, and informed our group of our situation. I had them board the taxis. We drove to the garage, where the bus was being repaired. Everyone took one small bag from the luggage compartment. We filled the trunks in the cabs and strapped bags on the roofs. Then off we went, a drive of about 150 miles to Venice. While we were on our way, the restaurant owner phoned our hotel and informed them that we would be a couple hours late. We arrived at our hotel. While porters took our bags directly to our rooms, we went immediately into the dining room before it closed. After a few sips of wine and a fine Italian dinner, we were all laughing about our adventurous afternoon!

Now of course, you wonder what did a 150-mile trip of 6 taxis cost?

When I approached the taxi drivers in Cortina, I negotiated with them for a round-trip fare of $20 for each taxi. However, when we arrived in Venice, I gave each driver a $5 tip. You may think this is very cheap, but remember it was 1960. The cost in 2021 would be around $175 for each taxi fare and $40 for the tip—a total of over $1200 for six taxis.

When we were in Rome, a week later, I went to the American Express office, sent a cable to Regina Tours in Chicago, and explained why I had spent $150 on a cab ride to Venice. I suggested that Regina Tours reduce their payment to the bus company by $150. That's MS about a $150 taxi ride!

Doge's Palace

St. Mark's Basilica

In Venice, we toured St. Mark's Basilica and the Doge's Palace. We went to Murano, to visit a factory where artisans skillfully blew glass and shaped it into pieces of art. We exited the factory through a store where items could be purchased and shipped home. After our group left the store, I asked them to wait a moment while I went back in to check if anyone was inside. I was in fact, going to collect 10% of the gross sales, from my group's purchases. It was my commission, for bringing these customers into their store!

*Talented Glass Blower*            *Chapter Four: Genesis I*   105

*Blown Glass Horse Art*

From Venice, we drove 125 miles southwest to Florence for two nights. Along the way, we stopped briefly in Padua and Bologna. Most of the time in Florence was spent in visiting galleries, museums, and churches. We did take a trip to the factory and store of Salvatore Ferragamo. I'm not sure if any of my group bought any shoes, but many purses were purchased. I even bought myself a leather wallet and managed to collect my 10% commission!

*St. Peter's Basilica and Salvatore Ferragamo store*
*Florence, Italy*

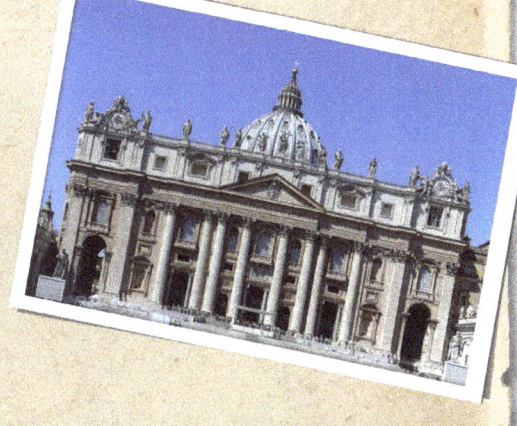

We left Florence and went 150 miles southwards into Rome, for a 3-night stay. I cannot tell you how many churches we visited on Saturday or Sunday! I don't remember which one we went to for Sunday Mass. I know it wasn't St. Peter's Basilica.

Monday, August 8, was our day devoted to St. Peter's and the Vatican. I told my group to eat a hearty breakfast. We arrived at the Basilica early. Each one was given a ticket to the Basilica and Vatican Museum. My group was left free to wander about St. Peter's, the largest church in the world. They walked, gazed, and read from a pamphlet I'd given them. They viewed Michelangelo's Pietà, and took all the pictures they wanted.

106 *My Marvelous Memories*

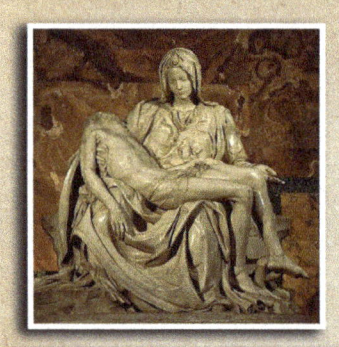

*Pieta & Sistine Chapel*

We gathered at the Sistine Chapel at 12:45 pm. Shortly after 1:30 pm, we lined up in a hall near this Chapel. Along with about 400 other people, we entered a small chapel and sat in pews. On a platform in front was a railing, behind which was the altar. We waited in silence. About 2:00 pm, Pope John XXIII entered and stood behind the railing and spoke to us. He greeted and thanked us for coming. He then gave a short 10-minute sermon and his blessing. He left, and our private audience with the Pope was over! I allowed another hour of sightseeing before we boarded our bus and returned to our hotel. There was time for a short nap before our supper at the hotel.

The next morning, after breakfast, we left Rome, and began our journey northward!

Chapter Four: Genesis I    107

We drove 160 miles to Pisa where we stopped for the night. The next morning, Wednesday, we toured the Cathedral of Pisa, its Leaning Tower, and visited a few other historic sights. We then drove 90 miles to Genoa, the birthplace of Christopher Columbus and our stop for the night.

Most of the drive to Genoa was along a scenic, coastal road. We saw many beautiful views of the Ligurian Sea, an arm of the Mediterranean. I recall stopping for lunch, at a lovely restaurant, high on a bluff, overlooking the sea. Tables were setup outside, and we looked down to the shore, about 300 feet below. A special choice for lunch that day was fresh, cold shrimp. Many in our group, as did I, ordered this selection. When the food was served, there were 8 very large shrimp on a plate. However, none had been peeled! Each came with shell, tail, head, eyes, and tentacles. I relished every morsel! However, half the orders were not eaten. Some people couldn't find the courage to remove the shell, especially the head!

## Yes? No? Maybe?

When we left Genoa, we drove 40 miles north to Alessandria. We went to visit the Giuseppe Borsalino Hat factory and store. In 1960, women still wore hats when going to church on Sunday. However, my 10% commission was rather small that day!

Back south to the coast we went, and again had lunch overlooking the Mediterranean. Afterwards, we continued southwest to Nice for two nights. One evening, we drove to the famous casino at Monaco. My group wanted to try their luck at the gaming tables.

I recall that one nun in our group, dressed in her black habit, came along. She wanted to see the famous Monte Carlo Casino. I well remember an elegantly dressed doorman blocking her entry into the Casino. He kept repeating, "L'Eglise ne vous permet pas!" ("The Church does not allow you to enter!"). I intervened and asked her to sit with me on a bench by the entry. She calmed down and told me she only wanted to see and take a picture of the famed Casino. She also hoped to catch a glimpse of Prince Ranier III and Princess Grace Kelly.

She lent me her camera and waited while I went into the Casino. I took a few pictures for her. While there, I learned that the Prince and Princess only come to the Casino for the opening of a special event, never to gamble. I came out, returned the camera, and told her what I'd just learned about the Royal family.

# Chapter Four: Genesis I    109

We sat on that bench for over two hours, chatted, and watched many a car, taxi, or limousine arrive to drop off or pick-up passengers. We gazed in amazement at elegantly dressed women and men that passed before our eyes. At 11:30 pm, our bus came to pick us up, and we returned to our hotel in Nice.

On Saturday, August 13, we drove 130 miles to Avignon. After some sightseeing and lunch, we drove another 50 miles to Montpelier for the night. The next morning after Mass, and a bit of sightseeing, we drove 210 miles to Lourdes.

*Lourdes Basilica*

On Monday, August 15, all tourists were free to visit the Shrine, Grotto, and Sanctuary of Lourdes. They participated in Mass and processions. They bathed in the waters, if they wished. Many obtained bottles of the water to bring home. We left Lourdes on Tuesday, August 15, and drove 210 miles to Limoges for the night. The next morning after some sightseeing, we traveled 150 miles into Paris for a 3-night stop. We toured the city during the day, visiting all the usual sights, i.e., Notre Dame, the Eiffel Tower, the Louvre, etc. We spent more than ☐ day at Versailles. One day, we drove to the Normandy coast and back to Paris. I forget where we went, but I think it was near Rouen.

Notre Dame        The Louvre         Eiffel Tower

## My Marvelous Memories

*Versailles*

Saturday morning, August 20, we all flew from Paris to London. My trip to Europe was nearing an end. Shortly, after landing at Heathrow Airport in London, I assisted about half of my group in boarding a flight back home. Most of these folks were teachers. They wanted to get home, rest a few days, and start to prepare for the new school year.

The rest of my group and I took a chartered bus into London for a 1-night stay. The next day, we were scheduled to take the boat train to Liverpool. We we were scheduled to board the **Isle de France** for a 5-day cruise back to Montreal. There the tour would end! I looked forward to this cruise as a time when I could have a little R & R. Unfortunately, it was not to be!

In July, dock workers in Britain had gone on strike, and it was still in effect on August 21. No ships were sailing from or into England! This caused havoc in the airline industry, as many tours were coming to an end. A traveler who had an airline ticket to fly home was just fine, but hundreds and thousands, expecting to sail home, were stuck. I saw people at the airport sitting in chairs and sleeping on the floor. I saw the same thing in hotel lobbies, congested with people. They were in chairs and on floors, waiting to find an airline seat home. Many didn't have enough money left, after their tours in Europe to pay for a hotel room. I managed to extend our rooms at the hotel for a few days. In dribbles of 1, 2, or 3 seats on a flight, I sent them off to Montreal.

On Wednesday, August 24, the last two people in my group and I boarded a KLM flight to Montreal. Back in 1960, KLM airlines did not fly into or out of London. However, all airlines were working together to get stranded passengers back home from Europe. I took a nonstop flight from Amsterdam to Montreal. A window of

> opportunity was found, in which this flight from Amsterdam landed at Heathrow and taxied to an empty gate. While it topped off its fuel, it took 10 stranded tourists back to Montreal. I was among the lucky 10. Immediately on landing in Montreal, I found an evening flight to Chicago. By midnight of August 24, I was home, and my **Great Tour of Europe** was over!

Before **MS** about the summer of 1960, I wrote all the things I had been doing *professionally* at IIT. I need to say more about what was happening in my *personal* life.

Ron and I celebrated our parents wedding anniversary on Friday November 3, 1961. We all went to Phil Smidt's restaurant in Hammond, IN for perch and white fish. Ron took our parents home while I left to attend a First Friday of the month dance held at Beverly Woods restaurant in Chicago by the YCW (Young Christian Workers). Beverly Woods was located on Western and 119th Streets. It was there I met Mary! She came to the dance with her best friend Pat. I knew Pat and had dated her several times. Pat introduced us, but I didn't dance with or talk to Mary throughout the rest of that evening.

Our first date was two weeks later, Sunday, November 19. We went to an early movie at the Beverly theater on 95th Street. Then we went to a restaurant/lounge next to the Arena Bowling Alley at Cicero and 103rd Streets. Here we ate and talked for over three hours. I recall one thing that happened early on. We wanted to have a cocktail before dinner. The waitress asked Mary for an ID. Mary didn't drive at this time, so she had no driver's license to show her. However, she had her passport, which she'd used in 1957 to go to Europe. It showed her age to be 23. It also had her picture, which was not found on an IL driver's license in 1961.

The waitress had never seen a passport used as an ID and was reluctant to accept it. She went and checked with the Assistant Manager, who was a young man. He too was skeptical about this unusual document. He went next door with it, to check with the manager at the bowling alley. He came back and said it was acceptable. Mary and I finally had our first cocktail together! We also had one or two dates during the Thanksgiving weekend.

112  *My Marvelous Memories*

Friday, December 1, was a special *First Friday Dance* at the Beverly Woods. It was the annual Christmas dinner dance, for couples only. Ladies were to wear gowns or cocktail dresses. Men didn't have to wear a tux, but suit, shirt, and tie were expected. This night turned out to be a double date. Ed escorted Pat while Mary and I were the other couple! We continued dating through the Christmas holidays. It was during this time, that I met her parents and family. It was a delight meeting everyone.

We were engaged in late February 1962 and began plans for an August wedding. Instead, we eloped on Saturday, June 9, and were married in Little Flower, her parish church in Chicago. Ed was the best man. I've forgotten Mary's Maid of Honor. The next day, Sunday we drove to Columbus, OH for our honeymoon. In the back of my car was Ed, and another graduate student from India. We were going to an International Conference of Scientists held annually at Ohio State U. Mary and I honeymooned at the Stouffer's Hotel on the Olentangy River in Columbus. I attended the conference in the morning and afternoon hours. One of the days, I presented the 15-minute paper I mentioned earlier about my research.

We returned from Columbus and began settling in. We first rented a small, furnished apartment near Marquette Park. By October, we were living in our home at 7945 S. Austin Avenue. As mentioned earlier, I taught my first course at Wilbur Wright College this summer.

*Chapter Four: Genesis I*

# Wilber Wright
## (September 1962 – March 1967)

••••••••••••

I began the academic year teaching full-time, as an Associate Professor of Physics at Wright. In 1962, the college was still part of the public-school system, under the Chicago Board of Education and Dr. Benjamin Willis, Superintendent. Consequently, I had to go downtown to the Chicago Board of Education to complete a lot of paperwork, personal interviews, and even a written test. In addition, a complete physical examination was done by a doctor, in a clinic at the Board's headquarters.

*Wilber Wright College*

At Wright. I was a member of the Physical Science Department. We taught courses in astronomy, chemistry, geology, meteorology, and, physics. In addition, we offered two courses which were part of the general education requirement. They were Physical Science 101 and 102. We did not teach any of the Biological Sciences. Our department consisted of about 17 to 18 full-time teachers. Four of us were physics teachers, and I was the junior member. Consequently, I was assigned most of the department's night courses. They were easy preparations for me, with one exception, Physical Science 101. It consisted of 50% geology, 25% meteorology, and 25% astronomy.

Since I'd never taken a course in geology, this was the problem. Fortunately, our department had a wonderful colleague, Forest Etheridge. He'd earned his BS from Virginia Tech and his MS from the U of Illinois. Both degrees were in geology. He took me under his wing. In a matter of 5 to 6 meetings, he gave me the essential basics of geology which prepared me to teach this course.

My memories over the next few years in **MS** are a blur and a haze. So much was I doing and accomplishing, that I can't remember clearly when they occurred. To name a few . . .

- In 1962, I was married, and began to teach full time at Wright.

- In 1963, Colleen, was born. At this time, Mary and I made a pact. She would stay at home and raise our children. I would work my butt off to be the family supporter.

- In 1964, Robert Jr. was born.

- From 1962-1965, I kept on writing my thesis. Finishing this, I received my PhD in June, 1965.

- Throughout 1963 to 1967, I taught part-time at the U of Illinois. Classes were initially held at Navy Pier but moved to the new Circle Campus in 1965. Occasionally, I taught a class at Roosevelt U.

- From 1963-1967, I was involved with Channel 11 (PBS) and TV College. You will hear more about this shortly...

In November 1962, I found a memo in my mailbox at Wright. It asked two questions . . .

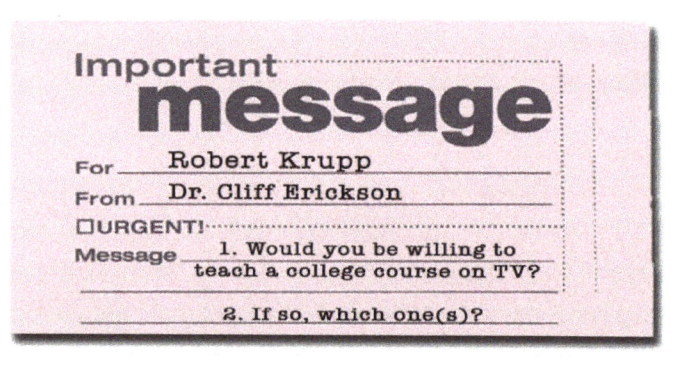

**Important message**

For: Robert Krupp
From: Dr. Cliff Erickson
☐ URGENT!
Message: 1. Would you be willing to teach a college course on TV?
2. If so, which one(s)?

## Chapter Four: Genesis I

I answered in the affirmative and sent it on to the appropriate office. The following March, Dr. Cliff Erickson, Dean of TV College, phoned and asked me to meet him in his office at Channel 11.

*WTTW – 1960*

In 1962, Channel 11 and TV College, operated in a wing of the Museum of Science and Industry, in Jackson Park. At our first meeting, Dr. Erickson told me that from a potential of 70 to 75 physical science teachers in the entire city system, I was the only one to respond to his memo. He was intrigued by my suggestion to teach a physics class, with a laboratory included. He asked me to return in April, to make a 5 to 10-minute audition tape. I did so. He, Dr. Hymen Chausow, Assistant Dean of TV College, and Bob Carolan, Chief Producer, liked my audition. They were extremely pleased with a visual demonstration that I included and explained.

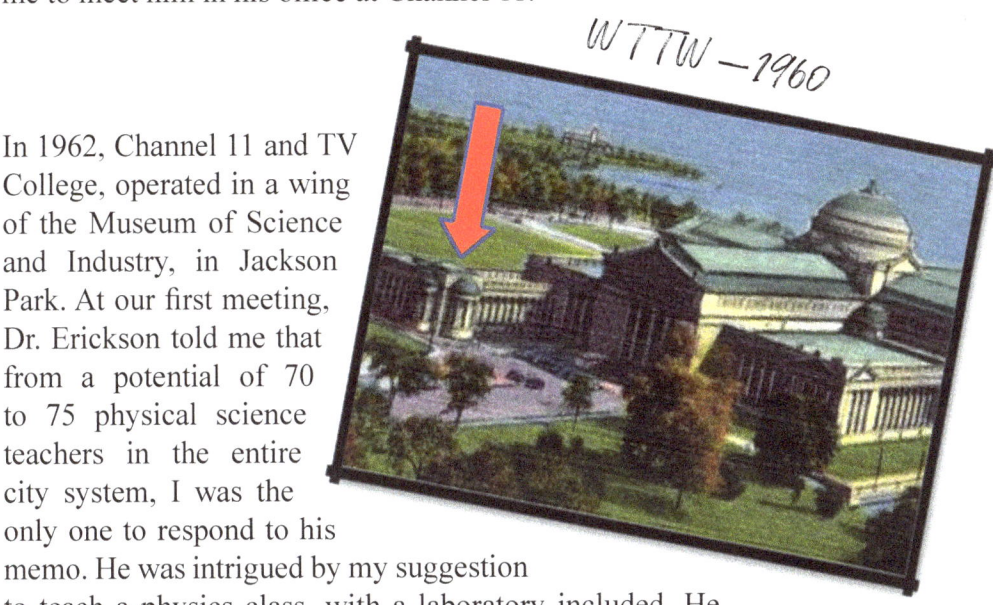

Before going further, let me give you some background. WTTW (Windows to the World) began in Chicago in 1955. During the 1960's, Channel 11 began airing educational programming, during the daytime hours. Among the programs broadcast, several were produced by TV College, a division of the City Colleges. The campus of TV College was in the studios of WTTW, and the faculty were drawn from one of the City Colleges, such as Wright. Throughout the 1960's, Channel 11 was only black and white.

In the fall of 1963, my good friend, Forest Etheridge was teaching Physical Science 101 on TV College. Each week he recorded live, two 43-minute lectures, for fifteen weeks. A videotape was made, and each lecture was shown twice during evening hours, and once on the weekend. In addition, twice a week, Forest was in his office on the Wright campus, where he held his *telephone office hours*. Students could phone in and ask him questions.

*WTTW – 2018*

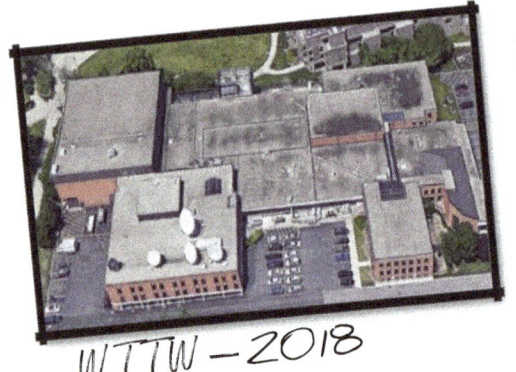

In the winter of 1964, Forest was now teaching Physical Science 102 on TV College. In February, when he held an office hour, I would meet and talk to him. The second half of Physical Science 102 is about physics. We planned for me to do his last 6 lectures on TV, so that I could get my feet wet. I did these lectures in late April and early May. Shortly thereafter, WTTW and TV College moved its studios and facilities to the north side of Chicago. It was adjacent to the new campus of Northeastern Illinois University.

In the summer of 1964, I taught no classes but received full pay. This was for preparing a workbook and lab book for Physics 221. In the fall semester I taught this course on TV College. For the lab book, I developed 10 experiments. Five were to be done at home with materials we provided. The other five labs would be conducted at one of the City Colleges.

The fall semester of 1964 began, and I taught no classes at Wright. My assignment was to teach the Physics 221 on TV College. For this assignment, I videotaped two lectures a week, which went out live. The videotape for each lecture was re-shown three times a week, twice in evening hours, and once on the weekend. This would accommodate students whose schedules prevented them from watching the live presentation.

On Monday, the day before my Tuesday lecture, I met at TV College with my producer, Bob Carolan. He would time my lecture, which had to be exactly 43 minutes. He critiqued my presentation, offered suggestions, and taught me that TV was a *visual medium*. Consequently, I always had 2 or 3 demonstrations for every lecture. I went through the same process with Bob on Wednesday, when we prepared the Thursday class. The semester lasted 15 weeks, and we produced 30 videotapes for the class.

TV College was hoping to enroll at least 100 students for my physics class. When the semester began, we only enrolled 70 students. However, the course was permitted to run. This was an era when we were all experimenting in using TV as an educational medium. This was the first time a laboratory was offered in any TV course in the country. Dr. Erickson wanted to see how this could blend into a video course.

## Chapter Four: Genesis I

This first TV course brings back several interesting memories . . .

-Some colleagues from Wright College helped to run the laboratories at different campus locations. For this, they were given overtime pay. Five Friday evenings during the semester, a lab was held at Wright (NW) and Bogan (SW) Colleges. Five Saturday mornings, labs were conducted at the Loop (downtown) and Wilson (SE) Colleges. I received overtime pay for conducting the lab at Wilson. More on this later.

-Jake Moelk, from Wright, conducted a very special lab on Friday mornings. He went out to the Illinois State Penitentiary known as Stateville (near Joliet). Three inmates had registered for my Physics 221 TV class. They were not permitted to attend any of the labs held in Chicago so we took the labs to them. I'll never forget the Friday night of Jake's first session at Stateville. He phoned me at home and said, "Bob, we've got to redesign the next 4 labs!" He went on to tell me how it took him over an hour to get cleared into the prison. The Chief of Security and two guards inspected, counted, itemized, and wrote down every piece of equipment Jake bought into the jail. I had forgotten about security.

-My Saturday lab at Wilson, had five or six students. One student I want to tell you about was a young man, about 30-years of age. He already had a BA degree from Lake Forest College. He was married, had four young children, and was a co-pilot flying commercial aircraft for United Airlines. He told me he'd recently suffered an eye injury which prevented him from flying in the future. He was receiving insurance that supported his family and he was now taking my physic course to beef-up his science credits. He wanted to enter a medical school and become a doctor!

-At our last lab session, I told him it would be difficult for him to be accepted into a medical school. This was a time when medical schools did not accept students over the age of 30. I also told him I would be happy to write any letters of recommendation he wished. In the semester after the course ended, I sent out several letters at his request. At the end of May 1965, he was accepted into the medical school at Wayne State University in Detroit. The following Christmas I received a card from him. He told me that his studies were going well. He mentioned that every weekend he commuted back home to Lake Forest to see his wife and children. I do not know if he ever succeeded in becoming a doctor. All I can say is I hope he did!

-In preparing for my live lecture, Bob Carolan and I would go into the recording studio an hour early. We'd set up the demonstrations, teacher's desk, and a board on which I could write. Thirty minutes before starting class, someone came in to put facial make-up on me, usually powder to remove shadows. Five minutes before we went live, I'd make my last visit to the Men's Room. One day, while I was in the restroom, the stage crew moved a table that contained the first demonstration. They only turned the table slightly to get a better angle on shooting the experiment. I didn't know they'd done this. The class began. I went to turn on the motor that was used as part of this demonstration. During the move, a setscrew had loosened, which caused the motor to turn too slowly. A cord became entangled in the gears of the motor. I spent two minutes trying to increase the speed of the motor but failed. With the camera taping it all, I gave up and said, "Now that I've managed to set physics back a 100 years, let's go to the board and see if I can bring it back to this century!"

-A few months later, I became aware that TV College used this short segment in their marketing campaigns. They wanted to show that video education was sometimes like a real classroom, where things could go wrong!

In the winter semester of 1965, I was back at Wright teaching physics and physical science classes, all of which were evening classes. Things were changing at TV College and I will tell you about this shortly. Before I do, I want to share a story that occurred in the spring of 1963, my first year at Wright.

Four students were taking their second class with me. They all were engineering majors taking calculus physics courses. One evening we shared a cup of coffee in the cafeteria. They told me that when they finished their courses at Wright, they were going to continue their studies at my alma mater, IIT. They were shocked when I advised them not to go to IIT. I knew they were good students and I explained why I gave them this advice.

*Chapter Four: Genesis I* 119

In their junior/senior level classes at IIT, they would find exceedingly bright and talented classmates. As I mentioned earlier, engineering students at IIT took calculus physics as freshman. They would have completed four courses, 16 CH, by the time they finished their sophomore year. By comparison, my Wright students would have taken two courses, 10 CH, in basic physics using calculus. I told these four young men, that ultimately the choice was theirs. However, I was fearful they might get discouraged if they got "C" grades, in advanced courses, while their classmates earned "A" and "B" grades. The spring semester ended, and these four students all earned an "A" grade. I never saw them again! However, a year-and-half later, in December 1964, I received a Christmas card signed by all four. They thanked me for the advice I had given them. They also wanted me to know that they had heeded my suggestion. In six months, they would graduate from New Mexico State University, and receive their engineering degrees, one in civil, one in electrical, and two in mechanical engineering.

I don't know what happened to any of them. Did anyone return to Chicago to work professionally? Where did their careers take them? Who knows? But I feel I was there for them when they needed some good advice!

I mentioned a moment ago about things changing at TV College in the spring of 1965. It all started when Dr. Erickson left TV College and the City Colleges of Chicago. He went to Rockford, IL where he opened a new community college, Rock Valley Community College. He took Forest Etheridge with him as his chief assistant.

Dr. Hymen Chausow was the new Dean of TV College. He asked to meet with me. When we met, he asked me to completely redo all the courses in Physical Science 101 & 102 for TV College. He wished to do so because Forest was now gone from the City Colleges. He also asked me to add a laboratory component to the Physical Science 101 course. He showed me the catalog of courses that existed for *all* the City Colleges . . .

    Physical Science 101, 3 credit hours (lecture only).

    Physical Science 111, 4 credit hours (lecture and laboratory).

    Physical Science 102, 3 credit hours (lecture only).

    Physical Science 112, 4 credit hours (lecture and laboratory).

Dr. Chausow wanted to run the new TV 101 & 111 courses in the fall of 1965. This would provide students an opportunity for an extra hour of credit by doing laboratory work, if they wished. So, in the summer of 1965, I again taught no courses. I was given full pay for preparing two workbooks, one for the course and another for the laboratory.

The fall semester began. I taught no courses at Wright, as I was videotaping the new lectures for Physical Science 101/111. So just as before, I videotaped 2-lectures a week for 15 weeks, thus producing 30 lectures. We registered over 190 students for the 101/111 courses. Laboratory classes were held in three locations and the instructors all received overtime pay . . .

- A laboratory was held on Friday nights at Wright. Dr. Ed Rietz, Physical Science Chairman, conducted it.

- A laboratory was held on Saturday mornings at Bogan. My colleague from Wright, Milton Langer, taught it.

- A laboratory was held on Saturday mornings at Loop College. Someone from Loop ran it, but I've forgotten who it was.

- I also was getting overtime pay in the fall. I was preparing a new workbook for Physical Science 102, a course scheduled for the spring of 1966.

The spring semester of 1966 began, and I again taught no courses at Wright. I was videotaping the new lectures for Physical Science 102. Just as before, I videotaped 30 lectures. We registered over 170 students in this course.

What now follows is about other interesting aspects related to my involvement with TV College. First, I remind you that when I taught a TV course, I also would spend an hour, twice a week, sitting by a phone. These were my *weekly office hours*. It provided an opportunity for students to ask for help or further clarification on confusing topics.

*Chapter Four : Genesis I*

However, we had one problem, some of my students were inmates in prison. They were not permitted to phone me. We solved this problem by my going to them. So, what follows in ***MS*** is about the 21 times I've been in a state penitentiary!

Stateville Penitentiary in Crest Hill, IL is about 2 miles north of Joliet. It opened in 1925. In the 1960's, it held about 3,500 inmates. It is often confused with the nearby Joliet Correction Center built in 1858 which is only 2.5 miles away. JCC closed in 2002. Stateville exists to this day with about 3,300 inmates.

*Stateville Correctional Center (CC) & Cellhouse F*

These Physical Science courses were designed to have 3 major exams. The first two were given after lectures 1-10 and 11-20. The final exam was a cumulative one on all the material covered in the course. In the schedule, three weeks were designated as *Exam Week*. During this week, a student could go to one of four college campuses. Here, a librarian would administer an exam. In prison, a Director of Education (DE) would give the exam.

Since my students in jail couldn't phone me for help, I would go to each prison before *Exam Week*. There, I'd hold a 3-hour seminar, answering any of their questions. After my first session at Stateville, the DE led me to a dining room where we had lunch. I don't remember exactly what we ate, but I do remember the bread. It was very fresh and tasty! When I commented on this, the DE said it had been made just a few hours earlier, by inmates working in the kitchen.

During my second visit to Stateville, I arranged to stay a couple of hours after lunch. The DE took me on a tour. He showed me a facility in the prison, that had 3 to 4 classrooms with a rather small library. This was the elementary school, grades 1-8. Elsewhere, he showed me the high school. It consisted of 4 classrooms and a more extensive library. He was pleased to tell me how he had negotiated with both Cresthill and Joliet school Boards. All classes, grades 1-12, were now taught by certified teachers from the two districts.

In 1961, when TV College started on WTTW, it was the first opportunity for college credits to be earned at a prison. The DE had to scrounge around the prison to find some suitable space. What the Warden had given him was the basement of *Cellhouse F*, commonly called the roundhouse. Twice, I had been in that basement to conduct my seminars. To enter it, I passed through a locked steel door, and descended steel stairs into the *dungeon*. There were no windows and it was lit by bare incandescent bulbs. The *main room* contained 20 to 30 desk chairs. Three TVs were bolted to the walls, one on each side and one in front. Also, in front was a movable blackboard. In the back were two rooms. One was the DE's office, the other contained the *college library*.

In the spring semester, when I taught Physical Science 102 on TV, I arranged a *special tour* for Mary and two others. One was my colleague, Milton Langer, who I mentioned earlier. The other was Joy, Milt's wife. While I conducted my 3-hour seminar/review, they toured the prison. Later, while having lunch, the DE told us that he was not allowed to bring Mary and Joy into the roundhouse to see the TV college classroom. Cellhouse F had only one entrance/exit. It was classified as a *dead-end area*. Consequently, women were never permitted to enter it.

Pontiac Penitentiary in Pontiac, IL opened in 1871. From 1872 to 1893 it was a boys' reform school. At the beginning of the 20th century it became a facility for older felons by adding cellblocks. By 1931, it housed 2,500 inmates. In the 1960's, when I visited this facility, it had slightly more than 2,300 felons, most under the age of 25. About 50% were white and 50% black. *The gangs from the streets of Chicago were not yet present.* My first visit to Pontiac occurred in February 1965. The time was approaching for our first exam. I wanted to give my 20 students an opportunity to have a review and ask their questions. I called the DE for Pontiac and scheduled my visit. I told him I'd be at Pontiac at 9:00 am.

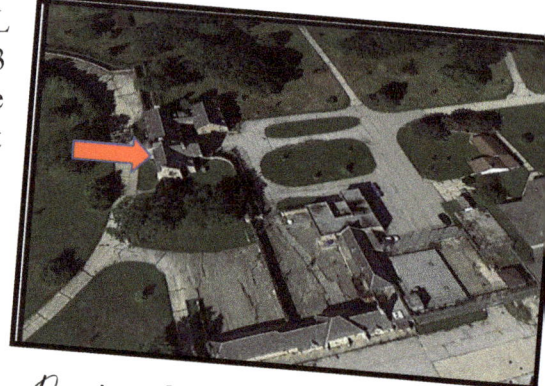

*Pontiac CC & Main Entrance*

## Chapter Four: Genesis I

From my home to this prison was about 75 miles. There was snow on the ground, but not snowing on the day of my visit. I left early enough to arrive at the prison around 8:30 am. I went to the reception area, signed in, and was told to wait in an adjacent parlor. My name was on the proper list, but the DE hadn't arrived. He had to escort me through security and the rest of the way into the prison. He arrived about 8:45 am, came into the parlor, and said, "Dr. Krupp, what are you doing here?" When I told him, I was there for my 9:00 am class, he laughed and said, "You have no idea what you've done! I'll explain at lunch what you achieved." He then led me through the maze of security to the TV classroom.

Later at lunch, he told me what had happened. He said, "No one from TV College ever shows up on time. When your students heard you'd be here at 9:00 am today, the betting started. The earliest anyone expected you was at 9:30. The man who had that time was declared the winner." He went on to tell me that due to being on time, I had gained the respect of all my students. Sad to say, he shared another story about TV College and one of its teachers. Over the previous few years, this instructor would schedule a visit to Pontiac. The day before his visit, he would phone and cancel, due to something that had come-up. This had occurred 5 or 6 times. As a result, his students at Pontiac called him "Professor No Show!"

A final memory regarding Pontiac.
One evening, around 1968 or 1969, I was walking down the halls of Bogan College, later named Richard J. Daley College. A student was walking towards me. When he was 10 feet from me, he looked up and shouted, "Dr. Krupp!" He came closer and I shook his hand. I said, "Hi! I'm sorry but I don't remember your name." He smiled and literally gave me a hug. As he placed his lips near my ear, he whispered, "I'm one of your students from Pontiac." He went on to tell me he had returned home about 6 months earlier, and was now taking classes to earn his AA degree. As we parted, he said, "Thanks for your help!"

Dwight Penitentiary for Women was in Dwight, IL. It opened in 1930, but closed in 2013. From my home to the prison was about 60 miles. In my first visit to Dwight, the DE took me first to meet the Superintendent of the prison, Ms. Margaret Morrisey. I had never met either Wardens from Stateville or Pontiac. We chatted briefly. She thanked me for coming out that day. One thing I recall from that visit, was a comfortable pet bed next to her desk. In it was a small, white furry dog. It had on a beautiful collar. It sparkled like diamonds, from the sunlight streaming through the windows.

Eventually, we left the administration building and passed through security. I was shocked when I entered the area where the inmates were incarcerated. I thought I was on the campus of a small, liberal arts college! I was on a pathway made of large, concrete slabs which surrounded a beautiful grassy quadrangle. Around the exterior part of the path, were eight buildings, 2 stories high built of limestone. Later, at lunch I learned that this women's prison was designed on The Cottage Model. Each cottage was built for 15 to 28 inmates and had a kitchen, dining room, parlor, lavatories, showers, and sleeping quarters. Each inmate had her own bedroom with a bed, dresser, rocking chair, and closet. Most of the wicker furniture had been made by prisoners in Stateville. Each parlor had a fireplace, piano, radio and TV for entertainment. Every cottage had its own female director or warden. The smallest cottage, designed for 15, was the only one with bars on the windows. It housed inmates requiring higher security.

*Remnants of Dwight CC, Main Entrance – 2018*

One of the parlors was used for my classroom, in which I met with my 8 students. After the 3-hour seminar, I was again treated to lunch in a small dining room in that Cottage. During lunch, I asked the DE a question. I said, "I've been to Stateville where there are over 3,000 male inmates. Pontiac has over 2,200. I know Dwight is the only women's prison in Illinois.

Earlier today, Ms. Morrisey, told me that there are now about 280 prisoners in this prison. She also said that you could accommodate only 20 to 30 more. Why such low figures for women?" The DE smiled and went on to explain that inmates at all penitentiaries, male or female, were convicted felons. The sentence for a felony was a year or more. A sentence of less than 12 months was considered a misdemeanor and was served in a county prison. She finished by asking me, "How often do you hear about a woman using a gun to rob a bank or kill someone?" These were the felonies commonly committed by most of the women in a penitentiary in the 1960's.

In the summer of 1966, I was given full pay to edit and make corrections to the workbooks for Physical Science 101 and 102. In addition, I edited and rewrote some of the experiments for Physical Science 111. The academic year of 1966-1967 began, and I was back at Wright teaching courses for the department.

At this point, I wish to review what I'd accomplished by January 1967. Things were to change again for this maverick. I had . . .

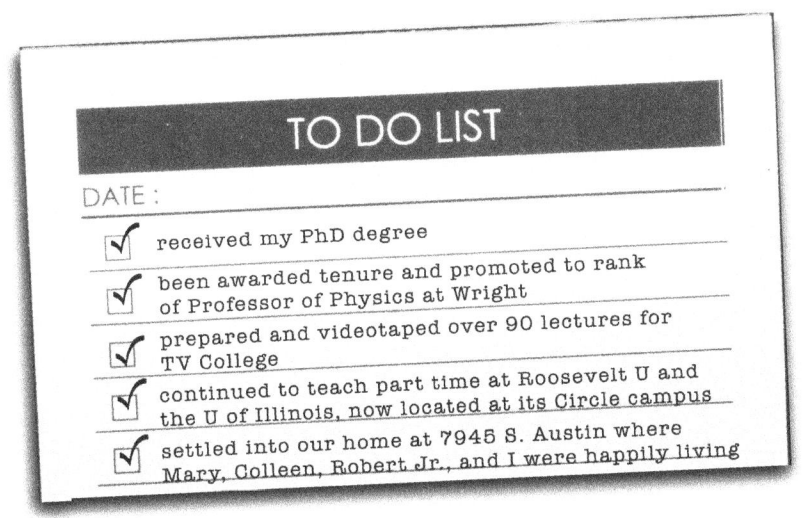

### TO DO LIST

DATE:

- ✓ received my PhD degree
- ✓ been awarded tenure and promoted to rank of Professor of Physics at Wright
- ✓ prepared and videotaped over 90 lectures for TV College
- ✓ continued to teach part time at Roosevelt U and the U of Illinois, now located at its Circle campus
- ✓ settled into our home at 7945 S. Austin where Mary, Colleen, Robert Jr., and I were happily living

In November 1966, I met with Dr. Chausow at TV College. He had become a good friend and trusted advisor. I told him that though I had tenure, I was considering leaving the City College system. My reason for contemplating such a move was that I'd been offered two full-time teaching positions in the Chicago area. One was from Roosevelt U and the other was from the UI, Circle Campus. The challenge of preparing, teaching, and developing senior level courses was of interest to me. After chatting a while, he asked me not to make any commitments until early February.

In mid-January we met again. He asked if I had considered working in college administration. He'd had several conversations with Chancellor Oscar Shabat about me. Chancellor Shabat knew me for he was the head of Wright when I was first hired. He approved my promotion to Full Professor in 1965. Both he and Dr. Chausow wanted to keep me in the City Colleges system. I discussed the advantages, both professionally and personally for such a move with Dr. Chausow. He gave me two weeks to think about it. I discussed it with Mary, Ed, and Bob. I phoned Forest Etheridge, who had moved into administration. Towards the end of January, I met again with Dr. Chausow and I agreed to remain in the system as an administrator. As we parted, he told me to be patient. Selecting and finding administrative positions in the Chicago College system took time to find the right fit.

Shortly thereafter, I was appointed Dean of Faculty at Bogan College. The head of the college was the Dean of the College. The Dean of Faculty was second in line and in charge of the college if the Dean was not present. Thus, in mid-March 1967, I was a college administrator. In the next chapter, I'll describe some of my memories during the next 3 years.

*Chapter Five : The Transition*

# Chapter Five
## Bogan College
## (March 14, 1967-June 30, 1970)

••••••••••••

*Bogan High School — 2018*

At this time, a new phase in my life started. I was now a college administrator. In one sense, I'd already served as a college administrator, because of my duties as chairman of the physics and math department at CBC, Memphis. The difference now was that 100% of my time, and over a 12-month period, I was an administrator. These next three years were a time of transition. As the Dean of Faculty at the college, I learned about the . . .

- scheduling of all classes for every term.

- hiring, evaluation, and retention of faculty.

- need to conduct meetings locally on campus with faculty and staff.

- requirement to attend monthly meetings at our central office in downtown Chicago for all Deans of Faculty. At these we received instructions and directives from the Board, Chancellor, and other administrators.

In early April 1967, our college was visited by an evaluation team from the North Central Accrediting Association (NCAA). This team was led by Dr. Isaac Beckes of Vincennes University. He was a national advocate of technical education for 2-year colleges. This NCAA team visited all seven City Colleges, as well as TV College.

In previous years, NCAA accredited only the Wright and Wilson colleges. All other campuses were approved as extensions of these two. However, in 1967 the NCAA team informed our Board about a significant change. Every extension would each have to undergo their own evaluation. Dr. Beckes and his team would return in 1968 to evaluate each one independently.

In the next three years, I became an evaluator for NCAA and served on teams which evaluated several public and private high schools, as well as a college in Iowa.

During his first visit to Bogan College, Dr. Beckes met with Dr. Sidney Teitelbaum, Dean of the Campus, and me. In that meeting, he suggested we visit Oakland Community College in Bloomfield Hills, MI. He said we would learn much about a modern 2-year college, with a very comprehensive vocational program.

In July 1967, Dr. Teitelbaum and I drove to Bloomfield Hills with two faculty members, the Chairpersons of Science and Language Departments. We went during the time of the 1967 Detroit Riot. We stayed in a Holiday Inn in the NW area of Detroit and followed the 9:00 pm curfew imposed on the city by the National Guard and Federal Troops. During the daytime, we visited various facilities of the college. It had begun in 1965, offering classes in an old renovated hospital and in a former Army Nike missile site.

We visited their first campus, Oak Ridge, due to open in six weeks. During our tour, I observed and wondered, but kept silent. Remember, I was new to administration and was just learning. The Oak Ridge facility had no classrooms, just one or two large lecture halls, in each of three academic buildings. Each building: Humanities, Science, and Vocational had its own library which stored books, videos, slide shows, etc. pertinent to its specialty. The educational concept was that a student would attend a class, in a large lecture hall once a week. The instructor would explain the plan for that week. Then the student would access books, journal articles, slideshow presentations, and videos found in the library of that building. Most of the space, about 75% throughout the building, was dedicated to

## Chapter Five: The Transition

study carrels. Here, a student could sit. At their own pace, students would use the educational materials from the library and proceed to learn the topics assigned for the week.

In the science building, I noticed that the laboratories were essentially two-walled enclosures. In place of the two missing walls were corridors. The idea here was that as students walked the halls and peered into the labs, they would see other students discovering marvelous things. The observers would then sign up and take these wonderful science courses! As I said earlier, I was *new to administration*, so I kept silent. Nevertheless, I wondered if this new approach to education would really work. Would it help students learn in an expeditious manner?

*Oak Ridge CC — 2018*

Ten years later, I met a biology teacher from Oak Ridge CC at a conference in Atlanta. We had coffee together and I told him that I had visited the new campus a few weeks before it opened. I asked how things were working out at his college. He laughed and said that he wasn't present for it's opening. He was first hired in 1969. He told me that he wasn't certain of the exact figures, but the original campus cost about $7 million to build and furnish. He went on to say that in 1974, the Board spent about $9 million to retrofit all the buildings, so that they would be more suitable to the learning process. I inquired if the President of the college was the same one from 1967. He said, "The Board fired him in 1972. He went elsewhere, to Georgia or the Carolinas, to peddle his garbage!"

I wish to mention one final event that involved TV College before I move on to the rest of **MS** involving Bogan college.

In early May 1967, I was invited to a special meeting at TV College. It was held from 10:00 am to 2:00 pm and included lunch on site. I parked in the college's lot, walked around to the front, and past a beautiful Rolls Royce limousine sitting by the entrance. I noticed the steering wheel was on the right side of the car. Behind it, sat a liveried chauffeur. As I walked past the limousine, he tipped the brim of his hat. I heard a heavy British accent say, "Morning, 'suh!"

I entered the conference room for the meeting and a woman greeted me. Again, I heard a lovely British accent say, "Good morning, Dr. Krupp! I've just been watching you on TV." I was introduced to Jennie Lee, British Minister of State for Education. She had been appointed by Prime Minister Harold Wilson and given a specific charge. She was to provide more opportunities for higher education throughout the islands of Britain and the entire UK. Since TV College was a pioneer in using television for educational purposes, she was here to learn from us. Before I arrived, she'd been shown videotapes TV College had produced. One of them was my failed experiment. Dr. Chausow, Bob Carolan, several other teachers, and I sat with her for almost four hours. We answered her questions and provided suggestions that might be of help. A secretary sat behind her and wrote down everything.

In 1969, thanks to the leadership of Jennie Lee, the British Broadcasting Company (BBC) began the Open University (OU). Today, OU is a public distance learning and research university. It is the largest university in the UK for undergraduate education. I am a consultant for OU because of the advice I gave the Baroness during our 4-hour meeting!

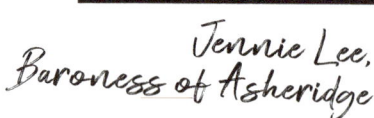

Jennie Lee, Baroness of Asheridge

I spent much of the summer of 1967, working with all departments at Bogan in hiring new faculty. A union contract signed that spring resulted in about a 20% increase in full-time faculty.

Chapter Five: The Transition 131

In August, Mary, Colleen, Bobby, and I drove west for a 3-week holiday. During this trip we visited . . .

- Lassen Peak, King's Canyon, Sequoia, and Yosemite National Parks in CA.
- San Francisco and St. Mary's College near Oakland, CA.
- Christian Brothers Winery in Napa Valley.
- Los Angeles, and met with many of my Jewish aunts, uncles, and cousins.
- Disneyland where the kids enjoyed It's a Small, Small World.
- Knott's Berry Farm.
- Las Vegas, where Mary and I went for a weekend, while Aunt Dorothy babysat the children.

Shortly before Labor Day, the 1967-68 academic year started. I began working with all departments to prepare for the NCAA visit. Dr. Beckes and his team visited us the following spring, after which, Bogan received its initial accreditation.

This same spring semester, Art Lerner, Art Department Chair, arranged for a guest lecturer to address our students. He was a young man, about 25 at that time. He'd recently been hired by the Chicago Sun Times as their film critic. His name was Roger Ebert. Roger had received his BA in 1964 from the University of Illinois (UI), Champaign. He earned an MS degree after graduate studies at UI and the U of Cape Town, South Africa. In 1966, he moved to Chicago and began pursuing a PhD degree at the U of Chicago. In his studies, he used film to document historic and art events.

Roger Ebert-1970

I met Roger and introduced him to the audience gathered in the auditorium. At the end of his program, I thanked him. While shaking his hand, I gave him an envelope containing a $50 honorarium. Two things I recall from his film presentation . . .

### 1. *Fountain of Time*
In the first part of his program, he showed the 1966 dedication of the Fountain of Time monument. It had been built in 1922 and had just been rebuilt. It is located at the western edge of the Midway Plaisance in Washington Park.

### 2. *Chicago Picasso*
In the second part, Roger showed a time lapse film of the construction of the Chicago Picasso. This monument was finished in August 1967.

## Chapter Five: The Transition

Dr. Chausow was now Vice Chancellor for Academic Affairs, and worked at the central office. He encouraged me to apply for an American Council of Education (ACE) Fellowship. This Fellowship program focused on preparing future leaders for colleges and universities. It did so by placing participants at another higher education institution. For one year, the Fellow observed various administrative activities. In May 1968, I was accepted as a Fellow for the 1968-1969 academic year.

In August 1968, the Democratic National Convention (DNC) was held in Chicago. It was a time of great political unrest due to the Vietnam War. I recall the week before the start of the convention. We had our monthly meeting for the Deans of Faculty. It was always held at our central office in downtown Chicago. Usually, I'd drive to this meeting. However, for this one I drove out to Beverly, took a commuter train to the La Salle Street RR Station, and walked a mile to the central office. Our meetings always ended at 12:30 pm. We'd then go to a nearby restaurant for lunch. For this meeting, I took a pass on lunch. Instead, I hastened back to the RR station and got out of town as fast as possible!

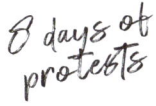

*8 days of protests*

Dr. Chausow and Dr. Teitelbaum appointed me to a special committee. I was the only one from the Chicago City Colleges on it. I was to represent all the southside colleges, i.e., Bogan, Southeast (at Chicago Vocational School), Fenger, and Wilson. The other members on this committee were from . . .

- Joliet CC in Joliet.
- Kankakee CC, Kankakee.
- Moraine Valley CC in Palos Hills.
- Prairie State CC in Chicago Heights.
- South Suburban CC in South Holland.

For want of a better name, I'll call it the *Upper Division University Committee.* You'll hear more about it shortly.

The academic year (1968-1969) began as usual, a week before Labor Day. This was the year in which I was on leave from the Bogan campus to participate in the ACE Fellows Program.

The program for all the Fellows began in early September, with a week of seminars at the Graham School on the U of Chicago campus. Our class consisted of 26 members from across the country. During this academic year, we met for a week of seminars in Denver, San Francisco, and New Orleans. We finished the program in May 1969, with a week in Washington, DC, at the ACE headquarters.

For these meetings, we would arrive and check into our hotel on Sunday evening. From Monday-Friday, we attended seminars and held formal discussions, all day and even into the evening hours. After lunch on Fridays, the meetings ended by 3:00 pm. We'd then return home. All expenses, i.e., travel, housing, meals, educational materials, speakers, etc. were paid by ACE. Some of the Fellows spent the year visiting another university. Others remained at their own campus. I did neither!

During my fellowship, I spent every day, downtown at our Central Office. I was assigned for 2 to 2½ months to different departments where I observed and worked for those in charge. Among those I worked for were . . .

- Dr. Hymen Chausow, Vice-Chancellor of Academic Affairs. This involved articulating all college transfer courses to a university.

- Dr. John Grede, Vice-Chancellor of Vocational Affairs. This involved the offering and special certifications required for all occupational programs.

- Dr. Irv Slutsky, Vice-Chancellor of Buildings and Grounds. This involved the construction of new buildings and the maintenance of all existing facilities.

- Dr. Henry Moughamian, Director of Computer Services. This involved using the computer for record keeping and research.

- Mr. Turner Trimble, Director of Human Resources. This involved negotiating all union contracts for faculty and staff. In addition, he was responsible for maintaining the archives and history of the Chicago City Colleges.

# Chapter Five : The Transition

During my time in Human Resources, I was given a *special assignment*. Using original documents from the archives, I was to write the early history of the Chicago City Colleges. Here's a brief summary of what I wrote . . .

> Chicago's first Junior College (JC) began in 1911, at Crane High School. This was a public high school operated by the Chicago Board of Education (CBE). It started with 30 students, most of whom were recent graduates of Crane. Crane JC utilized rooms in the high school building. By 1929, Crane JC had over 4,000 students and was the largest junior college in the country. It closed in 1930 due to the Great Depression. At that time, the CBE found difficulty in funding all its K-14 programs.
>
> Public pressure forced the CBE to reopen the JC within a year at the same location, Crane HS. However, it was given a different name. Because over 75% of the students were Jewish, it was called Herzl JC to honor Theodor Herzl, founder of the Zionist Movement. By 1934, Wilbur Wright JC, on the north, and Woodrow Wilson JC on the south were opened. Just like all its other schools, the CBE charged no tuition for these college classes. Consequently, the number of students significantly increased before WWII. During the war, the US military used all three colleges to train their personnel. After the war, enrollments at Herzl, Wilson, and Wright grew significantly, due to the GI Bill. In 1956, the three colleges opened extensions on the NE, SE, SW, and downtown areas of the city. A few years later, they all cooperated in establishing TV College.

*ACE Headquarters Washington, D.C.*

Earlier, I mentioned that five meetings were held for the ACE Fellows during the year. Towards the end of May 1969, we met in Washington, DC for the end of our Fellowship year. Our sessions were held in the ACE Headquarters near DuPont Circle. I recall two seminars from this final week . . .

## Dr. Coleman's Seminar

Dr. John R. Coleman was President of Haverford College from 1967-77. During his seminar, he told us how he would put his academic knowledge to the test, by working a variety of blue-collar jobs. One summer vacation, he'd worked as a garbage collector. Another summer, he worked on rural highways, paving holes in the roadway.

In 1971 or 1972, he took a sabbatical from Haverford. During this time he worked as a ditch-digger, prison warden, and a salad-and-sandwich man at the Union Oyster House in Boston. He wrote about his experiences for the *New York* magazine in a book called, *The Blue-Collar Journal: A College President's Sabbatical.* It received the 1974 award from the *Athenaeum of Philadelphia Literary Society.*

I mention hearing about Dr. Coleman speak on this subject in 1969. In a later chapter you will hear about an event in my *MS* wherein I heeded his advice. After following his suggestions, they *bit me in the butt!*

## The Priest's Seminar

Another seminar was given by a priest from the Association of Catholic Colleges and Universities (ACCU). I mention him not because of what he said in his seminar, but with something that happened afterwards.

He had done a *little homework* about the members in our Fellowship class. About four or five of us had attended a Catholic college or university. He asked that we join him at lunch in the ACE dining room. During this time, he told us that many, many Catholic colleges currently needed experienced and trained administrators. It was a critical time in Catholic higher education, when men's and women's colleges merged. Others changed from single sex to coed, and still others closed. He asked us to consider positions of leadership among some of these colleges, as our careers moved forward. You will hear more about this in the next chapter.

# Chapter Five: The Transition

These last few pages have dealt with my professional life. I'd now like to describe a few things that happened in my personal life . . .

Christine, my third and last child, was born in December 1967.

Since I was an administrator, I had greater flexibility in scheduling my working hours. In the fall of 1967, I was persuaded to volunteer and provide a community service. I entered my name and was elected to the public elementary School Board, District #111.

*Office of School District #111*

When first elected in 1967, the district had 9 elementary schools. In my first year, I was a member of the Board, and in the second year I served as Secretary. This was the only year I was paid by the school district. Twice a month, the day before payday, I went into the District Office to sign every paycheck given to the employees. By law, the Superintendent and Board Secretary had to sign each check. For this service, I was paid $20 a month. During the third year of my term, the payments stopped because I was elected President of the Board.

Though we were not paid as school board members we were encouraged to attend national meetings and workshops. The Board paid for these expenses, i.e., travel, housing, meals, fees, etc. As a school board member, I attended national meetings for school board members in Atlantic City, Seattle, and Phoenix.

I recall attending another workshop, but at no cost to the Board. Around this time, General Electric (GE) was selling the idea of heating buildings and offices using light bulbs. GE invited a board member and an administrator, to an all expense 3-day workshop in Cleveland, OH. One evening Don Hon, Assistant Superintendent, and I boarded a special charter flight out of Midway Airport. It was a small jet with about 150 seats. All were filled with school board members or district administrators. Shortly after takeoff, the captain spoke on the loudspeaker. He said, "I wish to welcome all you school board members and administrators to this special flight. I also want you to know that every nut and bolt, every piece of equipment on this aircraft was installed by the lowest bidder."

The GE workshop was held at the National Electric Lamp Association (NELA) Park. This was the first industrial park in the world when it opened in 1901. The initial goals of NELA were to do research and set the standards for the electric light bulb industry. The Association dissolved in 1911. GE absorbed the Association and developed the 92-acre site into a campus that emulated a university setting.

*NELA Park, Main Building*

From 1964, I was getting my haircut at a barber shop a half-mile from home. My barber was Louis Viverito, a Korean War veteran, who had received three decorations. Besides cutting hair, Lou was politically active. In 1969, he was elected as a Stickney Township Democratic Committeeman. Lou encouraged me to run for the public-school board in our community. Besides helping me to file on time, he assisted by leading my campaign. In 1972, Lou was an elected delegate to the DNC. From 1995-2011, he was a member of the Illinois State Senate.

*Einstein Visits NELA Park, 1922*

I mention Lou because in 1967, a new community college started, in our suburban area. It opened a temporary office in Oak Lawn, IL. Classes began in an old abandoned warehouse in nearby Chicago Ridge. A year later, a contest was held to give the college its name. Lou arranged for me to be on the committee delegated to find a suitable name. At our first meeting, the committee decided to advertise in local newspapers and to hold a contest requesting names. I asked if anyone on the committee could suggest a name. I was told, "Yes, but leave your name off what you write. We don't want to appear to favor someone on this committee."

## Chapter Five: The Transition

In 1968, I met the first President of the College, Dr. Robert Turner. At that time, he could not reveal the site the Board was planning to purchase for the college campus. However, he did tell me it was in Palos Heights, or Palos Hills, or Palos Park. One Sunday, Mary and I spent over four hours driving through these three communities. Remember, I had taught geology at Wright and TV colleges. I recognized the unique geographical features that produced all the hills and valleys in these three communities. They were ice age deposits called *moraines*. Mary was the first person to read the one sheet I typed up for the committee. I suggested the new college be named *Moraine Valley CC*. I submitted this sheet with no name on it. It was one of three names the committee submitted to the Board at its February meeting in 1969.

I'll never forget that meeting, which I attended. For over an hour the Board discussed and debated another name, not submitted by our committee. About 6 weeks earlier, during the Christmas holidays, one of the Board members had died suddenly. The Board members deliberated using his name for over an hour. Then they called on the College President, Dr. Turner, for his thoughts. I remember he first explained that he could accept any name they selected. The decision was theirs to make. He told them that, in his experiences, he had never heard of a college or public school ever being named for a Board member. He went on to suggest that at a future meeting the Board could consider naming a building on the campus after this deceased Board member. He also mentioned the Board had not yet heard from our committee. After he spoke, the Board read the names our committee had submitted. They liked the name Moraine Valley and within ½ hour they voted to accept it. Later, when I got home, Mary and I had a glass of wine to toast our new baby!

*Moraine Valley Community College in 2018*

Earlier, I mentioned my appointment to a special committee, which I called the *Upper Division University Committee*. I would like to tell that story now, but first I need to provide you some background.

In July 1965, the state of Illinois passed legislation that affected higher education immensely. Throughout the state, new community colleges were to be built. They were to provide the first two years of higher education. Within 4 years, 9 new CC started in the Chicago metropolitan area . . .

1. Triton CC, 1965
2. Kankakee CC, 1966
3. DuPage CC, 1967
4. Moraine Valley CC, 1967
5. Waubansee CC, 1967
6. McHenry CC, 1968
7. Harper CC, 1968
8. Lake County CC, 1969
9. Oakton CC, 1969

In that new legislation, two senior or *upper division universities* were approved. These unique universities were to offer only the last two years of undergraduate education. They were to be *commuting schools*, since no funds were budgeted for housing. One was to be located near Springfield, the State Capital. It began classes in the fall of 1970, as *Sangamon State University*.

The second senior university was to be in the suburban area of Chicago. The committee, on which I served, represented four southside Chicago city community colleges, and five south suburban community colleges. Our mission was to recommend and encourage, that this *upper division university* serve the students of these nine community colleges.

I well remember the meeting that was held before a special committee of congressmen, senators, and educators who made the final decision. It was held in a large assembly hall on the UI, Circle campus. It was an open meeting and was filled with 500 to 600 people. They were local community leaders and representatives. However, only the three *Upper Division University Committees* could speak or answer questions, about their reports and recommendations.

## Chapter Five: The Transition

The first report was from the committee representing the north and northwest suburbs. They really had brought out a powerful political person to make their presentation. It was Donald J. Rumsfeld, who served in the US Congress from 1963-69. I had never heard of him before this meeting. He had grown up in Winnetka and attended the Baker Demonstration School in Wilmette.

*Congressman Donald Rumsfeld*

This was a private, independent, progressive laboratory school, run by National Louis University. He later graduated from New Trier high school and received a BA in Political Science from Princeton, in 1954. He served three years as a Navy aviator and flight instructor and returned home in 1957, to begin his political career. I particularly recall a statement he made during the presentation. Rumsfeld said, "Our statistics show that 85% of our high school graduates go on to study at colleges and universities." These statistics were correct! What he didn't mention was that most of these students went on to private, first rate universities like, Harvard, Yale, Princeton, Dartmouth, Cornell, Northwestern, Stanford, etc.

The second report dealt with the western suburbs of Chicago. This committee had also called upon a well-known, powerful educational leader as their spokesperson. It was Dr. David D. Henry, President of the University of Illinois from 1955-71. During the first decade of his tenure, he'd seen to the growth and development of Navy Pier into the UI, Chicago. At the same time, he had expanded and strengthened the UI Medical School in Chicago.

*Dr. David D. Henry*

He made an excellent presentation. However, this committee had overlooked one important feature. In De Kalb, Northern Illinois U already existed, and it was a large, public university. This campus can be reached in a 1- to 1½-hour drive from the community colleges of DuPage, Elgin, McHenry County, Triton, and Waubansee.

Our committee's report was given last. We hadn't thought to bring out a big gun to make our case. Our report was given by our committee Chairman, whose name I've forgotten. He was from Joliet Junior College. At our first meeting, we'd elected him Chairman. We felt it was only right and proper. Joliet JC was the first junior college in the world, when it began in 1901. Our report had four main aspects . . .

1. We represented nine community colleges, four from Chicago and five from the south/southwest suburbs. All these community colleges would be excellent feeder schools to the new upper division university.

2. An excellent network of interstate highways had been built or planned in our area. These included: I-55, I-57, I-80, I-90, I-94, and I-294. The highways would provide access for students commuting to the new university.

3. The demographics of our area showed that blue collar workers constituted the bulk of the population.

4. There was no public university in the south-southwest suburbs. The closest was Illinois State U in Bloomington. This was anywhere from 90 to 120 miles from the homes of some of our students.

*Governors State University*

To finish this recollection in **MS**, our committee's recommendation was accepted. That's how Governors State U ended up adjacent to I-57 in the south suburbs of Chicago!

Chapter Five : The Transition

Some personal memories from the summer of 1969 . . .

On July 21, 1969, we all watched in amazement as Neil Armstrong stepped out of the lunar module onto the Moon!

On August 19, I took Colleen and Bobby to their first major league ball game at Wrigley field. We saw Ken Holtzman pitch his first no-hitter, as the Cubs beat the Atlanta Braves 3-0!

I'll now end this chapter. There are other interesting tidbits in the 1960's, but I need to move on. The next chapter deals with my migrating across the country, looking for just the right spot, as I continued my career in higher education. This was a period, when I sought to provide leadership, by serving as a college administrator, instead of an instructor!

My Marvelous Memories

*Chapter Six: The West Coast* 145

# *Chapter Six*
## The West Coast
## (1970-1973)

••••••••••••

*Modern Day Portland, Oregon*

## Marylhurst College, Oregon
## (July 1970-June 1973)

••••••••••••

In 1893, Marylhurst College began in downtown Portland. First named St. Mary's Academy and College, it was operated by the Sisters of the Holy Names of Jesus and Mary. The first college degrees were awarded in 1897.

*Main Hall built in 1930*

In 1930, it moved to a new location south of Portland near Lake Oswego (LO). The College was renamed Marylhurst, meaning Mary's Woods.

In 1959, it became an independent institution and formed a Board of Trustees, separate from the Sisters. On July 1, 1970, I became the first lay person to be the President of the College. At this time, the Board intended that Marylhurst continue as a college for women only.

Prior to accepting this position, I'd spent two years looking for a position in administration. In the last week of April 1970, I received two offers of a presidency at a Catholic College.

Besides Marylhurst, I received another offer from Mt. Senario College in Ladysmith, WI. After discussing this with Mary, we decided to go to Oregon. We wanted to visit and expose our children to the west and northwest sections of our country.

When I began at Marylhurst, I didn't begin with an agenda of change. I . . .

- kept Sister Fidelma, in her position as Academic Dean.
- kept Sister Elizabeth Jean, as Dean of Students.
- kept Mr. Richard Thomas, as Director of Development.
- kept Mr. Jim Corbett, as Business Manager.
- did not spend money to refurbish and redecorate my office with new drapery, floors, furniture, etc.

In early August, we hired David Connor, as our new Director of Admissions. His job was to visit high schools, especially all girls' high schools, in CA, ID, MT, NV, OR, UT, WA, and WY. He spent the month of August, planning his travel schedule. He came to me with a great idea! He had conducted a survey of farms within a 3-mile radius of the campus. It showed that there were stables to accommodate over 100 horses. Most of the farmers he contacted, agreed to rent space in their barns, for a horse or two. I asked him and Richard Thomas to develop a flyer that we could use for recruiting purposes.

At our September Board meeting, we presented a rough draft of this flyer to them. It encouraged new students to enroll at Marylhurst and to bring their horse along. Their beloved animal wouldn't be stabled on campus. However, on weekends, and other times, they could groom and ride their horse in a nearby facility.

## Chapter Six: The West Coast

The concept wasn't approved by the Board. The agreement in 1959, to form an independent Board required that one-third of the Board's membership consist of Sisters of the Holy Names of Jesus and Mary. I could see from the questions and discussion on this issue by the nuns, that they had an attitude. I was not going to be allowed to make a horse college out of their beloved Marylhurst! Forty some years later, as I reflect on this memory, I guess that was strike one!

About two weeks before Thanksgiving of 1970, Sister Elizabeth Jean, Dean of Students, met with me. She informed me that one of our resident students was pregnant. I said, "OK!" Then she asked, "When will you write the letter?" I said, "What letter?" She replied, "The letter expelling her from Marylhurst."

To say the least, I was a little taken aback by her reply. Nothing in all my experiences, including my ACE Fellowship, had prepared me for this one. After thinking about it, for a few moments, I said, "I don't want to know her name. Find out when her baby is due. Ask her what plans she's made for raising her infant. Finally, ask her if she'd like to get her bachelor's degree from Marylhurst."

The following week, Sr. Elizabeth Jean returned and told me . . .

- The baby was due around mid-January.
- Her parents knew about her situation.
- They'd agreed to accept and raise the child.
- However, a decision on whether they would adopt their grandchild had not yet been made.
- Yes, she would like to earn her BA from Marylhurst!

I then told Sr. Elizabeth to go back and tell her . . .

- We all wish her well on the birth of her baby.
- We also wish her entire family a Merry Christmas and Happy New Year!
- That she'd be welcome back at Marylhurst for the start of the second semester. It began in the third week of January. She did return about two weeks late for the second semester.

In case you're wondering if I brought this issue to the Board of Trustees, I did not! If they wanted to fire me, so be it. I signed a contract to run an educational institution called a college, not a convent!

One final memory regarding this story. A year later, in February 1972, I was on a fundraising trip in CA. I'd been to LA and San Francisco, calling on foundations and speaking to alumnae gatherings. I was at my last stop in Sacramento. The alumnae living in the area had arranged for a dinner. After the dinner, I spoke about what was happening at their alma mater. During the question period that followed, one of the ladies asked, "Is it true that you now allow pregnant women to remain in the dormitories?" That was one I didn't see coming!

As best as I can recollect, I said something like this, "You don't know much about my background. I've had over 12 years of Catholic education. This includes 8 years of elementary school by BVM nuns, and high school and college by Christian Brothers. In addition, I've done post-graduate work at a Jesuit and a Vincentian University. Somewhere in that journey, I was taught that Jesus said, *'Let the one among you who is without sin be the first to cast a stone!'* "

The academic year ended by mid-May. Graduation had been held. Summer school classes wouldn't start until mid-June. Our dormitories were empty. Richard Thomas and Jim Corbett tried to find ways to rent them out for short term meetings, retreats, etc. One group that stayed in our dormitories and had meals on our campus was the King Kamehameha (KK) HS Marching Band from Hawaii.

*King Kamehameha HS — 2018*

Since 1907, Portland has held an Annual Rose Festival in early June. The KK Band was touring the west coast in the late spring of 1971. They were scheduled to march in the Grand Floral Parade on Sunday and to give a concert on Friday evening at the Oregon Convention Center.

On Thursday afternoon, about 75 high school students and 12 to 15 adults, arrived on our campus. After checking into a dormitory, they had supper in our dining hall. I went there to greet them informally. No speeches, just going around to all the tables saying, "Hi! Hope you have a good time while you're here!"

# Chapter Six : The West Coast

On Friday, they all went off in their chartered buses to do some sightseeing. They went up to Timberline Lodge on Mt. Hood to see some snow. In the afternoon, they visited Lloyd Center, a shopping mall just NE of downtown Portland. This mall included an ice rink. Olympian, Tonya Harding, first learned to skate here. Of course, all these native Hawaiians had to try their skill at ice skating. The amazing thing was that only one student fell and broke a bone.

*Winter at Timberland Lodge*

*Lloyd Center Ice Rink*

I remember the call I got Friday evening at home. It was about 5:30 pm, when one of the chaperon's called. He said, "Dr. Krupp, can you please help us? I'm here in the emergency room at Providence Hospital in Portland." He went on to explain that one of their young ladies had fallen on the ice and broken her leg. He needed help to get her back to the dorm at Marylhurst. Here's what followed . . .

> Mary and I went to the college and checked out a 12-passenger van. Off we went to the hospital emergency room.
>
> When we got there, a cast was being put on the girl's leg. Mary waited in the emergency room while I drove the two chaperones to rejoin their group. They were having dinner at the food court in Lloyd Center.
>
> Afterwards, they went to the Convention Center to be part of an evening concert.

I returned to the hospital where Mary and the girl were waiting. Hospital staff helped us get her into the van and off we went to the college. Mary and I assisted her to her room. Mary settled her into her bed and sat with her until she fell asleep. The doctors had given her a mild sedative.

The next morning, Saturday, I went up to the college, while our KK visitors were having breakfast. I wanted to see how everything was going and how their young patient was doing. While having coffee with the Band Director, many of the chaperones came to thank me for the help I'd given the night before. I told them that Mary and I were planning a 2-week vacation on Maui, in mid-August. Many begged us to stop in Oahu, for at least a weekend, while in Hawaii. So, Mary and I changed our plans. On our last three days in Hawaii, we stayed in Oahu.

When we landed, our new friends from KK greeted us with leis. After a tour of the KK campus, they drove us to our hotel. Mary and I had dinner in the hotel and spent the night resting. The next morning, Saturday, our friends came and joined us for breakfast. They left us with a car to use for two days.

They suggested that we should visit the Polynesian Cultural Center (PCC) in Laie. After a morning visit to the National Cemetery of the Pacific in the Punch Bowl, we drove to the PCC. We saw an excellent, 3-hour live program, covering Polynesian history and culture. We returned to Honolulu to attend a luau at the Bishop Museum.

*Polynesian Cultural Center*

After Mass and breakfast on Sunday, Mary and I spent the day at Pearl Harbor. We visited various WWII Memorials, i.e. Arizona, Utah, and the Aviation Museum on Ford Island. About 5:00 pm, we went to a Chinese restaurant. There we met about 10 of our KK friends. They treated us to dinner. After driving us to our hotel, they took back the car they had provided us. However, on

*Arizona Memorial*

Monday morning, a couple came to our hotel, and drove us to the airport. After curbside hugs, they left us each draped in leis!

## Chapter Six: The West Coast

Since I've just mentioned the end of our trip to Hawaii, I should tell you about our first 10 days on Maui. Harry Kane, Chairman of our Board, had a vacation home on Maui. He let Mary and I use it. A car for traveling around the island was included with the house. It was in a gated community of 25 or 26 homes, on the NW coast of Maui. Only the gatekeeper's house and one other home were occupied during the time we were there. This community was situated on a bluff. Steps led down to a small sand beach. A swimming pool and deck chairs were located here. We could sun and swim in fresh or saltwater, if we choose!

*Fresh papaya!*

*Harry's House!*

At Harry's house, there were two papaya trees with ripe fruit. Every night, I'd bring in some papayas. After peeling and removing the seeds, I'd cut the fruit into slices. Into the fridge, they'd go for the night. I was always an early riser. In the morning, I'd setup the coffeepot, toaster, butter, plates, etc., on a table in the shaded patio. I'd read and wait for Mary to get up. When she did, we'd always have a light breakfast of papayas, toast, jam, and coffee. Our days were spent resting, reading, or maybe doing a little sightseeing. Every night we went out to a different restaurant for dinner. There weren't many channels on TV, and the reception from Oahu wasn't good. Instead, after a dish of ice cream covered with papaya slices, we read and went to bed by 9:00 pm!

One day, we went on a sightseeing adventure to Hana, on the east coast of Maui. It is one of the most isolated communities in the state. To get there, we drove along Hana Highway, a winding 64-mile-long roadway, on the northern shore.

*The road to Hana*

In Hana, we bought sandwiches and cold drinks at Hasegawa's General Store. We enjoyed lunch in Hana Bay Beach Park, gazing at the Pacific.

*Driving to Hana*

*Hasegawa's General Store*

*Hana Bay Beach Park*

*Seven Sacred Pools*

After lunch, we drove 10 miles farther south to visit the Seven Sacred Pools in Haleakalā National Park. Since I was wearing my swimming suit, I managed a dip into 2 or 3 of the cascading pools. Though cool, they were not icy cold. Mary did not get in the water. She sat on a bench, smoking and waiting for me.

Along our drive to Hana, we passed the ranch of Charles Lindbergh. He'd retired to this area in 1970. When he died in 1974, he was buried at a church, two miles south of the Seven Sacred Pools.

I think this is enough about our Hawaiian adventures! Let's get back to talking about Marlyhurst. In my second year, 1971-72, I was involved in several meetings with Dr. John Howard and members of his staff. I'd met John during my first year in Oregon. John was the President of Lewis and Clark College.

*Chapter Six: The West Coast*

Lewis and Clark College (L&C) was a private, liberal arts college in SW Portland, only a 15-minute drive from Marylhurst. At this time, it had about 1700 students in the undergraduate program. At a meeting, in the summer of 1971, some of the laymen on our Board encouraged me to meet with Dr. Howard. Larry Hilaire, a Board member, knew John and had recently met with him. During their meeting, Dr. Howard had said to Larry, "Is there any way we can help you at Marylhurst?" So, with their knowledge and at the behest of the Board, I began exploring cooperative ventures with L&C. One I'll relate now, another a little later in *MS*.

In September 1971, L&C had brought over from Holland, or maybe it was Belgium, a visiting professor. His specialty was a performing art, *mime*. During his three years at L&C, he was to teach courses in this art. His students were to give occasional performances. L&C was having difficulty in trying to locate the right space for him, on their campus, to conduct classes and hold recitals.

We, at Marylhurst had, many spaces that were not used. One I want to describe to you. I mentioned earlier, Main Hall, the first building constructed in 1930. The left wing of this building contained a small chapel. It'd been used by the students and nuns to attend Mass and other religious events. The interior was over two stories high and had a choir loft. A new, larger chapel was built in the early 1960's and this chapel was vacated. The altar was decertified and removed. All else, including the pews and an organ, were left in this chapel.

Prior to my arrival, and during my first year, it was designated as a movie auditorium. A projector was placed in the choir loft. In the front of the chapel, a screen which rolled up and down, was bolted to the ceiling. However, this *movie theater* was hardly ever used. Our library provided projectors to any classroom on request.

When I showed this space to the visiting professor, he became ecstatic. He said it was more than *perfect*! The two side rooms in front, where the priests had donned their vestments, would be used as dressing rooms. The choir loft would contain spotlights. Students could sit in the pews, while he taught a class. The same pews provided seating for an audience during any performance.

So, in the second semester, we scheduled all his classes to be held there. L&C provided a small bus that transported their students between campuses. Marylhurst students could register and earn art credits at no extra cost to them. I believe 6 or 7 of our students did sign up for the beginning class. It all started smoothly!

In the 3rd week of the semester, Sr. Fidelma, Academic Dean, came to see me. She began, "Dr. Krupp, you won't believe this! For four years, no one has used that old chapel as a movie theater. Now, I'm overwhelmed with requests by our faculty, to use it throughout the week. What I am going to do?"

It was our decision that the Marlyhurst faculty should be accommodated first. So, this program with L&C was cancelled. The unhappy professor returned to the L&C campus with his students. Our students had to transfer to another course on campus. Two weeks after this cooperative program was cancelled, no one on our faculty needed to use this chapel anymore to show a film. It again became totally unused. I guess this was strike two!

However, this second semester was not all doom and gloom. In February 1972, it snowed in Portland. Even though it was only a few inches, Portland and other communities didn't have equipment to plow the roads. Lay faculty and commuting students couldn't get to our campus. Classes were cancelled for two days.

On the first day I walked about a mile, through the snow to the campus. After warming up with a hot coffee, I met with Sr. Fidelma, and Richard Thomas. We planned and held our first *snow picnic*. We called the kitchen and talked to the Food Service Manager. He prepared potato salad, coleslaw, lettuce, sliced tomatoes, etc. for the noon lunch. Around 11:30 am, Sr. Fidelma, Richard and I started grilling hamburgers and hot dogs. Shielded from the falling snow, by an overhang outside the dining hall, we had two charcoal grills fired up. While a light snow fell, we three cooked the burgers and dogs for over 300 resident students. Occasionally, one of the young ladies would pop-out of the warm dining hall, to fling a snowball at us. We all had great fun at our first snow picnic!

# Chapter Six: The West Coast

Occasionally, I will stop writing about my professional life and shift to talking about my personal life. This is one of those times. I will now interrupt my Marylhurst tales, to tell you about things in our family's personal lives.

In early June 1970, Mary, Colleen (7), Bobby (6), Christine (3), and I began driving to Oregon. It was the start of our move. We took the long way to do some sightseeing. The 1st day we drove 500 miles and stopped in Joplin, MO. The 2nd day, we continued another 450 miles, and stopped in Amarillo, TX. We went to The Big Texan for a steak dinner. Though tempted, I did not order the FREE 72-oz challenge!

*The 72 oz. Monster!*

Another 500 miles on the 3rd day, put us in Flagstaff, AZ. We visited AZ's Meteor Crater, 40 miles east of Flagstaff. The next day, we drove 75 miles, to visit the Grand Canyon, and returned to our motel in Flagstaff for the night.

*The Grand Canyon*

We drove south through Oak Creek Canyon and Sedona the following morning. After lunch in Prescott, we continued to Quartzite for the night. The next morning, we drove to Riverside, CA where we stayed with Mary's cousin, Jerry Canavan. After 3 or 4 days in Riverside, we drove to LA. Here we spent a week visiting with my uncles, aunts, and cousins. I particularly remember a family picnic held on Sunday at Griffith Park and Planetarium. When lunch started, we couldn't find Mary and Bobby. We thought they were lost! They returned an hour later after their hike up to the Planetarium and Observatory.

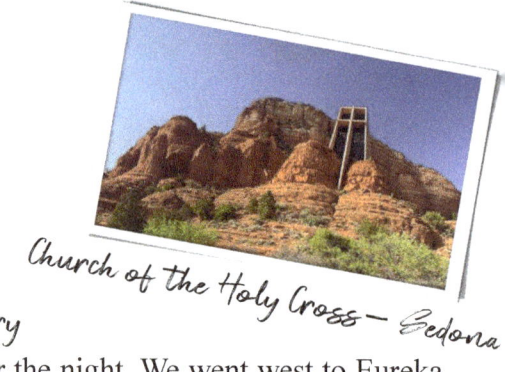

*Griffith Park and Observatory*

*Church of the Holy Cross — Sedona*

We left LA and stopped in Redding, for the night. We went west to Eureka on the Pacific coast and continued north. This was the last segment of our sightseeing adventure. We wanted to view the rugged coasts of northern CA and southern OR. We stopped in Florence for the night. In the morning, we drove 10 miles north of Florence to the sea lion caves. From an overlook stop, we hoped to catch a glimpse of some sea lions, in the ocean waters. Unfortunately, we didn't see any that day. We now went east through the coastal mountain range and turned north on I-5. That night, Sunday, June 28, we stopped at a motel in the Lake Oswego area. We had arrived at our new home!

*New home new adventures.*

*17075 Old River Road, Oregon! Our New Home!*

Our furniture was supposed to arrive on Monday or Tuesday, June 29 or 30. That didn't happen! We learned Monday that the furniture wouldn't be delivered until sometime the following week. The house was ready, cleaned and freshly painted, but no furniture! So, we checked into two dormitory rooms on the Marylhust campus. The kids loved it! It was better than a motel. The college even had an indoor swimming pool, that they used all day. I started my new job on Wednesday, July 1. Friday was the July 4th holiday. The furniture eventually arrived on Tuesday July 7. Mary and the kids unpacked and put the house in order. Our big summer move was over!

Chapter Six: The West Coast

The above story, about our move to OR, prompts me to expand it a bit. This was the start of a lot of traveling and sightseeing for our family. We had just driven through 8 states in our country. During the next 3 years, there were many more travel events that I recall . . .

In June 1971, we drove through WA to get to Vancouver, BC, Canada. Mary and the children boarded a Canadian National Railways train that took them eastward. It carried them through the scenic Canadian Rockies. Stops were made at Jasper, Edmonton, and Saskatoon. They got off at Winnipeg, cabbed over to the airport, and flew to Chicago for the summer.

Mary and I made two trips to Victoria Island, BC. On one of these trips, some of the children accompanied us, but I'm not sure if they all did. Here we visited the World Famous Butchart Gardens, a Historic Site of Canada. In these gardens we viewed the Salish Totem Poles. We learned that totem poles were found only among the natives of the Pacific NW and northern Rocky Mountains. This was due to the presence of the Douglas Fir tree, only growing in those regions.

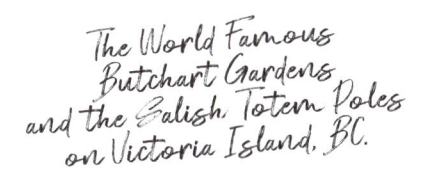

*The World Famous Butchart Gardens and the Salish Totem Poles on Victoria Island, BC.*

On one of these trips, we had high tea at the Empress Hotel, another Historic Site. It opened in 1908 and was built by the Canadian Pacific Steamship line. It was a terminus hotel. Its main dock for sailing vessels was only a block away.

The Empress Hotel

High Tea at the Empress

One summer, I had a week-long workshop in Boulder, CO. Mary and the children came along for our ride through OR → ID → UT → WY → CO. While I attended meetings, Mary and the children visited abandoned silver mines, and western ghost towns. My conference ended. We then drove through NE → IA → IL to arrive in Chicago. After a week visiting family and friends, I flew back to Oregon. Mary and the children stayed in Chicago for over a month.

In July and August of 1970, we often went sightseeing to many local sites. Several Sundays were spent in Washington Park. It contains the Portland Zoo, Children's Museum, Japanese Garden, and especially the International Rose Test Garden. This Rose Garden opened in 1918. It is the oldest, public rose test garden in the United States. Today, it contains over 10,000 bushes with varieties from all over the world. It is the reason Portland is called the *City of Roses*.

## Chapter Six: The West Coast

The week before the academic year began at the college, we had 3 to 4 days of orientation for faculty and staff. At one of the coffee breaks, one of the nuns on the faculty approached me. She asked how I and my family liked the northwest. I told her we were enjoying it immensely. I mentioned that the previous Sunday, we had made our 2nd visit to the Rose Garden in Washington Park. She responded, "Oh my! I haven't been there in 25 years. I should go again." I tell this now and it will be mentioned again in the next chapter.

### Crater Lake

Other sightseeing trips included four to Crater Lake. The children only accompanied us on two of these. They were with us the first time, which occurred on Memorial Day weekend in 1971. I'll never forget that trip! On Monday, May 29, I drove up the northern side of Mt. Mazama. Halfway up, we encountered a snowstorm. While the flakes fell, we arrived at the northern entrance to the park. We couldn't enter because the roadway was not cleared of snow. We later found out that from late September to mid-June, the north road is not plowed. So, we descended the mountain. The snow stopped. We drove around to the southside and drove up the mountain again. As we ascended, the snow started, however it wasn't as heavy. We arrived at the cleared south entrance to the park and drove in to see the lake. This was our first view of this gorgeous site. We didn't drive the 24-mile trip around the crater, since the roadway wasn't plowed at this time.

In September 1970, Colleen and Bobby began 2nd and 1st grades, respectively. They attended Our Lady of the Lake (OLL) parochial school. Christine was in nursery school and went to a swimming program for infants at Marylhurst.

I think this was the happiest three years of Mary's life. The kids were in school and she didn't have to work! However, she was needed at OLL. She volunteered to work there and was a go-for, librarian, and chauffeur. The teachers ordered educational films from a county library. On Monday afternoons, she would drive 13 to 14 miles to get them. On Fridays, she'd return the films. The school had a small library, but no librarian. Mary spent 1 to 2 hours a day, putting books back on the shelves in proper order. She drove a very large station wagon at this time. So, she and other parents took classes on field trips. Every time she had one, she'd tell me all about it that night at supper.

Because of her work, Mary was well known by parents in the school. I recall two memories which happened because of her volunteer work. We were invited one Sunday afternoon, to a reception at the home of Frank Leahy Jr. It was a reception, honoring the baptism of their 4th child. An hour after we arrived, the grandfather came in. It was Coach Frank Leahy! I didn't know he was living in Lake Oswego. After retiring from Notre Dame in 1953, he moved to Lake Oswego in 1963. I enjoyed chatting with him for over an hour, letting him recall some of his experiences at ND.

*Coach Frank Leahy*

The second recollection I had concerned another couple, whose names I've forgotten. They had 2 or 3 children in OLL, some of whom were classmates of our children. This entire family loved to snow ski. The parents had taught their children to ski. They took Colleen and Bobby up to Mt. Hood, where both learned how to ski. We didn't even have to buy equipment. Their garage was loaded with skis and boots, of all sizes. If it had been left to Mary or me, our kids would never had learned that skill!

*Chapter Six: The West Coast*

Other recollections of this time also have no relation to Marylhurst. Some of these now follow . . .

Harvey Dick was a man after my heart, a scallywag, a maverick, and an adventurer. He made his fortune in the steel industry in Portland. In 1941, he bought the old Hoyt Hotel, directly opposite the Union Railroad Station in the downtown area. Built in 1912, this six storied building was used by him to house his steel workers during WWII. In the early 1960's, he renovated all 175 hotel rooms. On the ground floor, he added a nightclub called the Barbary Coast Lounge, and the Roaring 20's dining room.

*The Hotel Hoyt*

*The Dining Room at Hotel Hoyt*

Occasionally, Mary and I went there for dinner. We enjoyed bringing our out-of-town visitors here for a meal, and some unique sightseeing. When the ladies went to the restroom, they were entertained by a harpist. While they powdered their faces, she played soft melodies on her harp.

In the men's restroom, there was a 12-foot long urinal, decorated like a rock grotto. In the middle, stood a 3-foot statue of Fidel Castro, his mouth open, one arm raised with a finger pointing upward. If a man could direct a stream of urine into Fidel's mouth, things would happen! His eyes would light up, other lights in the restroom would flash, sirens went off, and a huge cascade of water flushed the entire 12-foot wall!

Harvey had purchased a replica of an old steam locomotive, from the 20th Century Fox movie studio. He placed this locomotive in a corner window of the Hoyt Hotel, right next to the entrance to the Barbary Coast Lounge. At times, it went missing from the window. It was back in Hollywood, being filmed in various scenes for the TV series Petticoat Junction. It was the Hooterville Cannonball! Unfortunately, due to declining business, the hotel closed in August 1972.

To meet businessmen in the community, I joined the Lake Oswego Rotary and Country Clubs respectively. Some recollections of these now follow . . .

The LO Rotary Club met weekly for lunch, at a restaurant in town. In the summer of 1972, I arranged to have a meeting held at Marylhurst, with a special program for the day. The Oregon City Rotary Club, which met on a different day, changed their meeting so they could join us.

Lunch was served in our dining hall. Five or six of our students served as waitresses. We'd set up a stage, with a runway down the middle, for a fashion show. The program was hosted by Jantzen Knitting Mills.

This Portland based company, began in 1910. At first, they produced only knitted scarfs, gloves, and hats. By 1916, they'd begun making swimsuits for men and women. A spokeswoman from Jantzen, gave the program that day. She traced the history of women's swimsuits, over the period of 1916 to 1972. While she spoke, a model appeared onstage, walked down the runway, modeling the swimsuit she was currently describing. I recall one comment the speaker mentioned.

In the early 1950's, Jantzen designed a special bathing cap for Esther Williams. The cap was made of rubber. However, the outside was covered with rhinestones. Each gem was individually sewn onto the cap. Jantzen made 50 of these special caps and sent 5 to Miss Williams. She used them in one of her movies. The others were to be sold to other customers. A model wearing a one-piece suit and the rhinestone cap, walked down the runway. As she did, the commentator said, "We still own 45 of these caps. I'd be happy to take your order for one at the end of the program!" Later, I learned that 4 or 5 nuns watched our show from a window in the kitchen.

Chapter Six: The West Coast

Another memory from the Rotary and Country Clubs is about John. He was my personal banker, at the Bank of America. In the summer of 1972, he arranged a personal loan of $3,000. I used this money to purchase a motorboat for $5,000. I recall his words to me, after we completed all the paperwork. He said, "Bob, I want to tell you what one of my customers told me. He too had gotten a loan to buy a boat. He said that the 2nd happiest day in his life was when he bought the boat. The 1st day was the one on which he got rid of it!"

Mt. Hood, only 45 miles from downtown Portland, was *our mountain*. Its peak was visible from our kitchen window. While we lived in OR, we took many trips up to it, and visited Timberline Lodge, Lost Lake, and Crown Point. Timberline Ski Trails was where Colleen and Bobby learned to ski.

Skyline Drive was a road on a bluff overlooking Marlyhurst. Here we could see Mt. St. Helens, just 60 miles away, and Mt. Adams only 80 miles distant. Both mountains were in Washington state. Before erupting in 1980, Mt. St. Helens looked like an inverted ice cream cone covered in white.

*Mt. St. Helens before the eruption*

*Mt. Adams could be seen from Skyline Drive*

A final experience occurred at Marylhust in the 1st semester of the 1972-1973 academic year. It had to do with L&C, and another cooperative arrangement. In 1970, L&C had merged with the Northwestern School of Law in downtown Portland. A new law library was built on the L&C campus, and classes were held there. It was anticipated that 60 to 70 students would start their three years in law at L&C. Instead, they were inundated with over 150 beginning law students. The college scurried to find suitable housing for them. They rented nearby apartments. The problem only got worse when the 2nd class arrived with over 200 students.

Meanwhile, we had a vacant dorm at Marylhurst that was never occupied by our students. We maintained it, and rented it out for retreats, and other short-term meetings. It had only one floor with 23 rooms on one side of a hallway, 21 rooms on the other side, and a small apartment for the dorm director. Each room held two beds, two desks/chairs, and a sink. Toilets and showers were at each end of the hall.

Over several months of discussions, we worked out the mechanics of renting this entire dorm to L&C for 88 of their law students . . .

- -L&C would place a Dorm Director in the small apartment to supervise the students.

- -L&C would furnish a bus service to transport their students between campuses.

Fortunately, both L&C and Marylhurst used the same food service corporation to provide meals on their campuses. In meetings with the food service corporation people, we worked out a *special deal* for these law students. Each student would be given an ID punch card. Just showing the card in the cafeteria line at Marlyhurst would get him breakfast and supper. On the L&C campus, the same card would be punched to give him his lunch.

*Marylhurst Cafeteria*

Since 90% of the law students at L&C were male, this dorm would have only been occupied by men. Would there have been any social interaction between these young men of L&C and the young ladies of Marylhurst in our dining hall? Of course!

Chapter Six: The West Coast    165

## Marylhurst — 2018

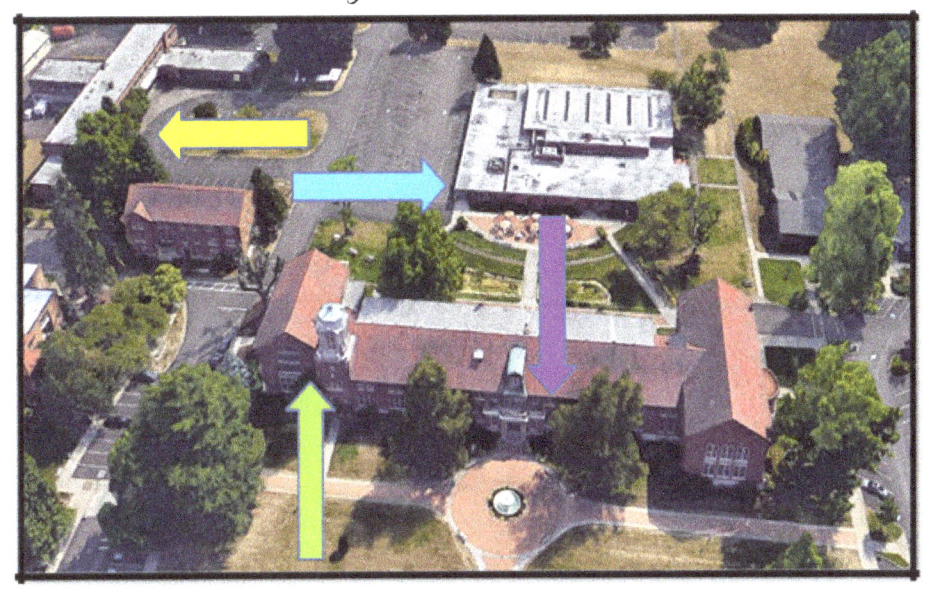

*Yellow: Empty Dorm*          *Green: Old Chapel, Mime Classes*
*Purple: President's Office*   *Blue: Dining Hall, Snow Picnic*

This proposal with L&C was not approved when brought to the Board of Trustees. Strike three! You're out! Enough of Marlyhurst!

During the spring of 1973, I interviewed for several administrative jobs. I accepted a position as Vice President of Academic Affairs (VPAA) at Dowling College on Long Island, New York.

In early June, our family started driving east. Mary and the girls led the way, in our station wagon. Bobby and I followed behind in a U-Haul truck, loaded with our furniture and boxes of stuff.

In the first chapter, I mentioned that I sometimes did stupid things. I did it again! Hitched to the rear of the truck, I pulled a trailer. On the trailer was my boat. From OR to NY, I hauled that damn boat. Along I-80, between Laramie and Cheyenne, lies the small town of Buford, WY. Sherman Summit is located here. At an elevation of 8,640 feet above sea level, it is the highest point of I-80 across the entire continent. I recall that the truck barely made it to the top, climbing the last 2 miles at 5 mph. At the summit, I pulled over because the radiator was overheating.

Mary drove into Buford and brought back many jugs of water. We filled the radiator to the brim and poured water over the engine. Once I got the truck going downhill, we had no more trouble getting through the Rocky Mountains.

A few weeks later, we drove through PA and the Appalachian Mountains. We crossed the 2nd Continental Divide on our move to Long Island.

Buford (aka Phin Deli) is a ghost town now. It's last resident moved out in 2017.

Buford was founded in 1866, and over time had a population of over 2000. But when the military outpost moved to another town, everyone slowly left, one family at a time.

Buford was bought in 2012 by a Vietnamese investor who opened a convenience store, but closed it in late 2017.

And ever since, Buford/Phin Deli has been an unincorporated ghost town.

# Chapter Seven
## The East Coast
## (1973-1978)

••••••••••••

## Dowling College, NY
## (July 15, 1973 - June 30, 1978)

••••••••••••

In 1955, Adelphi University, Garden City, NY began offering courses in Port Jefferson, Riverhead, and Sayville. Housed in an old public school in Sayville. It was the first 4-year degree granting liberal arts institution in Suffolk County. In 1963, Adelphi purchased the former William K. Vanderbilt Idle Hour Estate in Oakdale, NY. In 1968, Robert W. Dowling, a NY City real estate investor, city planner, and philanthropist, provided a grant of $3 million to Adelphi U. This allowed the Oakdale campus to become independent of Adelphi. He added another $3 million in endowment and renamed the college Dowling College. His close friend Allyn P. Robinson, was installed as the first President.

*Yellow:*
Main Mansion

*Green:*
New Library

*Purple:*
Mansion Rear Wing (Science)

*Blue:*
Connetquot River

Dowling College, 1973 – 1974

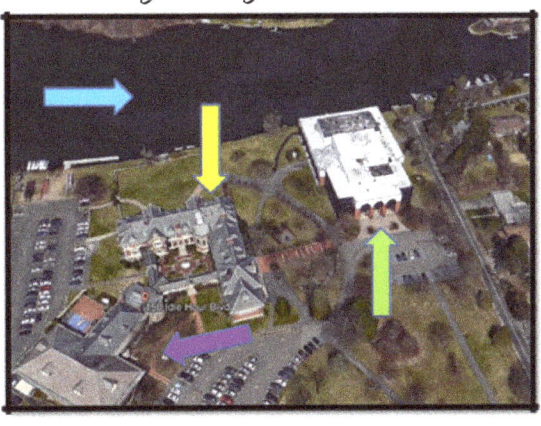

*View of Main Mansion from River —*

<u>*Yellow:*</u> *My 1st Office*     <u>*Blue:*</u> *My Office (after fire)*

Since I was not offered the position of VPAA at Dowling until mid-May, Allyn Robinson gave me a little slack. It wasn't until Monday, July 16, that I arrived on campus and starting working. This first academic year, 1973 to 1974, was one of many challenges and several successful accomplishments. I would like to mention two accomplishments related to the academic program . . .

The year before I arrived, the NY State Education Department denied the College's request for three graduate degrees. Their application was for an MBA, an MEd, and an MPA (Master's in Public Administration).

I reviewed all the documents related to their request. I realized that Dowling had made a fundamental mistake. It guaranteed denial! During my ACE Fellowship, I'd learned not to overload an arbitration or lawsuit with too many reasons for acting. If one didn't follow this concept, it would only take one weak reason, and your whole case would unravel.

Dowling's mistake was that all three degrees were submitted as one package. Their proposal for the MPA was very questionable. The college did not have a BA or BS in this field. No undergraduate courses in PA were currently

# Chapter Seven: The East Coast

offered, and no one on the faculty had a degree in this field. This is what the State Education Department (SED) found to be at fault. The entire proposal failed, including the MBA and MEd portions.

In mid-September, I met with John Fagan and Dr. Bob Hitzman, Deans of Education and Business. They were told to refresh their proposals for the MEd and MBA. Whichever one was ready by mid-January, would be sent to the SED in Albany. A few weeks later, Dr. Hitzman told me he was planning to retire in June 1974. He didn't want to spend his time shepherding the new MBA proposal forward. We agreed that the new Dean of Business would take on this responsibility. The MEd proposal was ready in January, and it went to Albany by February 1.

In early April, the SED scheduled a hearing on our proposal. Dr. John McConkey, Assistant VP of Academic Affairs, John Fagan, and I went to this meeting. The people in Albany did not know that I was doing a *little homework*.

We met with 4 people from the SED at their headquarters in Albany. In the first hour, the questions asked were easily answered. In the second hour it was obvious that one of the four was to be their devil's advocate. He focused in on the size and enrollments at Dowling. He questioned our ability to be large enough to offer any graduate degrees. I let him go on for about twenty or thirty minutes.

Then I started to speak, rather vociferously, my colleagues later told me. I questioned, why things had changed in the Education Department. I cited 5 schools in NY that all had enrollments smaller than Dowling's. One was ½ our size, another 1/3. They'd been approved to offer a MEd degree the previous year. The meeting ended shortly after noon. The committee chairman told us our proposal would be approved. We could begin offering the MEd courses in the fall of 1974.

*Nikita Khrushchev*

Later, that evening, McConkey, Fagan, and I celebrated at an Italian restaurant in downtown Albany. They kidded me about my response to the Education Department. They half expected me to take off my shoe, and pound the heel on the table, ala Nikita Khrushchev at the UN.

The following academic year, our MBA proposal was easily approved. Dr. Seyed Raji, the new Dean of Business, helped immensely. He had a PhD in business from NYU and was from Iran.

The second major accomplishment, in my first year at Dowling, started 10 months before I arrived. It began with Dr. McConkey, who supervised our evening programs. One of our students taking classes at night, met with him and requested credit for his life experiences.

*ATC Center, LI, NY*

In the early 1970's, the granting of college credits for life experiences was a big issue in higher education. This student was an Air Traffic Controller (ATC). He worked at an ATC center, located at McArthur Islip airport, less than 5 miles from our campus. However, this facility did not control any flights into McArthur airport. Instead, it directed all European flights, inbound and outbound, for the Newark and NYC airports.

Dr. McConkey began investigating how much credit he might be able to award this student. John told me about this when I arrived on campus. We discussed ways to bring this about, and how much credit to grant the student. Three faculty members, from the science/math department, were sent to Oklahoma City. They spent 3 days at the FAA ATC Training facility. In the meantime, I visited ACE Headquarters in Washington. The ACE was just beginning its CREDIT program (College Credit Recommendation), which started in 1974. This same year Dowling College began a new program. For lack of a better name, it was called our *upside-down-degree*. In this program:

- any FAA ATC graduate was granted 64 upper division credits. It was designated as her/his major or specialty.

- The student was then required to take 64 credits of general education at Dowling. Most of these credits were freshmen and sophomore courses.

- After satisfying this general education requirement, Dowling awarded a BS in Air Traffic Control. In 1975, 3 graduates were the first to receive this degree.

*Chapter Seven : The East Coast*

Sometime in 1976, the student who initiated this program with his request to Dr. McConkey, asked to meet with John and me. When we met, he thanked us for helping him get his BS degree. He then told us he was moving to the Boston area. He'd been promoted to be the new Director of the ATC center there. He promised us, he'd get his MBA from Harvard!

I recall two non-academic achievements I accomplished in my first year at Dowling . . .

In 1971-72, Dowling had started construction on a new library. Besides offices for staff, it contained several classrooms. It was to be finished by September 1973. But as often happens, it wasn't available until January 1974.

Since the library was my responsibility, I met with the director to plan the move. All library materials were housed in different rooms of the Main Mansion. Professional moving companies were contacted. Five companies submitted a bid for the move. The bids ranged from $30,000-$42,000. To our horror, we discovered that no money had been allocated in the current budget for this move. So, this is what we planned and accomplished . . .

- –We purchased 400 special, strong cardboard boxes for about $5,000.

- –We enlisted the aid of 50-60 faculty and student volunteers, to help us in the move.

- –Shopping carts from a local Safeway store, and 2 wheel dollies from a beverage company were borrowed. Our maintenance staff built a broad, wooden ramp sloping down the 5 steps from the Mansion's entrance to ground level.

- –Librarians headed teams of students. One team would take books off the old shelves in order and place them in a box. A librarian would write down on a sheet of paper the code numbers and place it on top of the books. The boxes were carted over to the new library. Another team, led by a librarian, placed the books on the new shelves in proper order.

After the move was completed, the library Director told me some of those boxes managed 10 round trips!

Dowling College had a 3-week break between semesters in January. On Monday, January 7, 1974, the parade started . . .

At 9:00 am, with TV News crews filming, the first cart went down the ramp. At 10:30 am, a break was called. We gathered in the Hunt Room, student lounge, where hot coffee, tea, Twinkies, and cookies were waiting. We resumed the move at 11:00 am.

At 12:30 pm, we stopped again and went to the Hunt Room. A cold-cut luncheon, with bags of potato chips, coffee, tea, and cold beverages was provided for all the workers.

We resumed working at 1:15 pm and ended at 3:00 pm. This cycle was repeated Monday-Thursday. Friday was a little different. Because this was new to all of us, we weren't sure about how long it would take to finish the move. We hoped to complete it by 3:00 pm on Friday, when something special was planned.

By 3:00 pm Friday we had completed about 95% of the task. The library Director assured me that she and her staff could easily complete the move next week. So, we stopped work at 3:00 pm. I asked everyone to go to the Hunt Room. I declared the move completed and thanked all for helping. Then we had a wine-n-cheese party until 5:00 pm!

A month later, Frank Banks, our new Business Manager, who was a bean counter, reported to the Board that I'd spent $10,000 which was not in the budget! I spent it on the library move!

*Chapter Seven : The East Coast*

The second achievement I recall from my first year was an odious task. In mid-November 1973, I was asked to attend a special meeting of the Board Finance Committee. The committee told me they were projecting lower enrollments for the 1974-1975 academic year. Consequently, to balance the budget they wanted a reduction in full-time faculty by 15%. My plan was expected to be completed by March 1, 1974.

To accomplish this, I did a lot of careful reading of the faculty union contract. The faculty at Dowling were organized as an American Association of University Professors (AUPP) union. Dr. McConkey was of immense help in this matter! We two would meet, read over sections of the contract, and debate what it meant. He accompanied me to all meetings I had with a faculty committee. By contract, this committee was to be informed on what actions I planned to take.

This distasteful task was completed by the deadline given me. The 15% reduction of the full-time faculty was accomplished, including one who was tenured.

To finish this tale, the enrollments for the 1974-1975 year did not decrease. The undergraduate program actually increased slightly. The enrollments in our new, graduate program in Education, were very substantial. What the Board did with the extra income, I have no idea!

I now wish to relate a very significant event that occurred during my first academic year.

Sunday, March 17, 1974 was St. Patrick's Day. John Fagan, our Dean of Education and college leprechaun, invited about 25 to 30 people from Dowling to his home, only two blocks from the college. His wife, Millie, had prepared a wonderful corned beef and cabbage dinner. About 8:00 pm, John, started serving his famous Irish coffee. I don't know how many I had, but I had too many! Mary drove us home, only a mile away, around 11:00 pm.

About 3:30 am Monday the phone rang incessantly. Mary answered it. She handed it to me, and said, "It's for you. He said it's urgent!" And urgent it was! I was talking to an Oakdale Fire Marshall who informed me that Dowling College was on fire. I needed to get there immediately! Before I hung up, I asked if he had called Allyn Robinson, the President. He said yes, and that Allyn said he should call me. I quickly dressed. Mary drove me to the College and let me off.

Fifteen minutes later, I was standing in front of the main building of the Mansion. Flames were raging along the entire roof. Coupled with my hangover, it made me sick, literally! I scurried down the bank to the Connetquot River and vomited, which was probably a good thing.

I returned and talked to the Fire Marshall. He told me the fire was very bad and his men had not yet got it under control. He saw that someone brought me some aspirin and water, which helped. I told him I'd be back in ½ hour. I found Allyn and we went into the new library. We went into the office of the library Director and spoke briefly. He would stay in that office, where he spent the morning calling and speaking to every Board member. I assured him I would take care of everything else!

I found another office, desk, and phone. I spent almost two hours calling every newspaper, TV, and radio station from NYC and Long Island. After identifying myself, the message was the same, "There is presently a fire at Dowling College. Right now, we do not know how bad it is. All classes are cancelled until further notice." No comments! No answering of further questions. It took me some time to look up all these phone numbers in the Yellow Pages.

Around 7:00 am, I'd finished that task and went outside to watch the fire. The sun had risen, and it was now daylight. Most of the flames had subsided and were seen only on the south end of the roof. I found the Chief. He told me his men were making great progress and believed the fire would be under control in about an hour. He also asked me to stay close by. After the fire was struck, I would be the first person from the college allowed to enter with him and some of his men.

Faculty, staff, and students began to arrive. The questions were always the same, "What are we going to do? How can I help?" My answer was, "I don't know! I'll let you know when I figure it out." Meanwhile, Mary, as she often did, drove the kids to school. She then stopped at a local deli and got me a cup of coffee and a bagel. She was smart enough to park at John Fagan's house. She walked the two blocks to the campus to make her delivery, which was most welcomed!

About 9:30 am, the Fire Marshall sent for me. He said the fire was now struck. No flames anywhere, just smoke from charred wood. His men were carefully monitoring these smoldering timbers, so that the coals wouldn't reignite. He and two of his men escorted me into the ruins. We walked through every part of the Mansion that had been damaged by the fire. The basement, which contained several administrative offices, was flooded with water. The first and second floors, that contained about 25% of our classrooms and the student lounge (Hunt Room), were destroyed. The worst though was the third floor or attic of the Mansion. The roof was gone. One of the two stairways was completely gone. The other was rather hazardous to ascend and descend. This attic contained my office and the offices for about 45% of our faculty.

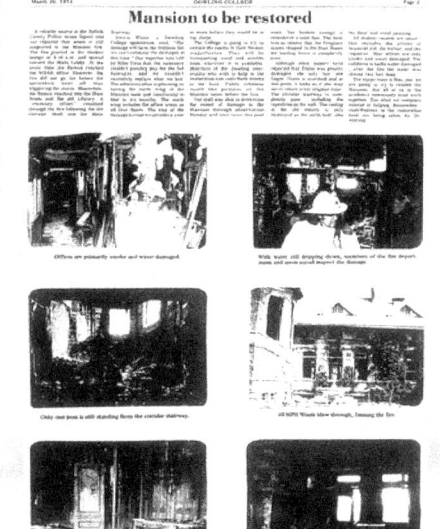

I now knew what had to be done . . .

I found 3 or 4 faculty members who earlier had offered to help. I directed them to build a large wooden bulletin board at the main entrance to the campus. They were to find a couple of maintenance men to help them with the structure. They also were told to go to the local lumber yard, use my name and account number, and obtain materials they needed.

I got George Germain, Registrar, for the past 7 to 8 years. He was very familiar with all the classrooms and laboratories, their size, and location. We went off campus somewhere, I forget where. We wanted to be alone. No distractions, no phone calls, no interruptions!

For 3 hours, we moved classrooms around so that those with larger enrollments had adequate space. We found temporary office locations for 35 faculty, for me, other administrators, and staff whose offices were gone. Around 1:00 pm, we returned to the campus and found my two secretaries. I asked one to make copies of our plans and see they were posted on all existing bulletin boards, especially the new one being built at the entryway. I had my other secretary call all the news media, I had phoned earlier. The message she read to them was, "Dowling College has had a major fire that destroyed the interior of the Main Mansion. It will be restored! Classes are cancelled for Tuesday this week and will resume at 8:00 am on Wednesday morning, March 20." Then George and I left campus again! We stopped along the way to get a cold 6 pack of beer and 2 pounds of French-fried shrimp.

We drove about a mile from the campus to the south end of Vanderbilt Blvd. There was a small marina here on the Connetquot River. Outside this marina were a few picnic tables and benches. I opened two beers and handed one to George. Before taking a sip, we clinked the bottles together. I said, "George, we did it!" We ate our lunch, sitting outside viewing the river, and enjoying what we had accomplished!

*Marina on the Connetquot River*

# Chapter Seven: The East Coast

We returned to campus around 2:30 pm. George went off to organize his staff. I now had my secretaries arrange Tuesday meetings with each faculty member whose office was in the burned-out attic. Every one of them was eager to get up to their office and see what books, papers, personal items remained. I couldn't allow it! The Fire Chief had shown me that the one stairway left to get up to the attic was very treacherous. Late Monday afternoon, two of our maintenance people, under the direction of two firemen, placed wooden beams to shore up this stairway.

On Tuesday, after meeting with me, I scheduled each faculty member to go up to their office at a certain time. They could climb the stairway only under the supervision of two firemen. Only one faculty member was permitted to go up there at a time. A maintenance man, bringing some boxes, would assist each person to carry what could be salvaged to their new office.

So, this day's catastrophe came to an end. Things began to fall into place on Tuesday and classes started on Wednesday. The only pain I had to endure in this disaster occurred during the days following the fire. The pain came from impatient faculty who kept asking me such questions as, "Who will pay for this precious book of mine destroyed in the fire?" "When will I be paid?" The reason it was such a pain is that I didn't know the answers to those questions!

That's enough on this disastrous event! I'll come back to talk more about Dowling later. I now want to write about things in the personal lives of Mary, the kids, and me. The children were all in the public schools of Oakdale. Colleen in 6th grade went to Oakdale Middle School. Bobby was in 5th and Christine in 1st grades at Arthur E. Premm.

Mary didn't volunteer as much as she'd done in OR. However, I do recall one field trip in which she helped Bobby's 5th grade class. They went on a field trip into NYC. She oversaw Bobby and five other boys. The entire class, teacher, and chaperones took a train on the Long Island Railroad and left from Oakdale into Penn Station. They took a subway to the destination of their field trip.

| |
|---|
| NEW YORK PENN STATION |
| FOREST HILLS |
| KEW GARDENS |
| BABYLON |
| BAY SHORE |
| ISLIP |
| GREAT RIVER |
| OAKDALE |
| SAYVILLE |
| PATCHOGUE |
| BELLPORT |
| MASTIC-SHIRLEY |
| SPEONK |
| WESTHAMPTON |
| HAMPTON BAYS |
| SOUTHAMPTON |
| BRIDGEHAMPTON |
| EAST HAMPTON |
| AMAGANSETT |
| MONTAUK |

On their return, they entered the subway. One of the boys in her group needed to go to the bathroom. He delayed them enough so that everyone else got on the subway and left. There she was, lost in NYC with six 9-year old boys. Somehow, she managed to find the right subway train back to Penn Station. She rejoined the rest of the group for the train trip back to Oakdale. After that, I don't think she volunteered to take a group into the NYC again.

In early December one year, our family visited Rockefeller Center in midtown Manhattan. After touring parts of the Radio City building, we went to The Plaza to see the Rockefeller Center Christmas tree and watch skaters on the ice rink. I know we didn't go skating. After dinner in Manhattan, we took the LI train home. At other times, Mary and I took our kids into NYC to see 2 or 3 Broadway plays.

One summer, Ron and his family visited us. We went to Central Park and its Zoo. Afterwards, we had lunch in the General Motors (GM) building. In a simulated drive-in movie theater, we ate our meals and watched cartoons on the screen. Before returning home to Oakdale, we took a 3-hour cruise around the island of Manhattan, during which time we sailed past the Statue of Liberty.

*Chapter Seven : The East Coast*

Several Decembers, Mary and I went into the city to do some Christmas shopping. Most of the time, we went to Macy's. Once she and I attended a matinee of the Rockettes at Radio City Music Hall.

On another trip, Mary and I went to dinner at Luchow's. This famous restaurant opened in 1892. A sign over the entry read: "Through the doors of Luchow's pass all the famous people of the world." Since it was the holiday season we feasted on roasted goose, only served during the Christmas season. We often went to the Ukrainian Village on the lower east side of Manhattan,.

*Luchow's*

*The Ukrainian Village*

On two occasions, Mary and I attended the opera at the Lincoln Center in Manhattan. I do not remember which ones we attended. Though we were appropriately dressed, I *did not* wear a tux or tails!

*Lincoln Center*

On Long Island, we had a few restaurants we'd frequent. For seafood we'd go to the Snapper Inn, located only ½ mile from our home. Situated at the mouth of the Connetquot River and the Great South Bay, it was a gorgeous setting for our meal. This restaurant used a building built around 1900, as part of the Vanderbilt estate. It was originally the estate's Tea House.

At this time, Mary and I started our special *Saturday Night Out*! Once a month, we made an early dinner for the kids. We'd get them ready for bed and leave them with a bowl of popcorn to eat while watching TV. When they got tired, they'd crawl into bed. Around 8:00 pm, Mary and I left, to have dinner at the Lake House, only 2 miles away. When we'd arrive, the dinner crowd was diminished, and we were seated in a matter of minutes. We'd order a bottle of wine and Caesar Salad for two. While sipping our wine, the maître d' came to our table, prepared the dressing, and tossed the lettuce. It was a wonderful salad! We'd finish with a luscious dessert and coffee!

Once a week, on a weekday night, I'd call John McConkey around 10:30 pm, or maybe John phoned me. Whoever called, the conversation began, "Hi! What are you doing?" An answer came back, "Nothing." The caller then said, "Fifteen minutes." In 15 to 20 minutes, John, his wife Pat, Mary, and I were in the Sayville Diner. There we had a late night snack of pie and coffee.

Thanks to John Fagan, Mary became a Democratic Voting Judge at elections from 1974 to 1979. When John asked her to do this, Mary refused. She was a registered Republican. He told her not to worry and begged her to accept. He couldn't find anyone else in Oakdale, that had the time or would volunteer for the job. He did caution her not to vote in any primary election.

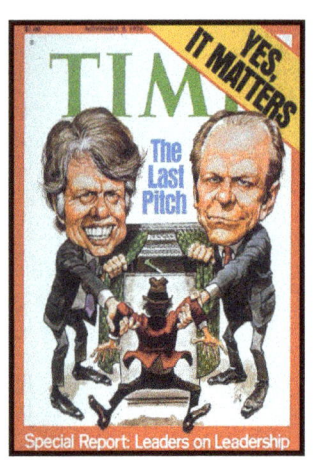

So, during this period, Mary was a Democratic Judge at all elections. The worst one I recall, was the national election for President on Tuesday, November 2, 1976. She left home shortly after 5:00 am. Judges had to report to their locations by 6:00 am, check all the machines, and open the polls at 7:00 am. They remained open until 8:00 pm. The counts at this election were close and had to be rechecked several times. She and a Republican judge then took all the ballots to the county seat in Riverhead, about 30 miles away. She came home exhausted about 1:00 am on Wednesday. Though hungry, she was too tired to eat! She crawled into bed and was sound asleep in a couple of seconds!

## Chapter Seven: The East Coast

I don't believe I've mentioned our residence in Oakdale. It was a 4 bedroom, 2½ bath home at 107 Lakeside Drive. It was only a mile away from Dowling, on a quiet dead-end street, and close to nearby schools.

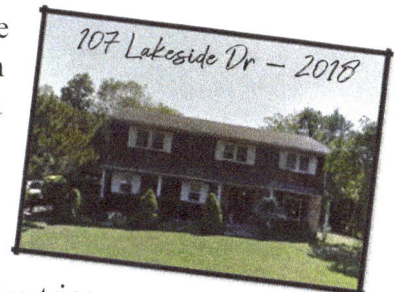

*107 Lakeside Dr – 2018*

While living in NY, we took many sightseeing trips. I recall several that I will now mention . . .

In 1973, over the Columbus Day weekend, we went north to see the leaves changing colors. We first drove through VT, and the Green Mountain National Forest.

*Green Mountain*

Near Montpelier, we gazed at a deep quarry where slabs of granite were being removed. In nearby Graniteville, we toured a factory and saw granite cut, shaped, and polished into monuments and headstones. We were told many were shipped worldwide.

*Rock Quarry*

We continued our trip through the White Mountain National Forest of NH. Here the colors of the leaves were gorgeous! Mary and I agreed, we'd never seen the colors so vibrant! After a night in Concord, NH, we went to Portland, ME. Of course, we all shared two large lobsters for dinner that night!

*White Mountain National Forest*

*Plymouth Rock*

On two occasions we went to Plymouth Rock during the month of November. All month long this area held a Thanksgiving Festival, so we enjoyed an early Thanksgiving Dinner!

*Free Kisses!*

We also made two trips to PA to visit the Gettysburg National Military Park, one

*Good–N–Plenty Restaurant– Yum!*

visit to the Hershey factory for the FREE chocolate ride and kisses, and two trips to the Kutztown Annual Folk Festival, which celebrates the Amish lifestyle and culture. During one of these trips we had dinner at the Good-N-Plenty restaurant.

On another trip to PA, we went to Philadelphia to visit Independence Hall (IH) and the Liberty Bell. I vividly recall how our tour of IH ended. After being led through several rooms, the tour ended in the Assembly Room, where the Declaration of Independence was signed.

*Assembly Room in Liberty Hall*

*Independence Hall*

At the end of his presentation, the docent asked, "Are there any questions?" A few moments of silence followed. No one asked a question. Christine, who was about 9 or 10, was standing in front by the railing. She raised her hand, and when recognized, she asked a question. Then she asked a second question, and a third. Mary was embarrassed. She whispered to me, "I don't know her!" Then she moved to the back of the crowd. Christine continued asking questions, maybe 4 or 5 altogether. They were all good ones! As we left, I overheard a man behind me speak to his companion. He said, "I'm sure glad that little girl asked those questions. I was wondering about some of those things myself, but I was too embarrassed to ask."

# Chapter Seven: The East Coast

1976 was the celebration of the country's bi-centennial year. Our OR friends, Ron and Carol Wyffels, and their 4 children drove across the country to visit and celebrate with us. Among the numerous sites we visited together, I recall, we took a trip to the north and visited . . .

Lexington, Concord, Boston, Faneuil Hall, the Old North Church, Old Ironsides (USS Constitution), Cape Cod, West Point, Lake Chaplain, and Ft. Ticonderoga.

*Lexington*  *Old Ironsides*   *Old North Church*

On our trip south, we stopped at Morristown National Park, NJ. This was the site of the winter campgrounds of George Washington and the Continental Army (CA) in 1776-1777 and in 1779-1780. It was where his Army went, after crossing the Delaware River, and defeating the Hessians in the Battle of Trenton, December 25, 1776.

Other sites visited were the . . .

- White House.
- US Capitol.
- Smithsonian Museum.
- Ford's Theatre.
- National Cathedral.
- Library of Congress.
- Supreme Court.
- National Archives.
- FBI Headquarters.
- Mt. Vernon, VA.
- District of Columbia.

## My Marvelous Memories

We also visited the Arlington National Cemetery & Tomb of the Unknown Soldier, as well as the Washington, Lincoln, and Jefferson Memorials.

When we lived in NY, we took several trips to FL for the Christmas holidays. While there, we visited Disney World, and the Space Center at Cape Kennedy. One spring vacation was spent at Myrtle Beach, SC. Driving home from SC, we stopped in Wilmington, to visit the USS North Carolina. On this trip, we drove home by way of the Chesapeake Bay Bridge and Tunnel.

Within six months of our arrival in Oakdale, we figured out how to leave LI when driving on a trip. I'd come home by 6:00 pm and have supper. Before taking a nap, I'd strap suitcases on top of our station wagon. Then I slept. Meanwhile, Mary and the kids laid out blankets and pillows inside the back of the wagon. I'd get up around 11:00 pm, and by 11:30 pm, we'd be leaving our driveway, the kids asleep in the back. Mary sat and slept in the passenger seat. In an hour, we'd be crossing a bridge leaving Manhattan, either the George Washington into NJ or the Verrazano onto Staten Island and eventually into NJ.

By 8:00 am, we'd have covered over 450 miles. The kids would wake up and get dressed. We'd stop for breakfast and a visit to a bathroom. Afterwards, Mary drove during the day, while I napped in the passenger seat. If we were heading south to FL, we always stopped for the night in Savannah, GA. No sightseeing here, but we always went to the world-famous Pirate's House Restaurant for dinner. It opened in 1753, as an Inn for seafarers. We always toured the basement to see the back door, through which drunken sailors were shanghaied out, to a waiting vessel!

Chapter Seven: The East Coast

*Pirate's House — Savannah, Georgia*

Before returning for more recollections about Dowling, I want to mention two other remembrances. The first, concerns the Rotary Club of Sayville, NY. In November 1975, a special meeting was held at our lunch. We deliberated on what the club should do for the upcoming bi-centennial year. Suggestions were offered, discussed, and eventually approved. I proposed one that had several aspects to it. Essentially, my idea was to sponsor weekend trips to historical sites on the East Coast. To avoid the heavy tourist season, I suggested our trips would go during the months of January, February, March, April, September, October, and November . . .

- A bus trip to the Boston area to visit all the historic sites related to the Revolutionary War.

- A train trip into Manhattan to visit the Washington Heights area, especially, Ft. Washington and Ft. Tryon in NY and Ft. Lee in NJ.

- A bus trip to the Lake Champlain area to visit Ft. Ticonderoga and the Saratoga battlefield.

- A bus trip to Morristown National Park and the Trenton Battlefield.

- A bus trip to Philadelphia to visit Independence Hall, the Liberty Bell, Benjamin Franklin's burial site, etc.

- A bus trip to Washington, DC, with unlimited sites to visit.

🎟️ Finally, a long bus trip of several days could be taken to VA. Here we could visit the burial sites of George Washington in Mt. Vernon and Thomas Jefferson in Monticello. Lastly, we could end this trip by going to Yorktown, where the Revolutionary War ended on October 17, 1781.

The Rotary Club discussed my suggestion, but it was not accepted. Instead, they voted to spruce up a small, old park near downtown Sayville. New sod, bushes, and trees were planted. A gazebo for holding band concerts was built. The entire project cost $10,000. Only two band concerts were held at this gazebo in the fall of 1976 and spring of 1977. I haven't heard of any since then, but I could be wrong!

*The Sayville Rotary Club Gazebo*

About 2 months after this meeting, I was at the weekly Rotary luncheon. At my table was an elderly gentleman, whose name I can't recall. But I remember what he said to me. "Bob, I was very interested in your suggestions for our bi-centennial activity. I grew up here in Sayville. For 40 years I worked in Manhattan and took the train into the City, 5 days a week. I'm retired now. When you spoke, I realized I've never been to the Statue of Liberty or to the top of the Empire State building. In two weeks, my wife and I are going into the City for 4 nights. We're staying at the Waldorf and plan to visit those two places. We're also going to visit the Metropolitan Museum and attend a performance of the NY Philharmonic at Lincoln Center!" When he told me this, I was reminded of the nun in OR, who hadn't visited Portland's famous Rose Garden in 25 years.

*Chapter Seven: The East Coast*

The second recollection I mentioned a moment ago, concerns Dowling, and yet it doesn't. It's about Dr. Irving Goldhaber, a specialist in Conflict Management and Win-Win situations. John Fagan introduced me to him during my first year at Dowling. We hired him as a part-timer, to teach two classes in the evening each semester. In his post-graduate work, he had specialized and did research in *Conflict Management* and *Hostage Negotiations.*

He had his own consulting firm. Organizations hired him to help resolve their differences. When he received a contract, he would hold a 2- to 4-day workshop, to assist groups in conflict, to a peaceful solution. He always had an assistant accompany him on these workshops. Over a 3-year period, John Fagan accompanied him on 4 or 5 of these workshops. I went on three. It was not part of our job to accompany him. Besides taking care of all expenses, i.e., travel, lodging, meals, etc., Dr. Goldhaber paid us $200-$400 for assisting him. I helped Irv with 3 workshops . . .

> -one at Sinclair Community College, Dayton, OH for Board and Faculty union people.
>
> -one at Moraine Valley Community College, Palos Hills, IL for Board and Faculty union people.
>
> -and one in Charleston, WV. This workshop was somewhat unique. It was held for personnel of the State Education Department (SED) and members from the School Boards of two or three small, local towns. The conflict had started a few years earlier, when the State Legislature directed the SED to close high schools that had small enrollments. Students from the closed schools were bussed to centrally located, district-wide high schools.

People from the small towns were rather unhappy and disgruntled with many actions taken by the SED. I vividly recall, one local Board member, with tears in his eyes, said, "They even took our lights!" He was referring to the lights at their school's football stadium. When the stadium was built, not enough money in the school budget provided for lights. The business leaders in the community led a fundraising campaign. Everyone in the community contributed a few dollars and lights had been provided. In his mind, as well as most villagers, the lights were theirs and not the State's to relocate!

I also remember the secrecy of this workshop. Dr. Goldhaber briefed me about this as we waited for our flight out of LaGuardia airport on Friday evening. He'd been told to arrive in Charleston in the dark of night, not in daylight. We were met by a state policeman, complete with a *Smokey the Bear* campaign hat. In a police car, he drove us to the WV State Police Barracks, about ½ hour away. For 48 hours we stayed there, sleeping rooms, meals, meeting rooms, etc., for all participants were provided. Sunday evening, the workshop ended. A state police Sergeant drove us back to the airport in the dark of night!

.....

I'll now get back to other recollections about affairs at Dowling College. This first one happened in the summer of 1974, a few months after the fire. But as I begin, I need to tell you about something that had occurred two years earlier.

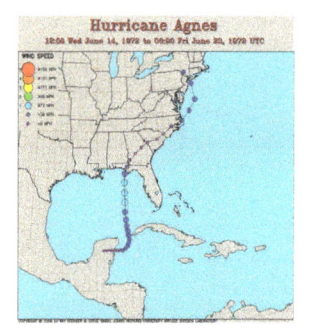

On June 19, 1972, Hurricane Agnes hit Panama City, FL. Over the next few days it moved northeast through AL, GA, SC, and NC. It went out into the Atlantic where it gained more energy. On June 21, it turned back west a bit and went through Long Island, NY. During this time, heavy rains fell on parts of PA and NY. Water from the Chemung River flooded the Corning and Elmira areas of NY.

The Department of Housing and Urban Development (HUD), provided temporary homes for victims of the flooding. Several thousand mobile homes were sent into the area to provide shelters. By 1974, restoration of flooded homes was completed. As mobile homes were vacated, they were placed in storage on a farm near Corning. In the spring of 1974, HUD began selling them to non-profit organizations. I became aware of this sale in mid-July. During the summer of 1974, I was very concerned about finding office space for about 35 (40%) of our faculty. On the day of the fire, I had placed them in one section of a new dormitory being built at the time. This dorm would be available to house only students by September 1974.

## Chapter Seven: The East Coast

President Allyn Robinson, was away on his summer vacation in the mountains of NC. I was in charge in his absence. His cabin did not have a phone. I reached him by calling a local store in the valley. When we spoke, he agreed with me that we could use trailers for faculty offices. He authorized me to purchase one.

John McConkey and I, immediately drove to Corning. The next morning, we went to the farm, where the trailers were on sale. Six or eight trailers were sitting on the farm. However, only 3 were left for sale, including the sales office. John and I went through them. Though some had slight damages, we agreed, they could be used as faculty offices. In the sales office I negotiated the purchase of the last three. I would've bought a fourth, if one was available. I was unsuccessful in several attempts to phone Allyn in NC. To summarize what I did and accomplished . . .

- ✓ I bought three trailers for a total of $28,000. Each was priced between $9000 to $10,000, due to interior damage.

- ✓ I arranged for each trailer to be driven to our campus for $3000 each. Later, we were billed an extra $500. Both the delivery company and I overlooked the tolls across bridges in getting to Long Island.

- ✓ These mobile units were placed next to the Mansion and made ready by Dowling's maintenance crew. Water, sewage, and electrical service from the mansion was brought in. Except for the bathroom, all interior walls were removed.

- ✓ John Hardy, Director of Buildings and Grounds once told me it cost about $3,000 per trailer to have it installed. He never did tell me what he got for selling the refrigerators, stoves, kitchen sinks and plumbing he salvaged. We used the kitchen cabinets for storage by the faculty.

- ✓ Each trailer had two wooden stairways, built up to an entry door. Inside, we squeezed in 12 desks, chairs, and bookcases. Folding chairs were left to accommodate students when they visited their professors.

- ✓ To my way of thinking, we spent $46,000 to $47,000 to provide office space for 40% of the faculty. Three years later the trailers were vacated, when the faculty moved into the rebuilt Mansion.

A few years later, I heard from John Hardy. For a while, the empty trailers were used for storage. In 1978, they were sold. He wasn't sure of the total received, since they went to different buyers, at different times. He estimated that it was probably $42,000 to $43,000. So much for my trailer tale!

·····

This next recollection in **MS** was not planned. However, it turned out to be much more fun and pleasant. At Dowling, the 1st semester ended before Christmas. The second one started in the 4th week of January. The first three weeks in January, were called an *Interim Semester*. No faculty member was required to participate. However, faculty were encouraged to design short, experimental 1 or 2-credit courses. If the course enrolled at least 6 students, it was a *GO* and the instructor received a little extra pay.

In my first semester at Dowling, two math professors, Dave Adler and Paul Abrams, developed a course for the *Interim Semester*. It had never been offered before. I think they did it as a lark. Its name was *Probability and Statistics with Applications to a Gambling Casino*. The curriculum was planned so that the . . .

- ♠ First week: the class met for two days for 3-hours. Students would be taught the basics of probability and statistics. During this week, each student selected a research topic.

- ♠ Saturday of week 1, the students and instructors would fly to the Bahamas. During an 8-day stay, students would collect data on their research project at a gambling casino.

- ♠ Third week: class would meet twice. Students would work on their research topic and submit their final report by week's end.

The faculty committee that reviewed any new course, approved it. I think the two wags who developed it were surprised. Another shock awaited them, when 10 students registered. Now it was a *GO* course. During the 1st week in January, while I was involved with the library move, they began the course. However, during that week, Dave and Paul found me. We had a brief discussion, in which Dave told me he couldn't go with the class to the Bahamas.

They asked if I would take his place. I accepted! So, here are some of the things that happened with this unique course . . .

At his expense, Paul Abrams, took his wife and two children along. He'd made reservations in a resort hotel, the Holiday Inn, on Paradise Island. It wasn't far from the casino.

I stayed with the students in a cheaper hotel on Nassau Island. I agreed to take complete charge of the class as their Laboratory Director. In the meantime, Paul didn't have to do anything that week. He could enjoy his family vacation!

On Saturday, our first day on Nassau, the students and I made use of our hotel pool and a nearby beach. We all had an early dinner together and walked 3 miles to the Paradise Island Casino. Calling on my experience as a tour escort (Europe, 1960), I knew exactly what had to be done.

I told the students to wait outside the casino. They should have their passports ready, to prove that they were at least 20 years old. While they waited, I went in, found the Head of Security, and asked to be taken to the Manager. I explained to him that I had brought 10 college students, who would like to come into the casino. They would stand behind the crowd around a gaming table, observe activity, and write in their notebooks. All they wanted to do was collect data, from each event at the table. If one of his patrons made a complaint to security, they could find me in the bar/lounge. If this happened, I would move the student elsewhere. This happened only once in three years.

The Manager was grateful, that I had first come to him for permission, to conduct this research in his casino. He quickly gave his consent! The Head of Security went off to alert his staff, and I went outside and escorted the students in.

So, there I sat, in a most unusual setting for a college class or lab, a bar/lounge of a gambling casino. I usually took a seat at a small table. I read or wrote, sipped an occasional cocktail, a cup of coffee, or water. At times, a student joined me to ask a question or simply to rest after standing for hours.

Later that night, around 11:30 pm, some of us shared a cab ride back to our hotel. The next day we learned that for only 10¢, a *water bus* would take us from Nassau to Paradise Island and the casino. These small craft carried about 25 to 30 passengers. There was often a guitarist on board. He may have been hired to be there. He played and sang native melodies on the crossing. We did have to watch the evening time though. This boat stopped operating at 10:30 pm.

Water Bus

This unique course was offered twice more. In 1975, we went again to Nassau and Paradise Island. In 1976, our trip went to Freeport. Nassau and Paradise Island was better! I went all three years as Laboratory Director, sitting in a bar/lounge, to advise and monitor the students. It was great fun!

.....

My community college experiences of the 1960's, uniquely prepared me for my next Dowling story. Over a two-year period, 1974-1976, I planned and developed a unique program for Dowling. I had much help from Dr. Seyed Raji, our new Dean of Business, who was born in Iran. However, I first need to provide you with some background material.

During his second term, President Nixon increased arms sales in the Middle East. This was a consequence of the *Nixon Doctrine*. Israel, Iran, and Saudi Arabia benefited from these sales. I want to focus primarily on Iran in the 1970's. The ancient name for Iran was Persia. It had been ruled by monarchs from 705 BC until 1979. The last monarch, Mohammad Reza Pahlavi, was known as the Shah of Iran.

Dr. Raji and I worked closely during my second year at Dowling. As mentioned earlier, we obtained approval of our MBA program by December 1974. In the spring of 1975, he and I visited the UN in NYC. We talked to Iranian dignitaries there, about an idea we were considering. Later that spring, he and I went to Washington, DC. There we discussed our plans, with representatives of the Iranian Ambassador.

One last point, about the arms sales to Iran, mentioned earlier. Among the items sold to Iran were 15 to 20 supersonic jet fighters. These were F-14 Tomcats, built by Grumman Aviation Corporation. During the Cold War, Grumman was the largest corporate employer on Long Island (LI). Every F-14 made, was built and tested on LI. So, Dr. McConkey, Dr. Raji and I began to meet and have discussions with Grumman executives.

F-14 TOMCAT

As part of the sales contract to Iran, Grumman had to provide flight instructors and maintenance personnel for 10 years. All these Grumman people were already working in Isfahan, 250 miles south of Tehran. The results of all our meetings resulted in the following plan . . .

> Dowling College would operate a 2-year extension program in Isfahan for native students. Freshmen and sophomore courses in accounting, business, English, history, languages, literature, mathematics, psychology, and sociology would be offered there.

> Grumman would sub-lease to Dowling space at the airport for 4 classrooms and 3 offices. We estimated that 75-80% of the instructors for this program would be hired locally, utilizing Grumman staff and family members living in Iran.

> Upon completing 60 credit hours in Iran, a student could matriculate to the Oakdale campus. All credits earned in Iran would be accepted, since they were Dowling credits. A student could then earn a BA or BS degree at Dowling. If interested, a student could remain to earn an MBA or MEd.

This is a brief, general description of what we planned. In one of my meetings in Washington, I'd learned that our program could not start, unless it was approved by Iran's Minister of Education (ME). In January 1976, I began writing to the ME in Iran. He liked the general concept, made a few suggestions, which we included in our final plans. In July 1976, he sent me a letter indicating our proposal was ready for his approval. He invited me to come to Tehran for a final discussion, after which, he would approve it.

I had, of course, kept President Allyn Robinson, informed about this proposal. In early August, he arranged a special meeting of about 8 to 10 Board members. I recall this meeting quite well! I outlined my plan, mentioned people I'd met with in the US, showed them letters from the ME, etc. I asked they approve Dr. McConkey, Dr. Raji, and I to be authorized to go to Iran and finalize the program with the ME. The Board members liked the idea, asked questions, and discussed it for about 30 to 45 minutes.

I remember what happened next. One of our Board members, I've forgotten his name, but he was a top Vice President with Pan American Airways. He sat silently for an hour. He began to speak and said, "Dr. Krupp, I like what you've done and the steps you've taken to bring it about. All of you know I work for Pan American. I am not at present allowed to elaborate, but I'm asking all of you to not approve Dr. Krupp's request at this time. Hold off for 12 to 18 months and see what develops in Iran. If things are OK, I'll be the first to move that we send our representatives to Iran." The Board members did not approve my trip!

Though disappointed, I finally understood two years later. In the fall of 1978, riots and strikes started in Iran. The revolution that followed led to the Shah leaving the country. By February 1979, his reign was over, and the monarchy ended!

Chapter Seven: The East Coast

My final Dowling story deals with some unhappy events and the most stressful period in my life. I do not relish recounting them. I wish I could forget them, but alas, I cannot!

In August 1976, Allyn Robinson announced his retirement effective June 1, 1977. The Board appointed a Faculty committee to advertise and receive applications. After screening and interviewing, this committee was charged to submit 5 names to the Board by February 1977. A special Board Committee would make the final selection.

I submitted my name for consideration and was interviewed by the Faculty committee. However, my name was not forwarded to the Board as one of the final five selected. I'm not certain that the person selected by the Board was even on the list of five forwarded by the Faculty committee. In any case, by mid-April the Board announced Dr. Victor P. Meskill, would be the new President. He assumed this position on June 1, 1977.

In the first week of June, President Meskill held staff meetings and private discussions with all administrators at Dowling. In my private conference, we discussed many things. But I do recall two main topics: (1) I would continue in my position as VPAA until May 31, 1978. He planned to bring in his *own person* the next day, and (2) He assigned me to join and take over the Administration's Negotiating Team as its Chairman. During the spring of 1977, deliberations had become sticky and little progress had been made.

Classes for the new academic year were to start on Monday, August 28. On Friday, August 25 negotiations broke off and the faculty went on strike. On Monday, I drove on campus through the picket line. I recall stopping my car and chatting briefly with some of the marchers. We exchanged pleasantries, and I didn't feel any animosity or ill-will from them.

During that last week in August, several off-campus meetings were held by the Board, at which I was present. On Wednesday afternoon of the 30th, two lawyers were present. They spoke at length to the Board. I had never met them before. They were *apparently labor law arbitrators* and were well known to some of the Board members.

On Thursday, August 31, we began another meeting at 10:00 am. The lawyers had done some research and informed the Board that the Union had engaged in an *illegal strike*. Consequently, the strikers could legally be fired, if they didn't return to work.

I'm not a lawyer, but I'll try to explain, the *illegality*, as best as I understood it. Since Dowling was a private college, it was governed by the Taft-Hartley Act. This federal law required a union to send notice to officials in Washington that a strike was imminent. This notice had to be sent 30 days before the strike started. Dowling's faculty union had failed to send the notice, hence the *illegal strike*. The lawyers advised the Board that the fired faculty could be replaced by new hires. The Board members discussed this information and its ramifications, before and during lunch.

After lunch, around 1:30 pm, the Board called an official meeting and acted. They voted that each faculty member on strike be given notice to return to work immediately! If not, she/he would be fired. New instructors were to be hired to fill any vacancy. Of course, I was directed to see that all this occurred! The Board meeting ended about 3:00 pm. I stayed and worked with the two lawyers for another 2 hours.

However, first I called my office and informed my two secretaries that I would meet with them at 8:30 am on Friday. I also told them to schedule a 9:30 am meeting for my entire staff, i.e., Dr. McConkey, Dr. Raji, John Fagan, my assistant, Joe Louzonis, George Germain, Registrar and the head librarian. I then returned and met with the lawyers. We composed two documents in legalese . . .

> A letter which was sent to every faculty member on strike. Within 48 hours of receiving this letter, the recipient was fired unless she/he returned to their teaching duties.

> A special advertisement to be posted in newspapers inviting applications for immediate teaching positions at Dowling College because of a current job-action.

At the meetings I held the next day, I begged all to keep secret what they learned that day! People at Dowling were about to be fired and they should not hear about it through the *gossip grapevine*. One of my secretaries spent the day typing up that special letter addressed to each faculty member.

She kept two copies and addressed envelopes to their home address. My other secretary called all newspapers in NYC and LI to place that *special ad*. It was to run for a week and start on Saturday or Sunday. In the staff meeting, I informed them of the Board's action. Questions were asked, answered, and discussed. All of us were concerned about the future, and what the next few days would bring. I went home at 1:00 pm for a light lunch and a nap, I was exhausted!

I will now relate recollections of the next 24 to 48 hours. They were the most stressful of my entire life . . .

On Saturday morning, I went to my office around 7:30 am. All those letters were waiting on my desk for my signature. I don't know if I can find the words to describe the next 2 hours. I signed each letter, put it into its envelope, and sealed it. As I did so, each name haunted me. I knew every one of those faculty members. In many cases, I knew their families. Some had young children in preschool and elementary school, others in high school and college. About 25% of them, I had hired. I will not say that I wiped tears from my cheeks, but there were tears in my eyes and heart! Sometime after, I mailed those 75 letters at the post office before noon. They were sent *Special Delivery, Overnight, Return Receipt Requested*. I then went for a long walk through the Idle Hour neighborhood.

That night, Mary and I went to the Lake House for our special *Saturday Night-Out Supper*. I told her how troublesome this week had been. I told her how I wanted to quit my job at Dowling. I didn't know what to do, because I was concerned about how I would support her and the children! That night I had little sleep, as I continuously tossed and turned.

*Connetquot River State Park*

Sunday morning, I left early, and took another long walk through the Southside Sportsman's Club, now known as the Connetquot River State Park. About 11:00 am, I ended up at the Western Union office in Sayville. I remember sitting at a little table in that office. There I wrote a telegram, which I sent to 24-members of the Board of Trustees. I didn't know the addresses of 4 others. I did not keep a copy of that telegram.

The telegram went something like this . . .

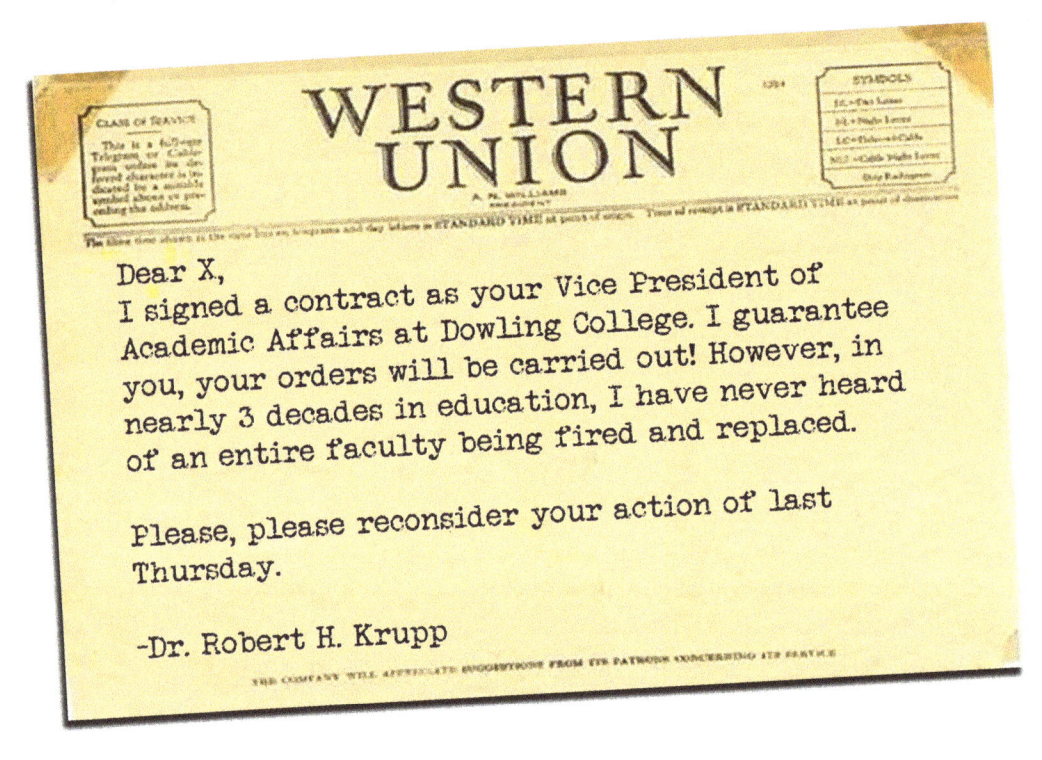

> **WESTERN UNION**
>
> Dear X,
>
> I signed a contract as your Vice President of Academic Affairs at Dowling College. I guarantee you, your orders will be carried out! However, in nearly 3 decades in education, I have never heard of an entire faculty being fired and replaced.
>
> Please, please reconsider your action of last Thursday.
>
> -Dr. Robert H. Krupp

I then called my best friend on Long Island, John McConkey. In 5 minutes, we met at the Sayville Diner. There, over many cups of coffee, I told John what I had done. He let me use his shoulder to cry on!

Monday was the Labor Day Holiday, during which I slept most of the day. In mid-afternoon, Pat and John had our family over for a most welcome dinner. On Tuesday, I was back at work and began receiving calls and applications to fill faculty positions. I scheduled some *special interviews* which I held on Wednesday, Thursday, and Friday afternoons. A Board member was always present at these *interviews*. If I approved an applicant, a contract was immediately offered to that person. I signed the contract, which was also co-signed by the Board member present. The lawyers assured the Board that this would then be a legal contract, approved by the Board. By Friday evening, September 8, we had hired 8 new faculty members!

*Chapter Seven : The East Coast*

Later that Friday night, about 8:00 pm, I received a call from President Meskill while at home. He informed me that the Board and Faculty union had agreed to reenter negotiations. As Chairman of the Negotiation Team, I immediately went to a motel in Hauppauge. I've forgotten its name. There I met two mediators who had just flown in from Washington, DC. We arranged for 3 suites of rooms. One was used by the Administration's Negotiation Team. Another was used by the Faculty union negotiators. Within them, each party could deliberate in private. In between these two suites was the 3rd one, where the arbitrators met with either side for private discussions.

The negotiations began around 11:00 pm Friday. We stayed there and went non-stop until Sunday night when we finally had an agreement. On Monday, both the Board and the union ratified the new contract. Classes resumed in full on Tuesday, September 12.

During the first week back, two faculty members sought me out. One was Dr. Byron Roth, a member of the union negotiating team. The other, was Dr. Irwin Oder, a senior member of the faculty. Both separately thanked me for having brought this mess to a conclusion.

I spent the rest of the academic year sending out my resume for administrative positions. I had a few interviews, but no offers until mid-May, 1978.

That's all I want to say about Dowling!

*Northern Lights in the Alaskan Skies*

# Chapter Eight
## The Frozen Tundra
### (1978-1979)

••••••••••••

## Kuskokwim CC, Alaska
### (July 1, 1978 – June 30, 1979)

••••••••••••

In mid-April 1978, I had an interview for the Presidency of Kuskokwim Community College in Bethel, Alaska. Bethel is 450 miles west of Anchorage, over the Alaskan Mountain Range and out on the frozen tundra! At my expense, Mary accompanied me on the interview trip. On our flight home to NY, Mary said, "If you get this job, I'm not coming with you to live in Bethel!" Of course, in early May, I was offered this position. Since I hadn't received any other offers, I accepted.

*Bethel on the Kuskokwim River*

Bethel lies on the banks of the Kuskokwim River. The college, of course, is named after the river. It was a public community college and part of the state system of higher education. In 1917, the University of Alaska in Fairbanks received approval to begin.

It opened for classes in 1922, and over the years, became a center for various aspects of Arctic Research. It was the flagship campus of the Alaskan system of higher education. At the time I was in Alaska, the head of this University was called the Vice Chancellor of AK University, Fairbanks. About 2 miles from its campus, was the campus of Fairbanks Community College. The head of the community college was the President.

In 1954, five years before Alaska became a state, Anchorage Community College started. By the late 1960's, there was pressure to expand it to a 4-year university, with some graduate degrees. By the late 1970's, when I was there, AK University, Anchorage existed. It was headed by the Vice Chancellor of AK University, Anchorage. Adjacent to its campus was the campus of Anchorage Community College. The head of the Community College was the President of Anchorage Community College. These two campuses even shared some common facilities, i.e., library, athletic gyms, and the major dining hall.

In 1972, the University of AK Juneau started classes. The head of this University was the Vice Chancellor of AK University, Juneau. Nearby, was the campus of Juneau Community College and its head, was the President of Juneau Community College.

In the early 1970's, there was an expansion of higher education to various parts of the State to provide opportunities for indigenous Native Americans. Community colleges were opened in Bethel, Ketchikan, Kotzebue, Nome, and Sitka. The head of each of these colleges was a President. The Vice Chancellor of AK Community Colleges supervised all eight community colleges. This Vice Chancellor held monthly meetings of all the Presidents. On odd numbered months, we met at Anchorage Community College. Even months, we'd meet at another of the community college. I vividly recall the October meeting held on the weekend of the Columbus Day Holiday. The temperature in Fairbanks was -10 °F. In Bethel, the river was already frozen solid.

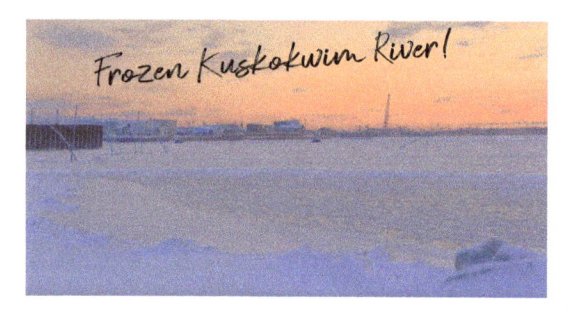

*Frozen Kuskokwim River!*

Though the position started on July 1, I took charge on June 1. At that time, the College was working on its 1978-1979 budget, which had to be approved by the Alaskan State Legislature. This was a rather unique impossible task, for the Legislature had stipulated a zero based budget for the upcoming year. This meant that the funds for the new fiscal year would be the same as the previous year. The Legislature expected an increase in educational services. In addition, the faculty were scheduled to receive a 6% salary increase, due to a new union contract!

*Chapter Eight: The Frozen Tundra*

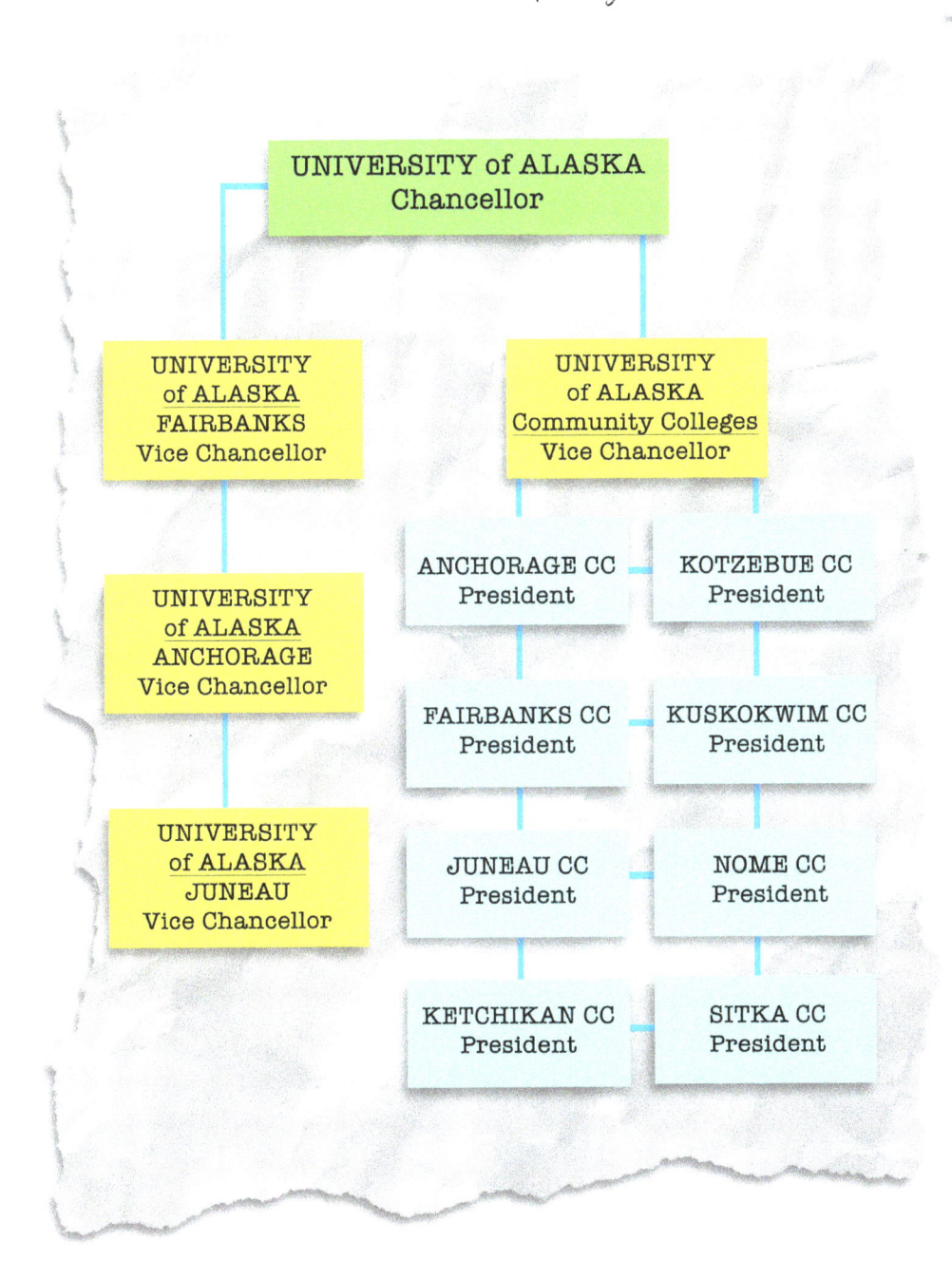

```
                    ┌─────────────────────┐
                    │  UNIVERSITY of ALASKA│
                    │     Chancellor       │
                    └─────────────────────┘
```

| UNIVERSITY of ALASKA FAIRBANKS Vice Chancellor | UNIVERSITY of ALASKA Community Colleges Vice Chancellor |
|---|---|

| | ANCHORAGE CC President | KOTZEBUE CC President |
|---|---|---|
| UNIVERSITY of ALASKA ANCHORAGE Vice Chancellor | FAIRBANKS CC President | KUSKOKWIM CC President |
| UNIVERSITY of ALASKA JUNEAU Vice Chancellor | JUNEAU CC President | NOME CC President |
| | KETCHIKAN CC President | SITKA CC President |

By the end of July, I finished preparing the new budget and returned to NY. Here I completed all packing in about a week. Mary and the girls stayed in our home on LI. By mid-August, Bobby and I were in Bethel for the year. He spent his freshman year at Kuskokwim HS, where 70% of the students were Native Americans. His new friends were Iñupiat, Yupik, Aleut, and Tlingit!

I'd like to describe Bethel and the college to you. In the late 1970's, Bethel was a community of about 5,000 residents. It was 80 miles upriver from Kuskokwim Bay and the Bearing Sea. Situated on the Kuskokwim River, it served as a regional transportation service center for over 58 Alaskan native villages. These Eskimo villages were spread out over a 57,000 square mile, road-less area. This is about the size of Illinois.

*Kuskokwim Community College*

The only hospital in this vast area was in Bethel. In the summer of 1978, the hospital was in the second year of construction for a new, 40-bed modern facility. It took 4 years to build, 3 for the exterior and 1 for the interior. I recall a few weeks after arriving in Bethel, I was invited to a Saturday evening party. There I met a young, black, hospital technician. As we shook hands he said, "Well Dr. Krupp, how does it feel to be a minority?" We both laughed as we clicked our glasses together!

*Bethel Hospital*

Later in the year, I arranged for the February (1979) meeting of the CC presidents, to be held in Bethel. On the first day, a snowstorm moved in. The meeting ended at 5:00 pm. Afterwards, a reception/dinner was scheduled at the only motel in Bethel. It was only a mile drive from the college to the motel. I've never had such a harrowing experience, as I drove through a whiteout. The person to my right, rolled down his window and looked out. He advised me if I was on the shoulder or a few inches from it. Behind me, someone leaned out the window, to tell me if another car was coming towards us. I crept along at a speed of 3 feet per second, which is 2 mph. Due to the blizzard, all flights were cancelled. Our visitors had to stay an extra night. When I finally took our guests to the airport, many swore they would never return to Bethel again. I recall other presidential meetings in Fairbanks, Juneau and Sitka. During that year we never had one scheduled in Ketchikan, Kotzebue, or Nome.

*Can you see the road? Neither could I!*

*Chapter Eight: The Frozen Tundra*   205

While in AK, I managed several meetings in the lower 48. In October, I was in Washington, DC. Mary joined me for 3 or 4 days. During the first week of December, I was in Reno, NV. The Northwest Accrediting Association held its annual meeting in Reno that year. Mary flew out and joined me for a week. She enjoyed her time at the slots! During the week, we discovered a Basque restaurant in Reno. We enjoyed it so much we went to it twice during our 6 days there! During the Christmas holidays, our family was together in Chicago. Bobby and I flew in, while Mary and the girls drove in from NY.

Since I was only in AK for a year, I do not recall many specific things about the college. However, I do remember many unique experiences I had during my AK adventure. I want to share some with you. Occasionally, some might have a college feature to it.

When I arrived at Dowling in 1973, I had two secretaries, one of whom was Robina Gibson. About a month or two after my arrival she invited Mary, the children, and I to Sunday dinner. When we got to her home, we met her husband John, as well as her son Michael and daughter Barbara. The chicken dinner served that day was excellent. Several vegetables she served had been homegrown by John. They were most tasty. Robina and John invited all of us for Sunday dinner, about every 4 to 6 weeks.

On November 28, 1975, Robina had a massive heart attack while preparing Thanksgiving dinner. She died the next day. Michael, who was now a freshman at Dowling and I, made all the funeral arrangements. John was too distraught to help. These measures were somewhat complicated. We scheduled a one-night wake and a funeral mass the next day at the local Catholic church. The casket containing her remains was taken to Kennedy Airport and flown back to Scotland for her burial. Over the next 4 years, John continued to invite our family over for Sunday dinners. In May 1978, Michael graduated from Dowling. I left for AK in early June. When I returned in late July to finish my packing and return to AK, John had us over for another Sunday dinner. I found out that Michael had not yet found a job. The country at that time was going through a minor depression when Carter was President.

To make a long story short, Michael bought a one-way ticket to AK. I had a job for him at the college. During that year, Michael lived with Bobby and me. We all shared several adventures together. In June 1979, Bobby and I left AK to return home to NY. Michael remained and became an Alaskan. He retired about 5 years ago in 2015. However, he still spends most of his time at his home in Wasilla, with his wife Mary, an Aleut woman.

The three of us always went to Sunday Mass at Immaculate Conception Catholic Church. We made friends with native parishioners. One family I wish to mention often invited us to their home on Sunday for brunch. In January, one of their parents died. Bobby didn't join us, but Michael and I went to the funeral. Following Mass, we went to the cemetery. I wondered what kind of burial I would see. At the cemetery, the body was taken from the casket, wrapped in thick canvas and tied with stout ropes. It was then placed on the surface of the grave site and we all left for a luncheon. Later, in June or July, when the tundra had thawed a bit, a hole was dug, and the body buried.

*Traditional Eskimo Family*

While in AK, I bought a snowmobile for recreational use. I could never get the hang of how to control it. Bobby and Michael caught on quickly, and they used it much, much more than I did! I'd now like to teach you at least one Eskimo word. It is irondoc (pronounced iron-dock). It means snowmobile and comes from iron and dog. It makes sense, when you consider that a snowmobile replaces their old means of transportation, a dog sled.

One Saturday in late January, our Director of Village Programs (DVP) planned for us to visit Hooper Bay. This was an Eskimo village on the coast of the Bering Sea. We flew out of Bethel, on our chartered 4-passenger bush plane. I rode in front, next to the pilot. Bobby sat in a rear seat next to the DVP. When we started, the sky was overcast but not snowing. As we flew westward it started to snow. I noticed our elevation was dropping and dropping. When we reached the coast, about 150 miles west of Bethel, we couldn't find Hooper Bay. The pilot made several passes, flying N→S and

# Chapter Eight: The Frozen Tundra

then S→N at an elevation of 150 to 200 feet. We never did find it. I recall the plane making several turns over the Bering Sea. I gazed down at some very cold, icy water. I was thankful when we returned and landed at Bethel. I did say a silent prayer!

The DVP and I went on another trip to Mountain Village and St. Mary's, two villages on the Yukon River. At that time, the population of Mountain Village was about 250 to 275. When we visited it, there were no dogs in the village. In the preceding month, the AK State Police had come into the village and euthanized all dogs. Several of the dogs had contracted rabies after being bitten by rabid foxes.

*Mountain Village*

That night we had dinner at the home of an Eskimo family. On the table was a bowl of oil. We'd dip a slice of bread in the oil before eating it. The oil was not olive oil for it had a slight odor of fish. The oil came from a seal. The main course was a fowl with dark meat, much like a duck or goose. It had been cooked by boiling it in water. The seasonings made it palatable. Ever inquisitive, I asked, "Is this a goose?" The answer was, "No! It's *Tundra Turkey*." Later, over coffee, I found out it was a swan!

The next day, the DVP and I went to visit St. Mary's. It had a population of 375 to 400 at that time. We visited and stayed at a small boarding high school, run by a Jesuit priest and several Jesuit volunteers.

While in Alaska, I also ate bear, moose, and reindeer sausage. I brought some of this sausage back to Chicago at Christmas time. It was much like smoked polish sausage. It just didn't have any garlic in it. Though I heard of it, I was never offered any walrus.

*My Marvelous Memories*

For many years, the school system in New York had a week-long holiday in mid-February. It was due to the birthday celebrations of Lincoln, February 12, and Washington, February 22. Coupled with two weekends, it often enabled one a 10 to 12-day vacation. While in Chicago, during the Christmas holidays, Mary mentioned she and the girls were going to FL that week to visit her parents.

As Bobby and I flew back to Bethel, after the first of the year, I thought about the girls and Mary going to FL. I decided that it wasn't "fair" to Bobby, to be stranded in cold AK in February. Since he was only 14 years old at that time, I had to make special arrangements for him. So, here's what I organized . . .

> On Friday night, I put Bobby on an Alaskan Airlines flight from Bethel into Anchorage. Waiting for him was Laurie Shimanek, the daughter of friends I'd made in AK. She met his plane, sat with him until after midnight, when he left for Chicago on his nonstop flight.
>
> When the plane landed, his aunt, Colleen met him. She escorted him to a different terminal at O'Hare and saw that he boarded a nonstop flight to Ft. Lauderdale, where his grandparents greeted him.
>
> Of course, all the above was arranged in reverse order when he came back to AK.

Many of the following stories occurred at different times during my year in AK.

In the first month I was in Bethel, I was invited to a potluck supper. Everything was loaded on a table so that you could help yourself. The featured item was a huge platter of grilled salmon. Someone had caught a 50 lb king salmon the day before. After filleting it, he'd broiled the fish on a charcoal grill. It was delicious!

## Chapter Eight: The Frozen Tundra

Another item on the table was in a large bowl. It was soft, white, and had blue marbling. I looked at it curiously. I said to a person behind me, "What's that?" He answered, "It's akutaq, Eskimo ice cream." I asked, "Is it a dessert?" He answered, "It's like Jell-O. You can eat it with your meal or eat it alone as a dessert." I put a bit on my plate. It had a slightly salty taste, as well as, a mild sweetness. I asked my friend, "What's in it?" He pointed to an Eskimo woman sitting in the next room and said, "Ask her. She made it." I went to her and introduced myself. I asked what was in akutaq (a-goo-da). She responded, "How do you like it?" I shrugged and said, "I'm not sure." She said, "Well, when you finish, I'll tell you."

**"ESKIMO ICE CREAM"**

**AKUTAQ**
äh koo tôk

Whip together 1 cup caribou or moose fat, ¾ cup seal oil or Crisco, and 2 cups sugar. Add ½ cup snow, 10 cups fresh berries and 1 cup fish chunks. Serve immediately.

Later she told me, "I finely chopped up a fresh, raw fish." I said, "That explains the saltiness. But what are the blue-purple streaks?" She answered, "I picked some fresh blackberries the other day. After mashing them, they were added and mixed in." "Ah-ha." I said. "That explains the sweetness. But what is all this soft, white stuff?" She looked at me, smiled, and said, "Crisco." I'd told that story many times over the next few decades. Then it dawned on me! Every time you eat margarine, you're eating Crisco. They're both hydrogenated vegetable oil.

When in my office working at the college, I usually had a small radio playing on low volume. I listened to KYUK 640 AM. Every morning at 10:00 am you'd hear drums beating. The Tundra Drums were on the air. This ½ hour program had no entertainment. It was strictly for informing a village that "Ivan would arrive by plane at noon the next day," or "Herb would be landing at 2:00 pm the next day," etc.

Once a week, I think it was at 11:00 am on Wednesdays, a test of the *Early Warning Emergency System* was conducted. It always concluded with the words, "If this was NOT a test you would be told what station to turn to for further information." The BIG JOKE in Bethel was: *What other station would they tell us to listen to*? KYUK was the only radio station heard in over 58,000 square miles!

People often ask what conditions were like living in AK, especially the 6 months of darkness. Bethel is 400 miles below the arctic circle. So, we never experienced 24 hours of darkness. From November to March, I would drive to work at 8:00 am in total darkness. If the sky was clear, one could see the Sun rise about 9:00 am. It would set around 3:00 pm. The drive home was also in total darkness.

Before I'd retire at night, I'd plug an extension cord into an electric plug attached to my truck's motor. A timer would go on at 4:00 am, and a heater would warm the oil and motor. This enabled me to start the engine when I left in the morning, to drive to work. When I parked in the college lot, there were electrical extensions adjacent to every slot. During the day, the oil was kept warm by plugging the heater into one of those extensions.

# Chapter Eight: The Frozen Tundra

Earlier, I mentioned Laurie Shimanek. She was the daughter of Betty and Verne Shimanek the best friends I made while in AK. Betty had started a health care program at the college. It was called the CHAP (Community Health Aid Program). In the 58 native villages surrounding Bethel, there were no healthcare providers, no doctors, no nurses, no technicians, no clinics, and no pharmacies. Her innovative program trained native students to: (1) read a thermometer, (2) apply a band-aid, (3) change a bandage, (4) dispense aspirin, (5) identify various symptoms, (6) keep a personal file for each patient, and (7) use a radio to send and receive messages to doctors located at the hospital in Bethel.

Each village provided a room to be used as the Village Clinic. Native students, trained at our college, met sick villagers, and provided them with the basic medical services mentioned above. Using the radio for communication, the clinician and doctor would decide if an illness or accident was serious. If so, a plane would be sent to bring the patient into the hospital.

Verne was the Superintendent of the hospital. He oversaw the day-to-day operation of the hospital, and supervised the construction of a new, 40-bed hospital being built. He managed all medical services in the surrounding villages. All these services were free to indigenous Natives. One day, while walking along a trail, Bobby stepped on a rusty nail. It pierced the skin. I took him to the emergency room at the hospital for a tetanus shot. I was charged a rather small fee for this service, because Bobby was not a Native American. I tell you this story, not as a complaint, but to let you know, that at times, your tax dollar is well spent!

Betty was the one who recommended our graduation speaker for May 1979. His name was Henry Brown and was one of Betty's first trainees. A few years earlier, he had returned to Mt. Village, his home village, to be its clinician. Thanks to Betty's assistance, he later obtained a complete medical scholarship to Brown University. At that time, he was in his first year of Medical School. I provided him with a round-trip ticket from RI to Bethel, to be our graduation speaker. The ceremony and reception were held at the college. During a reception after the ceremony, he came and thanked me for the airline ticket I'd sent him. Then he said, "When I left to go to Brown to get my doctor's degree, it was my plan to return to Bethel and work for the betterment of my people. But, Dr. Krupp, I don't know if I can live again in Bethel or in one of the villages."

I understood completely! He was a victim of what was, and still is, called *brain drain*! However, I learned recently that Dr. Henry Brown worked diligently in AK for many years before he retired.

*Our Alaska Home in the Trailer Park*

At our home in Bethel, Mike, Bobby, and I had our own dog, Bruno. He was a mixture of a St. Bernard and a Huskie. He had long thick hair and weighed about 220 pounds. The kids in the neighborhood called him The Bear, because he looked like a small, brown one.

When we first got him, I used a large plastic bowl as his food bowl. Within 2 days, the bowl was shredded into splinters. The metal bowl I bought next survived. But in a short time, it was covered with many indentations from his teeth. After eating his food, he'd toss it around like a frisbee. Inside our fenced-in yard, he had his own house to which he was chained. One night, the temperature was -55 °F. I brought him inside the house to keep him warm. He continually whimpered and cried to be outside. After 2 hours of this, I took him back out to his house. He curled himself into a ball of fur, put his nose under a front leg, and happily spent the night sleeping in that frigid air!

*Flat Bottom Boat like Verne's*

Bobby was heading home to NY in late May 1979 after completing his freshman year. Mike and I wanted to send him home with some special gifts for Mary and John. We wanted him to bring back two large, frozen king salmon. Of course, we had to go out and catch the fish.

I mentioned in chapter one, that at times I'm inclined to do something stupid. I did it again! We three went out fishing, in the Kuskokwim River, on a Saturday, when the waves were high and choppy. We used Verne's boat. Shortly after leaving shore, it started to fill with water and capsized. Fortunately, we were all wearing life jackets, so we survived. An Eskimo, in a larger boat saw us go into the icy water. He quickly sped over and got us on board his boat. He took us to our truck, parked along the shore. We drove home and took hot showers to warm up!

## Chapter Eight: The Frozen Tundra

The next recollection is my *honey bucket story*. But first, I need to describe some unique housing situations in the bush of Alaska. In 1978-1979 only about 40% of the homes in town had flush toilets. Our home was in a mobile home park, which had its own sewage system. It allowed us to have a flush toilet inside our home.

Sixty percent of the homes in Bethel contained an interior *outhouse*. Inside this room, a little larger than a closet, would be a wooden bench on which to sit. The top half was split in two sections. One section would have a hinge, so it could be swung up and down. This section also had a hole in it. When it was in the down position, one could sit on it, above the hole. Sewage could then drop through the hole into a 5-gallon bucket directly below the hole. These buckets were called *honey buckets*.

A cup of Clorox, to kill bacteria, was first placed in an empty, clean *honey bucket*. Another cup of pine scented soap, or other fragrant soap, was added to help alleviate odors. This *honey bucket* was then placed directly under the hole in the hinged seat. It then received the human offal. When the *honey bucket* was about 75% full, it was replaced with a fresh one.

Of course, you ask, what do you do with the material in the bucket? Bethel had a special *honey bucket service,* much like collecting garbage in a city. You were charged for this service. A family could arrange for 2 to 3 pickups a week, as needed. It all depended on the size of your family and how many buckets were evacuated. Most people had a supply of 3 to 4 buckets in their home.

The pickup crew used the town's *honey bucket truck,* which came to a home. A filled bucket was dumped into the truck, rinsed with warm water, and left as cleaned. When the truck was filled, it drove out to *honey bucket lake* and deposited its load. This lake was about 4 miles out of the town. Once a week, the crew added 200 to 300 lb of lime to increase the oxygen in the lake. Usually, no one in town went strolling out to this lake. It was only visited by the crew that ran the *honey bucket brigade.*

I also need to mention a unique room built into all homes in Bethel. Before you entered a home you passed through a small room called a wanigan. This was a small, unheated shed like structure, with an entry door. After entering a wanigan you'd hang up your parka, and remove your snow caked, muddy boots. It was a barrier between the cold, frigid air outside, and the warm air of a home. Filled honey buckets were left in the wanigan for pickup, never outside. In fact, residents had to take special steps to keep the material in the bucket from freezing. Usually, a wooden box, with a lid, was built to hold several honey buckets. Inside this box was a socket containing a light bulb. When one left a few honey buckets for pickup, the light was turned on. The heat from the light bulb prevented the offal from freezing. If a bucket was unheated, the material inside would freeze in an hour or two.

I'm now at the point, where I have a unique memory and story. We had hired a woman, who was our college counselor. She taught one course, served as an academic advisor, and supervised student housing. We rented an apartment to house students, who came to Bethel from the villages. She lived alone and consequently, didn't fill up many honey buckets. Her pickups were on Mondays and Fridays. When she left for work, she'd put out one bucket in the wanigan. Her home was located near the garage where the truck parked overnight. In fact, the honey bucket crew started their run at her home. Consequently, she never kept a bucket warm in her wanigan.

The tale begins on a Monday night, when she returned home and entered her wanigan. Her honey bucket was there, but not emptied. All its contents were frozen solid! But not to worry, she'd already placed another fresh bucket under the bench inside her toilet. On Tuesday, she phoned to inquire why her bucket wasn't taken care of the day before. She learned, that the crew had trouble starting the truck on Monday. They got to her home about 2 hours late and the material in the bucket had frozen solid.

Friday morning came. She got up, dressed and prepared to go to work. She put the honey bucket from the toilet out in her wanigan and saw the one still out there, with all the frozen sewage. She'd forgotten to bring it into her home the night before to thaw. So, she brought that bucket inside and put it on her wood burning stove in the kitchen. She planned to heat it a few minutes until it became a fluid. Shortly, after placing the bucket on the stove, she got a phone call. It was from someone at the dorm informing her of a problem that had occurred the previous night. She would have to deal with it that day. This call distracted her, and she quickly hastened to the college to deal with the crisis.

## Chapter Eight: The Frozen Tundra

When she got home that night, she saw a clean honey bucket in her wanigan. After removing her boots and hanging up her parka, she entered her home. She was greeted with an awful smell! What caused it? When she went into the kitchen, she realized what had happened. Her honey bucket had melted. All the contents had liquefied, flowed down the stove, and onto the floor where it had dried. In fact, some of it was still baking on the stove!

I wasn't the first one she called, but I did get a phone call from her. She asked, "Bob, do you have anything to drink?" Upon hearing her call for help, I hustled over to her home with a gallon of bourbon. Other friends soon gathered and brought vodka, gin, scotch, and rum. About 8 to 10 of us came to help her clean up!

Her kitchen was small, so only 3 to 4 of us could work in it at the same time. Those not working sat in her living room chatting, drinking, laughing, drinking, snacking, drinking, and preparing for our turn on the cleanup crew. Yes! You had to be inebriated to participate in this poop party!

What follows, will be the last of my Alaskan adventures. It is somewhat lengthy and deals with my departure from AK.

When I was young, I often read stories from two magazines published weekly. These were *Collier's* and *The Saturday Evening Post (SEP)*. In the SEP there were often stories about an adventurous woman named *Tugboat Annie*. I relished reading about her daring-do-adventures!

Soon after arriving in Alaska, I met a woman who reminded me of *Tugboat Annie*. She had lived in Bethel for many years. Her husband worked for the Bureau of Indian Affairs. He was responsible for building and maintaining all the structures in the 58 Eskimo villages in our area. Their two daughters were born in Bethel. This woman spent her summers working on one or more tugboats. No, she was not the Captain or First Mate. She would cook onboard the vessels. I mentioned to her how I had long admired the adventures of Tugboat Annie. I told her about my wish to work on a tugboat if the situation arose.

On Friday, June 15, 1979 my job in Alaska was essentially finished. Graduation had been held weeks earlier. Bobby's high school classes had ended, and he was already home on Long Island. The few summer classes the college offered were set to start the following Monday. Sometime that morning I got a call from the lady I just mentioned. She asked me to meet her for lunch.

During lunch she informed me that she'd just gotten a call from the Bethel Port Director. He asked if she was available to work as a cook on a tugboat over the next 4 to 5 weeks. She told him she was already committed to work on another boat, but offered to help find someone. To again make a long story short, let me mention what happened . . .

> I met with the Captain of the tugboat around 3:00 pm. The boat was docked in Bethel and unloading its cargo as we spoke. It was scheduled to leave at midnight.
>
> He offered me the job as cook, and I accepted.
>
> But I wouldn't be ready to leave at midnight, so we worked out an arrangement.
>
> The next day, Saturday, June 16, I completed all that I needed to do. By mid-afternoon, I left Bethel on a bush plane. I flew about 45 miles downriver, to the village of Tuntutuliak. After landing on the edge of town, I walked through the village. Over my shoulder, I carried my one large duffel bag.
>
> I got to the river where the barge was pushed onto the shore. The crane on the barge was off-loading cargo. The tugboat was not in sight. I approached a worker on the shore who was directing the crane operator on where to drop the cargo. I told him I was the new cook and asked where the tugboat was. He smiled and said, "We've been expecting you. Leave your bag here on the ground. We'll get it over to you."
>
> He signaled the crane operator. Down came the cable, on the end of which was a heavy metal ball, about a foot in diameter. He gave me a pair of leather gloves, told me to stand on the ball, and

## Chapter Eight: The Frozen Tundra

hold tight to the cable. I was lifted about 100-feet into the air and swung across the barge towards the river.

There was the tugboat below. It had pushed the barge onto the shore. The crane operator lowered me to the rear deck where the 1st Mate was waiting for me. We waited for my duffel bag to come over by means of the crane. The 1st Mate then showed me my sleeping quarters. I was given a quick tour of the boat. He showed me the kitchen, dining area, shower and toilet, and a storage locker in the hold. It contained cartons of various canned goods and other food supplies.

I only had time to make a quick supper of soup and sandwiches for the crew. I cleaned up the kitchen and dishes, took a shower, and went to sleep. I was exhausted!

Before I relate more of my adventures at sea, I want to give a brief description of the tugboat and barge . . .

The barge was about 200-250 feet in length. Cargo was carried in its hold below deck and freight was stacked up on its deck,. In addition, a steel framework supported an upper deck, on which more cargo was carried. In the rear of the barge was a crane for off-loading the material. Strong, steel cable, about 6 to 8 inches in diameter, was used to pull the barge by the tugboat. I later learned the naval term for this cable was a hawser.

*My Marvelous Memories*

The tugboat was about 45 to 50 feet long. It carried an 8-man crew, three of which were the officers, i.e., Captain, 1st Mate, and 2nd Mate. Each officer was paired with a seaman as a team. For example, Team A was the Captain and a seaman, Team B was the 1st Mate and his seaman, and Team C was the 2nd Mate and his seaman. The 7th man on board was the Engineer who made sure all machinery on the vessel kept operating. He also monitored and adjusted the tanks of fuel and fresh water located on each side of the boat. As these liquids were used, he made sure that the boat didn't list to one side and capsize. The 8th and last man on the boat was me, the cook.
I was responsible for providing three meals a day for the crew.

The teams I mentioned earlier worked a 4-hour shift and had 8 hours off. Later in the day, each team worked another 4-hour shift. Team A, the Captain, and his seaman, worked from 8:00 am to noon and 8:00 pm to midnight. Team B, the 1st Mate and his seaman, worked from 4:00 am to 8:00 am and 4:00 pm to 8:00 pm. The 2nd mate and his seaman worked from noon to 4:00 pm and midnight to 4:00 am. There never was a time when all members of the crew sat down and had a meal together!

I served breakfast at 7:30 am to three people, Team A and the Engineer. After their breakfast, this team began their 4-hour shift at 8:00 am. The Captain steered the vessel and plotted its course. His seaman did whatever he was given to do by the Captain, including fetching him a cup of coffee from the kitchen. The Engineer went about his duties of keeping everything running.

At 8:00 am, the 1st Mate and his seaman finished their shift and came down for breakfast. I usually joined them, so again I made breakfast for three. The 2nd Mate and his seaman never showed up for breakfast. They'd finished their earlier shift at 4:00 am by raiding the kitchen for coffee and leftover cake or cookies. They slept in until their lunch at 11:30 am, after which they started their noon shift.

*Chapter Eight: The Frozen Tundra*

Breakfast was usually eggs, cooked your way, hash brown potatoes, bacon, sausage, toast and coffee. On occasion, I made pancakes. Lunch started at 11:30 am and was simply soup, a sandwich, and cookies. Supper began at 4:30 pm and was the main meal with a salad, meat, potatoes, canned vegetables, and a cake for dessert.

After breakfast, I'd wash the dishes and bake a cake for supper. Then I'd take a 1 to 2 hour nap, and get up in time to prepare lunch. During this time, I'd bake cookies to keep the cookie jar fully stocked. My lady friend in Bethel had given me a couple of good tips. One was, "Keep the cookie jar filled and the coffee pot full and hot. Seamen drink coffee day and night and they love to munch on cookies or cake."

After supper, I'd wash and dry all the dirty dishes, clean the stove, scrub the counters and prep area. After all that, I'd wash the floor of the galley, on my hands and knees. Using a mop did not get the galley clean. A wet mop didn't pick up all the pieces of food that had dropped to the floor. It also did not do a good job with the grease, hence the hands-and-knees method.

After the cleanup, I'd take something out the freezer to thaw. Two large freezers on board were loaded with all kinds of meats: chickens, hams, steaks, roasts, bacon, sausages, cold cuts, cheeses, etc. No fish! Then I'd go down into the hold. Up front, near the bow was a storeroom. It was loaded with cases of canned goods and other dry food stuffs, such as sugar, flour, packages of ready-made cakes and cookies. I'd bring up to the galley, what I planned to use the next day.

After all this, usually around 7:00 pm, my day of work was over. Before I went to bed, I always went up to the bridge. There I sat, gazing at the sea around us. I chatted with the 1st Mate who was the officer on duty. He was very pleasant and showed me . . .

- the charts he used to plot our course.

- how the wheel turned the boat.

- how he'd set the automatic pilot.

- the radio he used to communicate with various locations on land.

- a portable radio he'd use to talk to his seaman.

He told me how every 2 hours, he would order the cable on the hawser adjusted. This long cable, used to pull the barge, would rub and slide along parts of the tugboat. A cable left in the same position for many hours would wear away, become frayed, and unravel.

I was amazed to see birds flying around our boat and landing on the ocean. They were looking for fish or other food. The 1st Mate told me that while on the Bering Sea, we were 100-120 miles offshore. Later, when we were crossing the northern Pacific, we were 200-300 miles from land and we still saw birds!

I would now like to mention a few other events that occurred during my tugboat adventure . . .

> I mentioned earlier how I boarded the boat and made soup and sandwiches for supper. That first night I was asleep by 9:00 pm. While I was sleeping, the tugboat pulled the barge off the shore and sailed down river into the Bering Sea. I awoke about 10:00 pm, went to the bathroom, and vomited. I retched again around 3:00 am with the *dry heaves*. I was seasick! On Saturday, a rainstorm had passed through the area. The storm had moved on, but the ocean was still turbulent with 2- to 3-foot waves that tossed the boat from side to side.

Chapter Eight: The Frozen Tundra

The seaman on duty came to awaken me at 5:00 am. I had left a *wake-up call because* I needed to get up and prepare breakfast. So, even though I was sick, I got up to do my job!

I was cooking bacon, sausage, and hash browns on the stove's griddle. When I opened the fridge to get the eggs, the boat was tossed in the wrong direction. Through the open door, a 5-gallon jar of mayonnaise came flying out. The glass jar broke. The floor was now covered with slippery mayo. I couldn't stand on the greasy floor, so on my hands and knees, I washed the galley floor. I finished this task so that I could complete cooking breakfast. Except for me, the 2nd Mate, and his seaman, all members of the crew had their breakfast.

During breakfast, the 1st Mate saw that I was seasick. He told me I'd get my *sea legs* within 24 hours. He advised me not to eat, but instead sip carbonated beverages, such as Coca-Cola or 7-Up. I followed his advice and had a short nap before and after lunch. By 2:00 pm, I was feeling much better. I then continued my preparations for the Father's Day special dinner I served that night . . .

On individual salad plates, a bed of fresh lettuce was topped with 6 to 8 chilled spears of white asparagus. I'd found two cases, all full, of white asparagus in the storage locker. None of the 7 men on board had ever seen or eaten white asparagus. Only two of them tried to eat one of the spears. Throughout the rest of the voyage, I often treated myself to white asparagus as part of my lunch or supper.

The entrée consisted of a prime rib roast. Everyone had a bone with lots of attached meat. The sides were mashed potatoes, gravy, and peas with carrots. The desert was a double-layered chocolate cake, covered with thick chocolate frosting. Between the two layers and on top, were maraschino cherries. The men were a well-fed and a happy crew!

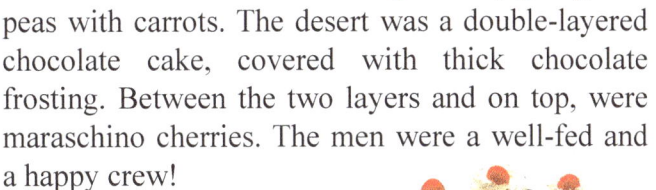

Early Thursday, June 21, we entered Norton Sound, the bay on which Nome is located. We were north of the Arctic Circle and experienced 24 hours of daylight. The Captain informed me that we would not dock at a pier. Instead, we anchored about ½ mile offshore. Smaller boats came alongside and our crew off-loaded cargo from the barge, onto these smaller vessels. These boats carried their cargo to shore, where it was moved to warehouses near the pier. Our crew worked throughout the night to deliver the shipment.

The Captain told me to plan and serve a *special luncheon* from 1:00 to 2:00 am. He advised me to keep it simple, so I prepared a luncheon of soup, sandwiches, chips, and cake. Throughout the night and morning hours, the coffee pot was kept full and hot. Next to the coffee service were piles of cookies. Around 7:00 am he told me to serve a *special breakfast*, special not in terms of the food, just the timing. He told me that I would be paid overtime for doing this. Also, I was to keep a count of the meals I served to men from Nome, who came aboard for both lunch and breakfast. I was paid extra for each one of the visitors served.

So, from about 9:00 pm Tuesday until around 11:00 am Wednesday, the crew and I worked a 24-hour shift. Shortly after breakfast on Wednesday, the Captain came and told me that we'd probably finish the cargo delivery by 11:00 am. There would be no more special meals. However, he sent me into Nome to purchase whatever fresh produce I could find in the local store. Fifteen minutes later, I got into a rubber boat. One of our seamen started the motor on the rear of the boat and told me to hang on to ropes along the sides. Off we went, bouncing across the waves into Nome. We walked about 2 blocks, to the local store where I purchased potatoes, lettuce, celery, and some apples. I remember paying $10 for two medium size cantaloupes. Back to our tugboat we hustled. We sailed out of Norton Sound before noon, heading south, and on our way *home to Seattle*.

A few nights later, while I was asleep, we left the Bering Sea as we sailed through the Aleutian Islands near Dutch Harbor. This was about 750 miles south of Nome. Now we headed east in the northern Pacific, on our way to Seattle—another 1900 miles to home.

As I chatted with different crew members, they all told me that this was the boring part of the voyage. Each day was the same 4 hours on duty, 8 hours of rest. Too far from shore to receive TV. Just sleeping, reading, doing laundry, and eating. It took us about 9 days to get to Seattle from Dutch Harbor.

## Chapter Eight: The Frozen Tundra

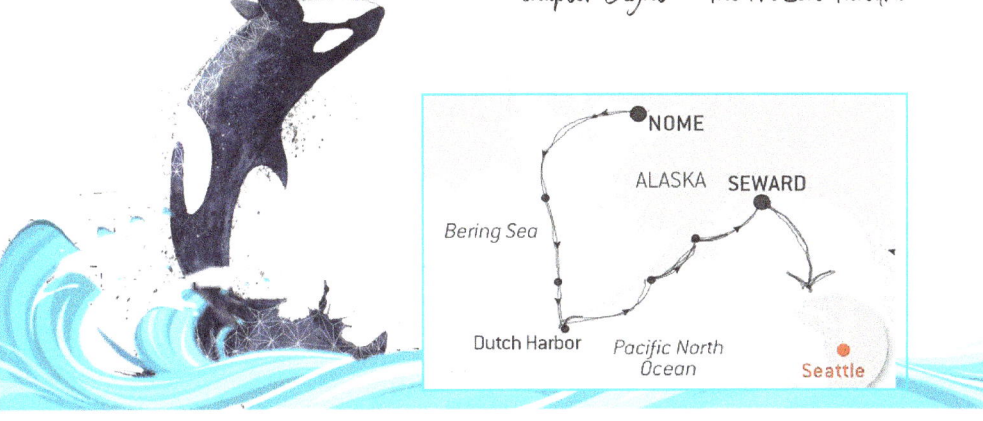

The night before we reached Seattle, the Captain called me to his quarters. He thanked me for the job I had done. He said I'd done a good job and he was pleased with my work. We finished with the following . . .

He gave me a letter of recommendation to the US Coast Guard. I needed this letter in order to register and receive my papers as a member of the US Merchant Marine. He'd promised me this letter, when he hired me in Bethel. It was conditional upon my doing a good job as the cook. He also gave me his phone number, in case I needed to reach him over the next few days.

He gave me a form to fill out. It was an inventory of all food items, still in storage in the food locker. Another form was used to inventory the contents of the two freezers. Both forms had items I could check to be added. He asked that I give the completed forms to him at breakfast. As part of his job, he had to provide these to a company quartermaster in Seattle, who then saw that the tugboat was resupplied for its next cruise.

He asked that before I left the boat in the morning, I gather all solid waste material, cans, empty cartons, etc., into green garbage bags. These were to be tied and left in kitchen/dining area. After the boat docked, a clean-up crew would take care of this waste.

He next cautioned me in the following matter. First, I should start cleaning out all food from the fridge. Leave what was needed for breakfast the next day. That night, I was to dump all this food in the ocean making sure that no other vessel was in sight. He didn't want to receive a citation for pollution, when all he was doing was feeding food that would be eaten by fish.

The next morning, Sunday, July 8, I made breakfast for all the crew. Cleaned the kitchen. Gathered the solid garbage. Packed my duffel bag. Took a shower. I was ready to leave the boat but couldn't. It was about 10:30 am. I sat on the bridge and watched us push the barge through the waters of Port Seattle. We docked it alongside a huge warehouse. On the dock, 30 to 40 men were waiting. As soon as the barge was secure, these men put down several ramps from the dock to the barge. Two movable cranes started to roll down the dock. They had 48 hours to fully load the barge with cargo for its next trip to Alaska.

After leaving the barge, it took us a ½-hour to get to the place where the tugboat was to be moored. Here a smaller crew was waiting to come on board. The tugboat would be first cleaned, then restocked with food, fuel, water, etc. My friend, the 1st Mate told me this usually took 30 to 36 hours. However, the Captain had ordered a new hawser for the rear deck. It would take 48 to 60 hours before our tugboat was ready to go to sea again.

My fellow seamen beat me off the boat when we docked. I shook hands with the Captain and 1st Mate, walked down the gangway, and set foot on land. My Alaskan and Tugboat adventures were nearly over, but not quite just yet!

I settled into a motel for two nights, called Mary in New York, and made a few other phone calls. Early the next morning, July 9, I was at the US Coast Guard headquarters, to start the process of acquiring my papers. The letter from the Captain was of immense value. However, since I was applying to be a *food handler*, the process took 2 full days, instead of one. The first morning I filled out many forms and documents. In the afternoon I underwent a complete physical exam, which included my leaving urine and stool samples for analysis.

On the morning of the second day, I returned to fill out a few more forms and have my fingerprints taken. I had to wait several hours because the results from the samples I left the day before were not completed. They would be ready at 3:00 pm.

*Chapter Eight: The Frozen Tundra*

I went out for lunch. To pass some time, I phoned the Captain to tell him of my progress. He was pleased it was going so well. Then he asked me, "Would you like to go to sea again?" He went on to tell me that he was leaving Thursday, July 12 on a tugboat. He invited me to come along as the cook. After further questions, I found out that he first was going to Bremerton, WA. There he would pick up a dry-dock, tow it down the west coast, and through the Panama Canal. After passing through the Canal, he'd sail to Puerto Rico, where the dry-dock would be delivered. I asked how long the trip would take. He said if his company didn't find something else to tow back from the Caribbean, we'd be back in Seattle in two months. I thanked him for the offer, but declined. I didn't say why. I had to get home to NY, brush up my resume, get it out, and find a new job!

I returned to the US Coast Guard facility. About 4:00 pm the decks were cleared. My picture was taken and printed on my papers. I was now a US Merchant Marine! My Alaskan and Tugboat adventures were over! That evening, I took a bus from Seattle to Portland, where I spent a few days visiting our friends, Carol and Ron Wyffels. On Sunday, July 15, I was back home in NY!

# Minuteman Press
# (September 1979 – July 1980)

Throughout July and August, I was at home in Oakdale, where I updated my resume. I sent it out to various colleges that had administrative vacancies, but had no interviews. Things were very slow because the country was still experiencing the depression mentioned earlier.

One position I applied for was the Provost at the University of Tennessee, Chattanooga. However, I didn't realize that UT, Chattanooga was the *Harvard of the South*! Many years later, I connected with my good friend, Dr. Edward Cahill, who was a Professor of Sociology at this university. Though he was not a member of the Provost Selection Committee, he knew all its members. He asked some of them why I hadn't been invited in for an interview. He was told, "We don't want a Provost who worked on a tugboat!" My adventure on the tugboat had an *adverse effect*!

However, to be fair, I am sure none of the faculty on this committee had any knowledge of Dr. John R. Coleman, President of Haverford College, who I earlier mentioned in Chapter 4. They probably would have also rejected hiring other members of the US Merchant Marines, such as Herman Melville, Louis L'Amour, Jack Vance, or Allen Ginsberg.

Though he was widely known at this time, this committee probably had no knowledge of another US Mariner. During WWII he had served as a seaman and navigator in the US Merchant Marines. Although his grades were only "C" average, Douglass C. North, managed to complete a triple major in *philosophy, political science*, and *economics* at the U California, Berkeley. He received his BA degree in 1942, and went to sea on merchant ships sailing from San Francisco to Australia. While at sea, he continued to read about economics. When the war ended, he returned to Berkeley and earned his PhD in 1952. During his academic career, he taught at such universities as Washington, Rice, Cambridge (UK), Washington (St. Louis), and Stanford. In 1993 he received the Noble Prize in Economics.

I did manage to find a part-time teaching position at the U of New York, Farmingdale. This university was only 15 miles from our home in Oakdale. I taught 2 calculus courses a semester in the math department for a year. Wages from a part-time teaching position were not enough to support our family. Mary and I decided to try our hand at running a business. We invested in a franchise printing shop in Sayville, NY, called Minuteman Press (MMP).

We first attended a week-long workshop at MMP Headquarters in Farmingdale, NY. We bought and ran a shop on Montauk Highway in Sayville, NY. We hired two young men, who were brothers, to do the actual printing and operate the other machines in the shop. Occasionally, Mary and I might run the folding or stapling machines. She stayed in the store, behind the counter, taking in walk-in orders. I spent much of my time going around Suffolk County visiting various businesses, marketing our products and services. I found out that I'm not much of a salesman, for I had minimal success in obtaining new clients. Mary had a great time in the store taking orders from the customers who walked in. She especially loved helping buyers who came in to order wedding invitations.

One story, about a *special group* we served, I do want to mention. In mid-June 1980, I returned to our shop one afternoon about 4:00 pm. I'd been out for over 6 hours marketing our services and when I entered, Mary was all smiles. She greeted me with, "You'll never guess who was in today and placed an order!" I said, "Who?" She said, "David and Randy. I drove them to the ferry. Victor and Alex are coming in tomorrow." I told her I didn't know what she was talking about. She explained that David Hodo and Randy Jones, of the Village People, had come into the shop. This singing group was spending their summer vacation at their home on Fire Island. On weekends, they would be giving performances at various restaurants/pubs on the island. We were going to print their weekly programs. Victor Willis and Alex Briley, other members of the group would be in the next day to see what we had set-up.

Mary found out that David and Randy had walked a mile-and-a-half from the Sayville ferry dock. She drove them back to the dock to get the ferry back to Fire Island Pines. Later that summer, she met the other two members of the Village People, Glenn Hughes and Felipe Rose.

*Our Dear Customers— The Village People!*

Over the summer, we printed 8 to 10 different programs for them while they were on Fire Island. Mary developed quite a relationship with all six of them. I think it all started that first day when she said to David and Randy, "Let me drive you down to the ferry. It's hot out there!"

The following Wednesday, Victor and Alex came in and quickly approved that first program which was printed and sent out on the ferry Thursday evening. By the end of the summer she called them all by their first names! I hardly knew them, and yes, we did go to the island one Friday night to hear them perform!

I want to mention a few aspects of our business . . .

- Every Friday, our two printers received their weekly paychecks.
- Every month, we paid the rent, bills from our suppliers, and the MMP franchise fee.
- Every quarter, the county, state, and federal government all received their taxes.
- Many months, Mary and I didn't have much profit left to share as our own.

In the spring of 1980, Mary and I decided that I should return to teaching, a task I loved! To make a long story short, I found a teaching job in NW Wisconsin. The 1980 academic year started, and I was an Assistant Professor of Mathematics at the U of Wisconsin, Stout. This college was in Menomonie, about 75 miles east of Minneapolis, MN.

This ends a major period in *MS*. The next chapter will be about a new beginning and further adventures.

# Chapter Nine

## Genesis-II
## (1980-1996)

••••••••••••

## University of Wisconsin-Stout
## (September 1, 1980 - January 15, 1981)

••••••••••••

This was a period when our family was fragmented . . .

Colleen had finished high school in the spring. She started her freshman year at St. Xavier's U in Evergreen Park, IL. She lived with her grandparents and only had to walk a half mile to be on the university campus.

Mary and Bobby lived in Sayville, NY. It was his senior year and he wanted to graduate with his friends at Connetquot HS. They lived in an apartment in Sayville. Mary and our friend, Joan Parsons, worked as cleaning ladies in offices and homes. Mary used her wages to pay the rent on the apartment.

Christine and I lived on a small farm near Colfax, WI. The farm was the *semi-retirement home* of Betty and Vern Shimanek, my good friends from Alaska. Christine attended 8th grade in the public school of Colfax. She took the yellow school bus and meandered through the farmland to get to Colfax. I'd drive about 25 miles into Menomonie to teach my classes at Stout.

*Colfax, Wisconsin*

At the university, I taught trigonometry and calculus classes. In the fall of 1980, the Math Department had hired 4 or 5 new teachers to join their 15-person department. I was the only new hire with a PhD. Why the turnover, I have no idea!

*Bowman Hall at UWI-Stout*

One Sunday afternoon in the fall, our chairman invited all department members and spouses to a social gathering at his home. While I walked around meeting folks, I noticed a young man. He was sitting on the stoop of the fireplace with a drink in hand. No one spoke to him and he talked to no one. I sat down next to him, introduced myself, and we began chatting. I found out he was the spouse of one of the new hires. His wife had been a high school math teacher. Since she had an MS degree in math, the university had hired her. He and his wife had been married about 3 years. They lived in a house on his father's farm. While his wife taught, he and his father ran the farm. Guess what they were raising on that farm? Pigs!

He was happy to have someone talk to him and was elated that I kept on asking about *pig farming*. After chatting for over an hour, we parted. Before we did, he invited me to visit his farm. Later that week, his wife sought me out. She thanked me for talking to her husband. She told me he didn't want to come with her to that reception. He was embarrassed to be among all *those eggheads*.

*We are invited for supper!*

Two weeks later, I visited that pig farm. My new friend gave me a complete tour. At the time, he and his father were raising over 400 pigs. Later, his wife served supper in their home. Of course, it was a pork roast. But, oh did that farm ***STINK***!

## Chapter Nine: Genesis II

What follows are personal stories from my Wisconsin adventure, nothing about teaching at the university . . .

There was no Catholic Church in Colfax. Christine and I would drive about 15 miles to attend Sunday Mass at St. John's Catholic Church in Bloomer, WI. Afterwards, we'd stop for breakfast in Bloomer or Colfax.

One Sunday, we drove about 30 miles to another church. We went to attend a special *Polka Mass*. Sure enough, when we entered the church, up front, near the altar, we saw a small band. It consisted of a drum, accordion, guitar, bass fiddle, keyboard, and singer. It was *fun* to listen to the chants and hymns sung to a *polka beat*!

We became friendly with many nearby farmers and their families. One of these families attended the Colfax Lutheran Church. This church had its fall fundraiser, a Lutefisk Festival. I bought a couple of tickets from them. So, one Friday evening, Christine and I went to our first, and last, lutefisk dinner. Before I go on with the rest of *MS*, I want to tell you about lutefisk (Norwegian spelling) or lutfisk (Swedish spelling).

Lutefisk is a dried white fish, usually cod. Before drying, it is soaked in water, then in a solution of lye. This process preserves the fish for years without refrigeration. Before cooking, it must be soaked and rinsed in clear water to remove the lye. It is then steamed slowly, without adding any water to the pot, as the reconstituted fish contains much water.

At the festival, Christine and I got in line to get our food. We soon received our plate of fish, boiled potatoes, and melted butter. After a few bites, we both went back to the line. We each got a plate of Swedish meatballs, served in a cream sauce, over noodles. We were thankful for this alternative! Otherwise, we would have left the festival starving!

Because I was a single parent raising Christine, I tried to plan something for us to do each weekend. I recall during October we visited an apple orchard to get apples and cider. We went to a pumpkin farm to get our *Halloween Pumpkins*. We carved several when we got back home. Friday nights, we often drove into Menomonie for a pizza.

One night, in early December, we were driving home from our pizza party. We were on a highway heading north. Christine noticed some unusual lights in the sky ahead. This was her first experience in seeing the *northern lights*. Of course, I had seen them many times while I lived in Alaska.

*beautiful aurora borealis*

Once a month, I'd leave Colfax around noon on Friday. I'd drive 300 miles south to Chicago. I usually stayed two nights and drive back to Colfax on Sunday afternoon. The purpose of these trips was to visit my mother. Christine usually stayed home and got babysitting jobs while I was gone.

Earlier, I mentioned we'd made friends with farmers who lived nearby. A pleasant memory occurred on the Labor Day weekend, either Sunday or Monday. We had a neighborhood picnic on a nearby farm.

I vividly recall sitting in the shade, chatting with an elderly farmer, who was 76 at the time. He'd started this farm, 50 years earlier. In 1975, he'd given the farm to his son. He continued to live on the farm in another house and was cared for by his son, daughter-in-law, and grandchildren. We watched as the young men fired-up the grill and cooked burgers, brats, and dogs. Meanwhile, the women prepared the tables with all other necessary items. He and I just sat in the shade, watched, chatted, and drank our beers. He told me a couple of stories I've never forgotten . . .

# Chapter Nine: Genesis II

He said, "Bob, farmers never have a good year! In the spring if the weather and rain work just right, I can produce a *bumper crop*. But everyone else does too. So, when I have a lot of grain to sell, the price I get is low. However, if the year is awful weather-wise, I don't grow much of a crop. Same thing for all the other farmers. Now the price is high, but I have *nothing to sell.*"

Then he said to me, "You know Bob, when I started this farm about 50 years ago, we ate inside the house. We went outside to shit. Now we shit inside and eat outside. I'm not sure if that's an improvement!"

The farm across the road from Betty and Verne's farm was run by a young couple, Mark and Chris. Christine often babysat their two small children. One Saturday, Betty, Verne, Christine, and I were invited to their home for dinner. Our hostess, Chris, served a dessert of homemade apple pie with ice cream. The pie was the largest pie I had ever seen. The baking dish was about 16 inches in diameter, and 2 ½ inches deep. After I tasted the pie I said, "Chris, this is the best apple pie I've ever eaten!" She started laughing. I asked, "What?" She replied, "There are no apples in this pie!" She told me she'd used zucchinis grown in her vegetable garden. It's still the best apple pie I've ever eaten!

In the last chapter I mentioned that, in the summer of 1980, I'd called friends in Chicago and asked them to let me know if they'd heard of any openings for teaching positions in the area. A few weeks before Thanksgiving, a former colleague from IIT, Wally Oberheim, called me. When I'd left Wright to go to Bogan in 1967, he was hired to replace me. Wally called to tell me that a situation was developing in the Physical Science Department at Wright. A physics teacher was about to be fired. He urged me to send my resume ASAP to the department chairman, Vince Sawinski. He promised to speak to Vince about me. After doing so, he arranged a meeting/interview for me on the Friday after Thanksgiving. I left U WI, Stout at the end of the first semester in mid-January.

After spending the Christmas Holidays in Chicago, Christine drove back to New York with Mary and Bobby. She finished 8th grade at the Oakdale Middle School and Bobby graduated from Connetquot HS in the spring of 1981.

On Monday, January 19, 1981, the second semester started. I was back at Wright College teaching in my *old position*. Many of my former colleagues had retired. However, a few others remembered me from the 1960's. I was very thankful to be back home in Chicago. Before she passed away in 1983, I managed to visit my mother many times!

In the summer of 1981, our family came together, but also separated. After a year at St. Xavier's College, and living with her grandparents, Colleen started attending classes at St. Mary of the Woods in Terre Haute, IN.

Mary, Bobby, and Christine moved from NY and joined me in Chicago. Because of a clause in the union contract, our new home was in the city. We moved into a condo in the *Ford City* area, located on 76th Street between Cicero and Pulaski Avenues.

Christine started and finished at Queen of Peace HS in Burbank. Bobby lived with us in Ford City. He did not initially go to college full-time. He got a job, found new friends, including his cousins Roger, Ken, and Ron Jr. He did go part-time to the Chicago City Colleges. One semester, he took an evening class at Wright and drove up north with me. Other times, he took a class or two at Richard J. Daley College, located only 2 blocks from our condo. He liked to play softball on a team with Frank, a new friend he made during this time.

I'll end this section about our transition from NY → WI → Chicago. The following section is about the next 16 years of **MS** before my retirement!

# Chapter Nine: Genesis II

# Wright Commnuity College, Chicago
## (January 19, 1981 – June 30, 1996)

*Old Wilbur Wright*

Back *home*, in my old position at Wright, Professor of Physics in the Physical Science Department, things were the same and yet there were many changes. Old colleagues had retired, a few remained. The Department Chairman was Dr. Vincent Sawinski, someone new to me. He and I got along very well! When he retired in 1989, I served as Department Chairman until 1995.

During these years, I taught astronomy, chemistry, meteorology, physics, and physical science. Occasionally, I taught an overtime class for the math department. All my classes at Wright were scheduled in the evening hours, i.e. 5:00 pm to 10:00 pm. I won't dwell on many Wright events, but I will mention a few.

By mid-May of 1990, I was completing the end of my first year as Department Chairman. I decided to confront a problem that had existed in our department for over six years. I recall it was a Thursday afternoon that I requested a meeting with *Arthur,* a colleague and fellow physics instructor. He was 15 years younger than me. The office for all department members, including the secretary and chairman, was in one large room. I wanted privacy for our discussion, so we went into one of our stockrooms.

I began our meeting by telling him a lie! I said, "I've had several students visit me. They had no complaints about your teaching. However, they said you often came to class with alcohol on your breath." I reminded him that the issue of alcoholism was covered in the union contract. It could lead to his being fired. Fortunately, the students had come to me to express their concerns. Had they gone to the Dean with their complaint, the Administration would have dismissed him. He did not argue with me or offer any excuses. Before we parted, he promised not to drink alcohol before his classes in the future.

The following Sunday our Department had a retirement dinner for one of our colleagues. Arthur had purchased his ticket and planned to be there. He didn't show up. In the middle of dinner, I quietly spoke to our two stockroom clerks about his absence. They knew Arthur well, and were aware of his drinking problem. They called his home but got no answer.

The next day, Monday, I arrived at my office shortly around 2:00 pm. Helen, my secretary informed me that Arthur had missed his morning class and hadn't phoned her about cancelling the class. She also gave me a phone message from a medical doctor requesting me to call back as soon as I came in. To make a long tale short . . .

> When we met on Thursday, Arthur didn't believe he had an alcohol problem. On Friday noon, he played golf with his friends, as usual. Afterwards, they all went to the 19th hole for some refreshments. He planned to show me I was wrong by having 2 or 3 beers before dinner.
>
> The next thing he knew he woke up on Sunday afternoon, around 3:00 pm with a terrible hangover. He didn't remember anything from late Friday until he awoke on Sunday. This shock convinced him to do something. He wasn't married and lived alone. He spent the rest of Sunday evening talking to his younger brother, seeking his help. They were able to contact his doctor by phone. Early Monday morning, he checked himself into a rehabilitation hospital, in a northwest suburb. The doctor who phoned me said Arthur had specifically asked that I come visit him. This doctor informed me, that if a patient requested someone to visit, it was very important to do so. The next afternoon I went to see Arthur. He first apologized for doubting what I had told him on Thursday. He told me about his golf game on Friday, and his lost weekend. We discussed his remaining classes for the week and his final exams for the following week.
>
> I left my meeting with Arthur and phoned our department secretary, Helen. She knew what was going on. In fact, she knew why I met with Arthur on Thursday. We informed the Administration and others that he was in a hospital under treatment. Substitutes met his classes during the first week of his absence. We arranged for some of his colleagues to administer his final exams in the second week.

I visited him several times during those first weeks. I brought him all his exams, homework assignments, and lab reports to him. He graded these assignments and phoned in his final grades to Helen.

During the summer, I also visited him several times. He left the rehabilitation hospital in mid-August and began the 1990-91 academic year, a sober, rehabilitated alcoholic. Twenty years after I retired, I learned he had gotten married. When he retired in 2010, they moved to CO where he continued to play golf and snow ski, his two passions! Most importantly, he stayed sober!

In 1991, while I was chairman, we began planning for a new campus. For 57 years, the college had been located at 3400 N. Austin. In September 1993, we began the academic year at our new, 23-acre campus, situated at 4300 N. Narragansett. The cost of this new facility was $93 million.

*New Wilbur Wright CC*

Wright's President, Raymond LeFevour, had significant political connections with the Democratic Party. In the fall of 1992, while still at the old campus, we were visited by Bill Clinton, Democratic candidate for President. Security before and during his visit was intense. But these security measures were nothing compared to the safety procedures a year later by the Secret Service, when President Clinton came to visit us at our new campus.

In May 1991, we had a retirement dinner for our colleague, Dr. Lillian Questiaux. Her 93-year-old mother was sitting at the head table with Lilian, Mary, and myself. Her mother started choking on a piece of meat. I jumped up and immediately performed the Heimlich maneuver. Mary told me later, that I literally lifted her out of her chair. The procedure worked! She coughed up the piece of meat and survived! She was more embarrassed at having caused a commotion during her daughter's retirement party.

One more Wright story, when we moved to our new campus, the college began expanding our Adult Continuing Education (ACE) programs. These were noncredit, community service-oriented classes. Most were offered on Friday evenings.

I tried to warn the Administration about using our laboratories for these ACE classes. My advice was not heeded. One Monday, I arrived on campus and was told that one of the physical science labs had drops of mercury all over the floor. Later, we learned that this laboratory was used on Friday night for a *knitting class*. One of the students in the knitting class was *pulling her yarn*. She'd tied one end of her thread to a mercury barometer on the wall. When she gave a good yank to her yarn, the barometer broke.

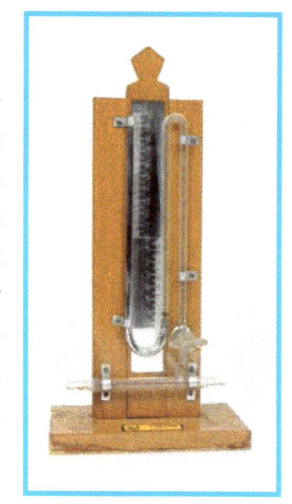

The Chicago Fire Department's *HAZMAT Team* came in to clean up the mercury spill. Later, they sent a $15,000 bill for their services. After this charge, the Administration didn't schedule any more ACE classes in a science laboratory.

{ Fun Fact:
$15,000.00 in 1991 is equivalent in purchasing power to about $28,686.56 today (January of 2021). That's the present cost of an awfully expensive knitting accident. }

Enough about Wright! Much more was happening in our family's lives. Though quite extensive, I'd now like to share these stories. However, they may not be in chronological order.

When we were living in Ford City, Mary decided to take some college classes at Richard J. Daley College, only two blocks away. She took classes and became a Certified Nursing Assistant (CNA). As part of her program, she had to do three internships at nursing homes. She did not like the environment that she found in these places. When she completed her program and was certified, she focused on taking only home health care positions.

Initially, she worked for JoAnn Sheehan who ran a service which provided home health care. Mary encouraged her old friend, Pat Nichols, to become a CNA. They both worked for JoAnn for about a year. It wasn't long before they realized they could earn a higher hourly wage by finding their own patients. So, Pat, Mary, and Margie Jurzina, another friend, helped each other find patients seeking home health care services. Margie lived less than a mile from us in Ford City. Mary worked as a CNA from 1986-1997.

Chapter Nine: Genesis II

Jo and Dan Rolewicz lived in a Ford City condo directly across the hall from ours. They were not only our new neighbors but became our very good friends. Mary and Jo both smoked, and they both loved to play bingo. So, two nights during the week, and once on the weekend, out they'd go to a local bingo hall. Of course, they'd like to win! But even if they didn't win a game, they enjoyed smoking, chatting, and covering the numbers on their cards!

For almost 25 years, 1982-2005, these two prowled the southside bingo halls. They also made five trips to the casinos of Las Vegas and three junkets to Biloxi, MI. They went to try their luck at the slots and other games found there! Mary's best friend Jo passed away in May 2005. Mary followed her in November 2006.

In 1984, Colleen, graduated from St. Mary of the Woods in Terre Haute, IN with two BA degrees. One in *Early Childhood Education* and the other in *Special Education*. She later earned an MA degree in Education from Governor's State U. Her specialty for a graduate degree was *Autism*. She has spent her entire career in providing education for children with special needs.

In 1989, she married TJ (Terrance John) Brown. Zachary was born in 1992, and Austin in 1998. Since 1996, the Brown Family has lived in Plainfield, IL. I have a 4-room apartment attached to their home, and live there from June to October.

In 1987, Robert (Bobby) graduated from Benedictine U in Lisle, IL. He married Jeanine Kies in 1985. They now live in Wauwatosa, a suburb of Milwaukee. Sabrina, their oldest daughter, lives near Columbus, OH. Quinlyn, their youngest, lives in Boulder, CO, where she recently (2021) was married. She also graduated from the U of Colorado.

Christine lived with us for several years in Ford City. In 1985, she graduated from Queen of Peace HS, in Burbank. She attended the U of Illinois, Chicago and received two degrees. She earned a BA in philosophy in 1989 and an MA in philosophy in 1991.

Later, she spent two years at Kendall College in Evanston to obtain a teaching certificate. Her specialty was Montessori Education. She moved to Champaign, IL and for over 30 years has taught 3- to 5-year-old children at a Montessori school in nearby Savoy. In the summer of 2003, she married Kevin Wolter. Laura Krupp Wolter was born on August 4, 2004. In 2017, they and all their pets moved into their new home in the Glenshire Estates area of Champaign.

My full-time job was teaching night classes at Wright. If it was equal to or less than ½ a teaching load, our union contract permitted another job elsewhere. From January 1983, until I retired in 1996, I taught part-time at several parochial high schools during the day.

From 1983 to 1986, I taught at Elizabeth Seton girls' high school in South Holland, IL. Two months after starting to teach here, I was visited by Mary Kay Adamczyk, the science department chairperson. She was apologetic when she talked to me about visiting my class. She told me her job required her to do this. She was embarrassed because she was only 29 at that time, and I was 54. In addition, she had only a BS in chemistry and I had a PhD in physics. After her visit, she met to discuss what she had observed. She began by saying, "Dr. Krupp, I just wish that you had taught at IL State when I went there. I learned more physics in the 45 minutes I sat in your class, than in any of my college physics courses."

Of course, from then on, Mary Kay and I became very good friends! Mary and I attended her wedding to Ed Wonders in Streator, IL. Over the years, we visited them often in their home near Bloomington, IL. I attended her daughter Holly's wedding a few years ago. In June 2018, I was delighted to attend her retirement dinner in Delavan, IL. She had devoted 30+ years to teaching high school science to students in the corn fields of Illinois.

In January 1986, the student body and faculty of Seton were assembled in the school auditorium. We were all excited! We were going to watch Christa McAuliffe become the first teacher launched into space. Not only was she an inspiration to our young students, she was raised a Catholic to boot! The entire assembly of 800+ went silent 73 seconds after the launch as we saw the *Challenger Space Shuttle* break up. There was no teaching of physics that day! My fellow teachers and I did the best we could to console these weeping young women!

*Chapter Nine: Genesis II* 241

From 1986 to 1987, I taught at St. Rita's HS, Chicago. This was the last year for the school to be located on 63rd and Oakley Avenues. My physics and chemistry classes, including labs, were held under the old enclosed football stands. During this year, I became quite friendly with Norb Lasky, math teacher. Unfortunately, over the years, we've lost contact!

From 1987 to 1996, I taught at St. Patrick's HS, Chicago. When I started, St. Pat's was only two blocks from the old Wright College on Austin Avenue. I made many good friends at St. Pat's during these 9 years. My best friend was Dennis Miller. Sad to say he passed away in June 2010, before his 65th birthday.

At Christine's suggestion, Mary and I started the Annual Krupp Pie Contest. It was held on the Saturday after Thanksgiving at our condo in Ford City. Mary and I made the dinner. Colleen, Bobby, and Christine would bake a special pie of their choice. They could bring a guest, who also could enter the contest with their own pie. A peach pie was banned from the contest! Everyone knew it was my favorite, and I was always one of the judges. After sampling the entries, decisions were made and awards passed out. Then we spent the evening drinking coffee and sampling more slices from the different pies!

In May of 1985, I tried to find a summer job as a cook on a tugboat, plying the rivers of the country. I visited a union office for seamen in Joliet, filled out application forms, and spoke to the director. He called a week later and told me there was an opening for a cook on a tugboat presently in New Orleans. However, I had only 48 hours to get onboard. Unfortunately, there was one week left to the semester at Wright. There was no way I could have given the final exams, graded them, and turned in my final grades in so short a time. So, another ship sailed without me. I never tried to work on a tugboat again!

I spent the summer of 1987 in Colfax, WI, living with Betty and Verne on their farm. They now had a small business in Colfax that sold bait, beer, and other sundries. I occasionally manned the store while they took a break.

Verne helped me build a movable food stand out of an old boat trailer. This stand had a gas grill, a small electric refrigerator, and a long extension cord. From it, I grilled buffalo burgers and sold them along with bags of potato chips. You know my name is Bob, so my T-shirts said *Buffalo Bob's Buffalo Burgers*. For 3 weekends, the stand was set-up in the parking lot, at Verne's Bait shop. Twice a month, I would drive 90 miles south to La Crosse, WI. A farmer in this area had a herd of about 200 buffalo. I would buy my frozen ¼-lb buffalo burgers from him. From mid-July, I took my food stand on the road. I served buffalo burgers at 5 county fairs in WI. From Thursday morning to Sunday night, I sold my burgers in Menomonie, Chippewa Falls, Neillsville, Rice Lake, and Oshkosh. I didn't make much money, but it was a lot of fun!

When I returned to Chicago in 1981, I reconnected with many old classmates from Glencoe. One especially, was George LaVaque. He, his wife Mary, my Mary, and I went on several memorable vacations together.

One summer, we went to Sioux City, SD and then on to the Corn Palace in Mitchell. After a brief visit to the Badlands, we stopped for our free glass of ice water at the famous Wall Drugs. Moving farther west, we spent a few days in Rapid City.

Chapter Nine: Genesis II    243

One day, we visited the four presidents at Mt. Rushmore National Memorial. Another day, we filled our coolers with ice, food, and beverages. Off we went for a picnic in the park, surrounding the Presidents. I had to maneuver through many bends and turns on the road through the mountains.

One night, we went for supper to the Circle B Chuckwagon Dinner and Cowboy Music Show. After a visit to Lead and Deadwood, with a stop at the graves of Wild Bill Hickock and Calamity Jane, we ended up in Spearfish, SD for a couple of days. One evening we went to the *Black Hills Passion Play.* This production was an American version of the Lünen Passion Play. It came to this country in 1932 by immigrants. They claimed it had been produced since 1242. George fell asleep during the last act. We kidded him on our ride back to the motel. He responded by saying, "I know how it ended!"

*The Badlands*

*Follow the Signs to FREE Water!*

*FREE Water! Get it Here!*

*Mt. Rushmore Monument*

*Circle B Chuckwagon Dinner*

*Deadwood*

Through George, I reconnected with Frank Myslewic, Gene Staub, Howie Baumert, and Hank Vaughn. Gene had a weekend house in Fox Lake, where we often met. We'd gather there early on a Friday evening for a *Boy's Weekend Out*. We'd go somewhere for crab legs or a fish fry dinner. After chatting and reminiscing awhile, we'd crash somewhere in his 2-bedroom home. Saturday we'd hang out, maybe do a little fishing from his dock. In the evening, we'd go out again, somewhere for dinner. After Mass and breakfast on Sunday, we'd all head back home to Chicago.

It was during this time we started our *Super Bowl* parties. Same pattern as before, we'd meet early Friday evening in Fox Lake. On Sunday, instead of heading home after breakfast, we stayed at Gene's pad. I'd make a big pot of chili to eat while we watched the game. We wouldn't get home until 11:00 pm or later. In 1986, when the Bears won the Super Bowl, we brought our party into Gene Staub's home in Lincolnwood. This was the first party in which our wives joined us. Henceforth, all Super Bowl parties were held so that the ladies could be present. Most of the time, we held them at the home of Hank or Gene.

George also got us connected to the Glencoe Club. In the summer, this Club had a picnic at St. Joseph's HS in Westchester. On the first Sunday in November, we met at Lewis University. First, we'd attend Mass and pray for all the departed souls of the previous year. This was followed by a scrumptious dinner, usually slices of a prime rib roast. During the Christmas holidays, the Club went to the *Mercy Home for Boys* on Jackson Blvd. We'd have a great cocktail party and dinner. Then we'd help Santa bring gifts to the boys in the home. In mid-March, the Club held their last event of the year. It was the St. Joseph Day spaghetti and meatball dinner at St. Patrick HS. My mother and father had been active members of the Glencoe Club from 1944 to 1960.

*Mercy Home for Boys — 2016*

## Chapter Nine: Genesis II

I would be remiss in not mentioning this next story. In 1985, Bobby and Christine were in college at the same time. To start the new school year at Benedictine U, they had to have their first semester tuition paid in full. In addition, money was required to pay for housing, meals, and books. I didn't have all the money needed.

Mary suggested I go talk to our brother-in-law, Bob Hriszko. I'd barely got the words out of my mouth when he reached for his checkbook. I recall he said, "How much do you need, Bob?" No promissory note was signed. No interest on my debt was ever charged. Bob stepped up like a true family member! He immediately wrote a check for $2500 to help us. For that I am forever grateful! To conclude this story, he was paid the full amount within 18 months.

Thanks to my friend Ed Wonders, I drove some unique, old cars he'd discovered on farms in central IL. One was a 1972 Golden Cadillac limousine with two jump seats in the back. In the fall of 1988, St. Pat's football team made it into the playoffs. I drove my limousine to the playoff game with six other faculty members, two students, and myself in the car. People who watched us pull into the parking lot roared with laughter when they saw us arrive. We were riding on the hubcaps!

In the spring of 1989, I was the chauffeur again. The two ladies in back, Mary and Jan, were driven by limousine to the Bismarck Hotel in downtown Chicago. The three of us went there to attend the annual faculty union dinner. I'd purchased the tickets from the Wright College union representative. Consequently, we sat at one of the Wright tables. In another section of the ballroom were tables of Richard J. Daley College (formerly Bogan) faculty. Before dinner, Jan and I went over to chat with some of our former colleagues. While there, Jim Kozicki, a member of the English Department, introduced me to his wife. They'd been married after I left Bogan in 1970. She had a glint in her eye and a broad smile on her face. As I shook her hand she said, "You don't remember me, do you?" When I said no, she laughed and said, "I was a student of yours 25 years ago. It was a physical science class you taught on TV."

*1970 Corvette!*

Before the Cadillac limo, I'd been driving a 1970 Corvette convertible. One summer, while away from Chicago, I gave Colleen the keys and permission to use it. One evening, she and some of her friends went to a local pub. They were there awhile when a young man came in. He began asking around, "Do you know who owns that blue Corvette outside? I want to talk to him." He eventually found Colleen. His name is TJ (Terrance John) Brown, my son-in-law. My blue Corvette was the *matchmaker*! Today their oldest son, Zachary, drives a white 1995 Corvette.

From 1989 to 1996, I became a *Workshop Junkie*. Our nest had become empty. All our children had finished college without a debt. I didn't have to take on summer teaching assignments to earn extra money!

Because I taught at St. Pat's, I was eligible to apply for workshops held for HS teachers. Among those I participated in . . .

- ✓ Three summer workshops at Argonne National Laboratory in Lemont, IL.

- ✓ Two summer workshops on astronomy at the University of Chicago. I loved these workshops. Twice a week, we had a laboratory scheduled from 10:00 pm to 2:00 am. During this time, we'd use remote controls and a radio link to operate different telescopes. The telescopes were located 75-miles away at the Yerkes Observatory in Williams Bay, WI.

*Yerkes Observatory*

Because I taught at Wright, I participated in workshops designed for college teachers. I recall . . . .

- ✓ In June 1992, I went to Tufts University in Boston for a 3-week workshop on astronomy. Mary came with me. We stayed in a dorm room for two and had breakfast at the college dining hall. In the evening, we'd go out for dinner together, or with fellow workshop participants.

In the morning, our lectures were at Tufts. After lunch, we'd spend time using telescopes to study sunspots and other features of the Sun. Three evenings, we drove 40-miles to Wellesley College to utilize the Within Observatory. Using its telescopes, we observed the night sky.

*Within Observatory*

✓ In August 1992, Mary and I drove to Kansas City, MO. I went for a 3-week workshop at the National Weather Service Training Center. While I attended the lectures and trained on equipment at the center, Mary relaxed, rested, and read at our motel. In the evening, we'd go out for dinner.

On Monday, August 17, we boarded a bus for a 160-mile drive to Offutt AFB near Omaha, NE. Only workshop people were allowed on this trip. Mary and other spouses stayed behind in KC. After arriving at the AFB and checking through security, we went to visit the Air Force Global Weather Center (AFGWC). We were greeted by a Colonel who was the Director of the Center. We learned that the Air Force had over 2-dozen satellites circling the Earth at that time. I was impressed when he provided some information regarding the Gulf War, Operation Desert Storm, of 1990-1991. He told us that all military forces, on the ground, in the air, or at sea, received their daily weather forecasts from the AFGWC during this mid-East conflict.

*National Weather Training Center*

We spent hours visiting this center and seeing various pieces of equipment.
Our tour ended in a large room the size of a small gym. It had a 24-foot ceiling and was partitioned off into many small cubicles. In each space sat two noncommissioned AF personnel. They sat looking at several TV monitors showing the weather conditions in real time for a sector of the Earth. We were split into smaller groups of two or three and told to wander about and ask questions.

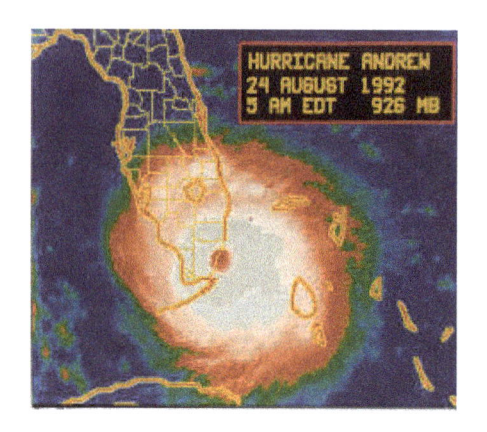

I remember going into one of these cubbyholes where a Sergeant was viewing the mid-Atlantic Ocean from Africa to the Gulf of Mexico. He was watching the growth and westward movement of tropical storms. He pointed to one in the lower part of the Gulf of Mexico and another just north of Haiti. He said that he didn't think these two tropical storms would cause any trouble. He then called our attention to a storm center that had just left Africa. It had moved westward, out into the Atlantic the day before. I remember him saying, "I think this one could develop into something dangerous." A week later, August 24, it went across southern FL and caused extensive damage in Homestead and Miami. This storm was named Hurricane Andrew! After stopping for dinner, we didn't get home to our Holiday Inn until around 11:00 pm. A long, but very instructive day!

A final story from this period happened in the summer of 1985. I was teaching an evening class in physics at Moraine Valley CC. This course was the first in a series of three designed for majors in science and engineering.

One of my students was a middle-aged woman. I've forgotten her last name, but her first name was Virginia. One day, she came to my office before class. She needed help with some problems she couldn't solve. Over the course of the summer, I learned she was a single parent, raising two boys. In fact, her younger son was taking this very same course, in the morning at Moraine. She worked during the day, as a hairdresser, and couldn't attend day classes. She worked diligently in my course and finished with an A.

I learned she'd decided to go to college, now that her boys were older. She planned to earn a BS in physics and become a high school teacher. The course ended and I never saw her again. However, I promised to help her achieve her goal. I phoned an old friend and colleague from my Glencoe days. Dr. Philip Hogan was now Chairman of the Physical Science Department at Lewis U in Romeoville. I told him about Virginia and her career goal, and I wrote a letter of recommendation for her.

*Chapter Nine : Genesis II*

She got a scholarship to Lewis and graduated a few years later with her BS in physics. Dr. Hogan told me that during her senior year, Loyola U offered her a full scholarship to earn her MS in physics. She accepted and went on to Loyola.

What finally happened to Virginia, I do not know. Did she earn her MS degree and become a high school teacher? Did she continue her studies, earn a PhD, and become a professor at a college or university?

I would like to count Virginia as one of the good deeds I've done in my life so far.

Let's return to Wright College. In the early 1990's, our Board was encouraging faculty to take Early Retirement. Their definition of early was before the age of 70.

In 1995, I resigned as Department Chairman. I wanted to assist Dr. Jane Guagliardo, the new Chairperson. On June 30, 1996, I retired from teaching at both Wilbur Wright College and my part-time job at St. Patrick.

*St. Patrick High School*

In mid-May 1996, the Physical Science Department had a retirement dinner for me and my colleague, Dr. Peter Metropolis. The banquet was held at Zum Deutschen Eck, a German restaurant in Chicago which no longer exists. Many family members came to celebrate this event with me. During my farewell address, I mentioned the proudest achievement of my life! My two daughters, Colleen and Christine were both teachers!

Starry sky over Saudi Arabia

# Chapter Ten

## Retirement
## (1996-2001)

••••••••••••

## Imperial Tutoring Service, Oak Lawn, IL

••••••••••••

In the first year of retirement I worked for Imperial Tutoring Service (ITS) of Oak Lawn. I coached several students in math or science. Two unique situations I would like to relate at length . . .

In mid-November AT&T, the phone company, was filming a special TV ad in Chicago. They planned to show it during the upcoming holiday season. Children who had run away from home were the specific targets. Any youngster, who had fled their abode, was encouraged to call home! From Christmas Eve to New Year's Day, they could call a special 800 number and have a *free* 10-minute conversation with their parents. AT&T assured runaways that no information would be given to parents, such as area codes, etc.

The company producing the ad was filming two scenes in Chicago. A teenage actor, flown in from Brooklyn, was the young runaway in the ad. He was assured a tutor would be provided to assist him with his geometry class while he was absent. I was that tutor! The first day was in downtown Chicago on the SE corner of Madison and State Streets. The background was the entrance to Carson, Pirie, Scott & Co. This entrance had been designed by Louis Sullivan in 1899. An outdoor phone booth on that corner was the main focus of the scene.

*Carson, Pirie, Scott & Co.*

On Monday, at 8:00 am, I was directed to board a motorhome parked on Wabash, just north of Madison. The young actor and his mother were elsewhere having breakfast. To keep the motorhome warm, the engine was kept running all day. Behind the driver's seat was a table, bench and seat. I was told to sit and wait for the young man, who would return shortly. In the meantime, someone brought me a hot coffee and Danish. Shortly after 9:00 am, the boy and his mother arrived. After introductions, I tutored him for less than 10 minutes. He was called to appear for a *shooting*. This was the pattern throughout the day, i.e., I would tutor him for 5 to 10 minutes. Then off he'd go for a *new shot* and return in an hour or so. That first day, I worked with him a total of 50 to 60 minutes.

In the meantime, I sat there in that warm motorhome, drinking coffee, eating pastries, and watching TV. However, around 1:00 pm everyone stopped working. We all went to lunch at a nearby restaurant. Filming and staging crews, actors, extras, wardrobe personnel, and other staff, a total of over 100 people, gathered for a nice luncheon, in a warm setting. The first day ended at 5:00 pm. I drove home and had earned $300.

The second day I reported at 8:00 am in a neighborhood on the NW side of Chicago. It was near Sunnyside and Pulaski. There in the motorhome I again sat, drank coffee, ate Danish and watched TV. I did manage to tutor my student for a total of about 1 to 1½ hours. The main scene today was a home with front steps, wooden porch, picture window in the front parlor, etc. The staging crew *had blown snow* around the steps, walkway, and bushes. The *main shot* was that of the young runaway returning home on Christmas Eve! Most of the shots were taken after 3:00 pm, as early evening fell. The Director wanted to film warm, soft, light coming from the front windows in the twilight and darkness of the evening.

Of course, we all took a break at 1:00 pm for lunch. The day officially ended at 5:00 pm. However, I was asked to remain for a few hours. Wardrobe gave me a hat, much like an Indiana Jones' hat. Along with 10-12 other extras, I got on a Greyhound bus parked in a nearby Jewel parking lot. This scene was to be of the young runaway making his way home for Christmas by riding on a bus. I think I was selected to be an extra because I was tall. That hat I wore appeared in the seat behind the boy, but not my face. The day for me ended at 7:00 pm. I went home and had again earned $300 for the day. In addition, I received $100 for being an extra for 2 hours.

*(You can see the final commercial with a link listed in the photo credits at the back of this book!)*

Scene from AT&T Commercial

In early December of 1996, the Director of Imperial Tutoring (ITS) and I went downtown to the headquarters of Metra, the suburban railroad system, in Chicago. At that time the headquarters were on Wabash and Harrison. We met with the Director of Training for Metra. He explained a problem he faced and was hoping Imperial Tutoring could help him deal with it.

He first explained that back in 1971, when Amtrak started, many US railroad companies went out of business. As a result, hundreds of trained mechanics for diesel, electric, and steam locomotives lost their jobs. Older workers retired. Middle-aged and younger mechanics had to find work elsewhere. Metra and other commuting railroads benefited from this pool of trained shop mechanics. But now, 25 years later, these mechanics were beginning to retire. Metra needed new, young, competent mechanics, but none could be found. Few were being trained anywhere across the nation. Consequently, Metra planned to start their own apprentice program in the fall of 1997. Fifty-sixty young people were to be trained in a 24-month-long program. It would lead to high paying jobs in repairing and maintaining all their railroad equipment. In early spring, Metra planned to advertise nationally for interested men and women, to apply for these paid apprentice positions.

However, in the fall of 1996, union representatives of Metra's service workers met with him. These workers cleaned and polished all of Metra's passenger cars. Their jobs included sweeping out cars, removing trash, washing windows inside and out, scrubbing toilets, and washing the exteriors of the cars. No repairs were done by these workers. The union representatives suggested that their workers be given preference for these apprentice jobs. Metra agreed to do so. However, the Director of Training, had pointed out that these apprentices would have to read shop manuals. These books contained a lot of mathematics. A math test had to be given to all applicants. The union agreed, and a mathematics exam had been given in early October 1996. Seventy workers took the test. Three passed and were assigned to the first class of apprentices. The union then suggested that the remaining 67 workers be given a second chance at the test. Metra agreed, but only if these people took a course to improve their basic math skills. Both the Union and Metra agreed to share equally the cost for this course. By the end of our meeting, the Director of ITS agreed to the following . . .

✓ ITS would provide a 6-week course of basic math skills.

✓ Each course would meet 1 night a week for 3 hours.

✓ Each class would have no more than 12 students and would meet at a Metra facility.

The Director of ITS and I left that meeting with a contract from Metra. We stopped in a nearby coffee shop to discuss what we had learned and agreed to. During this meeting, he gave me complete charge of developing the curriculum and overseeing the entire program.
Here's what happened . . .

# Chapter Ten: Retirement

- ✓ 40 men signed up and spent 3 hours, 1 night a week for 6 weeks. Instruction began in the first week of February.

- ✓ I taught two classes on the SE side of Chicago. We met in the cafeteria at the Metra shops on 111th and Pullman Streets. One class had 11 students, the other had 10.

- ✓ In the meantime, two other classes of 10 and 9 students met on the north side. These classes were taught by two other tutors from IT, who lived on the NW side of Chicago.

- ✓ At the end of March, the forty students took the math entry test that they failed in October. Twenty-three passed. As far as I know, they were all included in the first apprentice class, which began in the fall of 1997.

In January 1997, I saw an ad in a physics journal about teaching physics and chemistry overseas. I applied and within a few weeks I went to Houston, TX for an interview.

I'll never forget that Southwest Airlines flight I took out of Midway on Sunday, February 9, 1997. The plane took off at 6:00 am as scheduled. After takeoff, the co-pilot came on the intercom and welcomed us all. He told us that SW had 5 crew members on board, the pilot, co-pilot, and 3 flight attendants, who would serve us in the cabin. He finished by saying that the two passengers on board, including me, could select any seat we wanted!

We landed in Kansas City and then Oklahoma City. More passengers boarded the plane at each stop. The next stop was Houston. I got off and took a shuttle to a hotel near Hobby Airport. There I was directed to a small suite set up as a waiting room. Comfortable sofas, chairs and tables with newspapers and magazines were available. A large table was set with coffee, juices, and pastries. I waited about an hour and then I was invited into an adjacent parlor. Here I had a 1- to 1½-hour interview. Two of the interviewers had come from Saudi Arabia, a 3rd person was from Houston.

I was finished by 3:00 pm. As I left, the man from Houston said I would hear from him, within 1-2 weeks, and that I probably would be among those selected. I stopped at a restaurant in the hotel for a burger and beer. Then I took the shuttle back to the airport. I boarded a 7:30 pm flight back to Midway. When I boarded the plane there were only a few vacant seats left. 95% of the passengers were wearing beads and were in various stages of inebriation. The plane had started in New Orleans and it was Mardi Gras Weekend!

*Mardi Gras Revelers*

The following week I received a call from Houston, offering me a teaching job in Saudi Arabia (SA). I accepted. The caller informed me that I would receive a contract in the mail. Instructions would also be sent on what I had to do to prepare for my departure to SA. It took me three months to complete all the paperwork and other things to allow me to enter the Kingdom of SA . . .

✓ I updated my US Passport.

✓ It took two months before I received approval for a work visa from the Saudi Embassy in Washington, DC.

✓ I obtained an original, notarized copy of my birth certificate by going downtown to the Cook County and City Hall Building.

✓ I had to obtain proof from the Chicago Police Department that I'd never been arrested in Chicago. I went to the police headquarters at 11th and State Street to get this document.

## Chapter Ten: Retirement

✓ I went to the Reid-Murdoch Building on the north shore of the Chicago River. From the Illinois State Attorney's office located here, I obtained papers that showed I'd never been convicted of any crime in the state of Illinois.

✓ In Hinsdale, I found a doctor who specialized in diseases found in 3rd world countries. After visiting him weekly for 6 weeks, I was immunized by receiving various vaccines.

✓ Sunday, May 11th, was Mother's Day. We planned a small family brunch at Nikos Restaurant in Bridgeview. I was surprised when many other family and friends gathered to wish me well as I departed for SA. They sent me off with a gift of a small telescope. Everyone encouraged me to study the night sky from the desert sands of Arabia.

On June 1, I flew out of Chicago and landed at Heathrow Airport in London. I boarded a flight to SA and landed, in the dark of night, on the early morning of my 68th birthday. My new adventure in the Middle East had begun!

*Night Sky over Judah Thumb in Saudi Arabia*

# College Preparatory Center (CPC) Saudi Arabia
# (June 2, 1997 - December 23, 2000)

*Saudi Aramco Headquarters*

The CPC was a special educational facility located in Dhahran, SA, where the headquarters of the Saudi Aramco Oil Company were located. Before I tell you about this educational center, let me give a brief history of oil in Arabia.

In May 1933, an oil concession agreement was signed between SA and Standard Oil of California (SoCal). Geologists from SoCal were given five years to search for oil in a formation known as the *Dammam Dome.* Initially, their explorations met with little success.

*Max Steineke*

In 1936, Max Steineke was the chief geologist at SoCal. Despite repeated failures, he was convinced there was oil out in that vast desert. He came to Arabia. Through his efforts and persistence, oil in commercial quantities in SA was discovered. It happened in March 1938. SoCal's 7th exploratory well in Dammam was where oil was discovered. They named the well, Lucky 7, and later called it *The Prosperity Well*. The headquarters for Saudi Aramco then developed around Lucky 7. This community became known as Dhahran, SA.

Over the next 50 years, other oil companies joined in developing and operating the world's largest hydrocarbon network. Among them were SoCal (30%), Texaco (30%), Exxon (30%), and Mobil (10%). This conglomerate was called the Arabian American Oil Company (Aramco).

*Chapter Ten : Retirement*  259

Over the years, the Saudi Government acquired more and more of the Aramco assets. By 1976, it owned 100% of these assets. Aramco, the American Conglomerate, continued to operate and manage its former assets, including its concessionary interest in certain Saudi Arabian oil fields. In November 1988, a royal decree created a new company. The Saudi Arabian Oil Company, Saudi-Aramco, took over the management and operational control of all oil and gas fields from Aramco and its partners.

In the original documents granting the search for oil, words were included that would shape Saudi society for years. Article 23 of these documents said. . .

> *"The enterprise under this contract shall be directed and supervised by Americans who shall employ Saudi nationals as far as practicable, and in so far as the company can find suitable Saudi employees, it will not employ other nationals."*

From the beginning, the development of Aramco was directly tied to the betterment of Saudi Arabia.

Aramco began the first company school in Al-Khobar in May 1940. The following year the Jebel School opened in nearby Dhahran. Young native boys were hired into entry level positions. They went to classes from 7:00 am to 11:00 am. From noon until 4:00 pm they worked in the offices of Aramco. In 1950, Aramco built schools for 2,400 students in various locations. In 1959, the first group of Saudi students were sent to the States to attend college. By 1970, Aramco started hiring its first Saudi high school graduates and in 1979 began offering college scholarships nationwide.

I wish to tell you about Ali bin Ibrahim Al-Naimi, one of the early students. Born in 1935, he was the son of a pearl diver. At the age of four, he tended the family's flock of lambs. In 1944, at the age of nine, he and his older brother Abdullah, started attending the Jebel school. They studied English, Arabic, and basic arithmetic in the mornings. In the afternoons, both worked as office boys for Aramco. Utilizing various training programs provided by Aramco, he studied at the International College and American University in Beirut, Lebanon. In 1962, he earned his BS degree in geology from Lehigh U in PA. He then obtained his MS degree in hydrology and geology from Stanford. In the 1970's, he attended advanced management courses at Columbia and Harvard.

In 1983, Al-Naimi was the first Saudi to become president of Aramco while the company was controlled by the Americans. In 1988, he became the first CEO of Saudi Aramco. From 1995-2016 he served his King and country as Saudi Arabia's Minister of Petroleum and Mineral Resources. In his autobiography he shared the secret of his success. He wrote . . .

*"hard work, good fortune, and making the boss look good."*

Thanks to the leadership of Al-Naimi, Aramco began its College Preparatory Center (CPC) in 1985. This was a prerequisite to enter the College Degree Program for non-employees. It was highly selective! In June 2000, the last year I worked at CPC, over 5,000 young men took the required entrance exam in June. Only 220 to 230 students were chosen, to start the 10-month program in late August.

After finishing the program at CPC, students moved to universities abroad, either in the US, UK, Canada, China, Korea, Japan, or Australia. Upon acquiring their 4-year bachelor's degree, they were guaranteed a job with Saudi Aramco.

In 2006, six years after I left, CPC expanded its program to include women. For the 2006-07 academic year, CPC enrolled 251 males and 56 females. In 2013-2014, CPC selected 350 men and 82 women, from a pool of more than 20,000 students who took the entrance exam.

*CPC Main Classroom Building*  *Computer Labs and Faculty Offices*

I'd now like to focus on the programs at CPC, and what subjects I taught while in the Kingdom. This program did not offer any credit. It was intended to help native students become proficient in English. All instruction was in English, as were all the textbooks used. Most of the faculty, of about 30, came from English speaking countries, i.e. US, UK, Ireland, Canada, India, and Pakistan.

I taught physics, chemistry, and calculus classes. Each class was limited to 15 students. We used a separate building containing laboratories for chemistry and physics. These labs were managed by a staff of three men who provided a service far superior to that found at most colleges and universities in the USA. All I had to do was inform the director of the labs what experiment I wanted to run, the day, and starting time. When I went to the lab for a scheduled experiment, everything was set-up for my students. At the end of the lab, I did not have to clean-up or put anything away. The director and his two assistants did it all. If a piece of equipment broke, and could be fixed, they'd repair it. If not, they immediately made out a purchase order, faxed it to the Houston headquarters of Saudi Aramco, and within 4-6 weeks a new piece of equipment was in our laboratory.

Besides the courses I mentioned so far, students had computer courses and various English courses. These last included writing in English, speaking in English, and learning how to use the library for research. About 50% of our faculty taught English and speech courses. Each faculty member had his own office cubicle furnished with a desk, chair, computer, bookshelves, and one or two chairs for visiting students. During the summer, between teaching a class or two, we attended workshops on the use of the computer.

Throughout the next three years, I taught physics, chemistry, and calculus. In addition, I was given charge of the Science Club, which I will discuss in Chapter 12. In June 2000, at the end of the 1999-2000 academic year, I was given a new assignment. I no longer taught classes at CPC. Other than the tutoring job for the AT&T TV ad I mentioned earlier, this was the easiest task I ever had to earn my paycheck. I was assigned to the Testing Division of the Training Center at Saudi Aramco. Two other colleagues and myself, prepared exams for CPC in chemistry and physics. Our workday went like this . . .

> At 8:00 am, we met in a conference room, in which hot coffee and fresh pastries were always available. For a half hour, we'd discuss what area of chemistry or physics we were to deal with that day. Then from 9:00 am to noon, we'd go to our office and prepare three multiple choice questions on that topic.
>
> After our luncheon break, we'd meet again at 1:00 pm. For an hour or so we read, critiqued, modified, suggested changes, etc., to all the questions we had written that morning.
>
> From 2:00 pm to 4:00 pm we'd rewrite, change, or amend our three questions. When we ended the day at 4:30 pm, we left the final versions of our nine questions with the Director of the Testing Center. He'd use them in the final and mid-term exams he prepared for CPC over the next three years.

For the moment, this is all I want to say about my teaching activities at CPC. The rest of *MS* is about personal experiences while in Saudi Arabia.

...

When I landed in SA in the early morning of June 2, I carried the telescope I'd been given as a gift. It was confiscated by the authorities, when I went through customs. They thought I would use it to spy on the oil and military facilities. Six months later, when I returned to Chicago for the Christmas holidays, I brought it back. I gave it to Bobby as a gift and I believe he still has it. After passing through customs, I was met by a driver from Al-Falak, my employer in the Kingdom. He took me to an apartment building used by Al-Falak to house some of their employees.

## Chapter Ten: Retirement

We arrived around 2:00 am at my new quarters, a 2-bedroom, 2-bath apartment. I shared it with another man, also employed by Al-Falak. Each of us had our own bedroom and bathroom. We shared a dining room, parlor with sofas and a TV, a kitchen fully furnished with stove, refrigerator, sink, pots, pans, dishes, etc.

This building had five stories, a flight of stairs, and an elevator. The ground floor had only two apartments. One was a small unit occupied by Bahla, a Sri-Lanken. Al-Falak had hired him to be our in-house servant. More about him later. Floors 2 to 4 each had four apartments, each housing two employees. The 5th floor held utility and machinery rooms, and a small laundry with three washing machines. No dryers! We hung our laundry on lines setup on the roof, which also contained several plastic recliners. One could nap or catch a few rays, while doing his laundry. With the outside temperature around a 100 °F, clothes air dried in 2-3 hours.

Bahla was our security guard, as well as our servant. During the weekdays, when all of us left to go to our different jobs by 7:00 am, he would lock the entry doors to the building. This prevented any break-ins and robberies of our apartments. Every other day he would mop the elevator, stairs, and laundry room. He kept a schedule of once a week entering each apartment. There he would scrub and mop each bathroom, which contained a shower as well as a toilet, sink, and cabinets. Besides dusting, he'd vacuum the rugs in the parlor and dining room. He scrubbed the sink and mopped the floor in the kitchen. Doing dirty dishes was not part of his job!

However, there was one thing he did for us that was also not part of his job. In front of our building, 8-10 cars were parked overnight. They were provided by Al-Falak to transport us to work. During the night while we slept, the cars became covered by windswept sand particles. Bahla would rise an hour before the first car left for work. He'd fill a bucket with water and proceeded to give an exterior washing of all the cars. Since this was not one of his assigned tasks, we gave him a tip once a month. We were delighted to do this when we learned that he did not earn much money from Al-Falak. He hadn't visited his home in Sri Lanka in over 4 years. He'd send all his money back home to support his family and to pay for his daughter to attend a university.

As mentioned, it was early morning when I arrived at my apartment. I was exhausted from my long trip and quickly fell asleep. A few minutes before dawn, I was awakened. I heard the melodious chant of a muezzin (caller) singing out an adhan (summons to prayer) for the fajr (morning prayer before dawn) from a nearby mosque (place of worship). In the darkness of my room, and the night sky seen through a window, it took me several minutes to realize where I was, and what I was hearing!

*Al-Falak Headquarters*

In the morning, a driver from Al-Falak came for me. He drove me to company headquarters and my first day began. AL-Falak was founded in 1981 as a supplier of electronic equipment. It also provided manpower to service and install this equipment. In 1988, it received a contract from Saudi Aramco to provide trainers and educators for the oil company. I filled out all kinds of forms that first day.

I was taken next door to the Al-Franzi Bank. I opened my account and was introduced to, Abdullah, a Vice-President. He became my personal banker. Many a time he expedited my having to wait in long lines. We were never social, but he took great pleasure in handling my affairs. I think it was because he had a son, living in Indiana with his American wife. His 10-year-old boy was like me, a Cub fan. In case you are wondering, he also had a Saudi wife and children living in SA.

*Al-Franzi Bank*

# Chapter Ten: Retirement

After lunch I went through the ordeal of getting my driver's license. An interpreter from Al-Falak came with me and helped fill out all the paperwork in Arabic. As part of the process, I also had to have a sample of my blood drawn. I guess this was a requirement to provide a DNA data base. I didn't have to take a driving test. My IL driver's license was enough. Finally, my picture was taken, and I had my driver's license!

*Who is that handsome fellow? Yours Truly!*

On my second day in the Kingdom, a driver brought me out to the Saudi Aramco Training Center in Dhahran. He left me with the Director of Training for Saudi Aramco. I then proceeded down the staff pipeline, meeting various personnel. Eventually, I ended up at my ultimate destination, the CPC center. Here I met Daoud, the CPC Director, and his secretary, Mahfouz. Nine months later, in February 1998, I realized that all the administrators in the Training Center and CPC were *very happy* to have me as part of their teaching staff. After all, I had a PhD in physics! Only two other members of the 30 faculty at CPC had their PhD's. Both were in chemistry. One man, from Britain, taught chemistry and physics with me. The other man had a PhD in chemistry from Texas A&M. He was born in Pakistan and was a British citizen. Because of his knowledge and experience, he only taught computer science courses at CPC. I mentioned it took me nine months to become aware of this. I first realized it when I was selected to go to an educational meeting in the USA. The meeting was held for high schools that were teaching advanced placement courses and using modern technology, i.e. computers. It was held at Washington & Lee HS in Arlington, VA. I was selected because the Saudi's wanted to show that their oil profits were used on the best of instruction and training.

In mid-March 1998, a Saudi VP of Training and I flew business class from SA to Washington, DC on KLM Airlines. We first flew to Amsterdam, then on to DC. Since we flew business class, I ordered a couple of cocktails before dinner. I was delighted to see my cocktails served in Delft Blue miniature replicas of ancient Danish homes. I'd arranged for Mary and Zachary, my

5-year-old grandson, to join me in Arlington. We stayed at a nice hotel. My Saudi companion went to his home and American family. While I attended meetings at the 4-day seminar, Mary and Zach, did some sightseeing in DC. In the evenings, we had dinner together. When Mary saw the Delft Houses from KLM, she loved them and wanted more. I managed to get some additional ones on my return flight to the Kingdom. I still have these containers in a cabinet in my IL home!

I'd like to now mention other benefits that occurred during my Arabian adventure. Besides an annual salary in excess of $55,000, I was given free housing, access to a car for local transportation, and two round-trip airline tickets from SA to Chicago each year. One ticket I would use to take a 2-week holiday at Christmas time. The other, I'd use for my 3-week summer vacation in June or July.

Since I am writing this section during the Christmas season of 2018, I've recalled some of my holiday gifts during my time in Saudi Arabia . . .

✓ Christmas 1997. Following the biblical message of Matthew 2:11, gold, frankincense, and myrrh were among the gifts to Jesus by the magi. Of course, that's what I brought back when I flew home, i.e., gold earrings, bracelets, chains, and medallions.

Frankincense, an incense, was easy to find along with specially designed censers. Myrrh was a real problem. I couldn't discover any myrrh products in the stores or malls of Al-Khobar or Dammam. However, in Abquaiq's souq (marketplace), I found some myrrh resin chips. These had to do! I brought a few home and gave them to whom, I know not.

✓ Christmas 1998. This was the year of the *silk blouses*. In an Al-Khobar mall, I found a store selling women's clothing. It featured some beautiful silk blouses imported from China. Mary got all the sizes for me. So, the *ladies* in my extended family received a silk blouse. Depending on size, coloring, and manufacturer, I paid $20 to $30 for each one. My good friend Jan, the one with the inquiring mind, found out that similar blouses were selling at Marshall Fields's in Chicago for $100-$120!

# Chapter Ten: Retirement

✓ Christmas 1999. This was the year of the Irish Christmas. A colleague at CPC was from Ireland. He connected me with a knitting mill in Ireland. Again, Mary helped in getting correct sizes. So, from SA, I ordered and paid online for sweaters, scarfs, mittens, etc. all knitted in Ireland. The company shipped everything to our condo in Ford City. Mary and Jo, our neighbor from across the hall, wrapped all the gifts. When I came home for Christmas, Mary showed me a nice, *green plaid throw* that she'd draped across our sofa. She told me that it had come, with all my gifts from Ireland, in a separate box. When she opened it, there was a note from the owner of the knitting mill. He said he wanted to send this gift to thank us for our large, generous order. Mary always kept that blanket on the sofa and wrapped herself in it as she watched TV or took a nap!

*Cozy!*

✓ Christmas 2000. I don't recall what I ordered, if anything. I was busy planning and arranging the end of my Arabian adventure.

Earlier, I mentioned my salary and my personal banker Abdullah at the Al-Franzi Bank. I need to tell you more. Since I worked overseas for nine months of the year, I was classified as an expatriate. At that time, IRS allowed an expatriate to earn a maximum of $85,000 a year, tax free. On filing my tax returns, I reported this on a special form. I had to include additional financial benefits, such as housing, meals, automobile, airline tickets, etc. All my benefits never exceeded that $85,000 limit. So, everything I earned in SA was tax free in the US. In addition, SA did not have any tax, no income tax, no sales tax. Every penny I ever earned in these 3½ years was totally ***tax free***!

While in SA, I was generating a lot of income. In the US, my retirement benefits paid everything for Mary, all her living expenses and then some. She had money to increase her bingo activity to four times a week. She and Jo took 4-5 trips to Las Vegas and 2-3 trips to Biloxi, MS. They visited the casinos there to try their luck at the slots and Keno. I may be mistaken, but they never bothered with blackjack, poker, roulette, or craps.

After talking to Abdullah, he introduced me to a man who visited the Kingdom once a month. This man was from Britain and stayed only 4-5 days in SA. He was a financial advisor and was there to assist anyone looking to invest money. With his assistance, I opened a savings account in a bank on the Isle of Man. Later, this bank merged with another bank on the island of Guernsey. Both islands are among several referred to as the Channel Islands. Though under the protection of Great Britain, their banking laws were a little more liberal and flexible than those in the UK and US.

In the 3½ years I spent in SA, I met many men who were earning lots of money. Some used their earnings to fulfill a dream. In my first year, I recall meeting a man from CA. For four years he used his earnings to buy a 50-foot sailboat and equip it with every modern electronic gadget available. In our first meeting, he showed me pictures of his boat which was totally paid for and had no debt. It was waiting for him at a marina in Oakland. His dream was to sail around the world. He told me this was his 5th and last year in the Kingdom. He was using his current income to setup bank accounts in San Francisco, Honolulu, Sydney, Hong-Kong, Singapore, Cape Town, Rio de Janeiro, etc. When he sailed into any one of these ports, he could visit his bank, and obtain local funds for his expenses.

I also met men who lost their earnings by gambling it away in poker games. Others wasted their fortunes in frequent trips across the causeway to Bahrain. There they could spend their money on liquor and women in the brothels.

When I left SA in late December 2000, I had almost $50,000 sitting in a bank on the island of Guernsey. As you read the rest of **MS**, you will learn how I used these funds. I kept everything *legal* by reporting this on my annual filings to the IRS. I only paid taxes on the interest earned each year by this investment in Guernsey.

Besides my financial savings during these years in Arabia, Mary and I had several wonderful trips. You will read about these in the next chapter. There is more I wish to tell you about my Arabian adventure, but I will do so in Chapter 12.

# Chapter Eleven

## Phenomenal Travels

••••••••••••

As mentioned in the last chapter, I was making $55000 in Saudi Arabia. I also received two round trip tickets a year from SA to Chicago as part of my contract. I often arranged my trips for me and Mary to enjoy some outstanding excursions!

In the summer of 1998, I took my vacation home by going the long way to Chicago. I flew from Saudi Arabia → London → Los Angles. In the meantime, Mary and Christine flew from Chicago → LA. We stayed with my cousin, Gerry, in Burbank. Aunt Jimmie, my father's sister, was 98 and living with him. Christine enjoyed talking with her and queried her on the Krupp family history. Our timing was most fortunate because Aunt Jimmie died the following year.

Since we were so close, Mary, Christine, and I just had to stop in Las Vegas on our way home to Chicago. Chris's friend Donny flew in from Chicago to meet us in Vegas. We all stayed at the Luxor Hotel. Mary and Christine shared a room, as did Donny and I, in that glass pyramid.

*The Luxor Hotel in Las Vegas!*

# My Marvelous Memories

If you've never stayed in the Luxor, be prepared for a surprise! Our rooms were on the 12th floor. We entered a cubicle that looked like an elevator. I pushed the button, the doors closed, and it started to move. We did not ascend vertically as in an elevator. We went up the slope of the pyramid, riding in an *inclinator*.

Since I was not a gambler, I often went to bed early. One night I was aroused from my slumber. It was 3:00 am and Donny was shaking me awake. Once I was up, Donny sat on his bed. He was trembling and kept saying, "Bob, what am I going to do?" I asked him what was wrong. He held up a fist full of bills and said, "I just won this at the craps table!" I asked him how much. He counted it and said, "$2800." I asked him how much money he had brought with him to gamble. He replied, "$500." This is what we then did.

- ✓ After I got dressed, we went down to the lobby. I got a free safe deposit box at the check-in counter.

- ✓ I gave Donny $500 and said, "Gamble as much as you want, but do not ask me for more!" I put $2300 in the safe deposit box, locked it, and kept the key.

- ✓ Two days later, the four of us flew home to Chicago. After we claimed our luggage, I called Donny aside and gave him $2300!

While in Vegas, we wanted to go for dinner at a special restaurant in the MGM Grand Hotel. It was Emeril Lagasse's Las Vegas Restaurant. All of us had watched his programs on TV. We went to the restaurant early, about 3:30 pm. We were surprised to find out we couldn't get a table. The Maître D' informed us that reservations were full until closing. We would have had to book a year in advance to get a table in the dining room. Instead, we sat at their lounge/pub and tasted some of Emeril's gastronomical delights with our cocktails.

## Chapter Eleven: Phenomenal Travels

One final recollection from this trip. The Luxor Hotel had spas, for men and women, where various services were available. It was early June, and my birthday had fallen a few days earlier. Christine arranged for me to have a Swedish Massage as her birthday present. So, one afternoon I went to the spa. Its facilities were far superior to the bathhouse I went to as a child! After my massage, the masseur said, "Pardon me, sir! You are a man with a big body. Next time you have a massage, arrange for an hour, instead of a ½ hour. I didn't have enough time to finish you!"

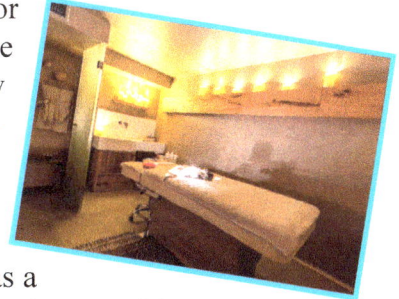

Two fantastic trips now follow. During both journeys, Mary and I *did not* travel with a group of 10 to 30 tourists. We always had our own private tour guide and traveled by car with a chauffeur.

On March 22, 1999, Mary and I began an outstanding trip through the Middle East. That afternoon, I was driven in a hired car across the causeway to Manama, Bahrain. This was about a 40-mile drive. I checked into a hotel and waited for Mary to arrive. She landed about 11:00 pm, from London. I was waiting for her at the airport.

Because so much occurred over the next two weeks, I am going to relate what happened briefly as follows.

## My Marvelous Memories

### Tuesday, March 23rd...

- we had breakfast at our hotel.
- went sightseeing in Bahrain.
- visited gold shops, perfume shops, and the souq (marketplace).
- had a middle-Eastern dinner at a Lebanese restaurant.
- used no tour guides in Bahrain.

Manama Souq, 1965

### Wednesday, March 24th...

- We flew to Amman, Jordan in the morning. Went sightseeing in this capital city using a car, driver, and guide.

Ammman, Jordan

# Chapter Eleven: Phenomenal Travels

## Thursday, March 25th...

- We toured the eastern desert of Jordan.
- saw Roman and Byzantine sites.
- visited castles and churches dating back to 3rd century AD.
- used a car, driver, and a guide to accomplish this.

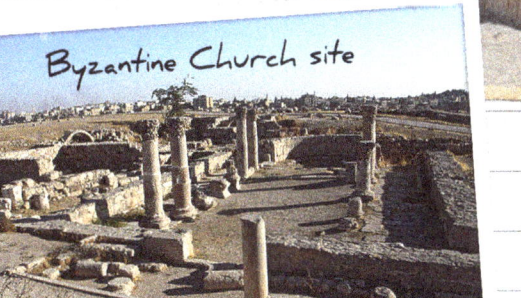

*Ajloun Castle in Eastern Desert of Jordan*

*Byzantine Church site*

*Ruins of the Roman city Jerash - only about 18 miles from Amman.*

### Friday, March 26th...

- We drove south to the Dead Sea, to Madaba, the City of Mosaics, to Kerak and its crusader castle, to At-Tafilah site of a major victory in the 1918 Arab revolt against Turkey, to Showbak, to visit another crusader castle.

- we stopped overnight at the Movenpik Hotel near Petra and had an outstanding dinner at the hotel.

### Saturday, March 27...

We spent the day visiting the Rose City of Petra, a famous archaeological site. This was the Nabatean capitol which dated back to 300 B.C. We spent the day in that narrow valley visiting the tombs, temples, and monuments carved into the pink sandstone cliffs. About 4:00 pm, we returned through the Siq, a narrow crack in the mountains. This was the entry/exit into Petra. We met our guide and chauffer. After a light supper, we drove 120 miles back to our hotel in Amman, along the desert highway. We needed to get back and rest for our big day on Sunday!

# Chapter Eleven: Phenomenal Travels

Ammman, Jordan is now a modern city but not far away is the ancient city of Petra.

The Siq, entrance to Petra

Modern Amman

The Treasury of Petra. It may have been a temple or library for documents.

The Treasury is huge and made famous in the Indiana Jones movie!

The Monestary is bigger than the Treasury!

The Corinthian Tombs

Caves of Petra

### Sunday, March 28th...

-Later, I will explain how I managed to arrange what we did on this Sunday. It was Palm Sunday for Christians. For Muslims, it was the main day of the Hajj, a pilgrimage to the Kaaba in the holy city of Mecca, SA.

Mary and I left about 6:00 am on a bus that took us to the Allenby Bridge crossing the Jordan River into Israel. The ride on the bus took an hour. It took over 2 hours to pass through Jordanian and Israeli passport and customs. Mary had her passport stamped at both centers, I did not. If I had, I wouldn't have been allowed into Saudi Arabia to return to work.

*Allenby Bridge*

*Garden of Gethsemane*

Finally, we were in Israel and met our driver, car, and guide. We drove to Gethsemane and managed to attend Mass at the Dominus Flevit Catholic Church near the olive gardens. After Mass, we toured the gardens and saw some trees that were nearly 1,500 years old.

## Chapter Eleven: Phenomenal Travels

From an overlook, our guide showed us the walls of Jerusalem and the Dung Gate through which we entered the old city. Through narrow cobblestone streets, our guide, Mary, and I climbed the hill to Calvary. We spent over an hour visiting the Church of the Holy Sepulchre. After exiting through the New Gate, we met our car and driver. Off we went to Bethlehem.

*Dung Gate in Jerusalem*

*Church of the Holy Sepulchre*

Only eight miles away was the Church of the Nativity. Because Bethlehem was a Palestinian town, it took us over 30 minutes to negotiate several Israeli roadblocks and checkpoints. It was March and not December, so the line into the church was short. We toured the church and grotto in ½ hour. Mary and I were tired, exhausted, and hungry. We stopped for a nice lunch at a Palestinian restaurant. An hour later we were refreshed and ready for the rest of our tour. We left the restaurant and within a block or two, we drove past the main entrance to Bethlehem University. There was no time in our schedule to stop and visit friends I knew there.

*Church of the Nativity*

# My Marvelous Memories

## Sunday, March 28th...

-We drove over to Bethpage, not far from the Mt. of Olives, where we had started our visit that morning. While we sat at an outdoor café drinking coffee and juice, we watched thousands of pilgrims pass by. It was the annual Procession of Palms. The walk starts at the Franciscan Church in Bethpage and ends at the walls of Jerusalem. Though the distance of the walk is only a little more than a mile, it takes about three hours to walk in this procession. Pilgrims from all over the world came to participate. We heard hymns and chants in various languages. Groups passed by reciting the rosary. Other groups would pass while a priest or cleric prayed the stations of the cross. Our guide suggested that Mary and I join the procession. We did and walked about ½-mile with the pilgrims.

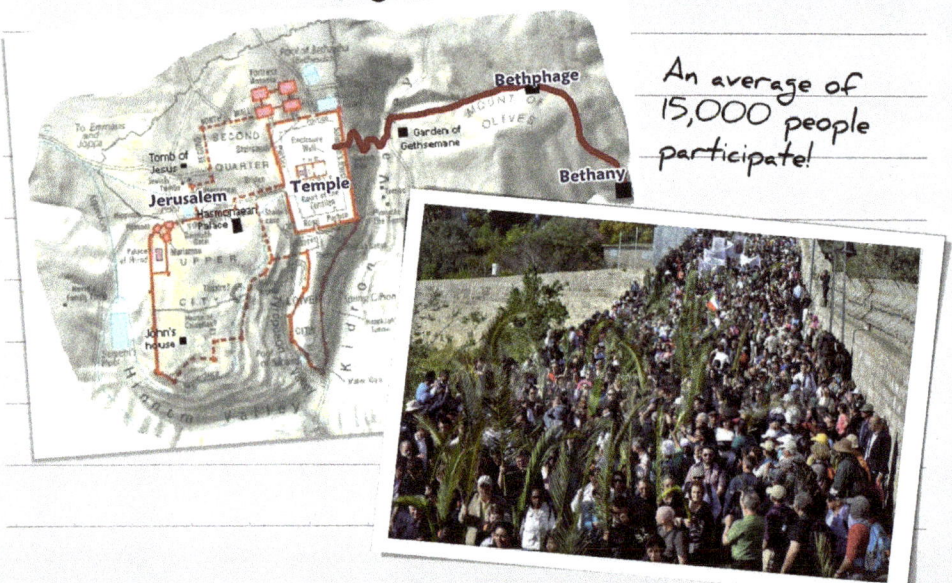

An average of 15,000 people participate!

# Chapter Eleven: Phenomenal Travels

Our car, driver, and guide were waiting for us at a designated location. We then drove a short distance and parked along the roadside. Our guide pointed out to us that across the road was the tomb of Lazarus. He'd hoped to have us make a short stop and visit at this site, but there was not enough time.

We drove to Jericho, near the Allenby Bridge, where later we would cross over to return to Jordan. However, we first stopped for supper. After that we had time for a short drive out of Jericho. Our guide showed us an archaeological dig where scientists were looking for artifacts from ancient times. We looked down into a shaft, about 30 to 40 feet deep. At the bottom were some stone slabs of rock believed to be the foundation stones for the ancient walls of Jericho which 'came tumbling down.'

*Walls of Jericho*

We drove a few miles into the desert, below some tall mountain bluffs. At the top was an ancient monastery our guide had planned for us to visit.

*Mountain Monastery*

However, we didn't have enough time to ascend the serpentine road leading to this monastery. Our guide told us that this was the location where Jesus was tempted by Satan after His 40-days and nights of fasting.

## Sunday, March 28th...

Just before parting, our guide told us that we were only two miles from the place on the Jordan River where Jesus had been baptized by John the Baptist. Since there was no convenient road there, we were not able to drive to that location on our tour. We would have had to walk there and back.

Finally, we arrived at the Israeli Passport and Customs Center. The process of leaving Israel and returning to Jordan went much faster than it had in the morning. We boarded the bus for the ride to our hotel in Amman. We arrived back around 10:30 pm. During the hour drive back, I slept most of the time!

I mentioned earlier on how I had arranged this one day trip to Israel. My Filipino travel agent and I planned and made all the tour arrangements in Al-Khobar. When I asked about a day or two in Israel, he told me he was not permitted to make those arrangements. Instead, he gave me the telephone number of an agent in Amman, Jordan. When we were in Jordan, I called her. She came to our hotel, spoke to us, learned of our planned schedule, and then arranged for this one day visit. Both agents warned me not to spend an overnight in Israel or to have my passport stamped by Israeli customs officials. If I did not heed their warning, I wouldn't have been allowed back into Saudi Arabia. In fact, I might even have been arrested as a CIA or Mossad spy!

## Chapter Eleven: Phenomenal Travels 281

### Monday, March 29th...

After a late breakfast, we drove about 30 miles north to visit Ajloun. Here we saw the Arabic Castle built in 1184 to defend against the Crusaders. It stands on the site of a monastery built around 550 AD. From this height we had a glimpse of the Sea of Galilee in Israel.

*Ajloun Castle*

*Sea of Galilee*

We returned to Amman and spent the afternoon visiting more sites in the city. We had dinner in our hotel and went to bed early. Tuesday was going to be a busy day!

### Tuesday, March 30th...

Following an early breakfast, we went to the airport in Amman. It was only a short 315-mile flight to Cairo. After passing through customs, our guide met us and assisted us quickly to the domestic terminal. We made it in time to catch our plane to Aswan, only a 425-mile flight. We landed about noon and were met by our guide for the next four days. She'd come down to Aswan from Cairo by train while we flew in.

*Cairo and Pyramids from the airplane! What a view!*

*My Marvelous Memories*

After lunch, our guide escorted us to our living quarters for the next four nights. It was our stateroom onboard a boat for our Nile River Cruise. We didn't have time to go for a visit to Abu Simbel. Instead, we drove across the Aswan Low Dam, built by the British in 1899.

Aswan High Dam

Next, we drove to the new Aswan High Dam, completed in 1970. This dam was built by Egyptian engineers with assistance from Russia. We walked out on the dam's surface and looked out at the Nile River flowing northwards, and Lake Nasser to the south.

Before leaving, we viewed a memorial monument commemorating Arab-Soviet Friendship. In this monument, the coat of arms of the Soviet Union is on the left and the coat of arms of Egypt is on the right.

At 4:00 pm, we returned to the docks near our boat and boarded a felucca. This is a traditional wooden sailing boat used on the Nile in Egypt and the Sudan.

Stunning Views from our felucca!

# Chapter Eleven: Phenomenal Travels

We spent two hours sailing among the islands near Aswan. We didn't visit, but viewed from our boat, the Mausoleum of Aga Kahn and the Monastery of St. Simone. We sailed close to the shore of Elephantine island on which several archaeological sites are located. A quarry on this island provided the pink limestone for Aga Khan's Mausoleum. In this region, on the west bank of the Nile, several quarries provided red, gray, and black granite slabs for ancient Egyptian monuments.

Among these are...

- Cleopatra's Needle, now in London.

- The Unfinished Obelisk, the largest obelisk ever discovered, still on site at a quarry.

- Several of the sarcophagi used in the burial chambers for Pharaohs of the 3rd and 4th Dynasties.

- Other structures that are found in the pyramids of Khufu, Khafre, and Giza.

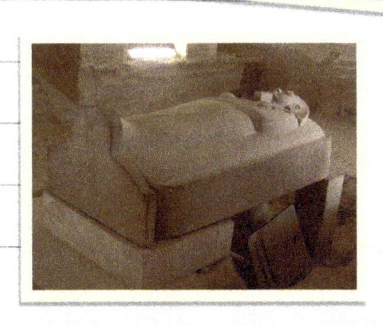

*My Marvelous Memories*

Date. _____ page. _____

We returned to our boat just before 7:00 pm when dinner was served. Afterwards, we sat on the deck and enjoyed the cool night air. We went to bed around 11:00 pm and, while we slept, our boat started its cruise down the Nile.

Wednesday, March 31st . . .

By early morning, the boat had sailed about 30 miles north and was now docked at Kom Ombo. It was only a short ¼ mile walk from the boat dock to the temple. We spent about two hours at the Kom Ombo temple and returned to our boat. While we had lunch, our boat started cruising again. Afterwards, we sat in the shade of a canopy and watched the sights flowing by. The afternoon temperature was about 85 °F.

Kom Ombo Temple

Chapter Eleven : Phenomenal Travels    285

Locks on the Nile

Date Palms along the farms on the Nile

By 4:00 pm we were docked in Edfu. The Temple of Horus is over 3/4 miles from the dock. Our guide arranged for a horse cab for a ride to and from the Temple.

We spent over two hours visiting the temple and returned to our boat for our 7:00 pm supper. That night, local musicians came onboard and entertained us with native melodies and songs.

Then          and Now

## Thursday, April 1st...

We awoke this morning docked at Esna. In less than a ¼-mile walk, we were at the Temple of Khnum for a 2-hour visit. Back for lunch on the boat as it continued to cruise northward.

*The Temple at Esna*

*A king offers wine jugs to Amun-Min*

After a cruise of 35 miles north, we were docked in Luxor on the eastern shore. After a very short walk we were at the Temple of Karnak. We returned to our boat for the 7:00 pm dinner. An enjoyable evening was spent on deck in the cool of the night. To bed by 10:30 pm.

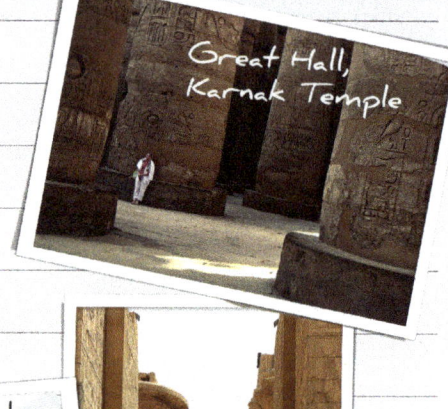

*Great Hall, Karnak Temple*

*The Temple of Karnak*

# Chapter Eleven: Phenomenal Travels

**Friday, April 2nd . . .**

Breakfast was our last meal on board the boat. We were expected to be out of our stateroom by 11:00 am. However, our packed bags were left in a storage area for pickup later.

Around 10:00 am, we went ashore where a car waited for Mary, me, and our guide. We now began our trip to the Valley of Kings. Though only four miles, as the crow flies, from our boat, it was a longer trip. The Valley of the Kings was on the west bank of the river. Luxor, the boat and dock were on the east side. Six miles to the south was a bridge across the Nile. It took 3 miles to cross the river and reach a north-south roadway on the western banks. Six miles to the north, we were at the dusty trails that led into the Valley of the Kings.

The Valley of the Kings

As we drove north on the westbank, we had a surrealistic experience. Walking on the right shoulder of the roadway, heading north as we were, was a donkey. Riding sideways on the donkey was a man dressed in a jalabiya or galabeya, the traditional Egyptian garment native to the Nile Valley. On the back of the donkey was a mound of fresh, leafy green vegetables, much like palm leaves. I thought we had been transported back 2000 years and were watching Jesus riding towards Jerusalem on Palm Sunday. Our guide told us he was just a farmer, taking his produce into the town's souk (market) for sale.

Musicians wearing jalabiyas

heading to the market

After the trip north, we turned west and drove another 3-4 miles along dusty trails. We arrived at the Valley of the Kings. However, before entering the valley, we stopped at the Mortuary Temple of Hatshepsut. She was the second confirmed female Pharaoh. This temple is over 3,400 years old. A relief sculpture within the temple tells the tale of the divine birth of a female pharaoh, the first of its kind.

Chapter Eleven: Phenomenal Travels    289

*The Temple of Hatshepsut*

*Inside the Temple*

On November 17, 1997, 16 months before we visited Hatshepsut's Temple, 70 tourists had been killed by Islamic militants. I'm not sure if this was the reason Mary did not join me and our guide. It also could have been the intense heat and long walk we had to take to get to the temple. In any case, Mary stayed in a small, air-conditioned café near the parking lot. Our guide and I toured the temple. Upon our return, we drove another dusty mile into the valley.

Most of our time was spent visiting the Tomb of Ramesses III, also known as Bruce's Tomb or Harper's Tomb. It is the largest tomb in the valley open to the public and is located near a central rest area. Because of this and its superb decorations, it is the one most visited by tourists.

We visited the tomb of Tutankhamun, King Tut, the Boy King. He died at the age of 18 or 19 and had reigned as King for only 9 years. To enter his tomb, one descended a ladder through a 3' by 3' opening. Mary refused to go down the ladder and stayed with our guide. I went down and spent about ½ hour looking around. Later, I described to Mary what I'd seen. I mentioned that I saw King Tut's mummy, still in his tomb. She shuddered and said, "Thank God, I didn't go down there!"

King Tut's Tomb

After this, we drove back to our boat in Luxor, got our bags, and stopped at a restaurant for a light supper. Then we all went out to the airport. Our guide saw that we got on our flight to Cairo, and we parted. She returned to Cairo by train.

We landed in Cairo and were met by a guide who drove us to the Sheraton on Gezira Island. The Island was in the in the middle of the Nile and downtown Cairo. After freshening up, we went for dinner to one of the hotel's restaurants. We sat outside, on a deck, right along the Nile. If I'd dropped my fork, it would have landed in the river.

# Chapter Eleven: Phenomenal Travels

We returned to our rooms and gazed down at a unique and lovely spectacle. It was still part of the Eid al-Adha holiday season and Friday night. Eid al-Adha is an Islamic festival celebrated by Muslims all over the world! We sat outside on our balcony and gazed at an amazing scene. The Nile was covered with hundreds of party boats. All the boats were covered with colored lights. Each boat was built to accommodate 50-75 passengers. Families with children boarded them. Throughout the night, the boats circled Gezira Island while the people sang traditional songs. They also feasted on food they'd brought on board. We enjoyed watching and listening to this festival.

Mary and I went to bed around midnight. I awoke about 3:00 am and still heard singing, though not as loud as earlier!

Boats on the Nile decorated with colorful lights!

### Saturday, April 3rd . . .

I'm not sure if it was a touch of food poisoning, or heat exhaustion from the previous day, but Mary didn't accompany me this day. My guide took me out to the desert, five miles west of the Nile. We were about nine miles southwest of Cairo's center. We went to the old river town of Giza to visit the pyramids and the Great Sphinx.

These and other pyramids were constructed to house the remains of deceased Pharaohs who had ruled ancient Egypt. At that time, people believed a part of the spirit remained with a corpse. A Pharaoh's remaining spirit assumed new duties as King of the Dead. A pyramid not only served as a tomb but also as a storage chamber for various items the Pharaoh needed for his afterlife.

The Great Sphinx of Giza is the oldest monumental sculpture in Egypt. It is a limestone statue with the body of a lion and the head of a human. Its face is believed to represent Pharaoh Khafre since it was built during his reign, 2558-2532 BC.

## Chapter Eleven: Phenomenal Travels

### Sunday, April 4th . . .

Mary and I had an early breakfast at the hotel. We were ready for the last day of touring Cairo, as well as our 2-week trip.

Cairo, the capitol of Egypt, is the largest city in the Middle East. It has long been the center of this regions' political and cultural life. It was nicknamed the city of 1000 minarets because of the preponderance of Islamic architecture.

Leaving our island hotel, we drove west across a bridge to the mainland. Within a few blocks, we stopped and walked around Tahrir Square. It is the center of the city and is surrounded by government buildings. The Egyptian Museum, which we visited later in the afternoon, is located there.

We drove about three miles south to visit Old Cairo. It contains remnants of ancient capitals of Egypt. We drove by but did not stop at the . . .

- Mosque of Amr, the Coptic Museum, and several Coptic Churches.

- Old Roman Catholic Cemetery.

- Ben Ezra Synagogue where baby Moses was brought after being discovered along the Nile.

*My Marvelous Memories*

Mosque of Ibn Tulun

Date.   page.

Fort Babylon

Amr Ibn al Aas Mosque

We stopped for short visits at Ft. Babylon, an old Roman fortress, and the Mosque of ibn Tulun, the oldest mosque in the city, surviving in its original form.

After lunch we returned to the Egyptian Museum and spent over 4½-hours wandering through its halls and galleries, until it closed at 5:00 pm. If you plan to visit this Museum someday, I urge you to set aside two full days, if you can, to tour this amazing Museum. It has the world's largest collection of ancient Egyptian artifacts, including the famous Tutankhamun collection. Mary and I spent more than half our time in viewing these treasures on display. We saw King Tut's beautiful gold death mask and much, much more!

# Chapter Eleven: Phenomenal Travels    295

The Egyptian Museum

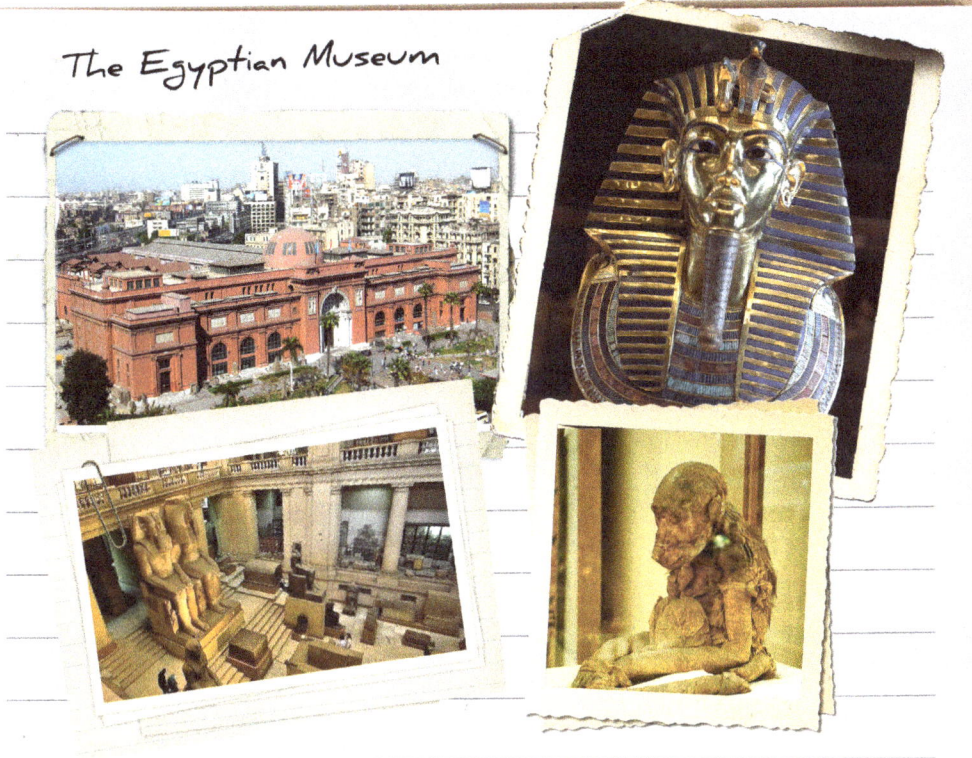

We returned to our hotel. Since we'd enjoyed our previous dinners there, we decided to again dine along the Nile. Towards the end of our meal, we noticed several patrons smoking a hookah, a water pipe invented in Persia around 500 years ago. The night before, we'd seen several men smoking a hookah, but no ladies. Mary said she would like to try a hookah sometime but did not know if ladies could smoke one in public. This Sunday evening, we saw one lady smoking a hookah. I encouraged her to order one and try it. She was too embarrassed and reluctant to do so. I ordered one for myself, took a few puffs, and shared our special dessert with her. Mary thought it was OK, but the scents were too flowery for her! This hookah was burning dried flower petals and not cannabis, or marijuana!

Monday, April 5...

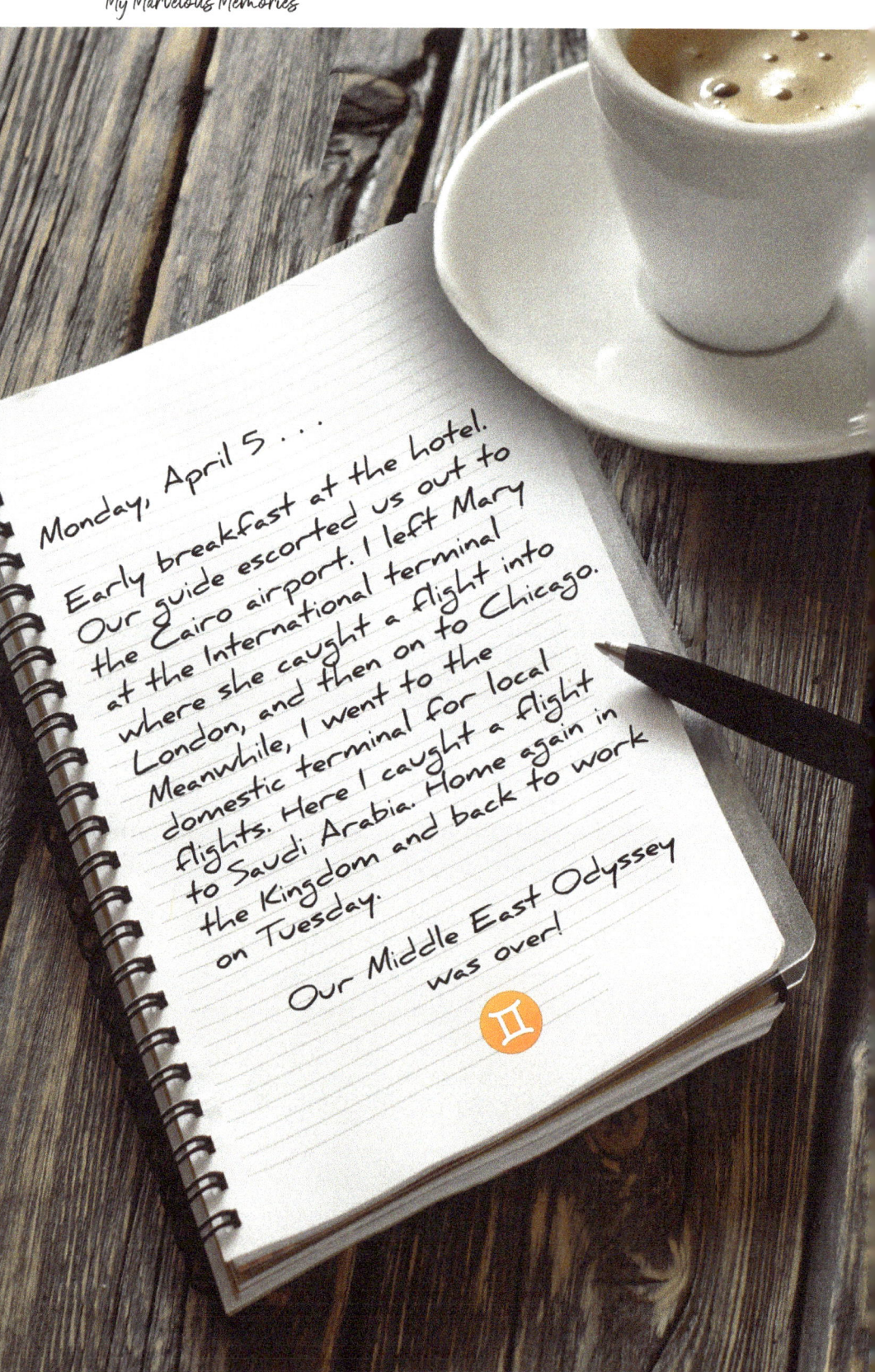

Early breakfast at the hotel. Our guide escorted us out to the Cairo airport. I left Mary at the International terminal where she caught a flight into London, and then on to Chicago. Meanwhile, I went to the domestic terminal for local flights. Here I caught a flight to Saudi Arabia. Home again in the Kingdom and back to work on Tuesday.

Our Middle East Odyssey was over!

# Chapter Eleven: Phenomenal Travels    297

Another wonderful trip happened in July 2000.

## Thursday, July 6 . . .

I flew from Arabia to London and boarded a flight to Dublin, Ireland. In the meantime, Mary, Colleen, Christine, and Zachary flew from Chicago to Dublin. We met at the airport and took a cab to our hotel in the city. We stayed here for the next four nights. This small hotel was near St. Stephen's Circle in downtown Dublin.

## Friday, July 7 . . .

After a full Irish Breakfast at our hotel, we boarded a tour bus for a 3½-hour drive through Dublin. Our tickets permitted us to ride, get off, re-board, and continue riding in this fashion for 24 hours.

So, we all rode back to visit Trinity College. It was founded in 1592 and is the most prestigious university in Ireland. It is modeled after the collegiate universities of Oxford and Cambridge. However, unlike these two ancient universities only one college was ever established. Hence, Trinity College and the University of Dublin are one and the same.

We got off the bus and walked about the campus. We visited the Old Library and its Long Room. We gazed in wonder at pages on display from the Book of Kells, the Book of Durrow, the Book of Howth, and other ancient handwritten texts.

Old Library at Trinity College

Trinity College is home for The Book of Kells.

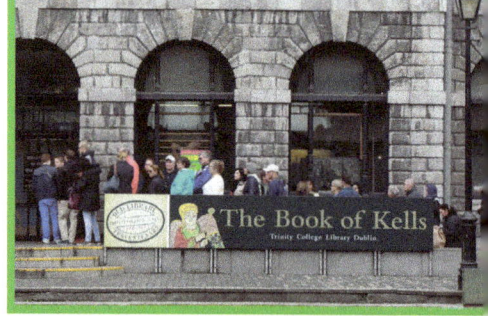

*Chapter Eleven : Phenomenal Travels*  299

After a 3½-hour visit at Trinity College, we were exhausted and hungry. We stopped for lunch, got back on the bus, and returned to our hotel. Mary, Zachary, and I went in for a short nap. Colleen and Christine, always full of spirit and energy, stayed on the bus. They rode back to the Guinness Brewery and took their tour. Afterwards, they spent several hours in the Guinness Pub sampling the many ales, porters, and stouts produced there. They also chatted up a few of the local lads. They returned around 9:00 pm in gay spirits!

During our bus tour on this first day, we drove past Áras an Uachtaráin, the White House of Ireland. In 2000, President Mary McAleese was in the 3rd year of her first term. We did not stop and go in for a tour. However, our guide called our attention to a 2nd floor window, directly above the main entrance. We saw a candle burning there. Our guide informed us that Mary McAleese had started the practice of having a lit candle, 24/7, 365 days a year placed in that window. It was a symbol to Irish people worldwide. If one's parents, grandparents, or great-grandparents were Irish and had emigrated, for whatever reason, the candle was lit to guide them back. It was meant to say, "Welcome home!"

*My Marvelous Memories*

Áras an Uachtaráin

The Obama's visit

*In Dublin's fair city,
Where the girls
are so pretty,*

*I first set my eyes
on sweet Molly Malone,*

*As she wheeled her wheelbarrow,
Through streets broad and narrow,"
Crying,
"Cockles and mussels,
Alive, alive, oh,
Alive, alive, oh,
Alive, alive, oh!"*

*Crying,
"Cockles and mussels,
Alive, alive, oh,
Alive, alive, oh!"*

Saturday and Sunday, July 8 & 9 . . .

Over the next two days we did a lot of walking. Many of these sites were near our hotel. I am not sure on which days we might have gone to these locations. Among those I recall, all of which were less than a mile from our hotel, we visited . . .

# Chapter Eleven: Phenomenal Travels

O'Connel Monument, site of 1916 Easter Rising

Ha'Penny Bridge

St. Stephen's Green Shopping!

Oscar Wilde Merrion Sq. House

National Gallery of Ireland

Fitzwilliam Square

Homes at Fitzwilliam Square

Christ Church Cathedral

St. Patrick's Cathedral

Inside St. Patrick's Cathedral

## My Marvelous Memories

Monday, July 10 . . .

This morning we spent time sightseeing. In the afternoon, everyone but me, went for a final shopping trip. I took a bus out to the airport to get a rental car for the next eight days. I came home, and we had our last supper in Dublin, at a nearby restaurant.

Tuesday, July 11 . . .

After breakfast, we drove north heading for Dundalk, only 55 miles away. Mary's paternal grandfather had been born in this city. However, we had no plans to stay there. An Irish colleague in Saudia Arabia had helped plan this trip. He told me that Dundalk is an industrial city with many factories. There would be little to see and enjoy in it. He suggested we go to Carlingford, only 10 miles east of Dundalk. It was a lovely, little fishing village on the south shore of the Carlingford Lough. A lough is a sea inlet, like a loch in Scotland or a fjord in Norway.

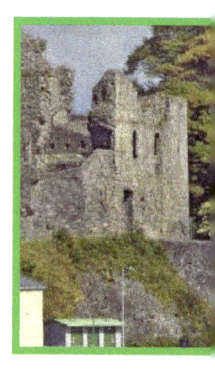

On the way north to Dundalk, we made an important sightseeing stop. It was Newgrange, the site of Neolithic Monuments. Here we saw tombs that had been built around 3200 BC. These monuments are older than Stonehenge (3000-2200 BC) or the Egyptian Pyramids (2630-2610 BC).

*Chapter Eleven : Phenomenal Travels*    303

This site consists of a large circular mound, with inner stone passageways and chambers for tombs. Many of the larger stones at Newgrange are covered in megalithic art. These artworks are carvings and drawings on large stones found in prehistoric Europe.

After 2-3 hours visiting Newgrange, we stopped for lunch and continued driving to Dundalk. It was only 25 miles to the north. We got there around 3:30 pm. Mary did not know where her grandfather's home had been, so we just drove the main road through town. As mentioned earlier, there was little to visit or see. I think we were in and out of Dundalk in 30-40 minutes.

We arrived at a lovely little hotel in Carlingford about 6:30 pm. It was right near the waterfront. I don't remember its name, but today it is called the Ghan House. We had dinner in the hotel and then got ready for bed.

GHAN HOUSE
CARLINGFORD

*My Marvelous Memories*

Carlingford is on the south shore of the Lough. Across the inlet on the north shore was Mt. Mourne in Northern Ireland (NI). A border crossing into NI was only five miles away. I was planning a 1-day trip into NI on the following day, July 12th. After entering NI, we were going to drive around the mountain, stopping in Rathfriland for lunch, and continue our drive back to our hotel. However, 16 miles to the north, the NI Orange Order was holding their annual march in Portadown. I wondered if we would be safe, even though we were not close to Portadown.

Colleen and Christine, as they often did, went at night to the hotel's pub for a wee draught. During this time, they of course chatted with a few of the lads. I asked them to speak to some of the local folk to see if our 1-day trip would be safe.

Wednesday, July 12 . . .

At breakfast, Colleen and Christine told us what they'd learned the night before. We were advised not to make the trip! So, instead we stayed in Carlingford and did a lot of local sightseeing. Though it was a cold, blustery day, we walked around town and visited . . .

King John's Castle — built from 1186-1190

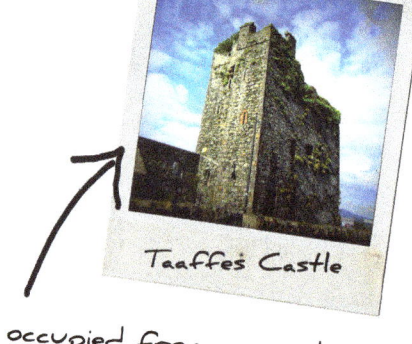

Taaffes Castle — occupied from around 1196 by one of the leading families of Ireland that had moved there from Wales.

# Chapter Eleven: Phenomenal Travels

*The Tholsel Gate*

ancient town gate, which is the only remaining example of its nature in Carlingford and one of the few left in Ireland.

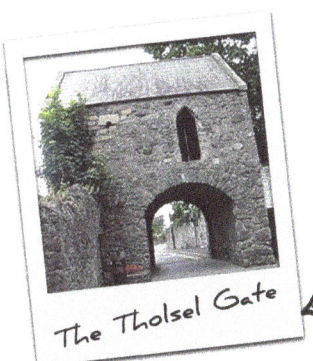

*Dominican Priory*

The Dominican Priory was started in 1305.

*Holy Trinity Church*

the Church of the Holy Trinity, a restored medieval church. Exhibits there displayed the history of Carlingford from Viking times. Inside this church and in the graveyard, we took some stone rubbings. What happened to those sheets, I do not know!

We returned to the center of town around 1:30 pm, cold and hungry. We were delighted to find P.J. O'Hare's Pub! Since Mary's maiden name was O'Hare, we of course had to go in and have lunch. I have several delightful memories of this time. We sat by a window overlooking the Lough. We were warmed by a fire burning in a nearby fireplace. And I swear I am not making this up. Sitting at the bar having a pint

## My Marvelous Memories

or two was a man who, except for the bowler hat, looked like the famous Hollywood actor Barry Fitzgerald, who played the character named Michaleen Oge Flynn in The Quiet Man!

And next to him was his younger brother Arthur Shields, also a famous actor! I'll never forgot the beautiful smiles I saw on their faces as they toasted each other at the beginning of each draught!

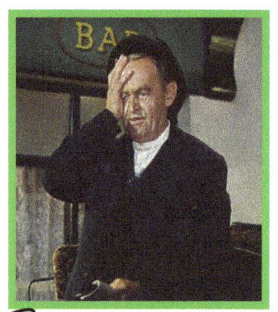

Barry Fitzgerald

Arthur Shields

One final recollection I have of this lunch. With a name like P.J. O'Hare and Mary's grandfather having been born 10 to 15 miles away in Dundalk, I was convinced there would be some family connection. I wanted to speak to the owner and ask about this. Mary refused. She said if I tried to do that, she would leave immediately, walk back to the hotel, and not talk to me for the rest of our trip. I did not want to ruin the next few days, so I kept my mouth shut!

Inside the cozy PJ O'Hare's famous pub.

# Chapter Eleven: Phenomenal Travels

307

*It's Yours Truly with the family sightseeing around Carlinford!*

In the early evening, we had a light snack at the hotel and went to bed early. Of course, that night, Colleen and Christine, had to share our adventurous day with their new friends in the hotel pub.

Thursday, July 13 . . .

After an early morning breakfast, we left driving southward. Our destination was Kilkenny. Though only 120 miles away, it takes some time to make this trip. Most of the roads were winding, two lane highways.

Kilkenny is a medieval town in southeast Ireland. Kilkenny Castle was built in 1195 by the Normans. We checked into our hotel, took a short drive around town, and had dinner at the hotel.

Kilkenny Castle

## My Marvelous Memories

Friday, July 14 . . .

Early morning breakfast. We arrived at Kilkenny Castle at 9:30 am, when it opened. We spent about four hours touring this beautiful, restored castle.

The Sea Court B&B

After a quick lunch we drove 30 miles to Waterford. We continued driving south another six miles to Tramore, a seaside town and fishing village. We stayed for three nights at a lovely B&B called the Sea Court. Our rooms had a beautiful view overlooking the Atlantic Ocean. We went to supper at a restaurant in Tramore called the Oakroom.

Saturday, July 15 . . .

We drove to Waterford after breakfast for our tour of the world-famous crystal Factory. Crystal production started in this city in 1783 but stopped in 1851. After WWII, almost a century later, a Czech immigrant established a glass works in Waterford. However, skilled workers were not available in Ireland. So, European workers, trained in Prague, were brought to Ireland. During this period, Miroslav Havel became the chief designer for Waterford crystal.

**WATERFORD®**
CRYSTAL

# Chapter Eleven: Phenomenal Travels

Born in Czechoslovakia in 1922, he was trained as a glass craftsman before the war. After our tour, we all had our picture taken at the factory with a large crystal vase. Christine has the picture today. After the tour, Colleen spent some time and money in the Waterford gift shoppe.

*Fun Time - Waterford Crystal*

Sunday, July 16 . . .

In the morning, we drove to Waterford and put Colleen on the train to Dublin. Later that day, she flew out of Dublin, back home to Chicago. The reason she couldn't stay longer was Austin was 18 months old at that time. She could only find babysitters for 10 days, hence her early return home.

After she left, Mary, Christine, Zachary, and I drove 40 miles west to Lismore. We went to visit the Mt. Melleray Cistercian Abbey five miles north of Lismore. We went there because Mary's maternal grandmother was raised on a farm 1-2 miles from the Abbey. When her grandmother was a teenager, she worked in the monastery's kitchen. As a young adult, she immigrated to the United States and settled in Chicago.

*Melleray Cistercian Abbey*

We visited and toured the main church of the Abbey. It was Sunday, so we stayed for the noon Mass. When we left, we drove around the grounds. Above the main entrance to one of the buildings we passed, I noticed the lunette or tympanum, a carved stone in the arch above a doorway. It read, Irish Scouts Centre. Zachary was a Cub Scout, so we stopped and took his picture standing in the doorway. Christine may have this picture today.

Irish Scouts Centre

I don't remember the maiden name of Mary's grandmother, but we spent about ½ hour driving around the nearby countryside. We looked at postal boxes to see if we could see a name Mary would have recognized. She didn't find any name familiar to her.

We drove into Lismore for lunch. During lunch, we were encouraged to visit the Lismore Castle, built in 1185. In 1753, it became the property of the Cavendish family, one of the richest, most influential, aristocratic families in England since the 16th century. It was the Irish home of the Duke of Devonshire. The public could not enter the castle.

Lismore Castle and Gardens

*Chapter Eleven : Phenomenal Travels*     311

Although we didn't tour the castle, we did visit the gardens and walked about the surrounding grounds. At one point, Zachary found a hill covered with grass. While Mary and I sat in the shade of a lovely oak tree, he and Christine had great sport in rolling down that hill. The climb back up was tiring, so Christine only managed two or three rolls. But Zachary was able to do a few more. Though he still had the energy and zest, we had to cut him off after five more rolls!

While touring this estate, we learned that Robert Boyle, The Father of Modern Chemistry, was born there in 1627. When we left the grounds, Zach and I posed for a picture under the plaque near the entry. I don't know what happened to that picture. We drove back for our last night at the Sea Court B&B in Tramore.

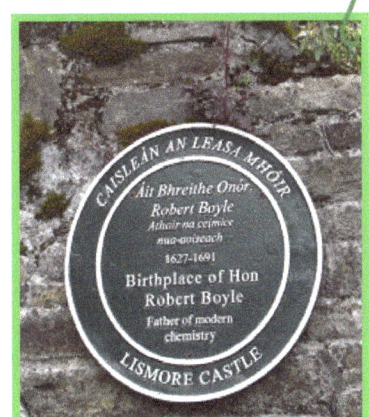

Monday, July 17 . . .

We left Tramore and drove about 20 miles west to Dungarvan, a coastal town with a beautiful harbor. We stopped for coffee and pastry along its picturesque quay.

Another 20 miles southwest, and we were in Midleton, just in time for a noon tour of the Jameson's Irish Whiskey distillery. We had our tasting experience coupled with our luncheon in their small café.

Ahhhh! Jameson Irish Whiskey Distillery & Cafe!

Afterwards, I slowly and carefully drove another 14-miles to the center of Cork, the third largest city in Ireland. Our hotel for the night was in downtown Cork, alongside the Lee River.

Tuesday, July 18 . . .

We didn't spend much time sightseeing in Cork. We drove from our hotel and went along St. Patrick Street, the main shopping area in downtown Cork.

Cork is known as the Culinary Capitol of Ireland!

## Chapter Eleven: Phenomenal Travels 313

We crossed the Lee River heading north. However, before leaving town we drove by The Church of St. Anne in Shandon. Even though it is an Anglican Church, we had to stop for a picture. Mary's favorite aunt, her mother's sister, had been named Anne.

Six miles from downtown Cork, and we were at our first major stop for the day.

In front of us was the remnants of Blarney Castle. This Castle, started in 1210, contains the Stone of Eloquence, better known as, the Blarney Stone. Christine and Zachary followed a long line up the steps to reach the top and kiss The Stone. Meanwhile, Mary and I sat below, drank coffee, and blew The Stone our kisses!

The legends say if you kiss the blarney stone, you'll be gifted with eloquence and persuasiveness!

One must lay on their back and put their head over the edge in order to kiss the stone!

We continued north from Blarney Castle for 50 miles for our next stop. We were now in Adare, renowned as one of Ireland's prettiest towns. We drove down several streets and took pictures of thatched cottages. We stopped in town and had a fine luncheon at one of the pubs on main street.

Pretty town of Adare

After lunch, it was only a 10-mile drive to the center of Limerick. We continued through town for another six miles northeast. We stayed at the Castle Oaks House Hotel, a wonderful resort hotel along the River Shannon.

*Chapter Eleven: Phenomenal Travels*   315

We had a very delicious dinner at the Castle Oaks. Later that night, I took a shower. I grabbed a towel off the rack next to the tub. Was I surprised! Not only was this the thickest, largest bath towel I'd ever used, it was very warm! I noticed the towel rack was really a pipe. When one turned on the lights over the bathtub, a heater also started to boil water. Hot steam was then sent through the pipe or towel rack.

Wednesday, July 19 . . .

Less than 15 miles from our hotel was Bunratty Castle, a national monument of Ireland. No longer used as a dwelling, it had been restored, and open to the public. We spent the entire morning viewing the many rooms in this Castle and had lunch in its former dining hall.

In the afternoon we walked a few steps from the Castle, and we were at the Bunratty Folk Park. This was an open air museum, featuring around 30 buildings. We learned that most of these buildings had been salvaged and moved from the Shannon International Airport area, less than four miles away.

Before WWII, many of the aircraft flying across the Atlantic Ocean were flying boats. Shannon Airport began as an airport, along the River Shannon Estuary, to service these flying boats. The land that surrounded this airbase was boggy. In 1936, the Government took steps to drain this land. Ireland was at peace during WWII, so construction on land-based runways continued. In late October 1945, the first commercial flight, New York → Gander → Shannon → London, landed at this airfield. In the development of this land, some homes on nearby farms were destroyed. Those that were salvaged were moved to the area adjacent to Bunratty Castle.

I remember several things from this visit to Bunratty Park. We went to a cottage surrounded by a fence. In the penned yard were chickens, ducks, and rabbits roaming and feeding. Upon entering the house, there was a fire burning in the fireplace. The entire home was smoky, and had an unusual, foul smell. I learned that peat was burning in the fireplace. As we walked around these buildings, I noticed many had thatched roofs. I asked some of the people who lived there about maintaining these roofs. I was told the roofs were quite comfortable and kept the rain out. However, it was becoming more expensive to preserve and replace them. The local folks thought that in time they would have to abandon their thatched roofs. After a long day, we returned to Castle Oaks for a late dinner and a good night's sleep!

*Chapter Eleven: Phenomenal Travels* 317

Thursday, July 20 …

We left Castle Oaks and drove about 30 miles west to our evening stop at Ennis. We did a little sightseeing by driving around town, had a light lunch, and checked into our hotel for a nap. We needed to be rested for our evening at Knappogue Castle. Only opened in the evenings, we were going to have a medieval dinner at this Castle.

We drove 10 miles east to arrive at the Castle for our banquet. We arrived about ½ hour before it started. While waiting to enter the banquet hall, we were served goblets of mead, a wine made from honey. On triangular toasts, we snacked on smoked Irish salmon with a cucumber/dill sauce.

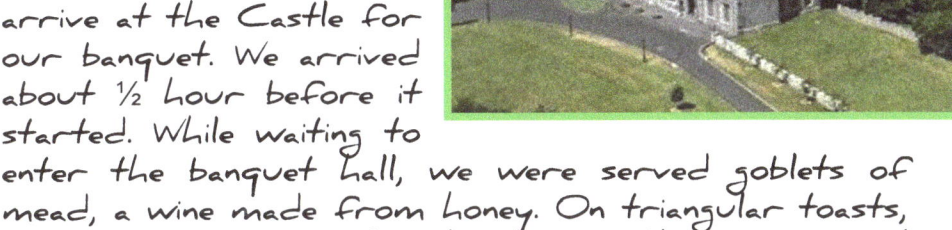

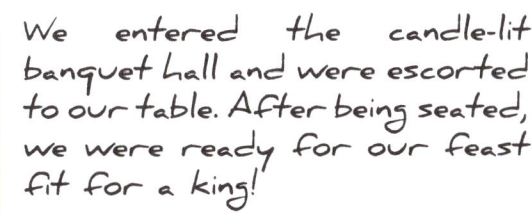

We entered the candle-lit banquet hall and were escorted to our table. After being seated, we were ready for our feast fit for a king!

A short welcome was given by the presiding Lord. Our serving wench introduced herself. She brought a pitcher containing a rich, hot, flavorful, steaming, delicious, soup—tomato basil. She filled each of our bowls. No spoon was provided, so we sipped directly from the bowl. Our wench was happy to refill our bowl, if we wished.

Yum! More please!

# My Marvelous Memories

We then ate a salad of fresh greens already set next to each of us. We did use a fork to do this. Our wench brought platers of fire roasted chicken, bowls of creamed potatoes, and dishes of roasted root vegetables. With coffee or tea, a delicious cinnamon apple crisp was served with a dollop of ice cream. Throughout the meal, minstrels and balladeers entertained us with various medieval melodies.

Friday, July 21 . . .

A morning drive of 25 miles and we were at the Cliffs of Moher. From O'Brien's Tower, the Cliffs rise 700 feet above the shore below. We had an excellent view of the Atlantic and the cliffs running southward. To the north, we could see the Aran Islands. A great sport done by young folk here is to defy the Law of Gravity. They hang by their fingertips from the edge of the cliffs Christine and Zachary both did this and survived. We took a picture of them doing this feat!

## Chapter Eleven: Phenomenal Travels

We continued driving north towards Ballyvaughan for lunch. While driving to Ballyvaughan, I made a turn, following a curve of a winding two lane roadway. I had to slam on the brakes! Luckily, I stopped in time! Crossing the highway was a herd of 20-30 sheep. Of course, they were being moved along by their shepherd and his dog.

We stopped and had a wonderful lunch at Monk's in Ballyvaughan.

Following lunch, we drove another 35 miles to arrive in Galway. We had to be sure to follow the signs along the way, for the roads were windy and tricky.

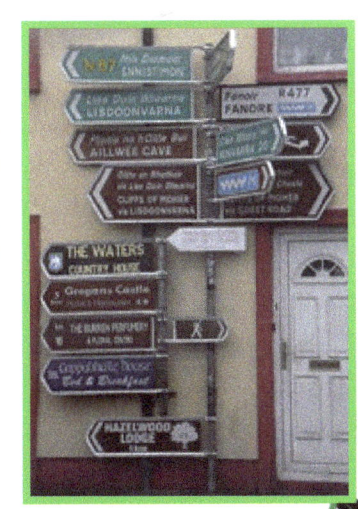

Simply follow the signs!

We stayed at The Galway Arms Inn, a lovely old hotel in the center of town. We were there for our last 2 nights in Ireland.

Galway Arms Inn

*"If you ever go across the sea to Ireland, then maybe at the closing of your day. You will sit and watch the moon rise over Claddagh, and see the sun go down on Galway Bay."*

From the song
'Galway Bay'
by Arthur Colahan.

Saturday, July 22 . . .

While in Galway we saw a ¾ moon rise over Claddagh and a sunset over Galway Bay!

After breakfast, I arranged for the return of our rental car, and we started our walking tour of Galway. In ¼ mile, we crossed the River Corrib on the Father Griffin Bridge and walked along the Claddagh Quay. We also took a stroll through the Father Burke Park. Back across the river we went. In less than ½ mile, we were at Eyre Square. Here we viewed the Kennedy Memorial and the Monument of the Galway Hooker.

# Chapter Eleven: Phenomenal Travels

The hooker is a traditional boat used in Galway Bay. It was developed for the strong seas and robust winds found there. Usually, the hull is black since it was coated with pitch. The sails are dark red brown.

*Hookers on the prowl!*

Around the perimeter of Eyre Square were many shops and restaurants. We just had to visit them for last minute shopping. We later returned to the Galway Arms for a shower and nap.

That night we had dinner in the inn's pub. Not only was the food wonderful, but the cheerfulness in the pub was amazing. A fiddler and other musicians played, people danced, and the crowd broke out in song. The lads sat at the bar discussing politics and sports, while sippin' their wee draughts.

Families were there with children. No babysitters at home! While the adults gossiped, sang, and danced, children played board games, i.e. checkers, chess, darts, or backgammon. We left around 10:00 pm because the next day was going to be long and busy.

*Cozy Pub Fun for All!*

## My Marvelous Memories

Sunday, July 23 . . .

Up early for breakfast. A car and driver came to the hotel. Bags were loaded on the car and we all boarded it.

We drove about ½ mile to the train station in Galway. I got out, took a train to Dublin, flew back to London, and then on to Chicago. In the meantime, the driver took Mary, Christine, and Zachary to the Shannon Airport, a drive of about 55 miles. They caught a flight to Chicago and were home hours before me.

Of course, you ask, why I didn't fly from Shannon with them? I could not make that arrangement. Because I had flown into Dublin from London, I had to fly back to London out of Dublin. I wasn't allowed to get an International flight out of Shannon, nor could I fly from Shannon to Dublin. Remember, this was in 2000, and I do not know what aviation regulations prevented it. As the saying goes, "It was, what it was!" In any event, I was home in Chicago for my summer vacation. Our fantastic trip to Ireland was over!

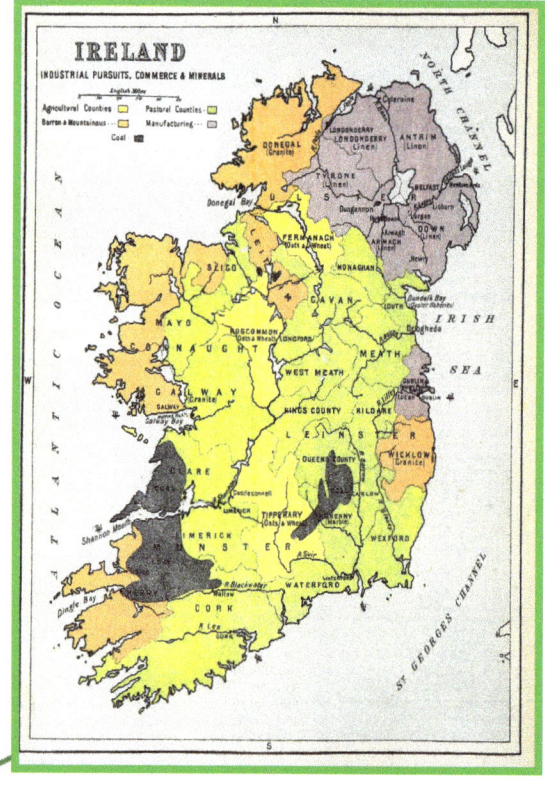

# Chapter Eleven: Phenomenal Travels

So far, I've written over 65 pages about my Arabian adventure, and the trips that resulted from it. In January 2000, I'd initially planned to leave my job at CPC in July 2000. I was going to come home to Chicago and stay after our trip to Ireland.

In the last chapter, I mentioned the new assignment I received in June of 2000 in SA. At Colleen's final dinner in Tramore, I told everyone about my new assignment. I went on to tell them that I now planned to return to Saudi Arabia for 4½ more months. I promised that when I returned for the Christmas holidays of 2000, I would remain home in the USA.

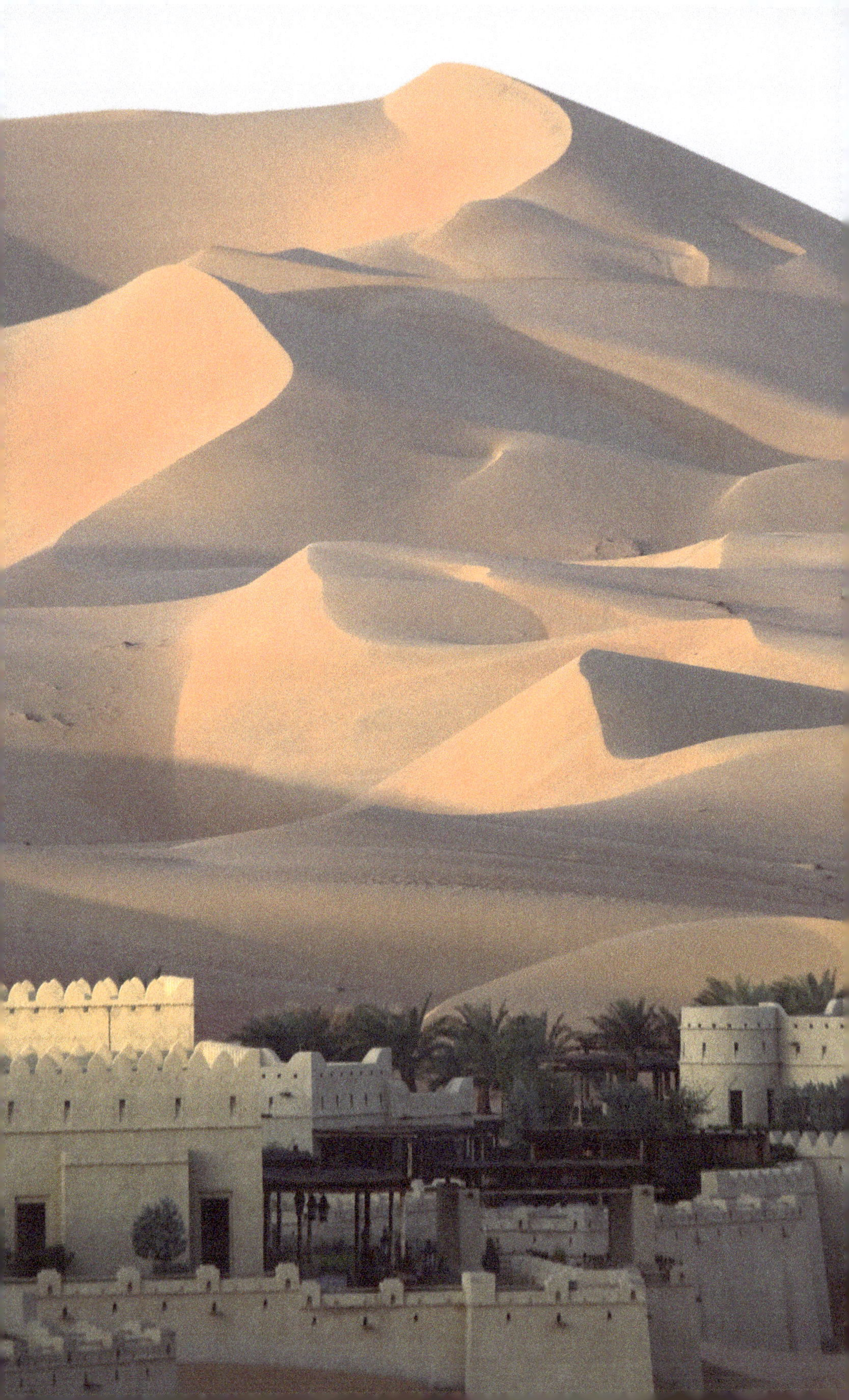

# Chapter Twelve
## The Searing Sands of Arabia
## (1998 – 2001)

••••••••••••

## College Preparatory Center (CPC), Saudi Arabia

••••••••••••

I'd now like to mention other recollections I have of my 3½-years in the Saudi Kingdom. I'll begin by talking about a few of the special friends I made while in Arabia.

***Pat Mahn:*** We were not close while we were teaching at CPC. We became acquainted, as fellow teachers in my 1st year. He taught business and computer courses and had been at CPC for 2-3 years before I arrived in 1997. A year after I arrived, he left the Kingdom to rejoin his family in CA. However, we kept in contact by emails. I will have occasion to talk more about him in the next chapter.

***Tom Stemshorn:*** He too worked for Al-Falak, taught math courses at CPC, and lived in the same apartment building I did. In fact, it was he who tried to teach reading to our servant Bahla. He left the Kingdom six months after I did. I later saw him twice in CA. During our last meeting in the summer of 2012, I found out he was having medical issues with cancer. I fear he is now gone, like so many of my friends and colleagues.

***Gene Wright:*** He was the closest and best friend I made in SA. I will mention him many times in this chapter, as well as the next. Gene taught math and science, so we worked on many things together.

Gene was a black man, 25 years younger than me, and was always physically active. In college, he'd been the starting quarterback for the Southern University football team, in Baton Rouge, LA. He was also a retired Army Captain.

Gene in his new garb!

*Mahfouz*: He was a Syrian Arab who was the secretary to Daoud the Director of CPC. I'd learned many years earlier, that if I ever wanted to get something done, I did not go to the president, principal, or director. Instead, I'd go to their secretary and discuss what I wanted to accomplish. I'd then learn how to bring this about. I was never in any social setting with Mahfouz. I just want to mention how I respected him, and how I am thankful for all the help he gave me while I was at CPC.

I want to now mention a few things further about CPC.

I was assigned to be the Moderator of the Science Club. Students were encouraged, but not required to participate in extracurricular activities.

We met twice a month after classes had ended. Usually, I'd arrange for a speaker from our faculty to relate some of their university experiences. Occasionally, I got someone from the other areas of the Training Center to give a presentation. Attendance at these meetings ranged from 8-15 students.

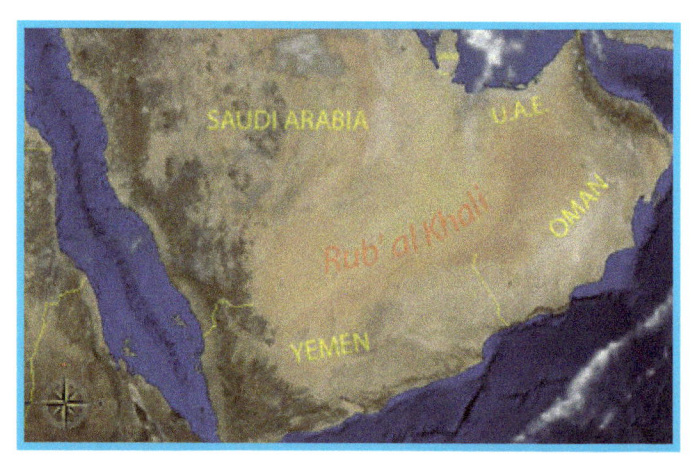

Rub' al Khali

*Chapter Twelve : The Searing Sands of Arabia*  327

In the Kingdom, our usual weekend holiday was held on Thursday/Friday. On one Thursday, I took 30 students on a unique field trip. Thanks to Mahfouz and other officials of Aramco, we went on a trip that had never be done before! Gene accompanied me and the students. We rode an air-conditioned bus out to the *Rub' al Khali, The Empty Quarter*. It is the largest contiguous sand desert in the world. It is also the location of the oil wells of Saudi Aramco. We were going to visit a drill site for a new well.

Security was very tight. No one, Saudi or non-Saudi, can go wandering, walking, or riding in this desert. It is patrolled by the Saudi military. There are few paved roads, mostly dusty trails. It took me, with the help of Mahfouz, 4-6 weeks to get a clearance for each one on that trip. Our ride was over an hour on dusty trails to the well site. Thank God the driver, a Saudi Aramco bus driver, knew where he was going.

We arrived at the drilling rig and were greeted by a young Saudi man in charge. He told us he'd earned his BS in Mechanical Engineering five years earlier at King Fahd University in Dhahran. How do I begin to describe what I saw and learned that day?

On the drilling platform 6-10 roughnecks were moving pipes, operating cranes, and in general drilling into the oil dome, about ¾-mile below.

Three teams of workers, referred to as A, B, and C, were assigned to the rig. Team A would start their 12-hour shift at 6:00 pm and worked until 6:00 am. They'd continue in this fashion for one week. The 2nd week, their 12-hour shift began at 6:00 am and lasted until 6:00 pm.

The 3rd week they'd return to their homes and had off for seven days to rest and take care of personal matters. On the 4th week, they'd be back at the drill site and start this 3-week cycle over again. Meanwhile, Teams B and C were going through similar cycles. During a 12-hour shift the crew stopped working for 15 minutes every 2 hours. This enabled the men a bathroom break and an opportunity to replenish body liquids with water, juice, or coffee. If a worker was a Muslim, he was allowed time for the proper prayer breaks, while the rest of the crew continued working. Six hours after a shift started a ½-hour break was taken for lunch. Breakfast was taken before one started his shift and dinner was served after a shift ended.

Besides the team of roughnecks mentioned earlier, there were cooks and other servants from India at the drill site. They worked in the kitchen, laundry, and housing units cleaning rooms and bathrooms.

Housing was provided in one storied structures that were mounted on huge wooden skis. Large Caterpillar tractors had pulled these buildings across the desert sands. I learned that this technique was not new to SA. It had been first used in the Mojave Desert in 1909. Two or three of these housing units were in place. Each one had about eight small bedrooms with toilets, sinks, and showers at one end. There were other units, also mounted on heavy wooden skis. These were the kitchen, dining area, laundry, storage, dispensary, and an office for the manager. All buildings were connected by short, enclosed walkways so that the entire complex was air-conditioned.

*1909 Tractors in the Mojave!*

Separate from the buildings I've just described were two huge electrical generators about the length of a diesel locomotive. Both of course, were mounted on huge wooden skis. One generator was running and making a lot of noise. The other was there as a backup, in case the first stopped running.

*Chapter Twelve: The Searing Sands of Arabia*

Now for the drilling rig and platform. It was mounted on huge rubber tires and pulled into place by the tractors. Once over the location for drilling, electro-pneumatic valves lifted the wheels up, and the platform down. When it was made level and in place, drilling began. These huge tires were 13-14 feet in diameter. My reason for saying so is Gene took a picture of me in front of one of those wheels. I am standing on the ground and the hub of the wheel was 3-4 inches above my head. During our tour of the outside it was difficult to hear. This was due to noise from the running generator. In addition, the drilling process added sounds of drilling and crane operations. During a lunch provided us, we could ask questions and hear the answers.

Before I continue, I want to mention a recollection I have about our luncheon. The dining area provided space for 15-20 people to sit and eat comfortably. Counting 30 students, Gene, the manager, and I, we doubled the capacity. We really had to squeeze together during our meal!

It was during this time we learned about the work-shift cycles, I described earlier. The manager told us a rig, such as this one, took 4-5 weeks to complete the operation. Once the drilling of a well was completed, they capped the well, and moved the drill to a new location. After they left, other crews came in to finish the process. A pipe crew came in and laid out pipelines and pumping stations. Eventually, the oil was brought into a large distribution center in the desert. From there, it was sent to refineries in the eastern or western parts of the Kingdom.

Other port facilities might receive crude petroleum to load onto tankers and brought to refineries throughout the world. Another crew would come to move the buildings and generators to a new location. Finally, a cleanup crew came in to do its job. Not so much *human waste*, which of course was dealt with, but the waste from the sludge pit. During our tour outside, we'd seen a huge pit, called the sludge pit.

In the process of drilling through rock layers, small chunks of rock are flushed up and deposited in this pit. It must be dealt with carefully since some of it was radioactive!

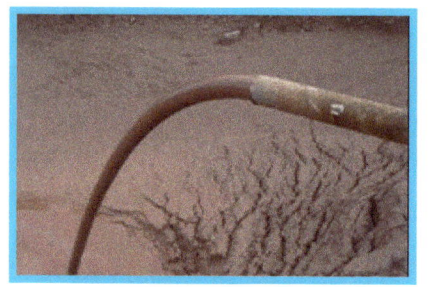

*Radioactive Sludge*

A few final points to finish this long story. One of the students asked the manager, in jest I think, about the bed we'd seen in his office. He laughed and told us that usually there wasn't a bed there. He explained that each team had its own manager. About four months earlier, one manager had gotten ill, was on sick leave, and was not sure when he'd return. So, the company asked our speaker to do double duty and manage two of the shifts. The manager said when he had his week off at home in Dhahran, he spent all his time sleeping. When he returned to the drilling rig, there were many days he was on a 24-hour shift, followed by another 24-hour shift. So, he put a bed in his office. If he became exhausted, he would fall into it for an hour or two and have a short nap. We all laughed. One of the students remarked, "I hope that they're paying you extra for doing this." The manager smiled and said, "Oh yes! Usually I earn $13,000 a month. Now I'm earning $30,000 a month." Then he said, "But, I'm too tired to spend it. Hurry up and get your degrees. We need you out here!"

• • • • • • • • • •

During my 2nd year in the Kingdom, I left my residence in the Al-Falak apartment building. I moved to a private compound and Al-Falak paid me a housing stipend. This gated secured compound accommodated about 70-80 residents.

I shared expenses for a 2-bedroom, 2-bath mobile home with Mitch, my mate from Sydney, Australia. He also worked for Al-Falak, but as a computer specialist for a bank. Though we lived together, we never were too social. He found a few blokes from Australia that he'd visit on weekends.

*1978 Chevy Blazer!*

## Chapter Twelve: The Searing Sands of Arabia

I continued to socialize with my friends from CPC. At this time, I bought and drove my own car, a used 1978 Blazer. Al-Falak paid me a transportation stipend for my own vehicle.

The advantages I found to this new arrangement of moving into a private compound were . . .

- ✓ Two hundred feet from our unit was the compound's in-ground swimming pool, surrounded by lounge chairs. The only pool rules were: (1) no glass around the pool, and (2) no use of the pool from 11:00 pm to 6:00 am.

- ✓ We could make our own *homemade wine* in our unit. I did take advantage of this privilege!

- ✓ In this compound, a Brit had rented two units. In one of them, he had set up his own little pub. In the evenings, and on weekends, I could always purchase a glass of *homemade wine, beer,* or *ale* there. Occasionally, he managed to serve gin or scotch. I also learned, wherever in Saudi Arabia you found 8-10 Brits living in a compound, there would always be an illegal pub to be found there.

Speaking of *illegal* reminded me that from October until the following April, one could buy tickets to a musical concert. Once a month, musicians and singers from Europe and the US came in for usually two evening performances. These were held in the gym of a private school in Al-Khobar. About 20% of the 200 to 300 in the audience were female, and of course, such a gathering in SA was *illegal*.

During the intermission at one of these concerts, my friend, Gene, ever the charmer, started chatting with one of the ladies in attendance. She always came to the concert alone, dressed as a native woman in a black abaya. At the last concert of the season in April, we were invited to her home for a post-concert dinner, and what a meal it was!

But first, let me tell you what Gene and I learned that night about this lady, named Rosa. She was born in Cuba in 1952. President Batista had appointed her father to be a member of the Cuban delegation to the United Nations. Consequently, she and her family were living in New York in 1959 when Fidel Castro became President of Cuba. The family could not return to Cuba, so they emigrated to France where Rosa continued her education. She could read and speak Spanish, English, and French. Raised Roman Catholic, she later married a Saudi man, moved to Saudi Arabia, converted to Islam, and raised her 13-year-old daughter in the Islamic faith. Her father had died years earlier, but her mother, Maria, was still alive. Maria spent most of the year living with her daughter in SA. During the summers she lived at her apartment in Paris. Maria had not attended the concert that night, but was present in the home, and had dinner with us.

The dinner that night was quite an experience! Six were present, Rosa and Maria, Gene and me, and a French doctor from the Saudi Aramco hospital and his wife. The doctor and his wife had attended the concert earlier. The dining table was elegantly set with gold-rimmed china plates and gold-plated dinnerware. Crystal glasses for water and cold juices were there—no wine or alcohol in an Islamic home. The food service was outstanding! Three waiters served us in *Service à la Russe*, service in the Russian style. This is a manner of dining that involves courses being brought to the table sequentially. This is in distinction to all the food being brought out at once in platters and bowls, *Service à la Française*.

On the plate in front of me, a waiter placed a warm bowl. A 2nd waiter held a tureen of hot soup while the 3rd waiter ladled soup into the bowl. When I finished the soup, both plate and bowl were removed, and immediately a plate filled with salad was placed in front of me. When I finished my salad,

*Chapter Twelve: The Searing Sands of Arabia*

the plate was removed, and a dinner plate, filled with chicken and vegetables, was placed in front of me. Later, this plate was removed, and immediately, a plate of lamb with different vegetables was before me. While the team of two waiters served the food, the 3rd waiter circled the table.

*Service à la Française*

From various pitchers, he filled our glasses with water and cold fruit juices. Later, we had coffee, cake, fresh dates, and nuts in the parlor. Gene and I left about 2:00 am well fed!

We never met or knew the name of Rosa's husband. He was not a member of the Royal Family, but he had a very important government job. He supervised all immigration for the entire eastern providence of Saudi Arabia. Except for US Military personnel, any non-Saudi in this region had to be approved by his agency. Rosa told us he was frequently away from home, because he attended many meetings in the capital of Riyadh, and he moved about the province evaluating the work of his subordinates.

I've mentioned Gene several times already. He was my best friend in SA and still is a good friend. During my Christmas Holiday in Chicago 1997, Gene and his 14-year-old son came to visit me for a few days in IL. Gene was divorced when we first met in 1997. While in the kingdom, he met Maria, a black woman from South Africa. She was working as a medical technician in one of the hospitals in Al-Khobar. They dated for about a year and were married in Bahrain in 1998. Their marriage could never have taken place in SA. My last 1½ years in SA, Maria, Gene, Tanzi, and I shared a 4-BR, 3-BA villa in a gated compound. Tanzi was Maria's 8-year-old daughter. They could now bring her from South Africa to live with a married couple. Of course, Gene and I were brewing our homemade wine in this villa. We never tried to make beer!

Because Gene was a retired US Army officer, he introduced me to *The Mission*. The Mission was a club/restaurant in a gated community that catered to active and retired US military personnel.

A military person paid no dues. I, as a US citizen could become a member of the club by paying an annual $25 fee. The restaurant was able to supply their stock with special supplies flown in by US Air Force transports.

Gene, I, and other friends had our weekly fix of bacon and eggs or sausage and pancakes at breakfast on Thursdays and Fridays. Besides dinners of turkey, chicken, beef, or lamb we attended many meals that featured pork or ham. The club's bar was always well stocked with alcoholic beverages. A large room was used to show current movies on weekends, which you could enjoy while munching on popcorn or sipping a beer. Do not get the wrong impression. Breakfast, dinner, movies, popcorn, beverages were NOT FREE. I paid for these things. The advantage was I had access to something not found elsewhere in Al-Khobar, Dammam, and Dhahran.

*Movie and Snacks!*

Gene introduced me to the *black community* in Al-Khobar. There was a gated community of about 400-500 residents in our area. About 50% of these residents were black US citizens. The men were aviation mechanics who had been trained in the US Air Force or Navy to service jet aircraft. These men were currently employed by McDonnell-Douglas to maintain and service the F-15 Eagles for the Royal Saudi Air Force. Gene and I attended many of the monthly parties this black community held.

*Maintenance on the F-15*

Besides meeting and talking to new friends, I enjoyed eating that *soul food* known as *greens*. I always sat, watched, and talked to the man who cooked the greens. One time while eating a bowl of his freshly prepared *greens* I said to him, "Don't get me wrong, these greens are OK, but they don't taste just right. Did you forget some seasoning?" He laughed and said, "I didn't have any fatback."

## Chapter Twelve: The Searing Sands of Arabia

A party in June always celebrated the Juneteenth holiday. I had never heard of this holiday. Also known as Juneteenth Independence Day, it commemorates the June 19, 1865, announcement of the abolition of slavery in the state of Texas. Lastly, in a harbinger of the future, (see Chapter 13) I tutored three or four men from this black community who were taking courses in math by correspondence, from Embry-Riddle Aeronautical U (ERAU). Not only did I get a tutoring fee from each student, ERAU gave me a stipend for administering their mid-term and final exams.

Gene and I were active in providing sports programs for our CPC students. Under the leadership of the Athletic Director at CPC . . .

> Gene and I each coached a student volleyball team and refereed the volleyball games. He also coached a student basketball team and refereed the games. During all these basketball games, I ran the clock, scoreboard, and entered information into the record book.
>
> We both arranged and helped with swimming instructions at a pool near the students' residence hall in the Munirah Camp area. Neither of us coached or refereed soccer games, but we were always in the bleachers cheering!

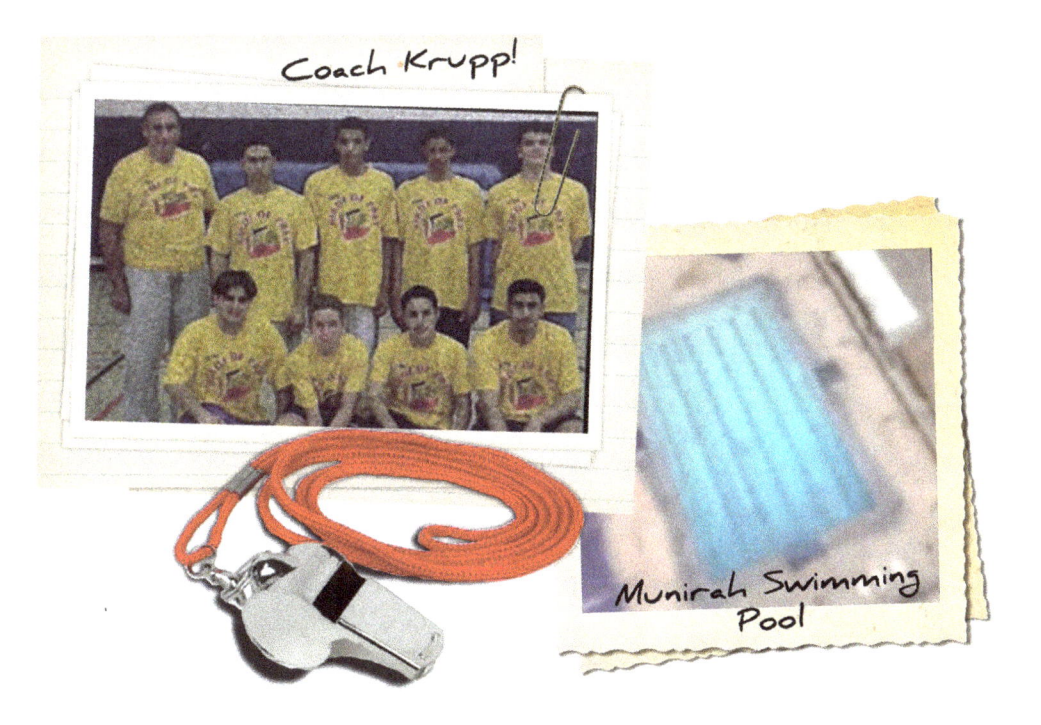

Coach Krupp!

Munirah Swimming Pool

## House Sitter with Ki

Occasionally, I would house sit a home of friends in the Saudi Aramco gated secured compound. This usually involved taking care of their dogs or cats while my friends were away on a family vacation. I've just mentioned the Saudi Aramco gated, secured compound. I need to elaborate.

Most of Dhahran is owned by the Saudi Aramco Oil Company and is totally secured. Twenty years ago, there were only two or three security gates through which one entered. Guards at the gates would stop every vehicle. Cars and trucks were inspected. A guard, with a mirror, looked at the undercarriage of every vehicle. Inside this first level of security was where most activities of the oil business were located. This area contained two mosques, a few tall office buildings, the company hospital, the Prosperity Well, 6-8 dormitories for hundreds of workers, several dining halls, the Training Center, etc. However, further inside this immense area was a second secure gated area. It was the residential compound for workers, mostly westerners, who brought their families to SA. This compound within a compound, housed about 7000 residents, including children. In it, there were three elementary schools each with a gymnasium. It contained soccer and baseball fields covered with grass and beautifully maintained. These fields had bleachers and lights. After all, in the hot desert, games were played at night. There were dining halls, a library, a theater, etc. There was even the Rolling Hills Golf and Country Club! It had its own, special rules of play, since the entire course was a *sand trap*.

# Chapter Twelve: The Searing Sands of Arabia

To enter this inner compound, one had to pass thorough another security gate. A resident's car had a sticker on the windshield and was immediately passed through without delay. A nonresident had to stop, enter a guard house, and obtain a pass to put on his car's dashboard. Only then could one gain entry. To get this pass, I had to fill out a card giving my name, my car's license number, and who I was going to visit. I had to wait while the guard called the phone number I provided. Once the phone was answered, the guard informed them I was seeking approval for entry. Getting that approval would then allow me to receive a pass for one day.

However, on Fridays, when I went to this inner compound to attend Mass, things got a *little sticky*. I may have not mentioned it yet, but our weekend started on Thursday. Friday was the *holy day* or *sabbath*. Classes were held at CPC from Saturday to Wednesday. Thursday and Friday were our *weekend*.

*Mecca*

Because Saudi Arabia is the Islamic holy land containing Mecca and Medina, no Christian churches are allowed anywhere. However, in order to attract western employees with family and children, the Oil Company makes special arrangements. The gymnasiums at the elementary schools are used on Fridays for counseling sessions. The leaders of these meetings are specially trained counselors who are paid by Saudi Aramco. Besides receiving a salary, these special counselors were provided with housing, transportation costs, and extra money for their *counseling expenses*. One of these counselors was a Roman Catholic Priest, the second was an Anglican Priest, and the third was a Protestant Minister, who I never met. The large home provided for these special counselors was always near an elementary school. In addition, this home always had several wings of smaller meeting rooms, for group counseling sessions.

I wanted to try to attend Mass while in the kingdom. It took me about three months to get myself set up. I had a little notebook in which I'd written names and phone numbers of friends inside the compound. On Fridays I could phone them for approval of my entry. Sometimes, the first name I gave the guard was not home when he called. I'd then try a second or third name, if necessary. Eventually, I'd be cleared and off to Mass I'd go. At first, I went to the Catholic Mass. This always had a large crowd, maybe 2,500-3,000 worshippers in attendance. The priest was OK, but the folks in attendance didn't provide what I was looking for. Most of those present were Filipinos. After Mass they quickly left the gym and parking lot to return to their own residential compounds. They would gather with fellow Filipino families to relax and enjoy their holiday together.

I tried the Anglican Mass, and it was just what I was looking for, and needed. The number of attendees was much smaller ranging from 300-400 people including children. The Mass always began with the choir, around a dozen men and women dressed in robes, singing and leading the priest to the altar. The seats were folding chairs set up on the gym floor with a central aisle. The priest greeted us, and the Mass started. Just after the gospel reading, all the children were led out by their teachers to conduct *Sunday School*. The Mass continued and was almost identical to the Mass found in a Roman Church. However, just before distributing Communion the priest had a saying I'll never forget. He held up the host over his chalice and said, "This is the Body and Blood of Christ! *ALL* are welcome to receive!" The Mass ended shortly, and the choir led the priest out to an adjacent room. There they removed their robes, while the priest took off his vestments. A worshipper could now leave, but most stayed and moved to the back of the gym. Here the "ladies of the church" had setup a table covered with cookies, cakes, and fresh fruit. On another table was a large coffee pot and a smaller pot with hot water for tea. It was time to snack and socialize! It provided just what we all needed, the sense of *community*.

I soon met the priest, Father Ben, and his wife, Helen. They were the embodiment of this sense of community. I met others who soon became my new friends. My very best friends from this inner compound, Cheryl and John Steiniger, were Catholic and continued to attend the Catholic Mass on Friday. But I was incredibly happy to continue going to the Anglican Mass.

## Chapter Twelve: The Searing Sands of Arabia

Some other memories from this time . . .

During Mass on Friday, November 7, 1997, Fr. Ben made a special announcement. He and Helen were inviting anyone in the congregation, who had no other plans, to come to their home on Thursday, November 27 to celebrate Thanksgiving. All they asked was to let them know by November 21. I accepted and went.

They planned to serve dinner at 3:00 pm and invited their guests to come at 2:30 pm for a glass of wine or cold juice. I arrived at 2:40 pm and while sitting in the parlor sipping a wine, a serendipitous event occurred. The phone rang and Helen answered in the kitchen. She spoke for five minutes. She called out to Ben to come and speak to the person who'd called. Another five minutes passed, and Ben returned to the parlor with a big smile on his face. I asked why he looked so happy. He said that was his daughter. She had called to wish her mother and father a Happy Thanksgiving. I thought she might be a student attending college in the US. I asked him if that might be so. He said, "No, she graduated last year. She's in her 1st year of teaching." I asked him where she was teaching. When he answered I thought to myself, OMG! He said, "She's teaching at Bethlehem University in Palestine." I told Ben that I had a colleague teaching there, Brother Dominic, my old friend Ed Everett (one of the Lucky 7 mentioned in Chapter 2). During dinner, I told Helen I knew someone teaching at Bethlehem University. She asked me to write Bro. Dominic's name on a sheet of paper. Here's what followed . . .

*Bethlehem University in Palestine*

I went home for two weeks during the Christmas Holidays.

During the holidays, their daughter came home to SA for two weeks. Because Bethlehem was a Palestinian town, and she was working at a university teaching Palestinians, she had no difficulty in getting through Saudi customs. She told her parents she knew Bro. Dominic very well! His classroom was across the hall from hers. Because his degrees were in Education, he had given her many tips to help improve her teaching skills.

After I returned in January 1998, they informed me of this. One evening, in February, they invited me to come to their home for dinner. Afterwards they phoned their daughter in Bethlehem. She and Bro. Dominic were waiting for the call. I spent 4-5 minutes chatting with him while he was in Palestine and I was in Saudi Arabia!

• • • • • • •

*The Skyline of Dubai*

Another recollection from this time involved my trip to Dubai. During my first year at CPC, Richard, an English teacher, and I became friends. In the summer of 1998, he moved to Dubai, the largest and most populous city in the United Arab Emirates (UAE). He found a teaching position at a college there.

We kept in contact by emails after he left. He encouraged me to come visit him in Dubai and look at his college. He thought I might be interested in teaching there. In April of 1999 I did go for a 4-day visit to Dubai and had an interview. The college was interested in me as a science/math teacher, but they had no vacancies at the time. So, no offer was given. I just enjoyed my trip as a brief vacation!

On Friday, my last day in Dubai, Richard and I went to a new hotel that had opened in 1997. It was a very modern hotel on the shore of the Persian Gulf. Its architecture was unique, in the shape of a wave. The southern end is only three stories high. It then curves smoothly upward to the north end that is 25 stories high. This beach had earlier been named the Chicago Beach,

## Chapter Twelve: The Searing Sands of Arabia

because for many years the Chicago Bridge & Iron Company had used it. Their barges and floating oil storage tanks had lined the shore for decades. In the early 1990's Dubai began a program to modernize their entire beach front. The Jumeirah Hotel was the first modern building opened in this stage of development. The road along the shore is now called the Jumeirah Street, and the beach has been renamed to Jumeirah Beach.

*The Jumeira Hotel remains one of the most recognized places in Dubai, even today!*

Jumeira Hotel

When Richard and I entered the main lobby of the hotel, we followed the sign to Western Dining. Following another sign would have led us to Middle Eastern Dining. Richard informed me that the signs were not intended to separate people. They were there to direct one to their choice of fare. We went to the western dining room that was offering a buffet breakfast. We filled our plates with bacon, ham, and eggs, potatoes, etc. On our second trip to the buffet we selected waffles and pork sausage. There also was a large selection of fresh fruit, juices, pastries, and coffee. We were satiated! I remember that the price was very reasonable. Had we so chosen, we could have gone to the Middle Eastern buffet where we would have been served traditional foods, and of course, no pork products!

After breakfast, we strolled along the ground floor, visiting shops that sold newspapers and magazines in many different languages. After an hour, our food had been digested, so we went to a locker room. Since we were not registered as guests in the hotel, we had to pay a small fee. This gave us access to a towel, sandals, and a locker. We changed into our swimsuits and walked out to the beach. Here we spent 3-4 hours on the sand or swimming in the Persian Gulf. While swimming I noticed a beautiful, new building being constructed about ½-mile south. It was almost completed and did open in December 1999. It was the Burj Al Arab!

When this hotel opened, it was ranked as the tallest hotel in the world. Now, it is the 5th tallest. Built on a man-made island in the Persian Gulf, its shape is designed to look like the sail of a ship. The rooftop contains a helipad, tennis court, and cantilevered restaurant. It has 28 double-story floors that accommodate 202-bedroom suites. The smallest suite is 1800 sq. ft. and rented for $2,000 per night. The Royal Suite is 8400 sq. ft. and costs $24,000 a night. These prices were for 2012. The Royal Suite is ranked #12 in the world according to a 2012 CNN report.

It took three years for the man-made island to be built and another three years to construct the building. To get to the hotel, a ¼-mile causeway was built. Security guards and gates at each end of the causeway were put there to ensure the safety of the occupants. One could also arrive at the hotel by air or water.

In January 2000, a month after the Burj Al Arab opened, I read an article about it in our local Al-Khobar newspaper. A few of my recollections from this article . . .

The hotel had a fleet of six Rolls-Royce limousines to transport people to and from the airport.

At that time, many of the wealthy jetsetters, arrived and departed Dubai, on the supersonic Concorde airplane from London, Paris, or Hong Kong.

The smallest room, not a suite, that accommodated two occupants, rented for $500 a night.

I think this is enough about the Burj Al Arab and the opulent wealthy who need such lavish accommodations!

# Chapter Twelve: The Searing Sands of Arabia

I have written many pages about my adventures in the first four years of retirement. As I end this chapter, and transition to the next phase in **MS**, I want to relate a *non-adventure*, something that could have happened, but didn't!

Shortly after my arrival in Saudi Arabia, I became acquainted with a large group of educators that I never realized existed. These were teachers who taught in schools around the world. However, they taught their students in English. Most of the ones I met, came from the US, UK, Canada, Ireland, and Australia. Many of them had majored in ESL (English as a Second Language). I learned that all over the world, usually in large metropolitan areas, there were American elementary and high schools. I heard about international meetings for ESL teachers, held annually in the US, UK, etc. Job fairs were always conducted during these meetings.

In the summer of 1999, I began looking for a teaching job at one of these American schools, but closer to home. I talked to some of my colleagues. They suggested I seek a job in Canada or Mexico. I quickly rejected Canada! I didn't want to live again, in a cold climate, like Alaska. To summarize what happened . . .

In May 2000, I was offered a job at the American school in Guadalajara, Mexico. It would start in September 2000.

Some advantages I saw in accepting this offer were . . .

    a) I would only be about 1800 miles from Chicago.

    b) Two 4-hour flights, nonstop to Chicago from Guadalajara were scheduled daily. I could fly home for Thanksgiving!

    c) About 25 miles south of the school was Lake Guadalajara. Many retired American citizens had moved and lived around this lake. I was certain I could find a condo or apartment to rent there!

It became a non-adventure because I declined the offer. Of course, you ask 'Why?' I knew from the get-go that I would earn less money by leaving Saudi Arabia. In 1999, my salary alone in SA was $55,000. The salary offered in Mexico was $37,000. This might have been acceptable if I considered the lesser pay would be balanced by my closeness to home. In addition, Mary could come and live with me during the Chicago winters. We might even have a few visitors from the Windy City drop by!

The thing that put a nix on the deal was that I found out that Mexico had an income tax. I would have had to pay 35% of my salary to the Government of Mexico. So, from the $37,000, I would only net about $24,000. You remember, I mentioned earlier, that in SA there was no income tax. So, my $55,000 salary would drop to $24,000, a 56% reduction. Consequently, in mid-May I said No Thank You to the folks in Mexico!

Two weeks later in early June, I was elated when I heard about the new job I mentioned earlier. In addition, at the end of June my salary increased to $58,000!

As I end this chapter, I want to mention one slight regret. During my years in Saudi Arabia I made four trips home for the Christmas holidays and three trips home for my summer vacations. All these air fares were paid for by my employer. My regret is not having supplemented one of these fares and bought myself an around the world ticket!

# Chapter Thirteen
## Genesis-III
## (2001 - 2021)

••••••••••••

### New Beginnings
### and
### Reincarnations

••••••••••••

In January, I was back home from Saudi Arabia and ready for some new adventures. However, Mary and I first took a little vacation together!

On December 27, 2000, we started driving to Florida. We spent a few nights, including New Year's Eve, in New Port Richey. We were guests at the home of Marie Mahn, the mother of the friend I had made in Saudi Arabia. Pat, his wife Tac, and their son Jason were also there. They had come to FL from CA, for the holidays. At this time, Pat suggested a new adventure for my consideration. I'll tell you more about that shortly.

January 2, Mary and I drove south along the Gulf Coast to Marco Island. We spent a month at a condo in the South Seas Development. In early February, we returned home to Chicago.

346 *My Marvelous Memories*

A moment ago, I mentioned Pat Mahn. He had an MBA from NYU in NYC. His expertise was in business, finance, and accounting. During our visit, he made several suggestions for me to consider. One I would like to tell you about in more detail . . .

> In the spring of 2001, Pat and I co-taught a graduate business course for the CA State University, Dominguez Hills.
>
> I ran the laboratory for the course. Before the class started, I prepared six experiments, or projects, to be done online using a computer and Excel, a spread sheet program. All of this was accomplished by use of the Internet and emails. I was in IL. Pat and 10 students were in CA. One additional graduate credit hour was awarded for this laboratory.
>
> Pat asked me to help him do this when we met in Fl. At first, I questioned him on my preparation to teach a business course. He told me that he would take care of all the lectures, tests, homework, etc. He knew what I could do with Excel. He saw this when we worked together at CPC. He wanted his students to begin to work with spreadsheets. So, I prepared and graded the 6 projects we agreed upon. This was the first course I ever taught online. It prepared me for some of my future activities.

During February and March, I worked on the graduate business course just mentioned. I also became involved with John *Jazzbo* Linden, a friend and former Brother. It was at this time he began to expand his Quicumque Club (QC) into an online, email platform. I recall we took 2 or 3 trips up to the north side of Chicago. We went to install wiring and computer jacks in the apartment of Luke "Connie" Lynch. This enabled him to be computer connected.

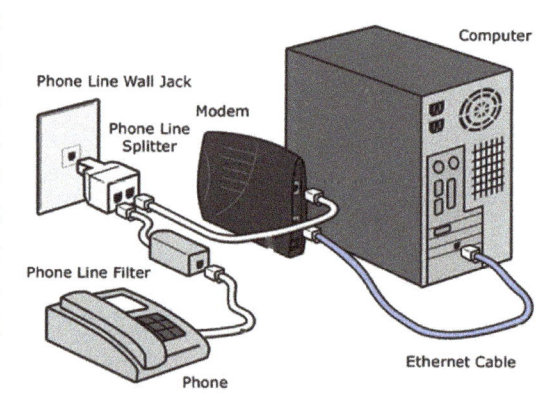

*Chapter Thirteen : Genesis III*

The winter months in Chicago were frigid. I had one cold after another. By mid-March, I was disgusted with being sick. One day I said to Mary, "If I'm retired, I don't want to spend my winters in Chicago." She encouraged me to seek a teaching job in FL or AZ. I went online and contacted a recruiter for high school teaching jobs. He set up two interviews for me in FL after Easter. I planned to fly down to FL on April 18. An interview was scheduled for the 19th at a private high school in Naples. A second interview was also set up for the 20th at a school in Ft. Lauderdale. On the Wednesday before I was to leave, he phoned and told me about a vacancy he'd just received. It wasn't even posted yet. He urged me to rearrange my schedule in order to make a visit to St. Stephen's Episcopal School in Bradenton, FL. Now for the rest of *MS* . . .

Monday, April 16, I flew into Tampa, rented a car, drove to Bradenton, and stayed overnight in a motel.

Tuesday, April 17, I arrived around 9:30 am at St. Stephen's. I went to the office of Jennifer Fox, Principal of the Upper School. She had been alerted to my coming but didn't know when to expect me. Her secretary, Jennifer Szabo, asked me to wait because Ms. Fox was at a meeting. Ms. Szabo soon returned. She asked me to come back at noon. The Principal would meet with me then.

I left the campus, did a little sightseeing, had some coffee, and returned at noon. After an hour interview, Ms. Fox said she was going to recommend I be hired to teach science and math. She set up a meeting later that afternoon with Mr. John Howard, Headmaster of St. Stephen's. He was the one that had to negotiate my salary and offer me a contract.

I met with John, a very kind and gentle man. He was the Headmaster from 1987-2003. We got along quite well! He offered me the job of teaching grades 11-12 math and science. I distictly remember in the middle of our meeting he said, "Dr. Krupp, help me here! What salary should I offer you?" Before I answered his question, I asked a few questions. I learned there were no PhD's on the faculty. Two or three of the faculty were working on earning a DEd but had not yet reached that goal. I then suggested he look at the budget, find the highest salary of any teacher, not an administrator. Next look at the lowest salary. Come up with a figure somewhere in between, maybe the average of the two. He looked in a book, did some calculating, and said, "How about $42,000?"

In my mind, I quickly recalled that this was less than Saudi Arabia. I expected that! However, it was more than Mexico with its 35% tax rate. I smiled and answered him, "John, that's very generous and I'm happy with it! I've liked everyone I met here today at St. Stephen's. I want to say YES to your offer. But would you give me 24 hours to call my wife in Chicago about this?" He laughed and said, "Of course!"

That night I called Mary, and we discussed this offer briefly. On Wednesday morning, April 18, I met with John and told him it was a YES! He asked me to stop by the Business Office and sign some papers. Before we parted, I asked him for two small favors. I told him of my interviews scheduled on the 19th in Naples and on the 20th in Ft. Lauderdale. He knew both Headmasters quite well. I requested he phone both, and give them a message, something like this, "I got a nibble, set the hook, and caught the fish. Dr. Krupp won't be seeing you!" We parted in good humor and we had a harmonious relationship for the next two years.

I returned to Chicago. In the next four months Mary and I hustled to accomplish the following . . .

In mid-June, Mary and I flew to Bradenton. We bought a turnkey, fully furnished condo on the Palm Aire Country Club. Our ground floor, 3 BR, 2 BA condo was an end unit. With windows on three sides it was very bright. We looked out to a pond of water, stocked with our own gator. Across the water was the 14th tee of the golf course. It was the furthest point from the club house. One hundred feet across the road from our condo was a swimming pool that I used frequently over the next five years.

# Chapter Thirteen: Genesis III

*Our Palm Aire home and our personal gator!*

*Our Plainfield home*

We sold our condo in Chicago on July 1. By July 15, we'd moved our IL residence to Plainfield. We were in our new 2BR, 1BA, 5-room apartment attached to Colleen's house. On our patio, we looked out at a ¾-acre lake where Zachary, Austin, and friends swam in summer and ice-skated in winter.

*Load up, Let's go!*

On August 23, I loaded up my truck with a lot of personal stuff, i.e., clothes, books, computer, pots, pans, etc. Mary stayed in IL and continued setting things up in our Plainfield home. Christine drove with me to our new condo in FL. She helped me unload and get things set up. She flew back to IL on August 26.

On Monday, August 27, I started several days of orientation at St. Stephen's. The first day began in the morning with meetings for all new teachers. The afternoon meetings were held for all the new Upper School teachers, which numbered about 8 or 9. Tuesday all teachers of the Upper School, new and old met. Wednesday morning meetings were again held with all Upper School teachers. In the afternoon, an all school faculty meeting was held. It was then I met my new Falcon (school mascot) Friend, Guy Cannata. He has become my best friend over the past 20 years! On Thursday, August 30, students arrived, and classes were held for half the day on Thursday and Friday. The Labor Day weekend started. Tuesday, September 4, the academic year was in full swing.

*My Marvelous Memories*

In the schedule for the Upper School, a ½-hour Chapel was scheduled every Tuesday and Thursday morning. Though these meetings were held in Christ Church, 75% of the time, the topics and activities were nonreligious. They were conducted much like a college seminar in which items of current interest were presented.

The Chapel on Tuesday, September 11, began as usual at 10:00 am. The first speaker was the rector of Christ Church. He began by offering a *strange* prayer for those in *dire straits*. John Howard, Headmaster, spoke for a few minutes and added to the confusion. Jennifer Fox spoke next and added to the muddle. I forget who the 4th speaker was, but during her remarks one of the teachers stood up and said, "Excuse me, but what are you folks talking about?" It was then, that all who had been speaking, realized that none of us in the congregation knew about the airplanes flying into the twin towers in NYC. Once we were informed about the events of 9/11, we prayed in earnest. At 10:30 am we left to resume classes. However, most teachers, as I did, spent the time consoling and counseling our students. It was quite reminiscent of the breakup of the Space Shuttle Challenger in 1986.

Shortly before noon on Thursday, two days after 9/11, we heard an announcement through the speakers in each classroom. All classes were being dismissed immediately. Everyone was told to hustle home and find shelter. Hurricane Gabrielle was on its way north in the Gulf heading for our area. Classes on Friday were cancelled. We were told to listen for further announcements regarding the resumption of classes. So, I rushed home and prepared to *weather* my first hurricane.

During the early morning hours of Friday, Gabrielle made landfall. It inundated the barrier islands at Ft. Myers Beach. It flooded Charlotte Harbor at the entrance to the Peace River. By the time the eye had reached Venice, the winds had subsided to 60 mph, so it was no longer Hurricane Gabrielle, but Tropical Storm Gabrielle. However, it did drop a lot of rain in our area. I sat Friday morning and looked out at the golf course. Though not excessively high, wind gusts of 60-70 mph lashed palm leaves back and forth. The trunks of the trees were bent violently. The rain was thick and heavy. I watched the pond in front of my lanai get higher. I wondered if my condo would be flooded. If so, what should/could I do? All the while, I listened to reports of the storm on TV.

Around noon, the power went off, and shortly thereafter, the rain stopped. The eye of the storm had moved to the northeast, the danger was over. But I had no power. I opened the entry door to look out at my parking lot. My truck was fine, the water was only up to the hub caps. However, the roadway was flooded, and I saw two abandoned cars.

In the afternoon, there was enough daylight to enable me to read, which I did. No TV. No radio. No power. I went to sleep early when it got dark. What else could I do? I was up early Saturday morning. The roadway was now clear of water, so I took a short ride in my truck. I drove around and saw many uprooted palm trees. The land was strewn with palm fronds. Stores, restaurants, gas stations were closed. No power yet! I returned home and a friendly neighbor, who had a gas driven generator, ran an extension cord into my condo. It didn't provide a lot of power, but it did run one or two small lamps and the TV. I ate nuts, dry cereal, and a lot of canned tuna which I opened with a hand can opener. I went to bed around 10:00 pm. Around 2:00 am Sunday, I was awakened by hearing my AC start up. Lights came on. My power was back. I had survived my first hurricane!

St. Stephen's resumed classes on Tuesday, September 18. The campus had suffered no damage to any buildings, but several toppled trees blocked walkways. The main entrance to the Middle School was blocked by a large branch from an oak tree. It took the maintenance staff Sunday and Monday to get the campus cleared. The rest of the academic year went smoothly, as far as I recall.

At St. Stephan's I taught AP calculus, AP physics, and general physics classes, on a full-time basis for two years. At my request, I taught half-time during the 2003-04 academic year and left St. Stephen's at the end of that school year. During this time, I also began teaching physics classes, on a part-time basis, at Manatee Community College, now called State College of Florida.

## My Marvelous Memories

For the academic year of 2004-05, I taught physics and math classes at Sarasota Military Academy (SMA) on a full-time basis. This charter high school started in 2001 and had about 500 students, all of whom were in a JROTC program. It was co-ed. Classes began at 8:00 am, but every morning the entire student body and faculty assembled on the parade grounds at 7:30 am. A trumpet played while the flag was raised. Officers did a quick inspection of the troops and reported to the battalion officers. The Pledge of Allegiance was said, followed by the singing of the National Anthem. The battalion was dismissed, and classes began.

In the first week of December 2004, Vera McClaugherty, Spanish and Language teacher at SMA, and I went on a special trip. We were the guests, along with another 80 teachers from Florida, of the US Marine Corps. They flew us to Savannah, GA and then bussed us to Paris Island. At the age of 75, I was a marine for 4 days! Under the tutelage of a sergeant, I even fired an M-16! Four of the 10 shots I took hit the target, not the bullseye. Being a marine for four days was quite an adventure for this old man!

I've just finished mentioning some of the things I did professionally during the first few years of the 21st century. I'd like to continue about several personal events that occurred during these years. These recollections may not be in chronological order.

In 2001, Mary and I became Florida residents. We got our driver's licenses and voter's cards. Mary, usually came down after the Christmas holidays, and was a snowbird from January to May. We'd spend our summers in IL, but I usually was in Fl from September to early June.

In 2003, Christine married Kevin Wolter. After some thoughts of having a wedding on the beach, on an island somewhere on the planet, we ended up having it at our home in Plainfield. On July 12, we did it all . . .

# Chapter Thirteen: Genesis III

✓ We set up the chapel in the shade alongside our lake. I escorted the bride down the grassy hillside. Our path was strewn with rose petals dropped there by Christine's nephew, Austin, and nieces, Sabrina and Quinlyn. A string trio played appropriate music. The wedding ceremony was conducted in the presence of about 100-110 family and friends.

✓ After the ceremony, we went to a tent where cocktails and hors d'oeuvres were served. My good friend, Dennis Miller, served as bartender. The best man, Chad, prepared some of his *special appetizers*.

✓ An hour later, we all moved to a larger tent. Here, there were linen-covered dining tables set with plates, silverware, napkins, etc. We had a wonderful dinner catered and served to us. All the while, soft music came from speakers mounted in the corners of the tent. A computer that Kevin had setup the day before, played soft music. Speaking of the day before, I recall how the family pitched in and helped . . .

- a) Zachary hauled dishes and other stuff around in his red wagon.
- b) Colleen, Christine, and Mary hung banners, flowers, and bunting in both tents.
- c) TJ set up 120 chairs in the chapel area and then helped me with the bar in the smaller tent.

After the dinner, wedding cake, and coffee, Kevin switched to more danceable music. People danced on the grass alongside the tents. I'm not sure if we did the Hokey-Pokey or Chicken-Dance, but we all had an enjoyable evening which ended around 9:30 pm with fireworks.

Of course, the next day, we all, except for Christine, Kevin, and Kevin's family, spent the day cleaning up!

Finally, I want to mention a great feeling of satisfaction and pleasure I experienced at the end of that weekend. I paid for most of the expenses of the wedding, about $25,000 to $26,000, using my mad money. This was my money in a bank on the Isle of Man. You recall that I hadn't paid a penny of tax on these funds. My spirit was ecstatic at this accomplishment!

One Friday night in October 2001, my new *Falcon Friend*, Guy, and I met at the Kangaroo Pub in downtown Bradenton. We smoked a cigar, nibbled on peanuts, and had several draughts of Foster's Ale. Guy suggested we meet for breakfast the next day, Saturday, at Robin's on Main Street.

The next morning, I joined him and his two children, Joey and Felicia, for breakfast. From October to May, a farmer's market was held every Saturday on Main Street. Guy was in the habit of bringing his two children down each Saturday for breakfast, after which they would wander through the market.

On that first Saturday, when I joined Guy for breakfast at Robin's, neither of us realized what we'd started. It was the birth of the Saturday Morning Breakfast Club. Over 19 years of existence, this club has met at times with only 2 or 3 in attendance and as many as 16 to 18. For the past 8 years it has met on the deck of the Riverside Café in Palmetto. Guy dropped out when the group decided to meet in Palmetto. He wanted to browse the farmer's market in Bradenton. A decade ago, Guy began providing a cooking demonstration on the 3rd Saturday of the month. Today, he is known as the Ambassador to the Bradenton Farmer's Market.

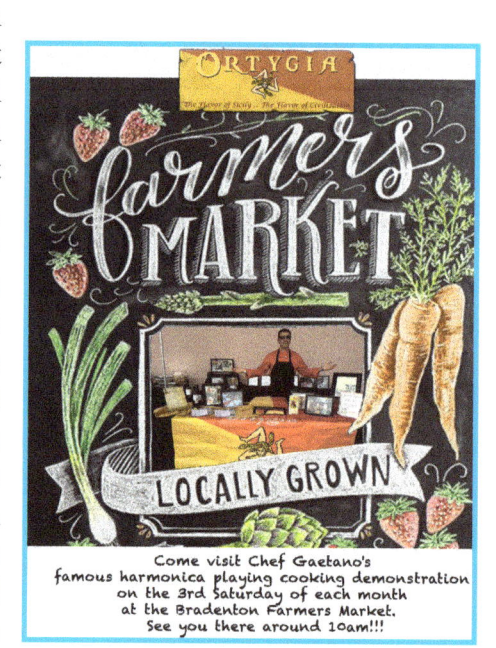

Come visit Chef Gaetano's famous harmonica playing cooking demonstration on the 3rd Saturday of each month at the Bradenton Farmers Market.
See you there around 10am!!!

Earlier, I mentioned I was only teaching half-time during the 2003-2004 academic year at St. Stephen's. In the fall of 2003, Bill and Brenda Fasciano arrived in their motor home from CA. Bill was at St. Stephen's to teach the physics classes I had relinquished. It was during this year that Mary and I became quite friendly with Bill and Brenda. I have many happy memories of . . .

*Chapter Thirteen : Genesis III*

- ✓ Dinners at the Fumble Inn and the Elks Club in Bradenton and the January 2004 Italian feast we had at our condo on the Palm Aire Country Club. Except for the cake, Guy, Bill, and Brenda cooked all those wonderful Italian dishes we dined on.

- ✓ The two visits to their home in Depoe Bay, OR overlooking the Pacific Ocean. Of course, during these visits we had to take Mary to the Chinook Winds Casino and Resort in Lincoln City. Only 10 miles to the north, we went several times so that she could test her luck at the slots.

- ✓ The four or five visits to Omaha, NE to participate in the Annual Martin Family Reunion in early June.

*Depoe Bay, Oregon*

Unfortunately, Mary died in 2006 and Bill in 2015. Both had initially contracted lung cancer but their passing was due to other complications.

Since I just mentioned Mary's death, let me handle that memory quickly and get it over with.

In late May 2006, Mary and I returned from FL to our apartment in Plainfield. During June, I noticed she was coughing a lot. Though I suggested it a few times, she refused to see a doctor. She said it was just bronchitis and she'd get over it.

I was scheduled for two classes in the fall at Manatee CC, so I returned to FL at the end of August. When I left, I asked Colleen to get her mother to a doctor if the cough persisted. Colleen finally got Mary to see a doctor in early October. I believe her first visit was in the week of October 16. She met the doctor, tests were taken, and other tests scheduled for the following week.

On Saturday, October 21, Mary was elated to attend the 50th Anniversary Reunion of her high school graduation. She was so happy to see close friends who she hadn't seen in many years. At this event, she was unaware she had cancer.

On Wednesday October 25, Mary received the news that she had lung cancer. It was diagnosed as small-cell carcinoma of the lungs. Her doctor was very upbeat and said it was treatable. When I spoke to her doctor on the phone, she told me that Mary would be cancer-free by mid-January, and probably would be able to travel to FL by February 1. Mary started chemotherapy (CT) on Monday, October 30. Her next CT treatment was scheduled three weeks later for November 20. She might also begin radiation therapy (RT) during that week. Tests taken later the first week, and the next, showed that the chemicals were doing a good job. The larger tumors had gotten smaller, and some of the smaller tumors were gone!

On Saturday, November 18, I landed in the early afternoon at Midway airport. My friend, Dennis Miller, picked me up and drove me home to Plainfield. I had to arrange this because everyone in Colleen's family was busy that day. Zachary had been confirmed that morning and there was a big family gathering/celebration in Plainfield. When we got to our apartment, Mary phoned down to Colleen. Colleen came up with sandwiches, salads, and beer for the three of us. Mary, Dennis, and I ate and chatted for about an hour. Dennis left to go home. Mary and I talked briefly, but then we both took a short nap. We both got up around 7:30 pm. I made some coffee while she went to the bathroom.

Shortly thereafter, Colleen came up, talked to Mary, and went into the bathroom. She immediately came out and said, "Dad, get dressed. Put your

*Chapter Thirteen: Genesis III*

coat on. We've got to go to the hospital." I asked, "Why?" She said, "I'll tell you in the car. Get a move on!" She later told me that there was blood in the toilet. The doctor had advised her to take Mary immediately to the hospital if that was observed.

What now follows are memories I will never, ever forget, but I must tell them even with the tears in my eyes . . .

> I was seated in the passenger seat with the window down. Colleen and Christine were helping Mary into the back of our van. Our 7-year-old grandson, Austin, came out in the cold of the night without his coat or hat. The words he spoke are seared into my memory. Three times he said. "Goodbye, Grandma!" I don't think Mary heard him, because she never responded.

> We got to the hospital and waited in the emergency room before seeing some medical people. Another hour passed before a doctor saw her. All this time, she was experiencing pain and begged for a shot of something to give her relief. About midnight, she was given a shot of something that put her to sleep. Just before she got the shot we spoke briefly. Those were the last words we ever had with each other. Shortly after that she went to sleep. They moved Mary to the Intensive Care Unit. Colleen called for Christine to get over to the hospital immediately. I may have gone into shock, but I managed to call my brother while Colleen called others in our family.

> Early Sunday morning my brother, Ron, and Mary's brother and sister, Dennis and Colleen, joined us. Our family had come together to give support, help, and comfort to each other. All were there, except one, our son, Bobby!

> To explain what had happened to Mary was that the strong chemicals that were destroying the cancer cells had lowered her immune system. She had gotten an infection and she was dying of sepsis. As a result, her organs were shutting down. Sepsis was the cause listed on her death certificate.

> She never awoke from the shot given her at midnight Saturday. Sunday evening, I held her hand one last time, kissed her forehead, and whispered in her ear. By 10:00 pm Sunday, November 19, Mary left us.

{breathe. just breathe.}

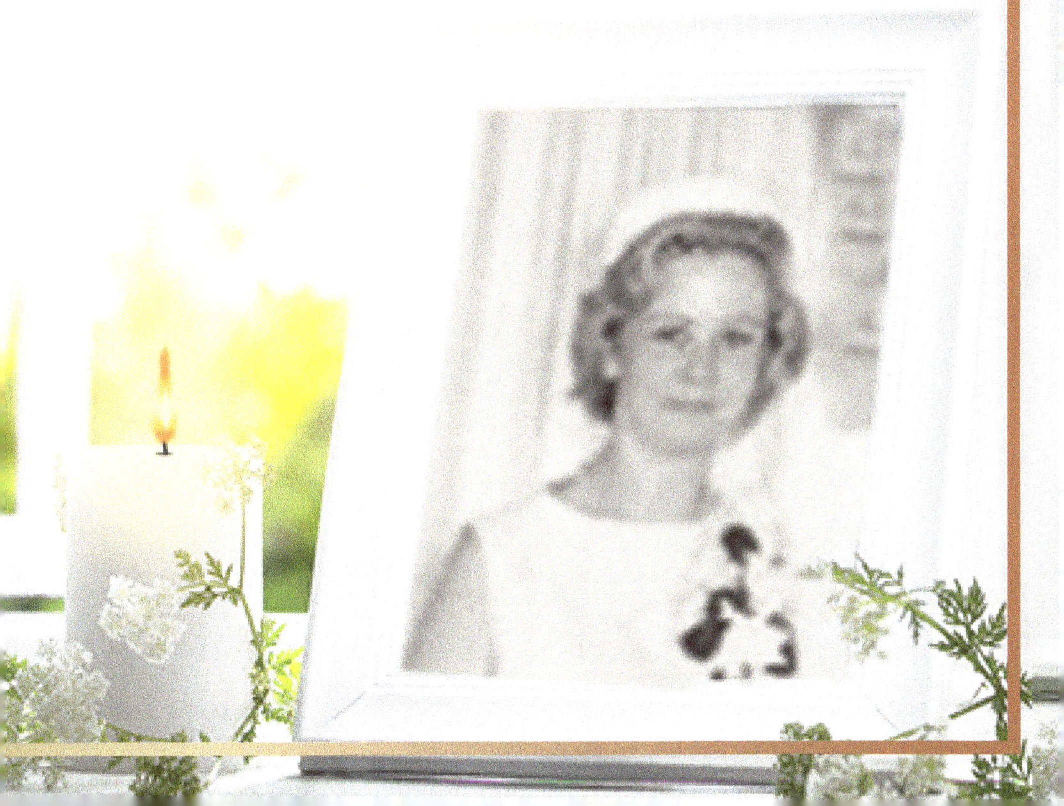

# My Marvelous Memories

On Monday, November 20, we all slept late, got up about 10:00 am, and began discussing what now needed to be done. During the late afternoon, family again stepped in to help. Mary's niece, Laura, was married to Paul who owned a deli in Naperville. About 5:00 pm there was an unexpected knock at the door. A delivery man was there to deliver a ton of food from the Schmaltz Deli on Paul's behalf. The sandwiches, cold-cuts, salads, and rolls he sent lasted the better part of three days. The other recollections I have of this week follow . . .

Friday, November 24, the day after Thanksgiving, we held a 1-night wake in Plainfield. Christine had brought her 2-year-old daughter to the funeral home. For most of the evening she'd been left in a playroom for children. Around 9:00 pm, Christine planned to take Laura home and put her to sleep. But first she carried Laura to view Mary in the casket. Unforgettable, are the words spoken by our granddaughter. While in her mother's arms, Laura pointed and said, "Look, grandma sleeping."

Saturday, November 25, was the day of the funeral and it went quickly. From the funeral parlor, it was ½-mile drive to St. Mary Immaculate Church for the funeral Mass. Ron gave the eulogy from notes I had given him. I don't think I could have delivered it. While we waited outside the church for the casket to be placed in the hearse, my niece Karyn came to me. She is Betty and Ron's special-needs daughter. Tears were streaming down her face. Karyn is short and I am tall, She put her arms around my waist and said, "I'm going to miss Aunt Mary!" From the church, it was only a 1½-mile drive to St. Mary's Cemetery on the Naperville-Plainfield Road.

Entrance to cemetary

Mary's Resting Place

*Chapter Thirteen: Genesis III*

Prayers were said at St. Mary's Cemetery and Mary was finally laid to rest. A luncheon for family and friends followed the burial. That's is all I want to say about this horrible week in my life.

I stayed in Plainview for two months to handle a lot of paperwork which was required after someone dies, i.e., insurance claims, social security, etc.

> KRUPP_Mary Krupp, nee O'Hare, age 68
> a resident of Chicago, died Sunday, Nov. 19, 2006. Beloved wife of Dr. Robert H. Krupp; loving mother of Colleen (Terry) Brown, Robert, Jr. (Jeanine) Krupp and Christine (Kevin Wolter) Krupp; adoring grandmother of Zachary, Austin, Sabrina, Quinlyn and Laura; devoted daughter of the late Dennis and Mary O'Hare; dear sister of Dennis O'Hare, Colleen (Bob) Hrisko; loving aunt to many nieces and nephews. Mary was a 1956 graduate of Mercy High School, Chicago and later chaired several annual alumnae dinners. She attended Saint Mary's of Notre Dame College. After raising her children Mary enjoyed traveling through Europe, the Middle East, and was proud to visit all 50 states in our country. Mary provided volunteer assistance to the elderly and later became a certified nursing assistant. Mary enjoyed spending her winters in Bradenton, FL. Visitation Friday, Nov. 24, 4 to 8 p.m. at Overman-Jones Funeral Home, 309 S. Joliet Rd., Plainfield. Closing Prayers will begin Saturday, Nov. 25, 10 a.m. at the funeral home and will proceed to a 10:30 a.m. Mass at St. Mary Immaculate Church, 15629 S. Route 59, Plainfield. Interment St. Mary Immaculate Cemetery, Plainfield. In lieu of flowers, memorials to: American Cancer Society, 17060 Oak Park Ave., Tinley Park, IL 60477.

A *Thank You* note was sent to all who had signed the Guest Book at the Overman-Jones funeral parlor. Similar *Thank You* notes were sent to those who had posted their names electronically on the Obituary page of the *Chicago Tribune*.

I finished up in January by sending a special letter of Thanks to 136 women I never met or knew. These were the members of the 1956 class of Mercy High School who had attended their Anniversary Reunion in October. I wrote a special letter on my computer, printed out copies, signed my name, and sent them out. Unfortunately, I didn't keep a copy. As best as I can recollect the letter said something like this . . .

# My Marvelous Memories

> Dear XXX,
>
> I am looking at a picture of 136 lovely ladies, all smiling beautifully. It is the picture of you and your classmates at the 50th Anniversary Reunion Banquet on October 21. In the 3rd row, just right of center, wearing a red dress and yellow scarf is Mary O'Hare Krupp, my wife.
>
> Maybe you knew her and spoke to her. Maybe not! In any case, on that evening Mary did not know she had lung cancer. Four days later she learned about this diagnosis and began treatments. On November 19, Mary passed and left us all.
>
> I am writing this letter to share this sad news with you. But most of all, I want to THANK YOU for making this reunion the last happy event in Mary's life. I am forever in your debt!
>
> Sincerely,
>
> *Robert H. Krupp*
>
> Robert Krupp

I mailed the letter with a Memorial Card to everyone in that picture.

After this, I packed up and flew back to Florida.

## Chapter Thirteen: Genesis III

In February 2007, I was back home at my condo on the Manatee River, near downtown Bradenton. Mary and I had purchased it at the end of December 2005. We moved into it in March of 2006. Mary lived in it for only three months.

At this time, my friend Guy was in the process of buying, renovating, and decorating his restaurant called *Ortygia*, in the *Village of the Arts*. He finally opened it in late October of 2007. He told me about another restaurant in the *Village*. It only opened for breakfast and lunch. It was owned and operated by Kim Hoffman. She had opened her *Charisma Café* in October 2006.

It was only ¾-mile from my condo, so I went there two or three times a week for breakfast or lunch. I always got a laugh from her when I opened the door, strode in, and shouted, "Kim, I'm here! I want a cup of your rich, hot, black, flavorful, steaming, delicious coffee!" Kim is only four months older than my daughter Colleen. She became my first *adopted* Florida daughter!

*The Charisma Cafe*

*Me with Kim at the Cafe!*

You may wonder how I coped with Mary's loss in the months after her passing. Did I find solace in alcohol? No! Did I suffer from deep depression? No! My salvation was in *work*. I had always worked hard. It was during this time that I realized, I'm a *workaholic*.

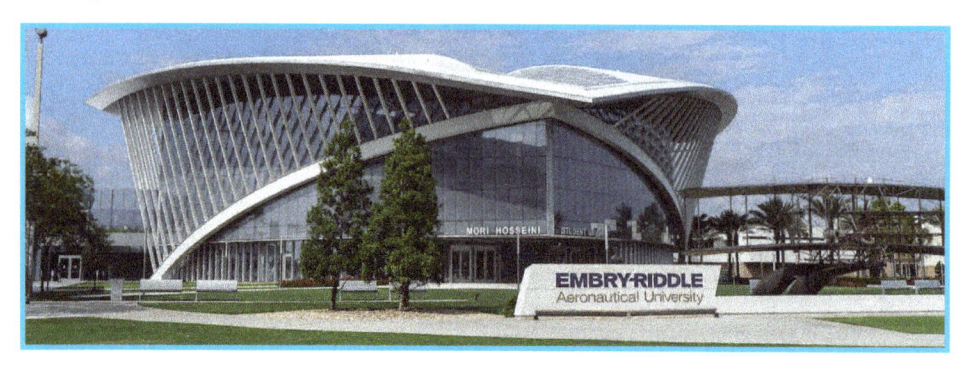

I need to now step back in time and tell you about Embry-Riddle Aeronautical University (ERAU). In the fall of 2004, I had made a connection with ERAU. First, let me tell you about this university. If you investigate Wikipedia, you will find these words . . .

*"ERAU is a private university system offering associate, bachelor, master's and PhD degree programs . . . It is the largest, fully accredited university system specializing in aviation and aerospace, and has campuses in Daytona Beach, FL and Prescott, AZ and other locations worldwide. It is considered one of the top aviation and aerospace schools in America."*

If you dig deeper into history, you'll find that in December 1925, Talton Higbee Embry and John Paul Riddle started the Embry-Riddle Company at the Lunken Airport in Cincinnati, OH. In the spring of 1926, the School of Aviation opened. However, it closed in 1930. In 1939 the Aviation School (AS) reopened in Miami, FL. It operated along Highway 41, at the old Tamiami Airport, nine miles west of the city center. During this time, the AS partnered with the University of Miami.

From 1938-1944, the US government funded and promoted a flight training program called the Civilian Pilot Training Program (CPTP). Though the stated purpose of the program was to increase the number of civilian pilots, it had a clear impact on military preparedness. It was during this time that the AS trained and certified its most famous alum, a young naval officer named John F. Kennedy.

After WWII, the AS continued to train pilots at this location. However, in the early 1960's, plans were underway to close the Tamiami Airport and move it elsewhere. In April 1965, the AS moved to Daytona Beach and changed its name to Embry-Riddle Aeronautical Institute. It is there today and the campus in Daytona Beach has grown significantly.

## Chapter Thirteen: Genesis III

During the 1970's, many programs and degrees were added. One of the programs established during this period was the opening of *mini campuses* worldwide. In 1978, a second residential campus was opened in Prescott, AZ. What began in 1925, as a regional school, for pilots and aviation mechanics, became a university that annually enrolls over 35,000 undergraduate and graduate students.

A *mini campus* was found most often at a US Air Force Base (AFB) somewhere in the world. Occasionally, one would be located at a Marine Naval Air Station (MNAS). What was it? It was simply an office provided at the military base. ERAU furnished it with a desk, chairs, filing cabinets, phone, and office supplies. ERAU hired civilian and military personnel to work there. Any military aviation person could drop in and enroll for a class. In the early years, a secretary would arrange for a teacher in Daytona Beach or Prescott to conduct a correspondence class. This is what I experienced in Saudi Arabia when I tutored some ERAU students while in the Kingdom.

During the last years of the 20th century, more AFB's were added worldwide, and the number of military personnel grew. The draft was eliminated, and the US moved to a *volunteer service*. Non-commissioned personnel usually do not have a degree. However, the government encouraged these service men and women to further their education. Government funds provided tuition assistance for college classes. Many more students came to the *mini campuses* seeking various classes.

In the fall of 2004, I became a member of the ERAU Tampa Campus. It was located on the MacDill AFB, six miles southwest of downtown Tampa. This campus consisted of two offices and a meeting room used as a classroom for 15-20 students. The Director of the campus was Hal Henning, a full-time employee of ERAU. Besides his administrative duties, Hal taught two classes each term. He sought out local, part-time faculty to teach different classes. He recruited, interviewed, collected resumes and transcripts, and checked on the teachers. Twice a year he held a faculty meeting. All the faculty were adjunct, part-time teachers.

I first met Hal in 2004. I had an interview and supplied him with all the documentation he needed. I was hired and became a member of the Tampa Campus as an Adjunct Assistant Professor. From 2004 to 2009 I taught physics classes in a classroom setting that enrolled 8-20 students. I recall . . .

- One class held at MacDill AFB.

- Four classes at the Coast Guard Naval Air Station at the St. Petersburg Airport.

- Five classes in an office complex near the Tampa Airport.

- Four classes at the Moody AFB north of Valdosta, GA. To enter any military or airport facility, I, as well as the students, had to go through a security gate to get on the site for each class meeting.

I've provided you this long, lengthy description about ERAU because of what now follows. I believe it was my salvation in the months that immediately followed Mary's passing!

In September 2006, two months before Mary's diagnosis, I received a newsletter from ERAU. One article in it intrigued me. I read it again and again. It informed the faculty that ERAU's Board had initiated a program of *faculty grants*. Money would be provided, up to a maximum of $10,000, for proposals on how the new technology, computer technology or Internet use, could be incorporated into ERAU's courses. I had an idea that fitted with the goals stipulated for the proposals. My main concern was, were these grants available to *adjunct faculty*? I went into Tampa and met Hal Henning at MacDill. We read that newsletter article together. He agreed that it didn't say the grants were for full-time faculty only. He suggested I wait until he checked with people in Daytona Beach. By mid-September, Hal called and told me to go ahead with a proposal. I started working on it immediately. In fact, in mid-October, I drove to Daytona Beach to meet with Dr. Tom Sieland and a few other administrators to obtain further information.

*Chapter Thirteen: Genesis III*

In case you wonder about the nature of my proposal, let me explain it simply. In all the physics classes that I had taught at ERAU, there were no experiments done. I knew of several simulated experiments available on the Internet. It was my idea to write instructions for doing simulated labs on the computer using the Internet. These would be added to the curriculum of the basic physics course ERAU was offering. By the time I left Florida on November 18, I had completed 50-60% of the proposal.

As mentioned earlier, upon my return to Florida in February 2007, work was my salvation. This proposal had to be finished and submitted by March 1. I had Dr. Tom Sieland review it and he helped with some suggestions. I submitted it two days before the deadline. Awards were announced in mid-April, and I was one to receive a grant of $10,000. Now my work really began!

From May-September, I found on the Internet 10 simulated physics experiments. All were suitable for ERAU's PHYS 102 course. In time, they became part of a course curriculum. I prepared 10 because in 2007, all undergraduate courses were scheduled as 12 weeks long. Dr. Sieland, Coordinator of the PHYS 102 course, made this suggestion of developing only ten.

For each experiment I wrote . . .

a) An instruction sheet containing specific, step-by-step instructions.
b) A data sheet with tables in which to record data.
c) A report sheet asking questions which utilized the data collected.

From September-November, I taught a PHYS 102 class at the Coast Guard Naval Air Station in St. Petersburg. As part of their assignments, students did the 10 experiments, gave their reports, and critiqued each experiment. This was the first field tests of these experiments. In a similar manner, a *second field test* was conducted at Moody AFB, in January-March of 2008. I wrote a final report on my research grant and submitted it by the deadline of March 31, 2008. During that summer, Dr. Sieland incorporated these 10 experiments into the PHYS 102 curriculum for all online offerings of this course. In mid-April, I was invited to attend the ERAU graduation ceremony held at the Daytona Campus in mid-May. At this ceremony, I received an award as *ERAU's 2008 Adjunct Teacher of the Year*. I later learned that in 2008 ERAU had over 1,800 adjunct teachers around the world!

In 2011, ERAU changed all its undergraduate classes to a 9-week term. Three experiments were dropped from the curriculum in the course. About the same time, the University began to shift most of its undergraduate classes into its Worldwide Division. Most of the offerings in Worldwide are presented online using the Internet in an asynchronous format. Occasionally, some courses are offered in a synchronous, *Skype* type fashion. Rarely, if ever, is an undergraduate course now presented in a *traditional classroom* setting.

Since 2010, I have taught over 60 classes for ERAU. Two of these were in a traditional classroom setting held in Tampa. All the others were online. This is all I have to say about ERAU!

Along with work, I also had the help of friends, new and old, to cope with Mary's passing. Thanks to my Falcon Friend, Guy, I met Joe Schmidt and Claudia Deschu.

Guy, Joe, and I started meeting for dinner on Monday nights. We didn't plan or foresee it, but this grew into the *Monday Night Men's Night Out* group. For 9 or 10 years, the meeting locations varied and the membership fluctuated. Besides Guy "the Chef" Cannata, Joe "the Gopher" Schmidt, and me "the Scientist," I recall . . .

    a)    Bill "the bald-headed Cuban" Aleman,

    b)    Cliff "the Schemer" Boltwood,

    c)    Kenny "the Stoic" Merritt,

    d)    William "Little Billy" Cannady,

    e)    Tony "the Merchant" Bua, and

    f)    Sal "the Obstinate" Alfonso.

## Chapter Thirteen: Genesis III

Due to movements out of state and other job requirements, this group no longer meets regularly. However, thanks to Joe Schmidt and Little Billy, six of us met again in early December 2018 and again in late March 2021.

There also was the group of Old Folks consisting of Guy's mother, Dorothy, Claudia's father, Casper, and Nicky Rysdale. We four would often go to the South Florida Museum for their . . .

 a) Monthly Wednesday night Think & Drink,

 b) Monthly Wednesday night Stelliferous (where stars, planets and constellations are headed in the next 30 days), and

 c) Weekly Friday night Old Time Movies.

All of these programs usually started at 6:00 pm or 7:00 pm. Afterwards, we'd go to a late-night supper, often at Casper's home a few blocks from the museum. Nicky was a very active member at the Museum and, because of her, I too became a member.

Nicky was also very active in a group called Save the Dogs which focused on adopting greyhounds. These animals were used in races at various dog tracks around FL. By the time a dog was 2-2½ years old, it was getting old and slow. If the dog was not adopted, it was put down. This group had an annual fund raiser and Nicky had purchased tickets for a table of six. So, I recall one Sunday our Old Folks group had brunch with the dogs. The event was held at the local dog track. In attendance were 400-500 people and about 200 greyhounds. The breakfast was catered in and was nothing to rave about. However, the most amazing things were those greyhounds. They laid or sat by the chair of their owners. During the 2½-hours of My Brunch with the Dogs, I never heard one bark!

*Beautiful Greyhounds!*

From 2007- 2013, I took a few trips, but I'm confused as to the exact years some of them occurred. Some that I recall . . .

-Several trips to Sun City, AZ to visit friends such as Shirley Silverman, Bonnie Kravitz, Shirley Barone, Frank & Carol Bowman, and Michael & Mary Gibson from Alaska.

*Sun City*

*Lake Havasu*

-Other trips to Surprise, AZ and Lake Havasu City, AZ to visit Brenda and Bill Fasciano. On one of these to LHC, I rode the Santa Fe Chief railroad train from Chicago and 44 hours later got off in Needles, CA where Brenda picked me up.

In September 2011, Ron and I flew to Las Vegas and rented a car. We didn't stop to gamble but headed east and drove past the Hoover Dam. Over the next two weeks, we visited several National Parks in AZ, NM, and CA. We stopped in Lake Havasu City to see Brenda and Bill. We went to see our cousin, Gerry Krupp, and his wife Judy, in Palm Desert, CA. We even managed an afternoon in Oatman, AZ to pet and feed the wild burros that came down from the mountains each day to be fed by tourists.

I took four trips to Omaha for the Martin Annual Family Reunion.

*Hoover Dam*

*Wild Burros*

# Chapter Thirteen: Genesis III

*Collepietro*

*Popoli*

In September 2010, Guy, Dorothy, and I went to Italy for 22-days. This was Dorothy's first trip to Italy. For Guy and me, it was our second. We spent a few days in Rome. Then we went east to Popoli, Collepietro, and Nevelle in the Appian Mountains. This is where Dorothy's mother and father had been raised. We visited family members she had never met before. We even got to Pescara on the Adriatic Sea. Returning briefly to Rome, we caught a flight to Sicily and stayed a week in Syracuse to visit family members of Guy's father. To sum up this wonderful trip, for our 22-nights in Italy we only stayed 5 nights in a hotel, all in Rome. During the entire trip, we only ate in a restaurant five times. How did we manage that? We were with family!

*Pescara on the Adriatic Sea*

*Piazza Duomo in Syracuse*

*Fountain of Diana at Piazza Archimedes*

In June 2011, I drove to Winona, MN to attend the 60th anniversary of my graduation from St. Mary's U. Fr. Bob Botthof drove with me. Flo Donatelli in Madison, WI was to join us, but he backed out at the last minute. Mary & Pete Schmit came by train from St. Louis for the weekend. We four had a great time at this reunion.

I failed to mention it earlier, but my wife, Mary, and I attended two anniversary gatherings at Saint Mary's. The first one was in 1996 for my 45th reunion. The second was in 2001 for the 50th reunion. I remember Pete Schmit was at this reunion, but I 'm not sure if his Mary was there as well.

In June 2012, Christine, Laura, and I drove to Fall Creek Falls State Park near Knoxville, TN. We went there to celebrate Betty and Ron's 50th wedding anniversary. Many family and friends gathered there to celebrate with Betty and Ron, including Paul and Ketut, both of whom came from Bali, Indonesia, to celebrate with us.

*Fall Creek Falls*

On the way down to TN, Christine, Laura, and I stopped in Hodgenville, KY to visit the Abraham Lincoln Birthplace Historical Park. During our tour, I recall reading a panel on a wall that had a quote from Lincoln. I'd never heard it before. It read, "I was born and grew up in a log cabin. Now I live in the White House."

*Birthplace of Abraham Lincoln*

After about five days of celebrating in the state park, we left and drove 45 miles south to Chattanooga. My good friend, Ed Cahill, gave us an excellent tour, with many comments, through
  (a) Chickamauga & Chattanooga National Parks, and
  (b) Lookout Mountain. Laura loved taking a ride up the mountain on the Lookout Mountain Incline Railway and her spelunking adventure to Ruby Falls. On our way home, we stayed at Falls Mill B&B. Here we saw a working watermill grinding grain. We stayed overnight in an old log cabin that had been restored and the interior modernized. Laura loved it and plans to revisit Ruby Falls and the log cabin.

# Chapter Thirteen: Genesis III

*Beautiful Ruby Falls and the Incline Railway*

In June 2013, I went to Glencoe, MO to attend a reunion. My good friend, Fr. Bob Botthof took a bus from Bloomington, IN to get there. Earlier, we'd made plans for me to drive him back home to Bloomington. After the reunion meeting in Glencoe, we stayed a night in St. Louis at the Dominican Aquinas Institute, a house of studies adjacent to the St. Louis U. While there, our friends, Mary and Pete Schmit, introduced us to Gian-Tony's Ristorante, a wonderful Sicilian restaurant on The Hill.

*Fr. Bob*

The next day, Bob and I drove to Springfield, IL and visited the new Abraham Lincoln Presidential Museum. After lunch, we drove to Taylorville, IL. We went to the Oak Hill Cemetery to visit the grave of his wife, Mary. She'd come from Taylorville and that's why she was buried there. We silently prayed for a few minutes. As we returned to the car Fr. Bob said, "You know, Bob, I was married for 23 years. I've been a priest for 25 years, 2 years longer than I was with her." A year later, October 2014, my dear friend Fr. Bob was laid to rest next to Mary in Taylorville.

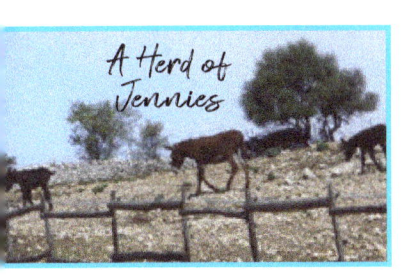

*A Herd of Jennies*

In September 2013, Guy, Dorothy and I joined 12 others on Chef Gaetano's first Culinary Tour to Sicily. It had all been arranged by April, Guy's new companion and business associate. In time, April became my *second adopted Florida daughter*! We stayed near Syracuse. I remember trips to Modica, Catania, Pozzallo, and Taormina. One day we visited an organic farm. Guy had an opportunity to milk some jennies (female donkeys) from a herd of 22 on the farm. Later, we were served an outstanding lunch in which all the food had been produced on the farm. One desert used the milk from the jennies!

- Nona Requests a Tarantella
- Guy & Nick making Pizza appetizers!
- Fresh tomatoes for Lunch!
- Guy & Marko preparing Lunch
- A few imgredients
- Individual antipasto serving! Yum!
- More fresh produce!
- Me with April!

## Chapter Thirteen: Genesis III

In April 2014, I fell and broke my right wrist. It wasn't too bad. However, it impaired my ability to walk. My sense of balance was greatly diminished, and my right hip and leg didn't function well. During the next 15 months, I spent...

- ✓ 2 weeks in Blake Hospital's Therapy Center.
- ✓ 3 months in Surrey Place, for continued physical therapy.
- ✓ 10 months in Verandas on the River, an Assisted Living Center.

*My Room at Verandas and View from the Dining Room*

Though I am now able to move around using a walker, my *traveling days* are over! In January 2020, I received a pacemaker and a new heart valve in April. In 2021, I survived Covid-19 and have received 2-vaccinations, but my driving days are over!

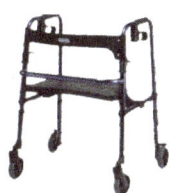

In June 2009, an event occurred that started me on a new, *major adventure* in **MS**. It was totally unforeseen and unplanned for. I'll tell you how it came about in the next chapter.

*Bob the Author
hard at work to write this very book!*

# Chapter Fourteen
## A Literary Artist
### (2009 - 2021)

••••••••••••

Laura, my granddaughter was five years old and in kindergarten at the Savoy Montessori School near Champaign. In early June of 2009, I attended her *Kindergarten Graduation*.

During the ceremony, I thought about Mary, her grandmother, who couldn't be present for this happy event. I sat there with tears in my eyes, but joy in my heart! I cradled a bouquet of red roses in my arms which I planned to give Laura. I thought to myself, what else could I have brought besides these beautiful flowers? Then it dawned on me!

- If you believe in a God, you will say His Spirit spoke to me.

- If you have faith in a hereafter, you will say Mary whispered in my ear.

- If you cannot accept these two beliefs, then it was simply a BBB, Big Bang in the Brain, as several neurons sparked together!

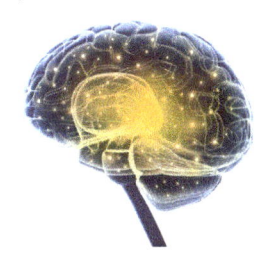

In any case, I thought to myself, *why don't I tell her what I know*? And *what do I know*? I know the physical sciences, physics, chemistry, astronomy, meteorology, and geology, as well as, mathematics. All my adult life has been devoted to teaching these subjects.

I will tell her *what I know* by writing short stories about a physical concept and explain it to her. I will use pictures whenever possible to help her understand the concept. Now I must tell you, I did not go home and immediately start writing. This is what happened over the next 12 months . . .

In August 2009, my friend, Bill Fasciano, was diagnosed with lung cancer. He and Brenda were living in Lake Havasu City (LHC), AZ. Surgery was planned for late October. I went out to be with him and help Brenda. I arrived in AZ in mid-October. His surgery was planned for the end of the month at the LHC Hospital.

Thankfully, Bill went to Mayo Clinic in Scottsdale, AZ for a second opinion. He decided to follow the recommendations of the doctors at Mayo, which did not include surgery. Instead, he received chemotherapy (CT) and radiation therapy (RT). He survived for 5 more years. His death in 2015, was not due to cancer, but other medical issues. In any case, during October to December he went to Scottsdale, 200 miles away, for his treatments. On his first trip to Scottsdale, Bill parked his motor home in an RV park near Scottsdale.

Brenda and Bill stayed two or three nights in their motor home while he went to the clinic. Meanwhile, I stayed in LHC, took care of the home, and their two Schnauzers, Sherlock and Watson.

It was during this period that I began writing stories about science for young children.

## Chapter Fourteen: A Literary Artist

Bill, you may recall, was also a science teacher. He and Brenda were the first to see the words I'd written. Bill gave me some excellent feedback, which I incorporated into my stories. In mid-December, I returned home to IL for the Christmas holidays. I arrived with stories that I thought would be 10 different books. I sent copies of these stories to publishers around the country, especially New York City. I never heard a word back!

During the holidays, I read all 10 stories to Laura. I wanted to see if she understood the words I'd written. I also wanted to see how she'd react to being introduced to new vocabulary words. She was now six years old. It took several days, but when I finished reading these stories, she told me that she'd learned about 30 new words.

In January 2010, I returned to FL and spent a lot of time mailing out my stories to publishers and agents. It was discouraging not to hear back from any of them. However, something happened in late January that was good to hear and encouraged me to move forward with this venture. I recall it was a Thursday evening. Christine called and said, "You'll never guess what she just did?" I thought to myself, "Oh-oh! What did she do?"

Christine went on to tell me, that the previous Sunday, she and Laura had gone shopping for school supplies. While they wandered through the store, Laura stopped and said, "Look Mommy, *acid*." Laura recognized the word acid. It was one of the new words she'd learned while hearing the stories I'd read to her. This store was selling vials of litmus paper. Christine spent $1 and bought Laura a vial of blue litmus paper and a vial of red litmus paper.

We now come to why Christine had called. A blizzard was coming into IL. All schools were closed on Friday in anticipation of a heavy snowfall. The snow had started falling on Thursday afternoon. Laura went out for an hour and played in it before supper. When she came in, she brought a glass filled with snow. She placed it on the kitchen counter. Christine asked, "What's that?" Laura answered, "It's a glass of snow. After it melts, I want to test it to see if it's an acid?" I ask you, "How many 6-year-old children are testing snow to see if it is acidic?"

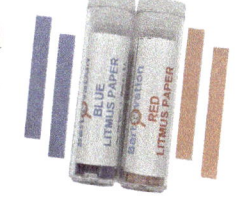

Advance forward several years to late January 2019. During this time, the Midwest experienced extremely cold weather. Laura, who was now 14, did an experiment I suggested to her. One day, when the temperature reached a high of -12 °F, she stepped out on her patio, and turned 2 cups of boiling water into instant snow!

*Science is 'cool'*

Since I didn't hear back from any publisher in 2010, I decided to *self publish*. There are hundreds of firms around the world that will help one publish a book. Most are available online. Since I didn't know much about the publishing business, I selected one locally. It was Pepper Tree Press (PTP) in Sarasota, FL.

When I first started working with PTP, I thought I would publish all 10 stories into 10 books. Each story would have 5 to 10 drawings depicting an experiment. Julie Ann James, at PTP, pointed out the foolishness in doing this. She first told me that if I was to be an author of children's books, I should never expect to make money. The reason was that children's books are usually priced very low, $5 or $10, and at most $15.

One Friday, I gave her 2 or 3 of my stories to read over the weekend. We met the following Monday. She said it would take about $1000 to setup the front and back covers of one book. So, 10 books would cost me $10,000, just for the covers. In addition, each drawing I planned to use would cost $80 to $100. An artist from her staff would draw what I wanted. Once I paid the artist, the drawing was mine to use as I pleased. She then said since my subjects dealt with reality, I could use free pictures available on the Internet. I signed a contract for $3500 with PTP. In 2011, I published Book #1 in my first series. I called this series **Laura and Grandpa, Discovering Science Together.** (L & G, DST).

*Chapter Fourteen: A Literary Artist*   381

Book 1, Published in 2011, includes 10 stories:
1. The Egg
2. Curds and Whey
3. The Cabbage
4. Cabbage Paper
5. Colored Pens
6. The Candle
7. The Rainbow
8. The Window
9. Roses are Red, Violets are Blue
10. Epsom Towers

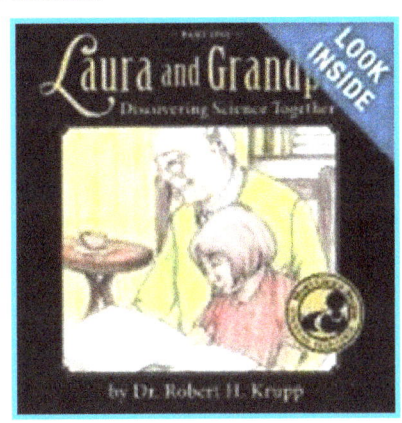

As mentioned earlier, my first book was published under contract with Pepper Tree Press. I soon learned that I could save a great deal of money by being my own publisher. For example, working with PTP Book #1 cost $8.50 to print and sold for $14.95. Book #2, which my company published, costs $4.50 to print and sells for $9.95.

However, I still had to utilize the services of a graphics person to find "free pictures," and to set-up each page to blend text and graphics. April helped me find Kristina of Kristina Edstrom Designs. She has been a true treasure and has helped in every book I have published since 2011, including this one! I will have more to say about her as we move along.

Book 2, Published in 2013, includes 3 longer stories:
1. Clouds
2. Time for Slime!
3. Hail

In L&G, DST Book #3, Kristina did an outstanding job! Because of her graphics, this book received a silver (second place) award by FAPA (Florida Authors and Publishers Association) in 2015.

Book 3, published in 2014- includes 4 stories:
1. Show and Tell
2. Dancing in the Jug
3. Floating Ice
4. Music, Music, Music

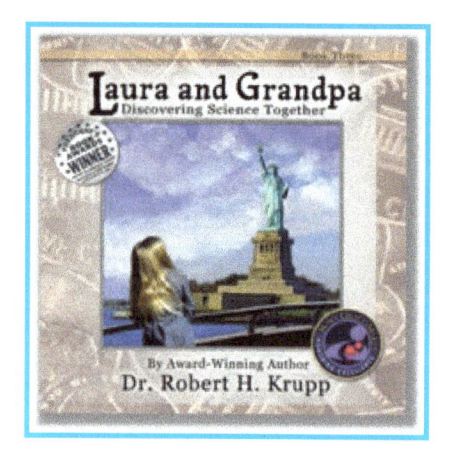

Book 4, published in 2015- includes 5 stories:
1. Blue Moon of 2012
2. The Blue Moons of 2018
3. Rotation and Revolution
4. The Fuse
5. The Diaper

Book 5, published in 2016- includes 4 stories:
1. Fog
2. Humidity
3. The Bottle
4. Ice Cream

*Chapter Fourteen: A Literary Artist*

In 2018, I decided to update the look of the first book, Laura and Grandpa, Discovering Science Together, Book 1, and publish a special anniversary editon. It includes all 10 stories with more graphics and updated text.

Book 1- Anniversary Edition, published in 2018-
1. The Egg
2. Curds and Whey
3. The Cabbage
4. Cabbage Paper
5. Colored Pens
6. The Candle
7. The Rainbow
8. The Window
9. Roses are Red, Violets are Blue
10. Epsom Towers

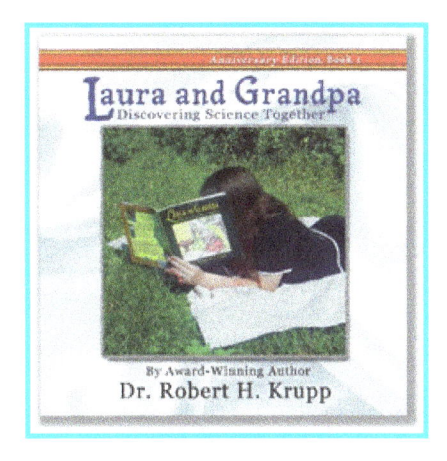

All these books were classified as *picture story science books for children,* written for the 4- to 8-year-old.

In 2014, an Exhibition was held in Bradenton called *The Da Vinci Machines Exhibit.* Ron and I went to see it in early March. Before leaving, I spoke to the manager and told him I was going to write a book about this exhibition. He asked, "Why?" I told him that I write books about science for young children. I mentioned that I planned to bring Laura to the exhibit later in the month. The manager was so pleased to hear this, he gave me a special pass. I could visit the Exhibition as often as I wished for FREE! During the spring of 2014, I often went to the exhibit to do research, take notes, and pictures. There was so much material, I soon realized that more than one book had to be written!

*The amazing and inspiring DaVinci Machines Exhibit*

In July 2014, my first book in this series called ***Laura and Grandpa, Discovering Da Vinci*** was published. This series has been completed with the publication of Books #2 and #3. Like the first series mentioned, all are classified as *picture story science books for children*. These books are written for the 8- to 13-year-old youngster.

Book 1, "Mechanics", published in 2014-
includes 11 stories:
1. Leonardo
2. Force
3. Mass and Force
4. Energy
5. Levers
6. Pulleys
7. Wheel and Axle
8. Inclined Plane
9. The Screw
10. The Wedge
11. Home Again

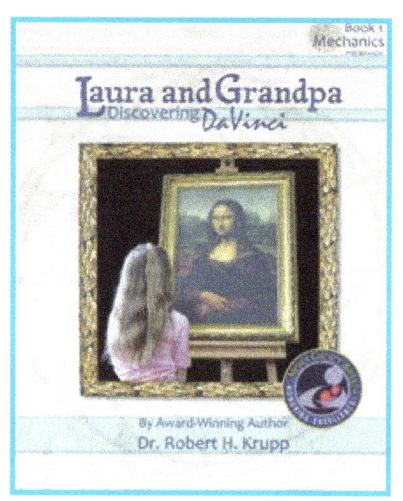

Book 2, "War Machines", published in 2016-
includes 9 stories:
1. Leonardo
2. The Wall
3. Bridges
4. The Tank
5. Cannons
6. Boats
7. The Diver
8. Viola Organista
9. Designer of War Machines

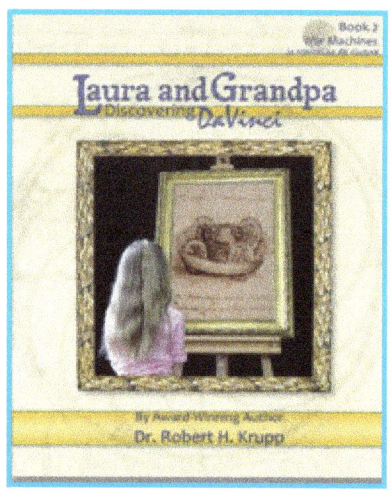

## Chapter Fourteen: A Literary Artist

This was the last book in the Da Vinci series, Kristina did another phenomenal job on its lay-out and graphics. In 2020, the FAPA awarded this book a First Place, Gold Award—the first time a book of mine ever earned a First Place!

Book 3, "Aviation and Art", published in 2019- includes 23 stories:

1. Leonardo
2. The Flying Machines
3. The Air Screw
4. The Parachute
5. The Baptism of Christ
6. Madonna of the Carnation
7. The Annunciation
8. Portrait de Benci
9. Benois Madonna
10. St. Jerome
11. The Adoration of the Magi
12. Vitruvian Man
13. Portrait of a Musician
14. Lady with an Ermine
15. La Belle Ferronniere
16. The Last Supper
17. Madonna of the Yarnwinder
18. The Virgin of the Rocks
19. Portrait of a Man in Red Chalk
20. The Virgin and Child with St. Anne
21. St. John the Baptist
22. The Mona Lisa
23. Sufmato and Chiaroscuo

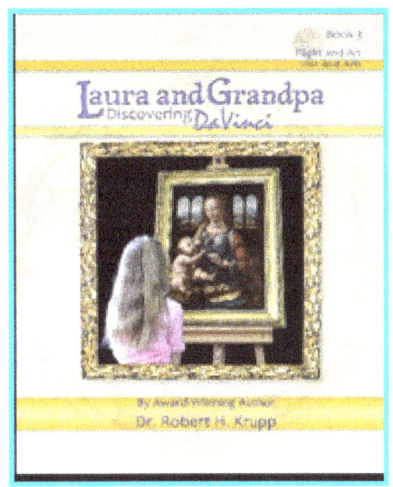

Three books in the 1st series (L&G,DST) and one in the 2nd (L&G,DDV) have been given a *Mom's Choice Award*®. Three of my books have received awards from the FAPA (Florida Authors and Publishers Association). As mentioned earlier, Book 3 in the Da Vinci series received a 1st Place Award from FAPA in 2020.

In 2015, my friend and colleague from Sarasota Military Academy, Vera McClaugherty, and I co-authored a unique book. It's title is the ***The Rainbow-El Arco Iris***. It is Story #7 from the first book I published. However, it is bilingual, in English and Spanish. It is the only book in the world that is a science book written for young children and also multilingual.

"The Rainbow—El Arco Iris", was published in 2015.

In the spring of 2020, a new series called ***Austin and Grandpa, Discovering Science Together, Book I***, was published. This book was written for the 8- to 13-year-old juvenile.

Book 1, published in 2020- includes 6 stories:
1. One Million Stars
2. A Billion Stars
3. Dropping In On Papa
4. Having a Ball at Papa's House
5. Reliable Research
6. Zero

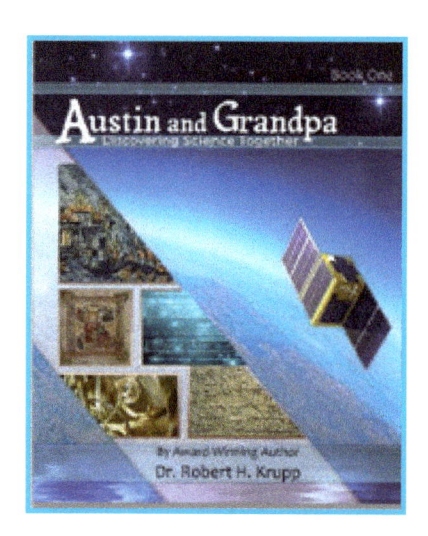

## Chapter Fourteen: A Literary Artist

In 2015, the first book in the Da Vinci series was a finalist in the *Writer's Digest® 23rd Annual Book Awards Competition*. Though it did not earn an award, I would like to share a critique written by one of the judges . . .

> *"The writing is straight forward and easy to understand. Grandpa puts this all in a language that children can grasp and understand. There are lots of photos of these simple machines and of the exhibition. There is a glossary in the back of the book to help with the understanding.*
>
> *I am the Librarian in a STEM elementary school, and this will be a great addition to our library and to our teachers. It would be great in any school!*
>
> *Krupp is a former teacher and it shows. He knows how to explain what can seem complicated in a language suitable for children."*

In summary, since 2011, I have published 11 paperback books and 20 electronic books. For 80 years of my life, I never thought of writing or publishing a book!

In 2021, these memoirs will be published—and just wait and see the terrific graphics Kristina and I have prepared for you!

At this point in **MS**, I wish to end this chapter. In fact, it is the end of **MS**. God willing, future adventures and memories await me!

# EPILOGUE

If you ever decide to write your memoirs—and you should—let me warn you. It is a daunting task!

Our mind and soul are filled with innumerable pictures and experiences. Many of them you may not have thought about for decades. As you dwell on certain periods of your life, you begin to recall happy events and experiences. However, during the night, as you are sleeping, you'll awaken with another memory from that time. You overlooked it, but your mind has brought it forth again.

You also will begin to remember unhappy memories that you have deeply buried in your psyche. My suggestion to you—leave them be! Let them go!

I've often thought about how we all have stories. Sometimes they're so short, you could fit them on the back of a 3 X 5 card. Other times, they're so long it takes a lifetime to write them, before they're finished.

Sometimes, everything that happens is connected to everything else that happens. These stories are so big and long they never finish. I like that kind the best!

During my lifetime, I have met a lot of people, both friends and students. I do not believe any came into my life by accident!

I would have loved to call **MS** *It's a Wonderful Life*, but Frank Capra beat me to it and used that title in his iconic movie.

Recently, I have discovered and adopted a new ***mantra***. Clint Eastwood first mentioned it to Toby Keith, who was inspired to write an award-winning song. Clint said to Toby, his partner at a Pebble Beach golf outing, "I get up every morning and go out. ***I don't let the old man in!***"

I beg your forgiveness in not always presenting events chronologically.

*Chapter Fourteen: A Literary Artist*  389

In conclusion, I wish to thank my parents and family for providing me with a *loving environment*. Because of them, I truly believe my life can be summarized with the two **L** words . . .

- **LEARN**— to acquire knowledge or a skill by study, experience, or being taught.

- **LOVE**— an act of the heart in which one helps another.

♊ *

*In case you've wondered about this orange icon, sprinkled around the text, it is the EMOJI symbol for a Gemini. In the very beginning of Chapter 1, I told you I was born in **early June**.

# APPENDIX
# KITH & KIN

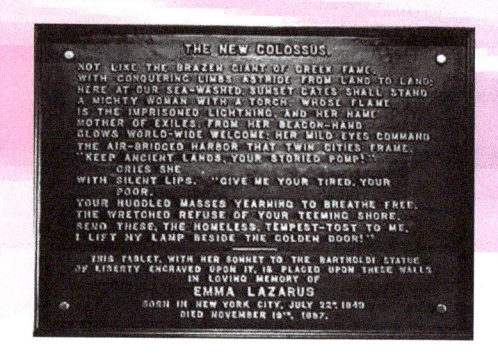

**THE NEW COLOSSUS**

NOT LIKE THE BRAZEN GIANT OF GREEK FAME,
WITH CONQUERING LIMBS ASTRIDE FROM LAND TO LAND;
HERE AT OUR SEA-WASHED, SUNSET GATES SHALL STAND
A MIGHTY WOMAN WITH A TORCH, WHOSE FLAME
IS THE IMPRISONED LIGHTNING, AND HER NAME
MOTHER OF EXILES. FROM HER BEACON-HAND
GLOWS WORLD-WIDE WELCOME; HER MILD EYES COMMAND
THE AIR-BRIDGED HARBOR THAT TWIN CITIES FRAME.
"KEEP ANCIENT LANDS, YOUR STORIED POMP!"
CRIES SHE
WITH SILENT LIPS. "GIVE ME YOUR TIRED, YOUR
POOR,
YOUR HUDDLED MASSES YEARNING TO BREATHE FREE,
THE WRETCHED REFUSE OF YOUR TEEMING SHORE.
SEND THESE, THE HOMELESS, TEMPEST-TOST TO ME,
I LIFT MY LAMP BESIDE THE GOLDEN DOOR!"

THIS TABLET, WITH HER SONNET TO THE BARTHOLDI STATUE
OF LIBERTY ENGRAVED UPON IT, IS PLACED UPON THESE WALLS
IN LOVING MEMORY OF
**EMMA LAZARUS**
BORN IN NEW YORK CITY, JULY 22ⁿᵈ 1849
DIED NOVEMBER 19ᵗʰ, 1887.

***The New Colossus*** is a poem written by American poet Emma Lazarus in 1883. In 1903, this sonnet was cast in bronze and mounted on the pedestal of the Statue of Liberty.

In the second stanza are found the words that are often quoted when talking about the Statue of Liberty . . .

*"Give me your tired, your poor,*
*Your huddled masses yearning to breathe free.*
*The wretched refuse of your teeming shore.*
*Send these, the homeless, tempest-tossed to me,*
*I lift my lamp beside the golden door!"*

As I wrote my memoirs, I thought of many, many different titles to call them. One I considered was ***The American Dream—Fulfilled***! I did so, because I wanted to thank and honor my ancestors, some of whom I never knew. They had the courage to leave Poland and the Ukraine with a dream for better lives for themselves and their progeny. My brother, Ron, and I are the fulfillment of their visions!

# Appendix

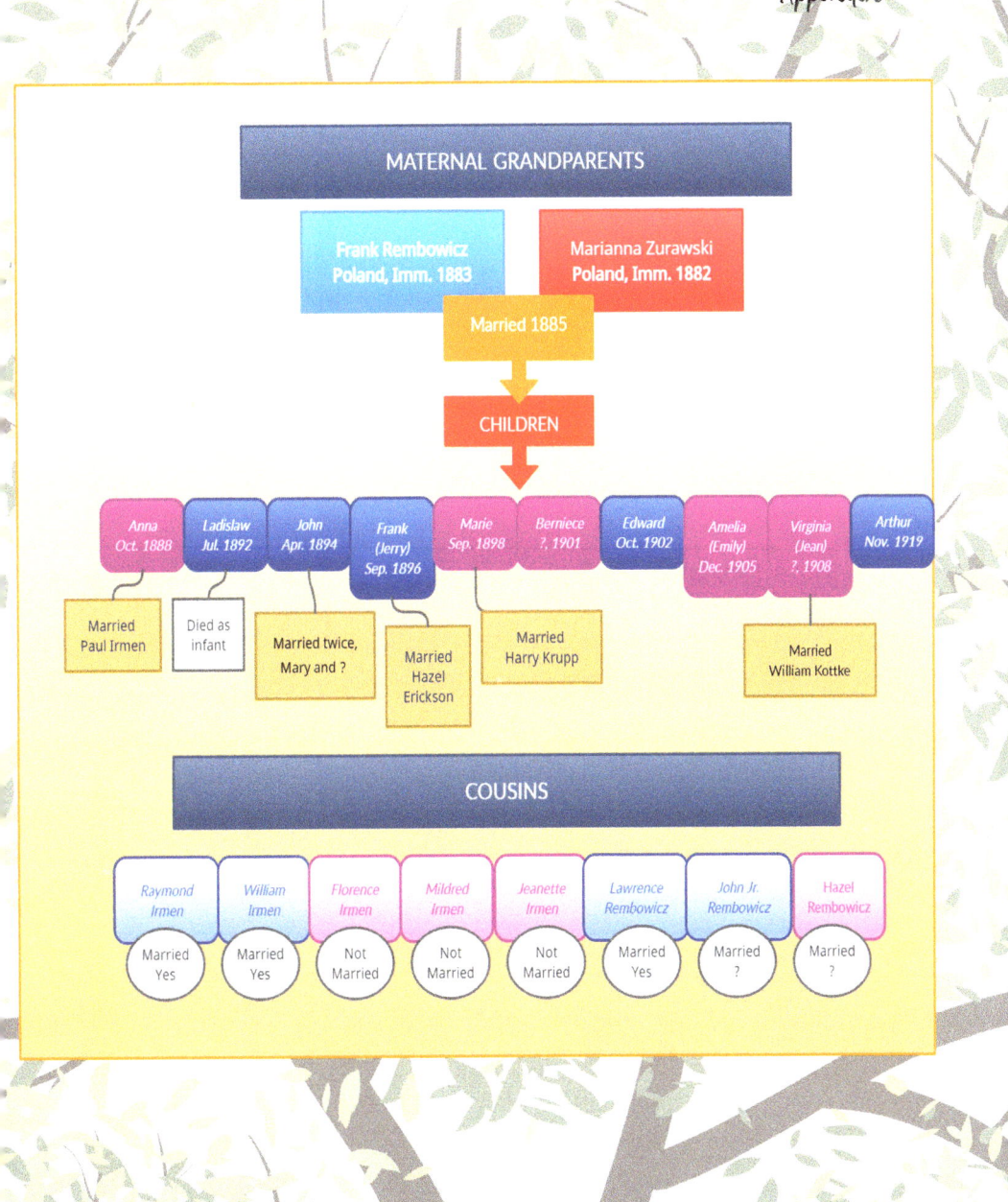

## MATERNAL GRANDPARENTS

**Frank Rembowicz** — Poland, Imm. 1883
**Marianna Zurawski** — Poland, Imm. 1882

Married 1885

### CHILDREN

| Name | Date | Notes |
|---|---|---|
| Anna | Oct. 1888 | Married Paul Irmen |
| Ladislaw | Jul. 1892 | Died as infant |
| John | Apr. 1894 | Married twice, Mary and ? |
| Frank (Jerry) | Sep. 1896 | Married Hazel Erickson |
| Marie | Sep. 1898 | Married Harry Krupp |
| Berniece | ?, 1901 | |
| Edward | Oct. 1902 | |
| Amelia (Emily) | Dec. 1905 | |
| Virginia (Jean) | ?, 1908 | Married William Kottke |
| Arthur | Nov. 1919 | |

### COUSINS

|  |  |
|---|---|
| Raymond Irmen | Married Yes |
| William Irmen | Married Yes |
| Florence Irmen | Not Married |
| Mildred Irmen | Not Married |
| Jeanette Irmen | Not Married |
| Lawrence Rembowicz | Married Yes |
| John Jr. Rembowicz | Married ? |
| Hazel Rembowicz | Married ? |

# Appendix

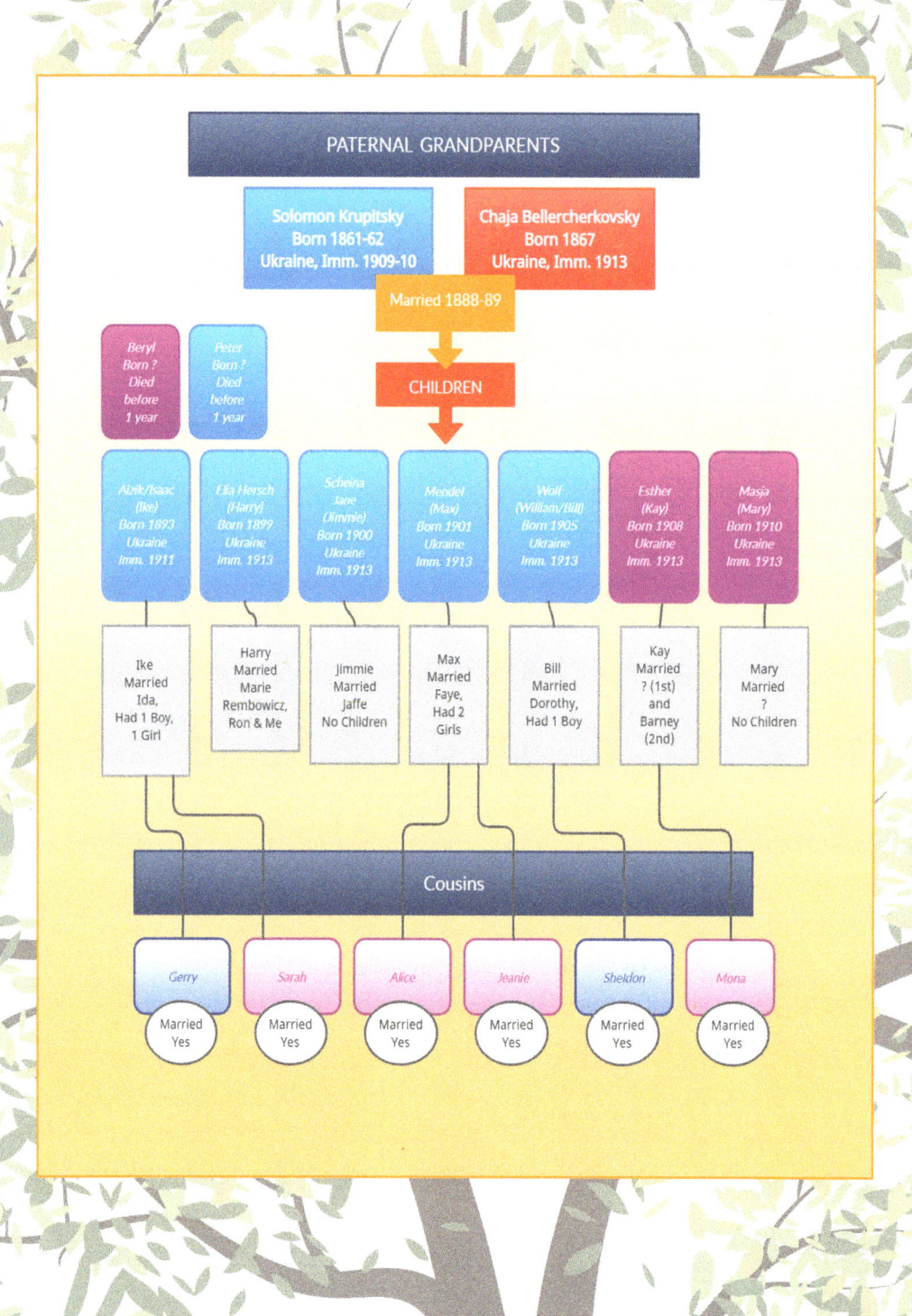

## PATERNAL GRANDPARENTS

**Solomon Krupitsky**
Born 1861-62
Ukraine, Imm. 1909-10

**Chaja Bellercherkovsky**
Born 1867
Ukraine, Imm. 1913

Married 1888-89

### CHILDREN

- **Beryl** — Born ? Died before 1 year
- **Peter** — Born ? Died before 1 year
- **Aizik/Isaac (Ike)** — Born 1893 Ukraine, Imm. 1911
- **Elia Hersch (Harry)** — Born 1899 Ukraine, Imm. 1913
- **Scheina Jane (Jimmie)** — Born 1900 Ukraine, Imm. 1913
- **Mendel (Max)** — Born 1901 Ukraine, Imm. 1913
- **Wolf (William/Bill)** — Born 1905 Ukraine, Imm. 1913
- **Esther (Kay)** — Born 1908 Ukraine, Imm. 1913
- **Masja (Mary)** — Born 1910 Ukraine, Imm. 1913

| Child | Marriage |
|---|---|
| Ike | Married Ida, Had 1 Boy, 1 Girl |
| Harry | Married Marie Rembowicz, Ron & Me |
| Jimmie | Married Jaffe, No Children |
| Max | Married Faye, Had 2 Girls |
| Bill | Married Dorothy, Had 1 Boy |
| Kay | Married ? (1st) and Barney (2nd) |
| Mary | Married ?, No Children |

### Cousins

- **Gerry** — Married Yes
- **Sarah** — Married Yes
- **Alice** — Married Yes
- **Jeanie** — Married Yes
- **Sheldon** — Married Yes
- **Mona** — Married Yes

# POSTSCRIPT

God willing...

1. ***My Marvelous Memories*** will be published by Christmas, 2021.

2. In 2022, Books #2-5 will be published and added to the ***Austin and Grandpa–Discovering Science Together*** series. These four new books will contain about 38 stories!

3. In 2023, a new series called ***Zachary and Grandpa–Discovering Physics Together*** will be launched. Three books, containing 24 to 28 stories, will be published for this new series.

*Yours Truly!*
*xO*

# Photo & Image Credits / Resources

Wikipedia
Wikimedia
The D.S.M.
imgbin.com
NASA.gov
pixabay.com
morguefile.com
Michael J. Collins, used with permission. pg. 93, Flickr
Benh Lieu Song, Wikimedia, pg. 107
NPS.gov
USGA.gov
picryl.com
pixy.com
flickr.com/Kirk K.
Cairo_dario-morandotti/unsplash
Kom Ombo_makalu/pixabay
freepik.com/Garry Killian
freepik.com
unsplash.com
Adobe Stock (purchased)

"Courtesy of the Oak Lawn Public Library"
the Tutoring Card Chapter 10 Kevin Korst (not used)

Chapter 10- AT&T Articles of Interest:
(Links valid at date of publication)
https://www.linkedin.com/pulse/most-memorable-att-commercial-i-ever-filmed-douglas-ritter/
https://vimeo.com/206614089

Kristina Edstrom- Art Direction/Graphic Design/Photo Editing/Personal Images
www.KristinaEdstromDesigns.com


My heartfelt THANKS to
Shirley Silverman, Lou Guillo, and Jim Frane
for the many hours they spent in proofreading this text.

CPSIA information can be obtained
at www.ICGtesting.com
Printed in the USA
LVHW070006201221
706671LV00002B/3